German Business Management

Toshio Yamazaki

German Business Management

A Japanese Perspective on Regional Development Factors

Springer

Toshio Yamazaki
Professor
Faculty of Business Administration
Ritsumeikan University
1-1-1 Noji-higashi, Kusatsu
Shiga 525-8577, Japan

Additional material to this book can be downloaded from http://extra.springer.com

ISBN 978-4-431-54302-2 ISBN 978-4-431-54303-9 (eBook)
DOI 10.1007/978-4-431-54303-9
Springer Tokyo Heidelberg New York Dordrecht London

Library of Congress Control Number: 2013935948

Printed on acid-free paper

Springer is part of Springer Science+Business Media (www.springer.com)

For my wife, Naomi and son, Tomotaka

Preface

How are German capitalism and German business management to be understood from the perspective of Japan as an Asian country? During a time in which different forms of capitalism have come under critical examination, the purpose of this book is to explore the German experience from a Japanese researcher's perspective.

Both Germany and Japan as defeated nations in the World War II received significant American leadership and support after the war. Both countries developed their enterprises, industries, and economy by deploying and adapting technology and management methods from the USA while establishing their own systems of industrial concentration. By these means, both nations became major trading countries. However, current economic and business conditions differ greatly between Germany and Japan.

In trade, American influence on Japanese business is still strong. Japan could not and cannot establish a complementary relationship with American industrial sectors and their products in the American market. Furthermore, a common market structure like the European Union does not exist in Asia. In contrast to Japan, Germany has developed independently of American influence and become part of a well-integrated regional economy. What were the driving forces that created those differences?

That question is approached from a Japanese point of view in this book, based on the assumptions that the origins of the distinct characteristics of German business management after World War II were developed in the 1950s and 1960s. The book analyzes the transformation of business management in Germany and explains the characteristics and structures of German management.

Three major factors that influenced Germany's independent development path are considered in this book. First, the effects of the deployment and adaptation of American management methods on the transformation of business management in Germany are analyzed by considering the overall influence of German capitalism. Second, the impact of the concentration of industries, such as seen in mergers and alliances, on business management and industrial structure is described. The importance of the big business system and cooperation mechanisms of postwar German capitalism is demonstrated. Third, the book describes how the development of German companies determined the current German condition, that is, "the Europeanization of Germany," while the world faced the globalization process. The origin of European integration at the level of business management during the 1950s and 1960s is determined. Moreover, the basic foundations of European integration are explored by analyzing market factors in Europe as well as the internal structural transformation of management in Germany.

To analyze the development of postwar German capitalism and German business management, this book introduces four unique viewpoints.

First, the overall structure of postwar German management style is examined in relation to German capitalism. In Japan, there is a school of management research that analyzes business management from the combined perspectives of political economy, industrial economics, and business economics. Using this school of thought, the author fully addresses the economic and industrial factors (the system of industrial concentration) without limitation to the factors inherent to the level of enterprises.

Second, a comparative analysis of Germany and Japan in Asia is provided, also from the point of view of Japan. Specifically, the author analyzes the differences between Germany and Japan in terms of the influencing factors on business and shows how these differences have existed in specific cases outlined in each chapter. This comparison reveals the significance of the German business management model, its characteristics, and contributing factors that make the overall management approach distinctive to Germany.

Third, the author analyzes German business management in relation to regional conditions such as market structure, the structure of competition in Europe, and the accumulation structure of German capitalism within Europe. Emphasis is placed on the transformation of business management in Germany during the 1950s and 1960s, while paying special attention to Germany's regional economic characteristics in Europe and the relationships between Germany and the USA. How German and European market structures regulate the system of competition is shown to be an important differentiating factor. The author then explores how Japan was not able to establish an accumulation structure in Asia as Germany did in Europe while remaining independent of American influence.

Fourth, this book provides a multifactorial analysis of business management applying the frameworks of the "total system of business management" and "reframing." The total system of business management refers to the fundamental conditional structures that regulate and determine an overall management style under a specific country's capitalistic economic system. Based on the author's original framework, the book analyzes business management in relation to the structure of German capitalism and the cooperative interdependent structures that arose from the concentration of industry. Applying the author's reframing framework, the implementation of American-style management is considered. Reframing refers to the process of how a management style that is well established in a particular country is transformed into a different style by adaptation, correction, and adjustment in order to fit into the capitalistic structure of the country where reframing is done.

By applying the author's two original frameworks to this analysis, we are able to provide a unique understanding of German business management and German capitalism.

The composition of this book is as follows. Chapter 1 introduces the purpose and significance of the book by explaining the various issues that are covered, such as current economic and business conditions between Germany and Japan, identifies research topics, reviews prior research and ensuant issues, and clarifies two original and key analytical frameworks. Chapter 2 discusses America's global strategy to build the capitalistic world post-WWII and the development of the US-led productivity movement. Chapter 3 examines changes in the relationship among nation, economy, and enterprises in Germany's political economy, which were significant to business management and the development of industrial concentration. Chapter 4 discusses post-WWII changes in labor relations under the codetermination system. It examines the new framework for labor relations in Germany called the "dual system," the mechanism of corporate governance based on the codetermination system and the codetermination system's significance. Chapter 5 analyzes the development of a new system of industrial concentration post-WWII. It discusses new developments in Germany's industrial systems based on industry–bank relationships and system restructuring of large corporate groups after the mid-1950s. Drawing on these bases, from Chaps. 6–10, changes in business management and the significance of the deployment and transfer of US management methods are considered. Chapter 6 discusses the deployment of American management education in relation to universities' role in management education, eligibility criteria for executive management, and the manager promotion system in German enterprises. Chapter 7 examines the deployment of American-style management and production systems. The major issues are human relations, industrial engineering (IE), and the Ford system. This chapter analyzes these issues in relation to German environmental factors such as labor relations, the codetermination system, management values and traditions, and the market structure in Germany and Europe. Chapter 8 analyzes the deployment of American methods for adapting to a mass market in relation to various factors such as the characteristics of domestic and European markets, production- and technology-oriented management values, the composition of executive management, and changes in the structure of competition. The major issues are marketing, public relations (PR), and operations research (OR). Chapter 9 discusses the deployment of a divisional structure in relation to changes in business strategies, management systems and practices, and managers' traditional attitudes. It considers the deployment of divisional structures using case studies of typical corporations from major industries. Following the previous chapters' topics, Chap. 10 reevaluates the changes in business management in postwar Germany through the early 1970s by applying the two original frameworks described in the Introduction—the total system of business management and the reframing of Americanization. It explains the significance of the German business management model that developed in the European environment by comparing Germany's situation in Europe with that of Japan's in Asia. Chapter 11 explains the origins of differences of the postwar development between Germany and Japan and how the transformation of German business management in the 1950s and 1960s underpinned the formation of today's European Union. It also suggests viewpoints for analyses of current problems affecting Germany's role and possible initiatives in the European debt crisis.

I extend my sincere gratitude to all those who have supported me while writing this book: Prof. Kyouichi Maekawa, my respected teacher who presented valuable insight and enlightening perspectives during my doctoral program at Doshisha University, Japan, and Prof. Masaki Nakata, emeritus professor at Ritsumeikan University, Japan, who provided me with important instructions and advice on writing this book. Without them this book would not have been possible. I also thank my family, my wife Naomi, who encouraged me, and my son Tomotaka, who gave me the strength and determination to complete my research. Without their understanding and support, completing this book would have been impossible. I dedicate this book to my wife and son.

Shiga, Japan Toshio Yamazaki

Contents

Chapter 1
Introduction: Research Topics and Analytical Framework

Abstract This chapter elaborates on the purpose and significance of this book. It first explains the issues discussed in this book by comparing current economic and business conditions between Germany and Japan, which were not only defeated nations during WWII but also major trading countries post war. Next, research topics are identified by examining major issues in postwar German capitalism and business management, the focal topic of this book's analysis; we do so by focusing on the postwar boom years, in particular through the early 1970s. This book explores the findings of previous research based on related topics and ensuant issues. Furthermore, in addition to clarifying two original key frameworks by the author and their significance, this section explains a "total system of business management" and "re-framing" as the frameworks for a multifactorial analysis of business management. These frameworks underpin this book's unique explanation of German business management and capitalism.

Keywords Americanization • German business management • Productivity movement • Rheinland model of capitalism • Varieties of capitalism

1.1 Awareness of the Issues of this Book

How is capitalism and business management in Germany, a European nation, understood from the perspective of Japan, an Asian nation? As a Japanese researcher of German business management for around 30 years, I have written this book to present unique perspectives on the very topic.

Today, many question the fundamentals of capitalism. Economic globalization, beginning in the 1990s, led to the "American standard" being claimed as a model capitalistic system and strengthened US influence. Against the background of the relatively long-term US economic development known as the "new economy," there emerged a corporate viewpoint oriented to shareholder value, increased capital market pressures on corporations, and further financial expansion based on the rapid

T. Yamazaki, *German Business Management: A Japanese Perspective on Regional Development Factors*, DOI 10.1007/978-4-431-54303-9_1, © Springer Japan 2013

development of financial globalization. Amid these changes, the phenomenon of Americanization returned. However, although various countries, including Germany and Japan, exhibited certain similarities in their versions of capitalism, they have not actually succeeded in fully adapting Americanization. This issue of the "varieties of capitalism" has generated important research issues. With the US-led financial crisis of 2008 increasing global impact and economic severity, US-style capitalism encountered marked limitations and failures.

In such circumstances, the "Rheinland model of capitalism" (Albert 1991) or a "coordinated market economy" (Hall and Soskice 2001) exemplifies capitalism in Germany. This market economy model differs from the US model in that the latter considers the full spectrum of market principles as the greatest good, whether in commodity, financial, or labor market. Issues regarding the German model of capitalism are deeply related to economic relationships with the US and gaining independence from its economy.

Although Americanization re-emerged while globalization progressed, in Europe, market integration and the unification of European currencies in the form of the EU increased and deepened with Europeanization through eastward expansion. Germany assumed a central role in Europeanization as the largest industrial nation in postwar Europe. Its actions clearly differed from those of Americanization and indicated that it pursued a unique direction in gaining independence from the US. Germany and Japan were nation defeated in World War II; however, they subsequently became the world's leading trade nations. What should Japan gather from this viewpoint? In the postwar era, both Japan and Germany were brought under the US global strategy, and by deploying US technology and management methods and building a unique system of industrial concentration, they achieved corporate and economic progress. However, today, situation in both countries differ greatly. Japan relied heavily on the US for trade purposes, and to this day, lacks complementary relationships between product areas and industries in the US market; it is noteworthy that Asia, on a whole, has not yet succeeded in establishing a common market. In comparison, Germany has gained independence from the US and moved toward European integration; integrative development into the European region was another form of Europeanization. However, the question remains as to what created these differences and how were they created. This book considers the origins of the system that regulated the postwar characteristics of German capitalism at the business management level and was formed between the 1950s and 1960s. By comparing the then changes in Germany's business management with those in Japan, we attempt to gauge answers to these issues from Japan's perspective.

1.2 Research Topics

First, we identify research topics by examining major issues in postwar German capitalism and business management during the postwar boom years, or the early 1970s, the focal topic of this book's analysis.

Prior to World War II, market problems were primarily the bottleneck of business management and impeded the development of productive forces; however, these circumstances significantly changed postwar. Domestic market conditions radically changed in the interest of protecting worker rights. These trends were seen throughout major European nations and created conditions for export markets on a European scale. International market conditions were not only supported by the US-led world economic system, that is, the free trade system and international monetary system, but also were complemented by the formation of a common market in Western Europe. Tremendous changes can be seen in postwar historical conditions, specifically regarding broader and deeper global market connections.

However, in the period immediately following the end of the war, productive forces and economic might significantly differed between European nations and the US. Thus, "catching up" became one of the most pressing issues in each country. The deployment of US technology and management methods greatly contributed toward addressing this issue; the requisite conditions for achieving this goal were created with US guidance and assistance. In addition, the productivity movement, part of the US global strategy, played a critical role in international expansion of organizational efforts. Under the Marshall Plan, "technical assistance" created a large-scale framework for supporting learning and introduction of US technology and management methods. This new framework enabled the deployment of US technology and management methods in Germany, tremendously changing business management.

In this way, the productivity movement led to each country's industrial development and the restructuring of their economies on the foundation of US-style productive forces. The movement gathered strength in the capitalist economic sphere of West Germany and attempted to build a collaborative circle of capitalistic economic systems beyond comparison with anything from the prewar era.

These changes transformed the prewar industrial structure, such that it no longer focused on producer goods but on the consumer goods sector, thus emphasizing a shift to mass production. West Germany's high economic growth from the 1950s through the 1960s warranted an economic structure characterized by US-style mass production, mass distribution, and mass consumption, which was appropriate to mass consumer societies. These changes represented a movement toward Americanization of the economy; the Americanization of technology and business management was key to these transformations (Kudo 1999, p. 453).

Industrial concentration also exhibited new postwar developments. German characteristics of industrial concentration, which were based on prewar industry–bank relationships, included new developments in the industrial system that coordinated interests and shared information between industry and banks and between corporations. Monopolies that had been dissolved by the postwar occupation policy reconcentrated. In addition, the system of large corporate groups began to re-emerge and re-concentrate, and with it came new developments in the system of large corporate groups. The system played a crucial role in the formation of the German capitalism's accumulation structure, the cornerstone of industrial concentration. The postwar era necessitated the restructuring of the system of large corporate groups that emphasized the benefits of division of labor based on specialization in response to oligopolistic competition. This phenomenon represented the transformation of the prewar system of industrial concentration that controlled markets on the basis of massive trust and wide-ranged cartels, which encompassed the entire industrial sector in the 1920s. From the perspective of market control, this new system, based on industry–bank relationships and large corporate groups, was an important element supporting the development of postwar productive forces and accumulation structures. Industrial concentration developed as an important process in the progress of German corporations while exhibiting new characteristics of cooperation in German capitalism.

Next, we will examine how business management changed with the deployment of US technology and management methods. Along with commonalities with the US, what types of unique developments emerged? From a structural analysis perspective, this research elucidates the overall view of changes in business management that accompanied the deployment of American management methods. These changes included the adaptations of systems to local conditions based on an overall structure of and relationship with German capitalism in business management. This being said, it is important to consider the implications on various economic and social conditions by US intentions and postwar German corporations' strategic intentions, business management traditions, management values, common labor practices, labor relations, and market structures.

American management methods often based on the principles of efficiency and productivity improvements and others that were related to business policy conditions or environmental factors (e.g., systems and practices, management values, and management culture). Therefore, it is important to consider the relationships between both aspects, analyze them, and understand them in regard to the deployment of American management methods. In this book, we will explain the overall view of business management through a complete and comprehensive understanding of these changes, and Germany's response to them. How were US management methods reformed to accommodate German conditions? And how were the German management style and characteristics created? What was the significance of these developments? We will explain these issues in this book.

Another research topic is the problem of industrial concentration that is deeply related to the characteristics of German capitalism and corporate development. By understanding the changes in industrial concentration from the perspective of accumulation structures, we will show the significance of the postwar system of large corporate groups and the cooperative nature of German capitalism (for "Cooperative Management Capitalism" in Germany, see Chandler 1990).

Further, we will consider regional conditions and relationships with the US by examining how the development of German corporations during the boom years of the 1950s and 1960s created the conditions that emerged in subsequent periods. In other words, through Germany's interpretation of Americanization of business management, how were economic relations (divisions of labor and foreign trade patterns) in the European region built based on different industrial structures and the strengthening of competitiveness in Europe? How were these related to the developments independent of the US and the Europeanization movement that resulted in today's EU? To address these questions, it is essential to further explore these points and understand the genesis of the European integration movement. We will discuss the European market structures and the resultant competition. Also, we will examine external environmental factors such as the characteristics and relevance of the German and European industrial structure. Furthermore, we will explore the origin of Germany's movement toward European integration from the perspective of internal structural changes in business management and the external environmental factors. The direction of European integration and the progress of an expansion rooted in an integrated Europe, from the perspective of Japan, was an important German feature. Since the beginning of the postwar era, there were no advanced economies in the Asian region that could be considered strong export destinations for Japan, particularly because many East Asian countries had previously been colonies with low levels of economic development. Thus, because Japan was left with no option but to rely on exports to the US, its most lucrative market, we will compare Japan's situation with that of Germany.

1.3 Prior Research and Issues Thereafter

In regard to the abovementioned research topics, we will explore the findings of previous research on related topics.

Regarding the relevance of these topics to this book's central research topic, we found internal corporate studies from postwar Germany to the early 1970s; however, to the best of our knowledge, no studies provide an overall structural analysis that fully addresses the economic and industrial factors (regarding the system of industrial concentration) without being subject to the limitations by factors inherent to the level of enterprises.

Most studies analyzing German capitalism do not sufficiently address specific changes at the business management level. For example, research dealing with varieties of capitalism covers basic issues, such as the characteristics of Germany's emblematic "coordinated market economy" and its institutional complementarities. These studies focus on macro-level issues and provide effective methods for analyzing capitalism. However, although they emphasize issues of production systems, their primary arguments do not identify issues at the business management level or analyze the specific processes of change in these systems (Hall and Soskice 2001; Crouch and Streeck 1997; Streeck 1992). In most research analyzing German capitalism, often the scope of the studies are is limited to macro-economic issues, US influence, and the issues of "Americanization of the economic system." Drawing on Germany's defeat in the war and the subsequent imposition of occupation policy by the allied nations, the primary issues addressed by the literature are those of competition structure, such as monopoly regulations and restrictions and the deployment of American economic systems. In addition, from the viewpoint of postwar reforms, problems of US influence on economic systems, German initiatives toward that reform, and system design are analyzed. However, corporate level issues have often been neglected in such research (Vgl. Jarausch and Siegrist 1997; Trommler 1986; Doering-Manteuffel 1999).

A large body of research has analyzed industry-level problems, such as the development of industrial concentration and problems in industry–banks relationships. However, it does not entirely examine the relevance of these issues to business management and German capitalism (Pfeiffer 1993; Gerhardt 1982; Eglau 1989; Edwards and Fischer 1994; Wiendieck 1992; Schönwitz and Weber 1982).

On the other hand, studies on business management do not address the relevance of business management issues to the structural characteristics of German capitalism and the market. Moreover, few studies sufficiently relate economic and industrial factors of business management to reproduction (accumulation) structures in German capitalism. It is only through such overall structural analysis that we can sufficiently explain changes in business management, the resulting mechanisms of corporate development, and their social and economic significance.

In fact, studies on corporate-level issues also seem to have omitted several factors. Drawing on these studies, the topics undertaken in this text are important aspects of the deployment and transfer of American management methods. The primary characteristics of US management methods deployed in the 1950s and 1960s were (1) management and production systems (human relations, industrial engineering, and the Ford system); (2) management education methods; (3) responses to markets coinciding with advancements in mass production (marketing, public relations, and operations research); and (4) the divisional structure. However, few studies provide an overall analysis of these primary management methods. For example, studies on production-level issues (Vgl. Wellhöner 1996; Edelmann 2003) focus on the deployment of the Ford system and neglect the overall dynamics of business management. Studies that examine the deployment of US methods in Europe or provide comparisons between Japan and Germany do exist; however, none provide a comprehensive analysis of various management methods. Instead, existing studies often limit their analyses to specific management methods or areas and provide only a rudimentary analysis of this book's overall subject, Germany (Schröter 2005; Djelic 1998; Kipping and Bjarnar 1998; Barjot 2002; Zeitlin and Herrigel 2000; Engwall and Zamagni 1998; Gourvish and Tiratsoo 1998; Kudo et al. 2004; Berghahn 1985; McCreary 1964).

Nevertheless, several of these studies provide outstanding analyses of issues on Americanization in German corporations. They cover various US management methods and problems regarding their deployment and provide comparisons of corporations, such as those of C. Kleinschmidt and S. Hilger (Vgl. Kleinschmidt 2002; Hilger 2004). However, even these researches and those citing the concept of "hybridization"—the combination of US elements with German or European elements for the deployment of US management methods (Zeitlin and Herrigel 2000; Kleinschmidt 2002; Hilger 2004; Feldenkirchen 2004)—do not sufficiently explain the details of hybridization or the process of modifying US management methods. They also do not individually or comprehensively explain the factors that caused hybridization and modifications. In this regard as well, we found no comprehensive structural analyses that explain business management through the deployment of US methods.

1.4 Analytical Framework

Next, we will attempt to elucidate an analytical framework. In Japan, a school of thought analyzes and understands the dynamics of business management on the basis of mutual relationships between political, industrial, and business economics, which comprise the structure of economics (Maekawa 1970, 1993, 1997; Kanbayashi 1976; Hayashi 1972; Yamazaki 2005). Among these mutual relationships, this school of thought identifies the causes of various problems and the unique styles and characteristics of business management, in particular those in developed countries. In addition, it discusses the societal significance of objective changes and the relationship between the law of change and development. In this book, going beyond specific corporate-level factors, we thoroughly analyze economic and industrial factors of business management and explain the process of corporate activities creating reproduction and accumulation structures, given a country's capitalistic nature. Using this type of analytical approach, we attempt to understand German capitalism by considering business management and its connection with the problem of industrial concentration. Thus, this book by nature is an analysis of business management as an element of economics.

Although we apply the abovementioned Japanese research methods, we consider various aspects and situations within a unique analytical structure, that is, a framework for a total system of business management, wherein we analyze overall business management. We also establish the idea of "re-framing," using which we analyze the various problems in deploying American management methods that created conditions that facilitated business management changes in the postwar era.

First, the total system of business management denotes a structural framework for conditions that define the established methods of business management within the characteristics of capitalism as implemented in a certain country. It is an analytical method for explaining the overall relationships and structure of business management. The concept of the total system of business management comprises the following two parts: first, are the external factors in business management, for example, external environmental factors such as the structure of a country's capitalistic system, industrial systems, and the framework of labor relations. Second, are the internal factors relating to corporate structures; these include structural factors of management, such as the system of labor relations, management, and organization in corporations, and executive management systems, such as single- and double-layered structures. The relationship between these two phenomena is defined by the state of business management and influenced by external factors of capitalism; these factors define the development of business management. The state of management is influenced by corporate-level institutional characteristics and mechanisms. Also, internal factors in corporate structures affect external environmental factors, such as the double-layered structure of executive management, defining corporate networks through the supervisory board function. Thus, the two sides are interconnected.

When we examine overall ties with business management, at the global level, we find a "world structure of capitalism" that reveals the mutual relationships within the capitalist bloc. However, given the leadership and aid of victor nations, this structure poses a problem in global relationships, particularly those in markets and capital, which can be seen in the framework for the global structure of capitalism that is centered on the postwar US. Although this world structure of capitalism is outside the total system of business management, it defines, or at least influences, the system. Under the global structure of capitalism, the total system of business management is a defining factor in a given country's established methods of business management.

The eight elements comprising these external environmental factors within the total system of business management are (1) state–enterprise relationships, (2) labor relations, (3) industrial systems based on inter-firm relationships, (4) financial systems, (5) the structure of productive forces, (6) industrial structures, (7) market structures, and (8) enterprise–market relationships. We will now discuss these eight elements on the basis of various issues in postwar Germany during the boom years.

State–enterprise relationships are comprised of state regulative policies, particularly anti-monopoly, trade, and industrial policies. In Germany, issues with the economic principles of social market economy and anti-monopoly regulations were related to regulative policy. Trade policy aimed at the integration of West Germany in capitalistic markets and the establishment of a common market through European integration. Industrial policy was faced with the issues of investment promotion measures and the state's intervention in the productivity movement.

The system for labor relations revolved around collective agreements, worker participation in management, and labor unions. According to corporate structures, these were external environmental factors and the specific state of labor relations within corporations were an internal structural factor. In Germany, in addition to the dual system of regional collective agreements and labor relations through codetermination at the plant level, industries were faced with the issues of codetermination at the corporate management level. The codetermination system is important for labor–management relationships, German production and marketing strategies, and the production structure and system that supported these strategies. It is important to examine the impact of labor relationships on business management through the codetermination system and the relevance of social redistribution in the postwar economic order, known as the social market economy.

We now discuss industrial systems based on inter-firm relationships or industry-level systems that were based on collaborative inter-firm relationships. In Germany such systems are exemplified by inter-corporate ownership and control structures, inter-corporate relationships, industrial systems based on industry–bank relationships, and the system of large corporate groups. In Germany, these industrial systems not only demonstrated collaborative capitalism with regulative functions and a new approach toward monopolies and industrial concentration, which supported the system of large corporate groups, but also formed mechanisms for governance.

Financial systems had issues related to corporate financing and the striking expansion of international ties in financial markets based on, what we would call today, information technology networks. The development of an interconnected financial system consolidated the universal banking system, which existed in prewar Germany, the house banks, a role of the large banks within the universal banking system, and the credit and securities businesses. This point is closely connected with the collaborative industrial (regulatory) system based on industry–bank relationships.

The historical development of productive forces, labor utilization, the system of vocational education and specialized skills reflected in production all influenced the changes in the structure of productive forces. In addition to the prewar tradition of "flexible quality production," which differed from the US mass production system, Germany had a history of developing mass production systems with production flexibility and scale merit with lower production volume (von Freyberg 1989; Siegel and Freyberg 1991; Stahlmann 1993). The foundation of a production structure relied on skilled workers that were supported by a system of vocational education and specialized skills, such as the Meister system. Although based on the deployment of US technology and management methods, these factors strongly influenced postwar changes to the structure of productive forces.

Regarding industrial structures, particularly those defined by the expansion process of Germany's capitalism, the nature of these structures, the composition of internationally competitive industrial sectors, and the characteristics of these industries were important issues. The issues included the following: the composition of key industrial sectors; industrial characteristics (technological, market, and product characteristics); each company's position within the national economy, demonstrated by their interconnectedness within industrial sectors and within international competition; and their relationship with (i.e. relative degree of reliance upon) the state. Among these, the changes in German business management were related to the level of transformation; for instance, the transition from an industrial structure based on producer goods to one developing the durable consumer goods sector.

Market structures include commodity, labor, and financial markets. For Germany's commodity markets, the nature of its target markets, the composition of the regions and export market products, trade policy in export destination countries, and competition structures were all closely related to corporate management behavior. In addition to German market characteristics, the nature and significance of the European market played a significant role, and such conditions for a common market were important issues that influenced the development of business management. When comparing German market conditions with those of the US, in which standardization was advanced, we note differences in market conditions such as a consumer emphasis on quality or functionality. These market conditions were deeply related to corporate product strategy, marketing activities, and labor utilization. In European markets, complementary relationships in industrial and product areas were based on German industrial structures, with the heavy and chemical industries and processing and assembly industries at their core. In addition, there were strong differences in industrial structures among European countries in comparison with those of other regions. This situation can be connected with the state of Germany's business management that adapted European market conditions.

In enterprise–market relationships, the impact of German marketization on business management and industrial concentration became a problem. As expressed by the term "coordinated market economy," there existed characteristics of marketization in postwar Germany and a market economy system that integrated measures to deal with the "limits of marketization." The characteristics of the system can be seen in social redistribution functions through social market economic principles, a framework for labor relations based on the codetermination system and its effects on the labor market, and a system for regulating interests in an industrial system based on the universal banking system and industry–bank relationships. Such characteristics of marketization are deeply integrated with the development of business management.

What were the types of business management changes in the overall structures and relevancies mentioned above and the interconnected factors in our eight elements? We address this very crucial question.

Re-framing, that is, the framework for analyzing various problems with the deployment of US management methods is explained below. Re-framing in this text refers to business management methods and systems that are defined by structural characteristics of a country's capitalism and how these are adapted, modified, and made compatible with the structural characteristics of capitalism in a country to which it is transferred. Among these, structural characteristics of this capitalism are related to the state of existence of the following items: a structure of productive forces, industrial structures, and market structures—these three characteristics of Germany are deeply connected to re-framing. In addition, management values, business management traditions, and cultural factors and definability from an institutional perspective are also closely related to re-framing.

The structure of productive forces, industrial structures, and market structures are factors included in the total system of business management. In particular, regarding the structure of commodity markets, a country's domestic market and export market characteristics, along with its regional and product compositions, are matters of market structure. These issues are closely related to price and quality competition and other competitive structures in a market. Thus, management methods must be developed according to differences in market structure. Labor markets are related to a country's regulatory mechanisms, the state of labor relations, and the system of worker participation in management. Financial markets are connected with market involvement in the credit business and securities market, their composition, and the system of financial institutions. In industrial structures, characteristics of industrial development and international competition are important issues, as are the structure of productive forces, adapted to market and industrial structures, and the characteristics of the structure of productive forces, reflected in the development process. Characteristics of the structure of productive forces are, to a certain extent, connected to systems of specialized skills and vocational education, and exert a tremendous influence on the deployment of foreign elements of productive forces and the state of labor utilization.

These various elements that comprise the structural characteristics of a country's capitalism are closely related to management values and business management traditions, culture, and systems. Business management traditions and culture interrelated with business management standards and values. Even regarding capitalism, wherein the pursuit of profit is the greatest goal, a country's corporate standards and values do not necessarily match those of other countries. For example, the US has traditionally emphasized standards and values based on pragmatism, and both the US and UK have placed significant importance on obtaining financial profit through interest-bearing capital; in contrast, the countries of continental Europe and Japan do not necessarily consider these their top priorities. Decisions on where to place value, that is, production, technology, quality, or marketing policies, which are more directly tied to profit, specifically short-term profit, greatly affect corporate behavior. However, management values and business management culture are not simply matters of general culture, but have deep connections with the structural characteristics of target markets identified by corporations. For example, if the commodity market in a certain country or region prioritizes product quality or functionality, corporations will focus on values and differentiation in technology or production because management values conform to market characteristics. Thus, market characteristics are closely related to management standards and values regarded important by corporations.

Institutional factors include legal systems comprising all types of regulations; labor relations; educational systems; and system for specialized skills. Labor relations define business management characteristics, such as investment in labor education based on labor conditions and employment security systems, corporate product and market strategies based on these investments, and production and management systems adapted to these strategies. A country's educational system is closely related with the cultivation of executives and managers and that of skilled workers. In addition, production systems also influence management standards and values. In discussions regarding varieties of capitalism, a country's production regime is deeply connected to institutional factors, the complementarity of education and training systems, labor market regulations and corporate governance, financial systems, and inter-firm relationships from the perspective of market competition and technology transfer (Hall and Soskice 2001). As a result, when a country's production systems and management methods that supported these systems are deployed in other countries, these institutional factors often influence the re-framing of management methods.

This concept of re-framing emphasizes the conditionality of structural characteristics tied to reproduction mechanisms of capitalism, particularly in the country where management methods and systems are created and that to which they are transferred and deployed. The management methods and systems of the originating country are adapted and modified to the capitalist structure of the country to which they are transferred. In addition, as these methods and systems begin to function, their circumstances define the structure and characteristics of capitalism and the aspects of reproduction structure in that country. Re-framing, in this text, focuses on problems that occur when the social system in an organization, specifically a corporation, is transferred to another country. Thus, the receiving nation's capitalistic characteristics are amended or modified to an adaptable form when the originating country's management methods, created for its own capitalistic structural characteristics, are introduced and spread throughout a foreign country using that country's methods. Accordingly, re-framing is the process of structural adaptation in response to different environmental conditions and a method of structural analysis, whereby the overall structure of business management is foundational.

To understand the issues of the international transfer of management methods, Abo (1994) provides a comprehensive analysis of "hybridization" and on the transfer of Japanese production systems outside of Japan. This research focuses on exporting Japanese systems, or system "application" (transfer) and "adaptation" (modifications adaptive to local conditions). In other words, it explains the problem of how two systems from different countries function when combined using certain proportions (Abo 1994, 2007). However, their analysis does not fully identify and present the factors that define hybridization. The same can be said of the abovementioned research on "hybridization" regarding in the deployment of US technology and management methods (Zeitlin and Herrigel 2000; Kleinschmidt 2002; Feldenkirchen 2004; Kudo et al. 2004). The analytical framework in this book differs from that used in the previous research. In analyzing the problems of the transfer of corporate management systems to foreign countries, Liker et al. (1999) attempts to explain the issues with "recontextualization," which means a reconstruction of the context of environmental and system elements for the modification and deployment of systems, such that they are compatible with specific market and societal conditions of the country in question. According to Liker et al., recontextualization is "the transformation of the meaning of firm offerings (e.g., technologies, work practices, or products) as they are uprooted from one cultural environment and transplanted to another." Recontextualization emphasizes how company deliverables are understood originally and how values evolve in new environments (Liker et al. 1999, p. 118). In contrast, the concept of re-framing used in this book attempts to explain factors governing the restructuring of management methods within overall structural relationships.

This book attempts to provide an overall structural analysis of business management on the basis of the unique structural analysis framework for the "total system of business management" and "re-framing." In addition, it presents an analysis of capitalism on the basis of a structural analysis of business management. Ideas based on these analytical frameworks attempt to explain the phenomena of amendments, modifications, and improvements to management methods, observed in the structural characteristics of capitalism in the countries in question and the various factors influencing business management as seen in the total system of business management. Through this analytical framework, we will discuss the overall structural changes to business management in Germany, the issue of what defines a country's unique state of business management, and how that is significant.

To provide a Japanese viewpoint and comparison of the analysis, we will present various items for consideration in each chapter, such as how Germany is different from and similar to Japan. Through this we will explain the conditions of Germany, the characteristics and factors that define these conditions, and the significance of German development.

Drawing on these premises, Chap. 2 will consider issues pertaining to the postwar world structure of capitalism, namely US global strategies and the development of the productivity movement in response to policy issues. In Chaps. 3 and 4, we will analyze political economy changes in domestic Germany that significantly influenced the development of industrial concentration and business management. In Chap. 3, we will examine the various changes in relationships among the nation, economy, and corporations. In Chap. 4, we will explore the new framework for labor relations under the codetermination system. Chapter 5 will explore new developments in the system of large corporate groups and industrial systems based on industry–bank relationships as an issue of industrial concentration closely tied to the characteristics of German capitalism. Drawing on these bases, from Chaps. 6–10, we will consider changes in business management and the significance of the deployment and transfer of US management methods.

The ideas herein are based on the following studies and reports, which are relates to the book's theme and various primary historical documents: annual reports of major corporations, activity reports of the German federal government, materials from the Bundestag, reports from the Marshall Plan organization and relevant US government documents, historical documents located in the German Federal Archives, The National Archives in Washington D.C., the archives of major German industrial corporations, and the Rhenish-Westphalian Economic Archives in Cologne.

References

Abo T (ed) (1994) Hybrid factory. The Japanese production system in the United States. Oxford University Press, New York

Abo T (ed) (2007) Japanese hybrid factories. A comparison of global production strategies. Palagrave Macmillan, Basingstoke

Albert M (1991) Capitalisme contre Capitalisme. Ed. du Seuil, Paris

Barjot D (ed) (2002) Catching up with America. Productivity missions and the diffusion of American economic and technological influence after the Second World War. Presse de L'université de Paris-Sorbonne, Paris

Berghahn V (1985) Unternehmer und Politik in der Bundesrepublik. Suhrlkamp, Frankfurt am Main

Chandler AD Jr (1990) Scale and scope: the dynamics of industrial capitalism. Harvard University Press, Berkeley

Crouch C, Streeck W (eds) (1997) Political economy of modern capitalism: mapping convergence and diversity. Sage, London

Djelic M-L (1998) Exporting the American model. The postwar transformation of European business. Oxford University Press, Oxford

Doering-Manteuffel A (1999) Wie westlich sind die Deutschen?: Amerikanisierung und Westernisierung im 20.Jahrhundert. Vandenhoeck & Ruprecht, Göttingen

Edelmann H (2003) Heinz Nordhoff und Volkswagen. Ein deutscher Unternehmer im amerikanischen Jahrhundert. Vandenhoeck & Ruprecht, Göttingen

Edwards J, Fischer K (1994) Banks, finance and investment in Germany. Cambridge University Press, Cambridge

Eglau HO (1989) Wie Gott in Frankfurt: Die Deutsche Bank und die deutsche Industrie. Econ Verlag, Düsseldorf
Engwall L, Zamagni V (eds) (1998) Management education in historical perspective. Manchester University Press, Manchester
Feldenkirchen W (2004) The Americanization of the German electrical industry after 1945. Siemens as a case study. In: Kudo A, Kipping M, Schröteret HG (eds) German and Japanese business in the boom years. Transforming American management and technology models. Routledge, London, pp 116–137
Gerhardt M (1982) Industriebezihungen der westdeutschen Banken. Sendler, Frankfurt am Main
Gourvish TR, Tiratsoo N (eds) (1998) Missionaries and managers: American influences on European management education, 1945–60. Manchester University Press, Manchester/New York
Hall PA, Soskice D (eds) (2001) Varieties of capitalism: the institutional foundations of comparative advantage. Oxford University Press, Oxford
Hayashi A (1972) Gendai Doitsu Kigyoron (Modern German enterprise). Mineruva Shobo, Kyoto
Hilger S (2004) „Amerikanisierung" deutscher Unternehmen. Wettbewerbsstrategien und Unternehmenspolitik bei Henkel, Siemens und Daimler-Benz (1945/49–1975). Franz Steiner Verlag, Stuttgart
Jarausch K, Siegrist H (eds) (1997) Amerikanisierng und Sowjetisierung in Deutschland 1945–1970. Campus, Frankfurt am Main/New York
Kanbayashi T (1976) Keieikeizaigaku Kigyo Riron (Business economics—theory of enterprise). Tokoro Shoten, Tokyo
Kipping M, Bjarnar O (eds) (1998) The Americanization of European business. The Marshall plan and the transfer of US management models. Routledge, London
Kleinschmidt C (2002) Der produktive Blick. Wahrnehmung amerikanischer und japanischer Management- und Produktionsmethoden durch deutsche Unternehmer 1950–1985. Akademie Verlag, Berlin
Kudo A (1999) 20 Seiki Doitsu Shihonshugi (20th-century German capitalism). Tokyo Daigaku Shuppankai, Tokyo
Kudo A, Kipping M, Schröteret HG (eds) (2004) German and Japanese business in the boom years. Transforming American management and technology models. Routledge, London
Liker JK, Fruin WM, Adler PS (eds) (1999) Remade in America. Transporting & transforming Japanese management systems. Oxford University Press, New York
Maekawa K (1970) Doitsu Dokusen Kigyo no Hatten Katei (Development of monopolistic enterprise in Germany). Mineruva Shobo, Kyoto
Maekawa K (1993) Gendai Kigyo Kenkyu no Kiso (Foundation of study of contemporary enterprise). Moriyama Shoten, Tokyo
Maekawa K (1997) Nichidoku Hikaku Kigyoron eno Michi (Comparative study of Japanese and German enterprise). Moriyama Shoten, Tokyo
McCreary EA (1964) The Americanization of Europe. The impact of Americans and American business on the uncommon market. Doubleday & Co., New York
Pfeiffer H (1993) Die Macht der Banken. Die personellen Verflechtungen der Commerzbank, der Deutschen Bank und der Dresdner Bank mit Unternehemen. Campus, Frankfurt am Main
Schönwitz D, Weber HJ (1982) Unternehmenskonzentration, Personelle Verflechtungen und Wettbewerb—Eine Unterschung auf Basis der 100 gröβten Konzern der BRD. Nomos Verlagsgesellschaft, Baden-Baden
Schröter HG (2005) Americanization of the European economy. A compact survey of American economic influence in Europe since the 1880s. Springer, Dordrecht
Siegel T, Freyberg TV (1991) Industrielle Rationalisierung unter dem Nationalsozialismus. Campus, Frankfurt am Main
Stahlmann M (1993) Die Erste Revolution in der Autoindustrie. Management und Arbeitspolitik von 1900–1940. Campus, Frankfurt am Main
Streeck W (1992) Social institutions and economic performance. Studies of industrial relations in advanced capitalist economies. Sage, London/Newbary Park/New Delhi

Trommler F (ed) (1986) Amerika und die Deutschen, Bestandaufnahme einer 300jährigen Geschichte. Westdeutscher Verlag, Opladen

von Freyberg T (1989) Industrielle Rationalisierung in der Weimarer Republik: Untersucht an Beispielen aus dem Maschinenbau und der Elektroindustrie. Campus, Frankfurt am Main

Wellhöner V (1996) „Wirtschaftswunder" —Weltmarkt—Westdeutscher Fordismus. Der Fall Volkswagen. Westfälisches Dampfboot, Münster

Wiendieck M (1992) Unternehmensfinanzierung und Kontrolle durch Banken, Deutschland–Japan–USA. Gabler, Wiesbaden

Yamazaki T (2005) Gendai Keieigaku no Saikoutiku (A study of the reconstruction of business management study). Moriyama Shoten, Tokyo

Zeitlin J, Herrigel G (eds) (2000) Americanization and its limits. Reworking US technology and management in post-war Europe and Japan. Oxford University Press, Oxford

Chapter 2
America's Global Strategy and the Development of the Productivity Movement

Abstract This chapter discusses America's global strategy to build the capitalistic world post WWII and the development of the US-led productivity movement. Regarding America's global strategy, it considers the Marshall Plan and Germany's position in it and elucidates the historical characteristics of the Plan compared with those of the Dawes Plan after WWI. In addition, it examines the restructuring of the US-led global capitalistic economic system in relation to the Bretton Woods system and the framework for the free trade system. Also, it analyzes Germany's position in the US-led capitalist system. Regarding the productivity movement, this chapter discusses its international expansion under the US Technical Assistance Program, institutional efforts within the movement, Germany's response to the expansion of the US-led productivity movement, and its historical characteristics and significance.

Keywords Bretton woods system • European productivity agency • GATT • Marshall plan • Productivity movement • Technical assistance

In Chap. 2, we will discuss America's global strategy and the development of the productivity movement specific to the restructuring of the US-led world economic system after World War II. In particular, we will examine the following: (1) the framework for rebuilding and restructuring the capitalist world under the Marshall Plan, (2) how the restructuring of the US-led world economic system shaped the global structure of capitalism after the war, and (3) its significance for the subsequent development of German capitalism and corporations. In addition, we will analyze the significance of capital aid under the Marshall Plan in the rebuilding efforts of 16 Western European countries and the Technical Assistance Plan in shaping European markets. Specifically, we will explore the role of the Marshall Plan in the formation of an accumulation structure under German capitalism, which was the cornerstone of many European regions, and Germany's efforts to gain independence from the US. Further, we will address the issues faced with the productivity

T. Yamazaki, *German Business Management: A Japanese Perspective on Regional Development Factors*, DOI 10.1007/978-4-431-54303-9_2, © Springer Japan 2013

movement specific to America's global strategy and European policy. We will also address the following questions: Together with the support of the framework, how did the productivity movement develop and what was its significance? How did Europe, in particular Germany, respond to these issues? We will shed some light on these important topics in this chapter.

In Sect. 2.1, we will first discuss the historical characteristics of the Marshall Plan and Germany's stand on the policy embodying America's global strategy. In Sect. 2.2, we will show Germany's position in the restructuring of the US-led world capitalistic economic system. Finally, in Sect. 2.3, we will consider the development of the US-led productivity movement and its historical characteristics and significance.

2.1 Marshall Plan as America's Global Strategy

2.1.1 US-Led System of Capitalism and the Marshall Plan: Historical Characteristics of the Marshall Plan

We will first examine the Marshall Plan and consider its historical characteristics on the basis of its relevance to the restructuring of the US-led system of capitalism and compare it with the Dawes Plan.

In the case of the Dawes Plan post-World War I, US aid policy was limited to the defeated nation of Germany and focused on capital assistance through private funding. US capital assistance was economically and politically motivated in three ways: (1) keeping Germany in the realm of capitalism; (2) receiving the highest possible interest payments from the strikingly capital-poor Germany (Maekawa 1970, pp. 11–14); and (3) reclaiming US war loans from both England and France (Yoshida 1976, pp. 26–27). By contrast, post-World War II, aid was primarily from public funding rather than private due to the impetus of the Marshall Plan itself (Kudo 1996, p. 250). Based on the understanding that the reconstruction of the framework in Europe, the "joint action" and "initiative" of recipient countries were considered prerequisites for assistance (Suzuki 1977, pp. 395–396); however, these would be impossible if each country functioned independently. The Marshall Plan's objectives were the economic rebuilding and invigoration of Western Europe, with its protection from the effects of communism using economic methods. The latter objective was tied to the embargo policy against the Soviet Union and its satellite countries (Karlsch and Stokes 2003, p. 258). Further, in the 1950s, there was a large chasm between Western Europe and the US regarding possible production and demand; thus, another objective of the Plan was to take advantage of the unsatisfied demands for US production in Western Europe (I.P.W.-Berichte 1978, p. 4).

The primary aim of the Marshall Plan was the provision of capital for a maximum of 4years on import transactions exceeding Europe's capacity to pay (Carreras 2006, p. 311). According to a 1950 report of the third quarter by Germany's Federal Ministry for the Marshall Plan, assistance through the Plan was invaluable to Germany due to the paucity of raw material, capital, and foreign currency (Bundesminister für den Marshallplan 1950b, p. 9). Two sectors benefitted from the Plan: (1) imports of daily necessity products, foreign raw materials of high utility, and critical finished good such as special-purpose machines (Bundesminister für den Marshallplan 1952, p. 13) and (2) exports from West Germany, which strongly increase in the machine industry, transport equipment industry, metal processing industry, and other industries (Bundesminister für den Marshallplan 1950a, p. 48).

Another significance of the Marshall Plan was the effect on promoting investment through counterpart funds (Bundesminister für den Marshallplan 1951a, p. 19; Bundesminister für den Marshallplan 1953, p. 22), which not only were used in infrastructure and for industrial (producer) goods but also facilitated the mobilization of additional credit from banks (Abelshauser 1983, pp. 57–58). Especially since 1954, large-scale investments for automation and mechanization became important, and credit from the special assets of the European Recovery Program (ERP) acted as a detonator in the explosion of capital investment (Zieschang 1959, p. 77). ERP capital tended to be used in raw materials industries, and was particularly concentrated in the areas of coal mining, metals, and chemicals, all of which were faced with bottlenecks (Baumgart 1961, p. 59). However, although the percentage of self-financing was relatively higher in sectors such as the electrical industry, funding through the Marshall Plan remained significant. According to the *Handbuch der Deutschen Aktiengesellschaften* of FY 1952/1953, the continuation of a large-scale expansion of AEG's factories was first made possible through the provision of credit by the ERP (*Handbuch der Deutschen Aktiengesellschaften* 1953, p. 4229).

Third, the Marshall Plan played an important role in the restoring and laying the foundation for productive forces in European countries through the Technical Assistance Plan. Even among the creators of the Marshall Plan, the transfer and deployment of US-style mass production into Europe was seen as obligatory (Djelic 1998, p. 114). Funds from the Marshall Plan were given to each country, undertaking overall planning for productivity improvements, and methods of technical assistance and the exchange of mutual experience were promoted in the program (Albrecht 1952, p. 49). The US-led economic system and technologies as well as management methods were held as models.

Another initiative of the Marshall Plan was realizing the integration of and free trade in Western Europe countries (Stolper et al. 1964, p. 272). The Plan aimed at establishing a multinational order for global trade and payments (Buchheim 1993, p. 78). Various policies to promote international cooperation in Europe and strengthen the capitalist system were coordinated by the Organization for European Economic Cooperation (OEEC), which was established with the goal and regulatory intent to gradually remove trade barriers, such as the allotment system in global trade, and similar discriminatory barriers (Schröter 2005b, p. 366; Postan 1967 p. 98). While the US worked to create conditions for economic restructuring in European countries under the Marshall Plan, it compelled these countries' governments to open their markets to free trade and international competition

(Schröter 2005a, p. 8). By laying the foundation for economic rebuilding based on the influx of dollars to many participating nations, capital aid under the Marshall Plan served as an important condition for the creation of the international monetary system after the war, which recognized the dollar as the world's key currency.

The Marshall Plan was also a core element in the rebuilding of Germany's economy, its return into the Western European economy, and the complete removal of policies that allowed the weakening Germany by occupation authorities (Furuuchi 2007, pp. 65–66). Thus, from this perspective, West Germany occupied a central position. In relationship to the anti-socialistically inclined political and economic policies, West Germany received capital aid, technical assistance, and grants for balance of payments, aiming at a membership with other Western European economic organizations such as the OEEC and European Payments Union (EPU) (Borchardt 1978, pp. 71–72).

2.1.2 Germany's Position in the Marshall Plan

Therefore, due to its opposition to the socialist camp and being a defeated country in World War II, Western Germany acquired special consideration in the Marshall Plan. Extensive congressional research on ERP repeatedly emphasized that the Ruhr was the economic heart of Europe, and Germany was the pillar of the entire restructuring system (Kitamura 1973, p. 33); Germany's high industrial production and its foundation that made it possible were the primary reasons for this importance. Moreover, as aid from the Marshall Plan was kept to a minimum due to the principles of "independence" and "mutual assistance" for European countries, promotion of German rebuilding was required to pick up the slack (Manabe 1989, pp. 174–175, 177–178, 188, 226). In other words, based on the US government's understanding that the revival and expansion of German industries was necessary for the rebuilding of economic conditions in Europe (Barjot 2002, p. 49; Crouzet 2002, p. 435), Germany occupied a central role in technical assistance under the Marshall Plan and the productivity movement.

The Marshall Plan was designed to integrate the overall German economy and that of the Ruhr region with the economic system of the West through large-scale financial aid (Schlieper 1986, p. 162). At the beginning of 1947, West Germany was supposed to be at the center of US stabilization efforts for Western Europe. The Marshall Plan proposed trade policy rules to ease Germany's return into the international scene, revive global markets in the mid-term, and develop international economic cooperation vehicles such as the OEEC (Abelshauser 2004, pp. 151, 153). The Plan aimed at bringing West Germany back into the European fold through the OEEC (Schröter 2005b, p. 369). One of the US' initial goals was to reduce resistance from each country toward Germany's economic rebuilding, by associating it to the rebuilding of Europe's overall economy, rather than simply focusing on the critical role of Germany and how much European countries were needed to restructure the European economy (Suzuki 1977, pp. 426–427).

Due to factors such as the division of Germany into East and West, West Germany's position at the axis of socialist bloc countries, and the relative strength of Germany's industrial productive forces, Germany became a necessary element in reorganizing the US-led system of capitalism.

2.2 Germany's Position in the US-Led System of Capitalism

Next, we will discuss measures specific to the restructuring of the US-led world economic system, and Germany's contribution to and position in the system. The primary pillars of restructuring the capitalist system were (1) the restructuring of the international monetary and financial system on the basis of the Bretton Woods system, (2) the establishment of an institutional framework for free trade as represented by GATT, and (3) systems for economic cooperation in European countries under the Marshall Plan, recommended by the OEEC and other mechanisms to promote the economy and trade, such as the EPU within the OEEC. The restructuring of the global capitalist economic system was promoted as part of the America's global strategy to open lucrative markets with their attractive, yet latent possibilities. To enable West Germany's return into the world economy after the war, various conditions were imposed by the US through the creation of this type of international economic and financial system (Abelshauser 1983, p. 149).

The Bretton Woods system was a new institutional framework created to guarantee free multilateral trade, with the objective of creating an international settlement system that could absorb income and expenditure imbalances from the countries. The International Monetary Fund (IMF) was the most important establishment within this system (Carreras 2006, pp. 308–309). The US dollar, pegged to the value of gold, became the key currency of the Western world, and currency convertibility was implemented in the vast majority of Western countries that relied on the dollar. This created a steady foundation that made possible comparisons of trade accounting and settlements for all countries participating in world trade. In addition, the agreement within the GATT framework brought about dramatic reductions in import tariffs for member nations, and did away with the restrictions on import and export volumes and other discriminative barriers within international trade (Plettner 1994, pp. 111–112). West Germany was included under GATT in October 1951, and had thus restored total sovereignty in tariff and trade policies. Around this time, the 38 nations participating in GATT accounted for 80% of global trade volume (Abelshauser 2004, p. 223). Thus, the restructuring of the world economic system was extraordinarily significant to the rebuilding Germany's economy post war.

OEEC had important implications not only on economic cooperation among European nations but also on the development of the productivity movement. The EPU was a component of the OEEC and a critical factor in the success of the step-by-step liberalization movement of international trade (Landes 1969, p. 506). The EPU was not merely a settlement institution, but acted as a credit organization as well (Hellborn 1963, pp. 124, 133). It eased European trade in goods and services, thereby expanding trade, and created the prerequisites for the gradual shift to global currency convertibility (Bundesminister für den Marshallplan 1953, p. 43). The EPU was also an important player in the formation of a regional economic zone. As the movement toward a free trade system gained steam, a "structured" regional economic zone, or an "organizational" interdependent economic body, was formed by the OEEC and EPU, which perhaps may have been termed the Western European economic zone at a time when regional economic integration, such as that brought about by the EEC, had not yet taken shape. As a "protected market" distinguished from the US, the Western European economic zone provided favorable conditions for West German exports, creating an export structure further reliant on Western Europe (Furuuchi 2007, pp. 89–91). Therefore, the entrance of Germany into European markets became possible through the EPU and OEEC (Neebe 1996, pp. 104–105).

In stark contrast with the period following World War I, the creation of basic conditions for the advancement of the capitalist camp into global markets with the restructuring of the US-led world economic system was significant. Opportunities for global exports allowed for the adoption of a scale merit theory in investment policies of German corporations as well as the successful promotion of mass production within German industries (Wellhöner 1996, p. 17). Thus, the development of mass production, the switch to an economic system that pursued economies of scale, the restructuring of the US-led world economic system, and Germany's inclusion in global markets are all greatly significant in business management.

In comparison with Germany, Asian countries, mostly being colonies, lacked mechanisms such as the OEEC and EPU that could contribute to trade promotion in Europe. Further, there was no emphasis on the creation of market linkages by opening markets within European countries. Nevertheless, Japan was given the position of a bastion of anti-communism in the Far East and the role of a factory in Asia. However, due to the conditions in each Asian country and the slow pace of development of Japanese productive forces, when compared with Germany's expected role as an economic engine for rebuilding economic conditions within Europe, Japan played a relatively smaller role.

2.3 Development of the US-Led Productivity Movement

As discussed, the economic rebuilding of the capitalist system under the new framework was specifically brought about by the productivity movement that expanded internationally due to US-led guidance and assistance. The productivity movement provided opportunities to learn about and deploy US technologies and management methods, as well as strengthened linkages among European markets. Thus, the movement was critical to the global structure of capitalism postwar. We will next discuss the expansion of the productivity movement.

In Sect. 2.3.1, we will first discuss the international expansion of the productivity movement under the US Technical Assistance Program. In Sect. 2.3.2, we will examine institutional efforts within the movement from the perspective of the US Technical Assistance and Productivity Program (USTA&P). Finally, in Sect. 2.3.3, we will consider Germany's response to the expansion of the US-led productivity movement.

2.3.1 International Expansion of the Productivity Movement

The productivity movement was developed during the postwar era as a means for economic rebuilding, and its greatest characteristic was that it expanded internationally, particularly in the capitalist countries where rationalization under the Marshall Plan was carried out by US-led direction and assistance. The US aimed at not only the revitalization and industrial development of the impoverished capitalistic economies within these major countries, but also the reconstruction of global markets and the maintenance and strengthening of the capitalist camp through economic rebuilding in each country. Thus, countries under the Marshall Plan were asked to adopt rationalization policies and measures. This led to the establishment of the Technical Assistance Bureau in Paris in 1948 and a productivity committee in the OEEC in 1950/1951, which were later reorganized into the European Productivity Agency (EPA) in 1953. These organizations implemented rationalization policies in countries under the Marshall Plan, in particular West Germany (Pavel 1957, pp. 12–13; Thalmann 1956, p. 91). The international expansion of the productivity movement due to the creation of the EPA was an inevitable result of the fusion of the two primary goals of US policy postwar: improvement in productivity and promotion of European integration (Boel 2002, p. 88). In the first few years of the 1950s, among the countries under the Marshall Plan, West Germany was the heart of capitalistic rationalization (Thalmann 1956, p. 91) and an important country within Europe for the expansion of the productivity movement (*National Archives*, RG469, Assistant Administration for Production, Productivity & Technical Assistance Division, Records relating to U.S. Advisory Group on European Productivity, 1952–1953, The Concept and Status of the Productivity Program).

Next, we will compare the productivity movement with the rationalization movement post-World War I and examine the important differences. The US was involved in the rationalization movement after World War I, but this involvement was limited to funding rationalization through capital exports under the Dawes Plan. The industrial rationalization movement was individually undertaken by each country, with no leadership or direction provided by the US for the movement. As a result, efforts to study and implement US technology and management methods were mainly carried out individually at the corporate level. In contrast, the US provided strong institutional support at the technical and management levels post-World War II, which was promoted through unified guidance from the US. This was characterized as a more comprehensive movement to stabilize a system of capitalism (Nakamura 1958, p. 260).

Improvement in productivity became key in US aid policies for Western Europe, and US anti-communist efforts made during the Cold War era became to provide political and economic stability in Western Europe after the war (Boel 1998a, pp. 37–38). However, at the time, independent efforts from each country were insufficient, and a speedy economic rebuilding within European nations was not possible without the international expansion of the productivity movement under the auspices of US technical and financial aid. A report by the Federal Ministry for the Marshall Plan pointed out that, among the countries under the Plan, productivity improvements could only be achieved through sufficient technical information and other assistance along with the necessary funding [*Bundesarchiv Koblenz*, B102/37052, Gründung einer europäischen Produktivitätszentrale. Dokumente PRA (52) 47 und PRA (52) 48 (8.1.1953), p. 1]. After the World War II, conditions for the study and deployment of US technology and management methods were put in place under US guidance and assistance. Moreover, the USTA&P, a part of the Marshall Plan, was a pillar of this assistance, which we will discuss below.

2.3.2 Development of the Productivity Movement and the US Technical Assistance and Productivity Program

2.3.2.1 Characteristics of the US Technical Assistance and Productivity Program

In contrast with capital aid under the Marshall Plan, US assistance for each country's productivity movement was termed technical assistance. As part of this technical assistance, the US shared technology with European countries for broadly-defined productivity improvements, intended to increase the effects of capital aid (Oba 1975, pp. 49–50; Takagi 1962, pp. 7–8). In other words, the objective was productivity improvement in European industries through the transfer of US technological and management know-how. The USTA&P was the specific program for promoting these means. The Marshall Plan and the productivity movement both provided unique opportunities to thoroughly research the transfer of management models to other countries from the standpoints of both usable volumes of knowledge and the scale and scope of know-how (Bjarnar and Kipping 1998, pp. 1–2). The USTA&P was created by ERP policy-makers and aimed at reforming European management practice as well as education and training (McGlade 1998b, p. 13). Further, in conjunction with the necessity to remilitarize because of the Korean War, the USTA&P heightened efforts to promote the large-scale transfer of US management models and industrial technology as a means to stimulate business and production reforms in Western Europe and increase munitions production capacity (McGlade 2011, pp. 170–171). On the other hand, from the perspective of European countries, a primary reason for the Americanization of Europe was the desire to catch up with US productivity and prosperity (Schröter 2005a, p. 221).

Under these circumstances, the productivity movement was an institutional effort to export US economic and management organization models to Western

Europe and the Far East in the 1950s (Kipping 2004, p. 31). The study and transfer of technology and know-how were the primary objectives of technical assistance projects [*National Archives*, RG469, Special Representative in Europe Office of the General Council, Subject Files, 1948–1953, Technical Assistance Criteria (6.4.1951)]. It was held that productivity improvements, carried out especially through a thorough the transfer and deployment of US management methods (Neebe 1989, p. 67) and advanced technologies, were primary issues.

The purpose of technical assistance was to realize the vast improvements in productivity through the promotion of proficient US technology standards through concentrated and unique experiences within economic sectors at the national and international level [*Bundesarchiv Koblenz*, B102/37021, Internationaler Erfahrungsaustausch im Rahmen des europäischen Wiederaufbauprogramms (15.11.1954), p. 1, *National Archives*, RG469, The Productivity and Technical Assistance Program for Europe, pp. 9–10, *National Archives*, RG469, Productivity and Technical Assistance Division Office of the Director, Technical Assistance Country Files, 1949–1952, A letter to the Security for advancement of management (New York) from Dr. C. Kapferer (20.9.1950)]. The USTA&P aimed at achieving the necessary production levels in the capitalist realm of the world economy as well as implementing productivity advances by working with the productivity centers of each country and providing financial assistance and know-how for them (Kleinschmidt 2007, p. 54). In addition, its objective was the improvement of production and distribution methods in European industrial and agricultural fields, amongst others (*National Archives*, RG469, Assistant Administration for Production, Productivity & Technical Assistance Division, Records relating to U.S. Advisory Group on European Productivity, 1952–1953, The Productivity and Technical Assistance Program for Europe, p. 1), and it attempted to instill the US principles of mass production and consumption among Europe's business leaders (Kipping 2004, p. 32). The US intent of economic rebuilding in Germany by inculcating new values was not only limited to economic education but also included exportation of US culture (Schröter 2005a, p. 54).

The concept of productivity held two meanings. In the narrow sense, it meant an increase in per capita production per hour or year by using new production technology and management techniques; whereas in the broader sense, it included an attitude toward production, human relations in corporations, and consumption (Barjot 2002, p. 48). An essential goal of US productivity propaganda in Europe, particularly in West Germany, was the evangelization of the legendary benefits of the "American Lifestyle" (Wettengel 1963, p. 110).

The USTA&P was primarily responsible for the promotion of mutual cooperation between US and European corporations and industries. However, after 1949 there were many efforts to spread US-style business management practices, models for human relations in the workplace, and labor relations through various programs (McGlade 1998a, p. 26). In the fall of 1951, US politicians and business executives invited leading industrial executives and representatives from 17 European countries to tour US cities and factories, and sponsored a joint meeting of the two countries' manufacturers. This meeting was the first highly conscious effort by the US in the postwar era to ingrain the "gospel of productivity" in Europe's corporate leadership (Kipping 1998, pp. 55–56).

US technical and management assistance under the framework of the Marshall Plan and USTA&P was particularly provided to small- and medium-sized firms (Kleinschmidt 2007, p. 110). USTA&P-sponsored productivity missions were more effective for medium-sized corporations than large enterprises directly connected to US corporations (Crouzet 2002, p. 437). Moreover, institutional opportunities for study and deployment were also important for large enterprises.

Based on the above, we see three types of projects within the content of the Technical Assistance Program: dispatch of observation teams from various European countries for study trips to the US (project type A); visits by US experts to Europe for consultation and seminar instructions (project type B); and study trips within Europe to facilitate exchanges of experience, information, and knowledge gained by the Europeans during their visits to the US (project type C) (*Bundesarchiv Koblenz*, B102/37023, Bericht über Produktivitäts-massnahmen in der Bundesrepublik Deutschland, pp. 9–10; RKW 1956, p. 36). Objectives of these projects were as follows: promoting rationalization and contributing to productivity improvements, implementing rationalization and productivity improvements that would serve economy-wide interests, and reporting of benefits by the trips' participants, which would then be made public [*Bundesarchiv Koblenz*, B102/37262, Wirtschaftliche Studienreisen nach USA zu Export- zweck und zur Marktforschung (4.6.1954), p. 1].

2.3.2.2 European Framework for the US Technical Assistance and Productivity Program

Next, by examining the European framework of the USTA&P, we will observe that the greatest potential for economic improvement in Europe is through industrial production. The primary objectives of the European Cooperation Administration (ECA) were to increase industrial production (*National Archives*, RG353, The Interdepartmental Advisory Council on Technical Cooperation and its Predecessore, Subject Files, 1938–1953, Technical Assistance to Countries participating in the European Recovery Program, p. 8). In addition, mass production, productivity improvements, and the creation of a competitive environment in Europe were within the main scope of the program set by ECA for Western Europe (Djelic 1998, p. 115).

In most cases, the ECA took the initiative for exchanges of experiences between the US and participating nations and those directly between participating nations, as well as efforts to learn from the US under the Technical Assistance Program. These efforts took the form of proposals for specific projects in each country's productivity centers (Schröter 2005a, p. 51). Entrepreneurs and managers in large corporations, with an interest in US management details and methods or new technologies, were not very interested in financial assistance; however, they held strong interests in USTA&P and OEEC programs (Kleinschmidt 2002, pp. 309–310).

Among these programs, the Article 13 programs formulated by the ECA in 1950 built a foundation for German policies to implement technical assistance. Some of the main strategies were as follows: the establishment of a productivity center;

advice from US experts on the German economic sector, study trips by German experts to the US and other countries; communications for technical advice; and expanding the use of statistics (productivity comparisons), educational films, and publications as educational materials (Bundesminister für den Marshallplan 1951b, pp. 49–51). These programs provided the possibility to learn from and implement all types of experiences from foreign countries, particularly the US, to develop the German economy [*Bundesarchiv Koblenz*, B102/37022, Etatvorschlag für die Produktivitätszentrale (PZ), p. 2]. Specifically, these were further expanded to include concentrated educational seminars for executives and managers, test projects providing special assistance to European corporations implementing US-style management and labor relations practices, consultant programs, and US industrial visits to European corporations (McGlade 1998a, pp. 27, 30; McGlade 2000, p. 67). Small research committees, created within US advisory groups, analyzed productivity issues and the most effective methods for analyzing problems that had a direct effect on productivity improvements (*National Archives*, RG469, Assistant Administration for Production, Productivity & Technical Assistance Division, Records relating to U.S. Advisory Group on European Productivity, 1952–1953, A letter to Mr. John, W. Nickerson from H. B. Maynart on 14 March 1952). Even in Europe, education and relevant materials for instructors provided as part of assistance from the US was being seen as necessary (*National Archives*, RG469, Assistant Administration for Production, Productivity & Technical Assistance Division, Records relating to U.S. Advisory Group on European Productivity, 1952–1953, A letter to D. L. Cole from R. L. Oshins on 25 June 1952, p. 3).

Within this framework of assistance, the Mutual Security Agency (MSA) made funding of 117,800,000 Deutsche Marks (DM) available from ERP special assets to promote German economic productivity [*Bundesarchiv Koblenz*, B102/37099, Produktivitätsprogramm (5.8.1953), p. 1, *Bundesarchiv Koblenz*, B102/37100, Produktivitätsprogramm, Dezember 1954, p. 1, *Bundesarchiv Koblenz*, B102/37099, Endgültige Richtlinien zum Produktivitäs-Kreditprogramm der Bundesregierung—Rundschreiben der Hauptgeschäftsführung vom 6 Juli 1953, pp. 1–2]. However, conventionally large industries, such as the iron and steel industry and the chemical industry, did not rely on the USTA&P for organizational development and financial assistance. ERP assistance emphasized small- and medium-sized firms, although the amount of credit available for assistance to these firms was relatively small. Of the aforementioned 117,800,000 DM aid from the counterpart fund, projects requiring less than 50,000 DM of credit accounted for the largest portion (37.4%); whereas those requiring credit supplies from 75,000 DM to 100,000 DM accounted for one third. Projects over 100,000 DM accounted for no more than 10% of the total (Kleinschmidt 2002, p. 70).

However, based on the nature of the Technical Assistance Program, the need for experienced personnel was relatively high, in contrast to that for financial assistance. For example, from 1952 to 1953, 24% of MSA personnel in the US and Europe were dedicated to the USTA&P (*National Archives*, RG469, Assistant Administration for Production, Productivity & Technical Assistance Division, Records relating to U.S. Advisory Group on European Productivity, 1952–1953, The Productivity and Technical Assistance Programs for Europe, pp. 1–3).

The OEEC was deeply involved in the productivity movement, and from 1949 onward, it aided USTA&P in organizing a series of programs for re-training and technical assistance for management of private corporations in Europe (McGlade 2000, p. 71). The purpose of these technical assistance projects within Europe was to foster mutual assistance among countries in the region and the exchange of technical information [*National Archives*, RG469, Special Representative in Europe Office of the General Council, Subject Files, 1948–1953, Intra-European Technical Assistance (12.7.1951)]. It was in this environment that study trips at the national and international level were undertaken within the framework of the OEEC program that provided technical assistance (Blücher 1952, p. 33).

In addition, within the OEEC and USTA&P framework for promotion of the US-style productivity model in Europe, in 1953, the EPA was established as a semi-autonomous organization through initiatives by the US and OEEC (Kleinschmidt 2002, p. 64). The Technical Assistance Program, previously conceived as a productivity committee within the EPA, fulfilled its role of providing opportunities for exchanges within Europe through the promotion of heightened human interaction among related organizations (Bundesminister für den Marshallplan 1951b, p. 14).

The EPA had four main functions: (1) channelizing US aid to OEEC nations, (2) acting as the OEEC's business department, (3) organizing information exchange among member nations, and (4) uniting the productivity centers of each country. Among these, it fulfilled the major role of improving business management from the outset of the program (Boel 1998b, pp. 36–37). The EPA's primary responsibility was coordinating the expansion of aid programs for industries that were being implemented by each country's productivity center (McGlade 2000, p. 72); however, it was planned as a means of transferring US technology, know-how, and ideas to Western Europe (Boel 1998a, p. 37). In addition, EPA activities included study trips to the US, sponsorships of international study trips and conferences within Europe, information and propaganda (e.g., reports, conferences, exhibitions, and films), research and development, education, information services, and exchanges of experiences between the US and European countries through technical assistance [*National Archives*, RG469, Deputy Director for Management Office of Organization & Methods Office of the Director, AFE Adm Budgets to France Organization European Country File 1954–1957, European Integration (1.3.1956), p. 5; Blücher 1954, p. 60; Harten 1953, p. 1013].

Thus, international projects for economic exchanges were undertaken on a large scale by the EPA in European regions [*Bundesarchiv Koblenz*, B102/37021, Internationaler Erfahrungsaustausch im Rahmen des europäischen Wiederaufbauprogramms (15.11.1954), p. 7, *National Archives*, RG469, Productivity and Technical Assistance Division Office of the Director, Technical Assistance Country Subject Files, 1949–1952, German-General, Technical Assistance Monthly News Report in February 1950 (9.3.1951)]. EPA activities were focused on disseminating values and attitudes related to modern management issues, in particular labor relations, marketing, and sales (Kleinschmidt 2004, p. 167). Among these, management education held a particularly crucial position. The core objectives of the EPA management education program were the creation of education centers in Europe and the "Europeanization" of educational content (Boel 1998a, p. 44).

Although the EPA did not become an important channel for implementing US management models, it functioned as a catalyst and promoter of a broad transfer of mechanisms, particularly aiding the creation and maintenance of various channels that did contribute to the spread of US models of productivity, management education, and labor relations (Bjarnar and Kipping 1998, p. 9). EPA activities did not focus on the implementation of various policies to improve productivity; instead, they acted as intermediaries in the development of necessary methods, specialized education, the promotion of experience exchanges, and the creation of favorable conditions for corporations to implement productivity improvements (von Lilienstern 1960, p. 1077; Harten 1955, p. 129).

2.3.2.3 Significance of the US Technical Assistance and Productivity Program

Based on the above points, we will next examine the significance of the USTA&P, particularly the relevance of institutional efforts to transfer and deploy US technology and management methods through strong US assistance.

After Germany's transition from the stage of recovery to that of rapid economic development, the emphasis on Americanization moved from the level of institutions to that of enterprise. Along with direct investment and technical cooperation (licensing), the productivity movement acted as the primary route for transfer and deployment of US-style management methods (Kudo et al. 2004, pp. 9–10). US programs and projects exerted a tremendous influence on the introduction of US-style management methods through the formation of networks for US and German corporations, associations, government organizations, universities, and individual intermediaries that served as the basis for information transmission and the spread of US management and production methods (Kleinschmidt 2002, p. 83).

However, direct transfer mechanisms such as the Marshall Plan aid, US technical assistance, and trans-Atlantic productivity missions had a very limited influence on European industries. Decisive postwar initiatives for the absorption of US technology and management methods needed to be tailored for local environments by deconstructing, editing, and reconstituting the elements of the US model. This was done by manufacturers, engineers, and bureaucrats who had implemented the imported mass production methods or had experience using them (Zeitlin 2000, p. 41). Between 1953 and 1958, the USTA&P allowed the creative conformance to European government and the industrial world out of its own necessity, rather than directly adopting US-style industrial strategies and practices (McGlade 2000, p. 74).

As for the orientation of German corporations to US corporations and the implementation of US technology and management methods, although information networks between the two countries differed, they shared two supplementary relationships. First, were the efforts of the US government, organizations, and corporations through the mid-1950s; they exported philosophies and models for management and production into Germany through the framework of the Marshall Plan and USTA&P, which acted as a type of development aid or self-reliance assistance for small- and medium-sized firms. Second, was the relationship of free-will orientation toward the US model within large corporations, which was a phenomenon that could not be appropriately expressed by the concepts of "Americanization" or "cultural imperialism in management." Regarding the former, the trend toward Americanization reflected a disproportionate power relationship between the two countries (Kleinschmidt 2002, p. 396). In particular, contact with the US, and the many opportunities for the research and deployment of US-style technology and management methods provided by the productivity movement, created important conditions that strengthened this free-will orientation to the US model. From the 1960s, changes in market conditions brought about the important trend of stronger adaptation to US know-how in German corporations (Vgl. Hilger 2004, pp. 281, 284–286). Thus, the free-will orientation became increasingly stronger. Nevertheless, the opportunities and channels for the learning and development within the productivity movement framework remained important.

Furthermore, the USTA&P promoted greater deployment and penetration of the US-style corporate activity mechanism of "efficiency" into German corporations. Even after World War I, the principle of "economic efficiency" was flagged as a problem, which is seen in the name of the organization that was the greatest promoter and supporter of rationalization, Reichskuratorium für Wirtschaftlichkeit (the National Board for Economic Efficiency). However, it can be safely said that the USTA&P fulfilled its role as a promoter of a more earnest pursuit of productivity improvements in German corporations in accordance with US-style management principles. It did so by "evangelizing/preaching the gospel of productivity" and creating favorable conditions for research, implementation, and transfer of US technology and management methods.

2.3.3 Germany's Response to the US-Led Productivity Movement

The US-led productivity movement and campaign was positively received by some European nations, although other nations that participated in the movement viewed it with skepticism, for example, England and other northern European countries (Boel 1998b, pp. 38, 48–49). Bearing this in mind, we will next analyze Germany's response.

As we examine the relevance of technology transfer or deployment of management methods, we will observe resistance to the Technical Assistance Program due to a weak belief in US political organizations and the possibility of incorporating US practices in Germany (Wend 2002, p. 133). However, at the end of the 1940s and beginning of the 1950s, promoters of Americanization open to and positive toward US philosophies and methods were no longer in the minority. In the first half of the postwar era, this was evident not only in US machinery and technology, paid for by the Marshall Plan, but also in the gradual transfer and dissemination of ideology at the heart of management practices and product exports. World War II resulted in the weakening of the formerly strong and conservative position of German industries, and this change in balance urged the importation of American culture on an even broader scale than that seen in the periods between the wars. However, instead of an overall adaptation, the US model was a peculiar mix of inherent German traditions and practices that imported US methods (Berghahn 1991, pp. 160–161).

The postwar pressure exerted by the US model was extraordinarily strong, and the wave of Americanization at the time was much larger in scale than that during the 1920s (Schröter 2005a, p. 62). Moreover, in comparison to the post-World War I era, the existence, role, and influence of the USTA&P and other US institutional programs in regard to Germany's response made Americanization particularly significant.

On the basis of the above discussion, we can state the following about the historical characteristics and significance of the productivity movement. The productivity movement created a path for Germany to become a major player in the economic development of Europe and laid the market foundation and basis for activities, through which German corporations and industries could enter Western Europe and thereafter the Western world. In other words, participation in the productivity movement led and assisted by the US created conditions that drew West Germany closer to capitalist markets, in particular European markets, by putting West Germany in a central rationalized position within the movement. In addition, the formation of a framework with conditions favorable to the deployment of US-style technology and management methods and the subsequent continuation of those deployment routes in the period that followed are particularly noteworthy. By creating the foundation for a domestic market and conditions in which West Germany could increase its role in international markets, routes for deploying US technology and management methods that were key to expanding productive forces were inherited during the 1960s. Unlike the period before World War II, the productivity movement created opportunities for Germany to catch up with the US structure of productive forces by providing the right market conditions.

Thus, a broader and deeper global linkage to capitalism was created through the international expansion of the productivity movement, with the aim of providing the most favorable conditions by combining productive and market forces under a US-centric framework and system of aid. It was under these circumstances that Germany was granted a foundation for a reproduction (accumulation) structure for German capitalism centered in European regions, which was based on its own interpretation and development of the Americanization of technology and management.

In the case of Japan, the Asian markets did not open up as they did in Europe. This was because many Asian countries implemented the productivity movement much later than Japan did and had limited trade partners after the war. Thus, Japan had no regional market linkages in Asia as did Europe, and Japan's trade reliance on the US had only heightened. The productivity movement within Japan began in 1955, and compared to Europe, it was not necessarily considered a direct method of economic rebuilding in the postwar period. These differing circumstances in the expansion of the productivity movement created the foundation for German independence from the US and the path to Europeanization through the formation of markets in response to an increase in productive forces.

In our discussions thus far, we have shown the significance of Germany in Europe by comparing with it that of Japan in Asia, and the restructuring of both in the postwar world economic system based on America's global strategy. Within Germany itself, there were major political and economic changes in the postwar era, such as the restructuring of the economic system and the development of competition policies and anti-monopoly policies thereafter and a new framework for labor relations based on the codetermination system. In Chaps. 3 and 4 we will discuss these issues at greater length.

References

Abelshauser A (1983) Wirtschaftsgeschichte der Bundesrepublik Deutschland 1945–1980. Suhrkamp, Frankfurt am Main

Abelshauser W (2004) Deutsche Wirtschaftsgeschichte seit 1945. C. H. Beck, München

Albrecht K (1952) Steigerung der Produktivität. Rationalisierung 3(2):49–52

Barjot D (2002) Introduction. In: Barjot D (ed) Catching up with America. Productivity missions and the diffusion of American economic and technological influence after the Second World War. Pressede L'université de Paris-Sorbonne, Paris, pp 13–50

Baumgart ER (1961) Investitionen und ERP-Finanziern (Deutsche Institut für Wirtschaftsforschung, Sonderhefte, Neue Folge, Nr.56). Duncker & Humblot, Berlin

Berghahn VR (1991) Technology and the export of industrial culture: problems of the German-American relationship 1900–1960. In: Mathias P, Davis JA (eds) Innovation and technology in Europe: from the eighteenth century to the present day. B. Blackwell, Oxford, pp 142–161

Bjarnar O, Kipping M (1998) The Marshall Plan and the transfer of US management models to Europe. An introductory framework. In: Kipping M, Bjarnar O (eds) The Americanization of European business. The Marshall Plan and the transfer of US management models. Routledge, London, pp 1–17

Blücher F (1952) Das Bundesministerium für den Marshallplan. In: Das Presse- und Informationsamt der Bundesregierung (ed) Deutschland im Wiederaufbau. Tätigkeitsbericht der Bundesregierung für das Jahr 1952. Kommissionsverlag, Bonn, pp 29–40

Blücher F (1954) Das Bundesministerium für wirtschaftliche Zusammenarbeit. In:Das Presse- und Informationsamt der Bundesregierung (ed) Deutschland im Wiederaufbau. Tätigkeitsbericht der Bundesregierung für das Jahr 1954. Commissionsverlag, Bonn, pp 57–70

Boel B (1998a) The European productivity agency. A faithful prophet of the American model? In: Kipping M, Bjarnar O (eds) The Americanization of European business. The Marshall plan and the transfer of US management models. Routledge, London, pp 37–54

Boel B (1998b) The European productivity agency and the development of management education in Western Europe in the 1950s. In: Gourvish T, Tiratsoo N (eds) Missionaries and managers: American influences on European management education, 1945–60. Manchester University Press, New York, pp 34–49

Boel B (2002) The European productivity agency and American policy toward Western Europe after World War II. In: Barjot D (ed) Catching up with America. Productivity missions and the diffusion of American economic and technological influence after the Second World War. Presse de L'université de Paris-Sorbonne, Paris, pp 87–97

Borchardt K (1978) Grundriβ der deutschen Wirtschaftsgeschichte. Vandenhoeck & Ruprecht, Göttingen

Buchheim C (1993) Marshall Plan and currency reform. In: Diefendorf JM, Frohon A, Rupieper H-J (eds) American policy and the reconstruction of West Germany, 1945–1951. Cambridge University Press, Cambridge, pp 69–83

Bundesminister für den Marshallplan (1950a) Dritter Bericht der Deutschen Bundesregierung über die Durchführung des Marshallplanes, 1. April 1950 bis 30. Juni 1950. Bundesminister für den Marshallplan, Bonn

Bundesminister für den Marshallplan (1950b) Vierter Bericht der Deutschen Bundesregierung über die Durchführung des Marshallplanes, 1. Juli 1950 bis 30. September 1950. Bundesminister für den Marshallplan, Bonn

Bundesminister für den Marshallplan (1951a) Fünfter und Sechster Bericht der Deutschen Bundesregierung über die Durchführung des Marshallplanes für die Quartale 1. Oktober 1950 bis 31. Dezember 1950, 1. Januar 1951 bis 31. März 1951 und Rückblick bis 1. Oktober 1949 bis 31. Dezember 1949. Bundesminister für den Marshallplan, Bonn

Bundesminister für den Marshallplan (1951b) Siebenter Bericht der Deutschen Bundesregierung über die Durchführung des Marshallplanes, 1. April 1951 bis 30. Juni 1951. Bundesminister für den Marshallplan, Bonn

Bundesminister für den Marshallplan (1952) Elfter Bericht der Deutschen Bundesregierung über die Durchführung des Marshallplanes, 1. April 1952 bis 30. Juni 1952. Bundesminister für den Marshallplan, Bonn

Bundesminister für den Marshallplan (1953) Zwölfter, abchschließender Bericht der Deutschen Bundesregierung über die Durchführung des Marshallplanes für die Zeit bis 30. Juni 1952 und Erster und Zweiter Bericht über die Fortführung amerikanischer Wirtschaftshilfe (MSA) für die Zeit vom 1. Juli bis 31. Dezember 1952. Bundesminister für den Marshallplan, Bonn

Carreras A (2006) The twentieth century—from break with the past to prosperity (II). The great stages. In: Vittorio AD (ed) An economic history of Europe. From expansion to development. Routledge, London, pp 289–334

Crouzet F (2002) Conclusions. In: Barjot D (ed) Catching up with America. Productivity missions and the diffusion of American economic and technological influence after the Second World War. Presse de L'université de Paris-Sorbonne, Paris, pp 427–438

Djelic M-L (1998) Exporting the American model. The postwar transformation of European business. Oxford University Press, Oxford

Furuuchi H (2007) Gendai Doitsu Keizai no Rekishi (A history of the modern German economy). Tokyo Daigaku Shuppankai, Tokyo

Handbuch der Deutschen Aktiengesellschaftn (1953) Allgemeine Elektricität-Gesellachaft. Handbuch der Deutschen Aktiengesellschaftn 1952/53 53(4):4227–4236

Harten KP (1953) Internationale Bestrebungen zur Steigerung der Produktivität. Stahl und Eisen 73(16):1009–1013

Harten KP (1955) Die europäische Produktivitätszentrale im Rahmen der Bestrebungen um Europas wirtschaftliche Fertigung. In: Brandt L, Frenz G (eds) Industrielle Rationalisierung 1955. Verkehrs- und Wirtschafts-Verlag, Dortmund, pp 128–129

Hellborn R (1963) Der westdeutsche Imperialismus erobert Westeuropas Markt. Akademie Verlag, Berlin

Hilger S (2004) „Amerikanisierung" deutscher Unternehmen. Wettbewerbsstrategien und Unternehmenspolitik bei Henkel, Siemens und Daimler-Benz (1945/49-1975). Franz Steiner Verlag, Stuttgart

I.P.W.-Berichte (1978) Wissenschaftlich-technischer Fortschritt und Entwicklungstendenzen des gegenwärtigen Kapitalismus. I.P.W.-Berichte 7(10):1–8

Karlsch R, Stokes RG (2003) «Faktor Öl». Die Mineralölwirtschaft in Deutschland 1859–1974. C. H. Beck, München

Kipping M (1998) Operation impact. Converting European employers to the American creed. In: Kipping M, Bjarnar O (eds) The Americanization of European business. The Marshall Plan and the transfer of US management models. Routledge, London, pp 55–73

Kipping K (2004) 'Importing' American ideas to west Germany, 1940s to 1970s. From associations to private consultancies. In: Kudo A, Kipping M, Schröteret HG (eds) German and Japanese business in the boom years. Transforming American management and technology models. Routledge, London, pp 30–53

Kitamura J (1973) Sengo Doitsu no Seiji to Keizai (German policy and economy after WW II). Horitsu Bunkasha, Kyoto
Kleinschmidt C (2002) Der produktive Blick. Wahrnehmung amerikanischer und japanischer Management- und Produktionsmethoden durch deutsche Unternehmer 1950–1985. Akademie Verlag, Berlin
Kleinschmidt C (2004) America and the resurgence of the German chemical and rubber industry after the Second World War. Hüls, Glanzstoff and Continental. In: Kudo A, Kipping M, Schröteret HG (eds) German and Japanese business in the boom years. Transforming American management and technology models. Routledge, London, pp 161–174
Kleinschmidt C (2007) Technik und Wirtschaft im 19. und 20. Jahrhundert. Oldenbourg Wissenschafts-Verlag, München
Kudo A (1996) Keizai Seichou to Chiiki Togo (Economic growth and regional integration). In: Hara T, Kudo A (eds) Gendai Yoroppa Keizaishi (Modern European economic history). Yuhikaku, Tokyo, pp 247–279
Kudo A, Kipping M, Schröteret HG (2004) Americanization. Historical and conceptual issues. In: Kudo A, Kipping M, Schröteret HG (eds) German and Japanese business in the boom years. Transforming American management and technology models. Routledge, London, pp 1–29
Landes DS (1969) The unbound Prometheus. Technological change and industrial development in Western Europe from 1750 to the present. Cambridge University Press, Cambridge
Maekawa K (1970) Doitsu Dokusen Kigyo no Hatten Katei (Development of monopolistic enterprise in Germany). Mineruva Shobo, Kyoto
Manabe S (1989) Amerika no Doitsu Senryo Seisaku (America's occupation policy for Germany). Horitsu Bunkasha, Kyoto
McGlade J (1998a) From business reform programme to production drive. The transformation of US technical assistance to west Europe. In: Kipping M, Bjarnar O (eds) The Americanization of European business. The Marshall Plan and the transfer of US management models. Routledge, London, pp 18–34
McGlade J (1998b) The US technical assistance and productivity program and the education of Western European managers, 1948–58. In: Gourvish TR, Tiratsoo N (eds) Missionaries and managers: American influences on European management education, 1945–60. Manchester University Press, New York, pp 13–33
McGlade J (2000) Americanization: ideology or process? The case of the united states technical assistance productivity program. In: Zeitlin J, Herrigel G (eds) Americanization and its limits. Reworking US technology and management in post-War Europe and Japan. Oxford University Press, Oxford, pp 53–75
McGlade J (2011) The Marshall plan realized? American aims and European re-industrialization. In: Fauri F, Tedeschi P (eds) Novel outlooks on the Marshall P. American Aid and European re-industrialization. Peter Lang, Brussels, pp 165–195
Nakamura S (1958) Nihon Seisansei Kojo Undoshi (History of the productivity movement in Japan). Keiso Shobo, Tokyo
Neebe R (1989) Technologietransfer und Außenhandel in den Anfangsjahren der Bundesrepublik Deutschland. Vierteljahrschrift für Sozial- und Wirtschaftsgeschichte 76:49–75
Neebe R (1996) German big business and the return of the world market after World War II. In: Berghahn VR (ed) Quest for economic empire. European strategies of German Big business in the twentieth century. Berghahn Books, Oxford, pp 95–121
Oba K (1975) Seisansei Undo (Productivity movement). In: Nihon Seisansei Honbu (ed) Seisansei Jiten (Productivity dictionary). Nihon Seisansei Honbu, Tokyo
Pavel K-H (1957) Formen und Methoden der Rationalisierung in Westdetchland. Verlag Die Wirtschaft, Berlin
Plettner B (1994) Abenteuer Elektrotechnik. Siemens und die Entwicklung der Elektrotechnik seit 1945. Piper, München
Postan MM (1967) An economic history of Western Europe 1945–1964. Methuen& Co., London
RKW (1956) Der Stand der Deutschen Rationalisierung im Jahr 1955. RKW, Frankfurt am Main

Schlieper A (1986) 150 Jahre Ruhrgebiet. Ein Kapitel deutscher Wirtschaftsgeschichte. Schwann, Düsseldorf

Schröter HG (2005a) Americanization of the European economy. A compact survey of American economic influence in Europe since the 1880s. Springer, Dordrecht

Schröter HG (2005b) Deutschlands Reintegration in die europäischen Wirtschaft. In: North M (ed) Deutsche Wirtschaftsgeschichte. Ein Jahrtausend im Überblick, 2, völlig überarbeitete und aktualisiert Auflage. C. H. Beck, München, pp 362–388

Stolper G, Häuser K, Borchardt K (1964) Deutsche Wirtschaft seit 1870. J. C. B. Mohr, Tübingen

Suzuki N (1977) Sengo Amerika no Taigai Enjyo (Foreign assistance by the USA after WW II). Shoken Kenkyu (J Finance Securities Market) 54:375–427

Takagi K (1962) Nishi Yoroppa ni okeru Seisansei Undo (The productivity movement in Western Europe). Nihon Seisansei Honbu, Tokyo

Thalmann H (1956) Durch Rationalisierung ohne Kapital zur verstärkten Ausbeutung der Arbeiterklasse in Westdeutschland. In: Behrens F (ed) Aktuelle Fragen der Ökonomie und Politik des wiederstandenen deutschen Imperialismus: Festschrift zum zehnjährigen Bestehen des Verlags die Wirtschaft. Verlag der Wirtschaft, Berlin, pp 87–114

von Lilienstern HR (1960) Das europäische Produktivitätsprogramm 1960. Der Volkswirt 14(23):1077–1078

Wellhöner V (1996) „Wirtschaftswunder"—Weltmarkt—Westdeutscher Fordismus. Der Fall Volkswagen. Westfälisches Dampfboot, Münster

Wend HB (2002) 'But the German manufactur doesn't want our Advice'. West German labor and business and the limits of American technical assistance, 1950–1954. In: Barjot D (ed) Catching up with America. Productivity missions and the diffusion of American economic and technological influence after the Second World War. Presse de L'universite de Paris-Sorbonne, Paris, pp 123–134

Wettengel EB (1963) Bürgerliche Legenden vom Wesen der kapitalistischen Rationalisierungin Westdeutschland. Jahrbuch für Wirtschaftsgechichte, Teil I, pp 61–126

Yoshida K (1976) Doitsu Gorika Undou Ron (The rationalization movement in Germany). Mineruva Shobo, Kyoto

Zeitlin J (2000) Introduction: Americanization and its limits: reworking US technology and management in post-War Europe and Japan. In: Zeitlin J, Herrigel G (eds) Americanization and its limits. Reworking US technology and management in post-war Europe and Japan. Oxford University Press, Oxford, pp 1–50

Zieschang K (1959) Grundprobleme der Investitionsfinanzierung in Westdeutschland. Akademie Verlag, Berlin

Chapter 3
Changes in National, Economic, and Corporate Relations

Abstract This chapter discusses changes in the relationship among nation, economy, and enterprises in Germany's political economy, which were significant to business management and the development of industrial concentration. It focuses on the issues of economic order, national industrial policy, competition policy, anti-monopoly policy, and trade policy. It considers the characteristics of postwar Japanese relationships among the nation, economy, and enterprises, and the subsequent changes in Germany. The major issues are Germany's social market economy and currency reform, the nation's investment aid policy, anti-monopoly policy, and European integration efforts by Germany's trade policy. It examines the anti-monopoly policy reform in relation to the US occupation policy, Germany's initiatives, basic characteristics of The Restrictive Trade Practices Act, and the cooperative characteristics of German capitalism.

Keywords Currency reform • European integration • Investment aid policy • Restrictive trade practices act • Social market economy

In Chap. 3 we will discuss changes in Germany's political economy that were significant to the development of industrial concentration and business management. We will examine issues relating to national, economic, and corporate relations in Germany's postwar economic system.

We will first consider changes in political, economic, and corporate relations from the perspective of economic order, national industrial policy, competition policy, anti-monopoly policy, market policy, and trade policy. In particular, the postwar European region became increasingly important as a German economic zone for market and trade policies. Further, determining the most effective strategy for creating a reproduction (accumulation) structure for German capitalism, the cornerstone of the regional economy, was considered a critical policy issue. Thus, we also examine the role of the state and identify changes in national, economic, and corporate

T. Yamazaki, *German Business Management: A Japanese Perspective on Regional Development Factors*, DOI 10.1007/978-4-431-54303-9_3, © Springer Japan 2013

relations that created the fundamental conditions for business management in Germany, as well as the significance of these changes.

3.1 Characteristics of Postwar National, Economic, and Corporate Relations in Japan

When comparing Germany's situation of postwar economic order with Japan's, the heavy and chemical industries in Japan developed at a much slower rate than those in Germany and the US before the war. Moreover, Japan inevitably had to adopt mechanisms that strengthened wartime economic control to increase munitions production. However, with the switch to a market economy in the postwar era, Japan did not adopt a special approach to a social market economy as did Germany. As a strategy to promote economic rebuilding, Japan prioritized increased production in specific industries and directed the investment of funds and materials to the coal industry, iron and steel industry, and other critical industries. Policy instruments included financing through the Reconversion Finance Bank and subsidies covering the difference between market prices and officially established prices (Masamura 1983, p. 49; Nakamura 1980, pp. 158–160). Further, in 1952, the Law for Acceleration of Rationalization of Enterprises was enacted to promote rationalization investment primarily through measures such as extraordinary depreciation and tax reductions (Tsusho Sangyo Sho Tsusho Sangyo Seisakushi Hensan Iinkai 1990, pp. 359–362).

Anti-monopoly policies, such as the 1947 Anti-Monopoly Act, were enacted early on under the strong guidance and pressure from the GHQ. Although several subsequent revisions to the law eased restrictions, the overall framework continued to follow the guidelines established by occupation authorities; holding companies were outlawed as were the buying and holding of treasury stocks (Miwa 2005, pp. 664–665).

In regard to market policy, particularly trade policy, few Asian countries allowed free trade immediately after the war. Thus, the development of a common market as a specific measure of trade policy could not be achieved in the region.

Germany's circumstances were markedly different from Japan's; the Nazi-controlled economy switched to the postwar economic system, but more fundamentally, a social market economy structure was established and largely remains till date. In addition, the state not only provided a set of national investment aid measures, such as the Investment Assistance Act, but also included currency reform, re-evaluations of corporate assets, and tax policies to promote economic rebuilding. Further, even with the US dominating anti-monopoly policies, Germany had more freedom than Japan throughout the process of enacting anti-monopoly regulations. For instance, Germany's Restrictive Trade Practices Act passed in late 1957 permitted holding companies, which served as a means of corporate control and intercorporate unions. These issues were, and have remained, fundamental to the harmonious state of German capitalism and corporate concentration and unions.

The trade policy facilitated the early formation of a common market in the European region, which had been skewed toward trade since before the war.

In Sect. 3.2, we will first consider the characteristics of Germany's social market economy and currency reform. In Sect. 3.3, we will discuss investment subsidy measures by industrial policy and the state's role in such an economic system. Next, on the basis of these discussions, we will examine anti-monopoly policy in Sect. 3.4. In Sect. 3.5, we will further consider efforts by trade policy toward European integration, an important policy issue from the perspective of opposing the US.

3.2 Germany's New Economic Order Post World War II

3.2.1 Principles of a Social Market Economy and a New Economic Order

Germany's federal government considered the social market economy in the framework of a postwar economic order as critical for economic policy, particularly to further expand and solidify the domestic market economy and competition (Erhard 1954, p. 150). Before the war, monopolies and cartels in the market were accepted under the Nazi-controlled economy, with the state meddling in economic affairs of a "politicized economy"; however, postwar, the state played a more regulatory role in economic policy. This economic policy was based on a philosophy that emphasized market mechanisms by limiting government to an auxiliary role and the strict separation of politics and economy (Noda 1998, pp. 196–197).

Within the concept of neo-liberalism in the social market economy, the following three objectives were included in a new social order: (1) stimulating overall prosperity by improving productivity through free-trade initiatives, (2) redistributing income for social equity through state intervention, and (3) regulating a market economy through the control of social order (Molitor 1958, pp. 60–63). Social market economies demand the redistribution of income to resolve social constraints in such market conditions, apart from which the state does not intervene in its socioeconomic affairs (Walter 2003, pp. 242, 244).

Thus, the social nature of government policy was evident in the creation of a framework for an economic order that guaranteed the equitable distribution of the product and benefits of economic activity (Bundesministrium für Wirtschaft 1959, p. 18). Social market economy was based on the combined principle of "freedom in markets" and "social equilibrium" (Müller-Armack 1956, p. 390). For the former, government assumed the responsibility of creating a framework that promoted competition and a system of economic laws and policies to prevent cartels and secure the functioning of essential market mechanisms. However, social policy systems, in particular those for welfare, expressed the "social" aspect of the social market economy and the principles of social equilibrium (Inoue 1992, pp. 18–19). Since the type of market economy demanded non-interference by the state, apart from the establishment and maintenance of the requisite conditions for a free market economy, the state would interfere neither in the coordination issues of daily economic activities nor in long-term economic planning. The framework for collaboration among associations complemented these principles. These fundamentally new elements of the political economy system of market liberalization in postwar West Germany were supported by the functions of coordination through social organizations that developed the framework for market competition (Noda 1998, pp. 199, 204).

Legislative measures for the social market economy were adopted in the first half of the 1950s, and national social elements began to be implemented from the mid 1950s (Roesler 2006, p. 81–82). In the trend toward global economic policy in the postwar era, based on Keynesian theory, the social market economy was seen as an alternative to demand management, with Germany taking a specific path of regulative policy (Abelshauser 2004, p. 94). However, in the latter half of the 1960s, the German government contemplated intervening in the coordination of the overall economy through the Law to Promote Economic Stability and Growth, and thereafter pursued Keynesian countercyclical fiscal and budgetary policies corresponding to annual national expenditures (Schröter 2005b, p. 387; Abelshauser 1983, p. 113). The significance of this law is that government policies in the social market economy, at the time, were losing their ability to be rationalized in a stable manner (Idemizu 1978, p. 188). Nevertheless, an economic system based on the principles of the social market economy continued, and the direction of the economic order in the early postwar period was critical for securing market stability through its social redistribution function.

The social policy of redistribution, reflecting the "social" element in Germany's social market economy, became a factor in the nation's financial burden, and certain measures taken in response became major issues. In Chap. 4, we will examine the codetermination system, which at the time was said to be very important.

3.2.2 Currency Reform

We will see that currency reform was one of the three great reforms, along with the abolition of government control and tax system reform (Triebe 2001, p. 21). Easing economic confusion over the abnormal inflation of currency distribution in response to product supply and settling the Nazi Government's huge national debt were pressing problems after the war. Currency reform implemented in response to these issues (Krieger 1988, p. 375; Benz 1999, p. 190) was indispensable for rebuilding the postwar economic system. According to calculations, after switching currencies of bank deposits and older currency with declaration requirements, the Deutsche Mark was traded at an exchange rate of 6.5 marks per 100 Reichsmarks, and 93.5% of the Reichsmarks were removed from circulation (Benz 1999, p. 193; Abelshauser 2004, p. 125; Walter 2003, p. 232).

Although currency reform was a condition for the liberalization and normalization of trade, it opened new paths for economic policy and order by managing wartime inflation, ensuring reliance of market competition mechanisms, (Abelshauser 2004, pp. 121, 127–128) and enabling a shift from forced control to a free market (Angster 2004, p. 124). Currency reform was a precondition for implementing a smooth liberal economy and market economy in the form of a social market economy and making pricing mechanisms more robust. In addition, the stabilization of wartime inflation and the creation of a stable currency laid the foundation for the broad participation of German industries in exports to foreign countries (Neebe 1996, p. 104). The low exchange rate of the Deutsche Mark against the US dollar also created favorable conditions for exports to the US.

In conjunction with currency reform, the re-evaluation of corporate assets also occurred because of the relationship of the currency switch with corporate assets, capital, and debt (Aizawa 1991, p. 63). Already appraised values of depreciated fixed assets were further raised, making depreciation possible for a second time, and corporate debt was set at a tenth of previous amounts (Heβ 1958, p. 159; D.W.I.-Berichte 1965, p. 14), establishing an important foundation for corporate revival and expansion. With tax exemptions covering the difference between current prices and re-evaluations of physical assets, and a favorable change in appraisals through relatively lower reductions of shareholder equity and reserves, conditions were created for self-financing at high rates based on later depreciation policies (Maekawa 1970, pp. 124–129, 132, 220; Aizawa 1991, pp. 64–65). The combination of re-evaluation and national policies promoting investment contributed to increased investments, and became a factor in influencing the roles of corporate financing and the securities market.

Economic reforms implemented in parallel with currency reform, along with the Marshall Plan, not only created preconditions for postwar West German economic expansion but also were central to subsequent economic rebuilding measures (Feldenkirchen 2004, p. 153; Mercedes-Benz 1990, p. 101). However, the German economy had been stagnant even after the Marshall Plan began to produce results in the West (Dienel 2004, p. 125). For this reason alone, West Germany's "great leap" toward economic rebuilding was regarded increasingly significant, which was possible through currency reform. This reform created the requisite environment for market mechanisms based on the characteristics of the social market economy.

3.3 National Investment Aid Policy in Germany

In the restructuring of the economic system, the essential aversion of state intervention in economic management was considered. However, the state intended to improve conditions for industrial expansion, economic rebuilding, and corporate capital accumulation through measures enabling the state's promotion of investment.

In 1952, the Investment Assistance Act was enacted as a comprehensive measure by state policy to promote investment. This act was the state's investment aid measure in response to the lack of capital, which at the time greatly obstructed rationalization

(Eymüller 1953, p. 9). The state exceeded its role as funders of investment and capital formation and functioned as the largest banker in the economy for investment financing (Wormer 1960, p. 127). The redistribution of state funds for corporate investment capital provided direct funding, whereas preferential treatment in the form of tax reductions and depreciation provided indirect funding (Keller 1979, pp. 112–113). Next, we will examine the measures of funding assistance.

3.3.1 Development of the Investment Assistance Act

The Investment Assistance Act of 1952 was a government measure that promoted investment in raw materials, a sector requiring special urgency, and fulfilled investment demand in response to capital market insufficiencies (Keichel 1951, p. 7). This law controlled the flow of financial capital from manufacturing industries to raw materials industries (Erhard 1952, p. 107). Except for corporations in steel, coal, and electric power industries, and those that were state owned, other industry corporations (132,700 corporations total) were required to invest one billion marks of their 1952–1953 profits and supply capital for investing in preferred industries, such as the raw materials industry. This law provided 80% of the credit for rationalization of large corporate groups in coal and iron and steel industries (D.W.I.-Berichte 1960, p. 19; Stahl und Eisen 1952, p. 156; Chemelnizkaja 1962, p. 126). In addition, the law allowed for the development of measures to prioritize the distribution of capital and investment; for instance, channelizing US capital aid provided under the Marshall Plan to bottleneck industries (Thomas 1951, p. 9; Blücher 1951, p. 22; Erhard 1951, p. 94).

The Investment Assistance Act facilitated the rapid increase in the amount of investment tied to assistance provided under tax policy (Petzina 1992, p. 534). The act not only promoted investment in important sectors such as raw materials and energy industries, but also expanded demand in related key industries such as the electrical industry. For example, strong revenue increases between 1952 and 1954 in Siemens, AEG, and BBC resulted from the increase in demand from the power, coal, and iron and steel industries, which benefited from high depreciation rates and capital distribution to supplier industries such as the power industry (Reindl 2001, pp. 116, 119); this ripple effect was also visible in the machine industry (Vgl. Der Volkswirt 1955a, p. 29; Der Volkswirt 1955b, p. 36). Thus, it is important to understand the significance of these policies based on their impact among related industries.

3.3.2 Depreciation System for Promoting Investment

Among indirect subsidy measures resulting from acknowledging depreciation methods with tax advantages, extraordinary depreciation through special regulations in the Investment Assistance Act and Income Tax Law was particularly important.

This system of extraordinary depreciation clearly delineated controlling interventionism contradictory to a liberal policy mentality (Schröter 2005b, p. 385).

Article 36 of the Investment Assistance Act recognized extraordinary depreciation for a specific period—from January 1, 1952 to December 31, 1954—for equipment assets that were purchased or produced (Stahl und Eisen 1952, p. 157; D.W.I.-Berichte 1955, p. 21). An extension of the act was passed in 1954, and similar investment assistance measures continued [*Historisches Archiv Krupp*, WA78/1506, §36 Investitionshilfegesetz (14.12.1954), p. 1]. Extraordinary depreciation had the greatest potential effect on major corporations (Wettengel 1963, p. 106). In particular, the raw materials industry was preferred for large-scale investments primarily from shareholder equity, which were prescribed by Article 36 of the act (D.W.I.-Berichte 1959, p. 2).

Federal finance courts had already acknowledged the use of degressive depreciation after 1952 (Krohne 1955, p. 17; Stolper et al. 1964, p. 285). This reduced taxable and distributable profits by the increase in depreciation for the initial period and enabled the use of interest-free operating capital (Ifo-Schnelldienst 1953, p. 9). According to an amendment in the tax law regulations of July 26, 1957, the government had the authority to legislate regulations on extraordinary depreciation in the coal industry (Erhard 1957, p. 49). The government further acknowledged degressive depreciation in 1958, enabling 25% in the year of investment and 75% in West Berlin as preferential treatment in response to the East–West competition (D.W.I.-Berichte 1960, p. 20). Many industries saw an increase in demand through the increased potential for depreciation, which was afforded by the Investment Assistance Act (Vgl. Zickler 1954, p. 448; Stelter 1955, pp. 11–12).

3.3.3 Preferential Tax System for Promoting Investment

Further examining the preferential tax system's role in promoting investment, Hafer (1949) noted that supporting capital formation in the framework of tax law to overcome investment difficulties and the shortage of production equipment was increasingly becoming an issue for the state (Hafer 1949, p. 12). With constraints in the capital market, promoting self-financing for business rationalization was considered both necessary and important, and tax measures were viewed as a particularly effective method for doing so (Rationalisierung 1950, p. 98).

From June 1948 to April 1950, a series of four tax law revisions granted preferential tax treatment for internal reserves on profit and a major expansion of depreciation (extraordinary depreciation). Due to these revisions, the demand for procurement of external funding decreased markedly (Möller 1976, p. 477) and significantly contributed to the promotion of investment. From 1940 to circa 1950, tax policy focused primarily on investments that strengthened private capital accumulation and encouraged saving; however, such broad preferential tax treatment for investment activities ended in the summer of 1951 (IFO-Institut für Wirtschaftsforschung 1953, p. 73). Nevertheless, government tax law was evidently important for forming large capital reserves from non-dividend incomes and enabling monopolistic enterprises to shift from financing in the capital market to self-financing (D.W.I.-Berichte 1959, p. 2).

The abovementioned policies focused on subsidies for specific large-scale industries and major corporations. The government investment policy in 1953 pursued two immediate objectives: (1) securing sustained investment financing and (2) promoting economic rationalization and modernization through enhanced productivity, thereby increasing competitiveness (Erhard 1953, p. 141). Government investment policy, nevertheless, began to shift its focus to more general investment measures. Various state policies that promoted investment through the productivity movement exemplified the state's role in corporate activities and the postwar economic system.

3.4 Deployment of Anti-monopoly Policies in Germany

Policies regulating monopolies were another important reform in postwar Germany. Therefore, we will next consider state competition policy and monopoly regulation issues, particularly corporate concentration and inter-corporate relations, and examine their similarities with the US occupation policy and US anti-monopoly policy.

3.4.1 Influence of the US Occupation Policy on Anti-monopoly Policy

The US occupation policy included the physical rebuilding of German industries as well as the shift to a German capitalist structure, whose obvious manifestation had been in the Third Reich (Berghahn 1985, p. 326). Eradicating the cartel-like nature of economic concentration, characterizing prewar German capitalism, was a method for achieving this objective (Yanagisawa 1991, p. 84). In Europe, cartels were an important practice of corporate cooperation (Schröter 2005a, p. 67); thus, England and France did not oppose them as long as they produced and distributed goods (Schröter 2005a, pp. 56, 212). The US, on the other hand, considered the elimination of practices that restricted competition by cartels and trusts in OEEC member nations (Takagi 1962, pp. 17–18). Thus, the US industrial policy that occupied Germany at the time emphasized the removal of the strong cartel tradition from the German business world, and the movement toward an oligopolistic market based on the principles of competition, such as that in the US (Berghahn 1985, p. 280). Structural reforms to rebuild the German economy and industries were designed by the US and focused on the creation of production units and corporate scale, such as those in the US, and regulation of economic activities that suppressed competition through anti-trust laws (Djelic 1998, p. 111).

Occupation authorities, particularly those in the US, questioned the benefits of a forced economic reform. A project to transfer US anti-trust laws and traditions to

West Germany was designed such that it could be taken over by West German's at a point in time (Djelic 1998, pp. 167–168), and economic and industrial structural reforms initiated by US occupation authorities were achieved in the context of West Germany (Djelic 1998, pp. 104, 109–110, 162). However, they were not transferred by force, rather the spontaneous imitations of West Germany by a group under the leadership of L. Erhard, Minister of Economic Affairs with guidance and education from the US, were effective transfer mechanisms in the early 1950s (Djelic 1998, pp. 168–169, 182). This group focused on the economic and industrial system, wherein mass production and mass consumption were linked to competition, and worked toward a set of objectives that closely conformed to US projects (Djelic 1998, p. 111). Based on this point, the US direction and compulsion of an Anti-Monopoly Act in Japan significantly differed from those in Germany.

3.4.2 Basic Characteristics of Anti-monopoly Policy

We will now examine the various characteristics of postwar anti-monopoly policy. The Restrictive Trade Practices Act was finally passed in 1957 as an anti-monopoly regulatory law. Although this law was influenced by the US, it was formulated to replace the Allies' anti-trust law [*National Archives*, RG59, 862A.054, Summary of German Press Coverage of Passage of Cartel Law (6.8.1957), p. 1].

The Restrictive Trade Practices Act aimed to destroy cartels originally recognized under the Cartel Ordinance of 1923, based not on the principles of "abuse regulations," but rather on those of "prohibition" [*National Archives*, RG59, 862A.054, Developments concerning the German Cartel Law (3.7.1956), pp. 1–2]. However, the Restrictive Trade Practices Act was an extraordinarily loosely conceived bill, leaving several loopholes for reviving cartels [*National Archives*, RG59, 862A.331, Correspondence to R. H. Harlan from Society for the Prevention of the World War III, Inc (22.5.1958), p. 3]. For example, many economic sectors, such as agriculture, banking and insurance, and shipping, were excluded from adaptation. In addition, in case restrictions on competition or other ordinances were believed to be in the best interests of the state, a clause in the law allowed the Ministry of Economic Affairs to recognize cartels on the basis of these individual cases [*National Archives*, RG59, 862A.054, Summary of German Press Coverage of Passage of Cartel Law (6.8.1957), p. 1]. These loopholes were particular to rationalization cartels and export cartels (Vgl. Deutscher Bundestag 1958). There were several limitations from the beginning, such as the lack of planning for regulations on mergers (Berghahn 1985, p. 280), and until a revision in 1973, the Federal Cartel Office merely had the authority to investigate mergers and not the authority to prohibit them [*National Archives*, RG59, 862A.33, Reconcentration in Iron, Steel and Coal Industries of the Federal Republic (5.10.1959), p. 5]. In addition, the Restrictive Trade Practices Act did not recognize market-dominating enterprises under the same criterion as cartels, thereby making it possible to avoid cartel regulations, but creating the risk of concentration (Mötteli 1961, pp. 99, 101).

The circumstances leading to the lack of effective anti-monopoly regulations under the Restrictive Trade Practices Act were further influenced by the strong opposition from industries, whose trade associations had long opposed the anti-cartel act from being passed [*National Archives*, RG59, 862A.054, Status of Decartelized and Deconcentrated German Coal and Steel Companies (23.6.1955), p. 1; Kipping 2004, pp. 40–41]. Due to this opposition, the Ministry of Economic Affairs was forced to reach a consensus when adopting a policy of limited resistance against more radical proposals by the Allies (Berghahn 1986, pp. 172–173).

Thus, the Germans exhibited a strong initiative with anti-monopoly regulations (Haley 2001, pp. 44–48), but created a political compromise in the conflicting approach to cartels, that is, "prohibition" vs. "abuse regulation" approaches (Haley 2001, p. 172). From an industrial perspective, the Restrictive Trade Practices Act weakened the principled prohibition of cartels to the extent that the industrial world was satisfied (Takahashi 1997, pp. 250, 256). As a result, the idea behind the original bill, which was thorough in its prohibitory provisions doing away with monopolies as well as granting authority to the monopoly office, had largely become a shadow of its former self by the time it was enacted into law (Stolper et al. 1964, p. 288). The Act even considered control through conditions wherein the formation of large corporate units within specific economic sectors was beneficial (Plettner 1994, p. 109). Evidently, Germany diverged from the US model in anti-trust laws between the 1950s and 1960s (Zeitlin 2000, p. 24).

3.4.3 Significance of the Restrictive Trade Practices Act

In practice, the Restrictive Trade Practices Act faced major problems and suffered significant limitations. For instance, courts adopted a theoretical legal approach that prohibition regulations could only be applied when there was clear evidence of cartel operator contracts or cartel resolutions of trade associations. Thus, many court cases brought by the German Federal Cartel Office against cartels were lost due to insufficient evidence (Uegusa 1975, p. 178). The Federal Cartel Office also tended to prioritize court decisions over rulings by administrative decree or make decisions with merger parties prior to making them public (Smyser 1992, p. 53). Further, the Restrictive Trade Practices Act aimed to decentralize economic power through the prohibition of cartels, and anti-trust laws and regulations in Germany allowed intervention only when there was a clear abuse of power in the market through a merger (Dyas and Thanheiser 1976, p. 132). These legal deficiencies were rooted in policies intended to strengthen the export competitiveness of large corporations and corporate groups, because exports were seen as the primary method for rebuilding the West German economy (Uegusa 1975, p. 202).

Subsequently, in 1966 and 1973, the authority of the Federal Cartel Office was expanded to include the regulation of mergers (Djelic 1998, p. 170). The revision in 1973, in particular, granted the Federal Cartel Office the authority to prohibit mergers, leading to the establishment and strengthening of market control. However, when merging corporations provided evidence that their mergers facilitated competition that sufficiently offset disadvantages through market control, the Office had no choice but to approve the merger (Sato and Jungfer 1997, p. 192). The creation of the Federal Cartel Office, responsible for the implementation of the Restrictive Trade Practices Act, was a symbolic systematization of US-style competition within Germany (Djelic 1998, p. 174). However, this organization could neither hasten or enforce corporate decentralization orders nor prevent or delay corporate mergers and acquisitions (Dyas and Thanheiser 1976, p. 54; Fack and Hort 1985, pp. 27–28, 30).

Compare with the prewar period, these reforms did in fact dramatically decrease the number of cartels. In 1929, the number of cartels had risen as high as 4,000, but in 1968, only 200 cartels were recognized as legal by the Cartel Office (Dyas and Thanheiser 1976, p. 54). Despite the political intent to ensure free market competition and free trade, the actual business environment from 1950 to 1970 was not sufficiently based these factors (Dyas and Thanheiser 1976, p. 48). As noted by A.D. Chandler, Jr., the characteristics of "cooperative managerial capitalism" (Chandler 1990) essentially remained unchanged. Many believe that anti-cartel liberal philosophies were far more lenient than was generally perceived (Tolliday 1995, p. 348). For example, H.G. Schröter argues that the complete dissemination of US anti-cartel beliefs throughout West Germany required more than one generation, and it was not until the 1960s that industrialists shared these views (Schröter 1997a, pp. 143, 152–153; Schröter 1997b, p. 151).

Rationalization cartels, important exceptions to anti-monopoly regulations, fulfilled critical roles in industry anti-recession and structural policies in certain cases. In the 1960s, state-led rationalization cartels were being developed; in particular, the 1963 measures that were implemented in the coal industry were a primary example (Burckhardt 1981, pp. 17–18). These rationalization cartels were also seen in the iron and steel industry, where excess capacity was an issue at the end of the 1960s, and the formation of rationalization cartels in iron and steel firms enabled production specialization in rolling mill products. Thus, they were successful in avoiding destructive competition by responding to market demands and lowering costs with such division of labor (Vgl. Schmitz 1974).

In our abovementioned considerations, we examined competition policy and new methods for regulating monopolies. If we analyze the implication of competition policy on trade policy and the global economy, we will see the important efforts made to form a common market through West European integration. For West Germany, admission into European international relationships, such as the European Coal and Steel Community (ECSC) and the European Economic Community (EEC), meant that they were participating in a European system to suppress cartel-like competition-limiting activities (Yanagisawa 2006, pp. 163, 167–169). Thus, the issues of state competition policy and anti-monopoly regulations were by character a response to the postwar framework in the European regions. Thus, we will now examine issues surrounding the formation of a European community, an antecedent to the EU, from the perspective of the German initiative and intent.

3.5 Efforts for European Integration

Integration issues leading to the formation of the EEC were part of the US-sponsored European integration policy related to the Marshall Plan. Since its inception, the European integration movement had the central aim of a Western solution to the German problem within the large framework of US global policy (Idemizu 1978, p. 148). However, European integration was an effort to create a common market for major European countries in response to the evident gaps in the postwar period and countermeasure US dominance.

The US attitude and contribution toward European economic rebuilding under the Marshall Plan, including that in German, was evidenced by the promotion of European integration through the foundation of the OEEC. However, France pursued the establishment of a "mini-European" customs union based on regionalism. One consequence of this was the formation of the ECSC under the Schuman Plan (Hirota and Nagamine 1992, p. 326). However, West Germany's Prime Minister, C. Adenauer, believed that Western European integration could initiate German re-emergence in foreign policy (Neebe 1996, p. 106). With the formation of the ECSC, caps on production were eliminated, and German coal and iron and steel firms were given the opportunity to reconcentrate with dissolved firms, making a restructuring of economic power possible. Germany was also recognized as having equal privileges as other countries, and regained the ability to emerge once again on the world, and in particular the Western European, platform (Hellborn 1963, pp. 14, 27, 43). The entry of West Germany into the ECSC and European Atomic Energy Community (EURATOM) decidedly contributed to the creation of trusting and warm relationships with its neighbors, particularly France (Auswärtiges Amt 1959, p. 6). In addition, under US pressure, the integration process began to build the basis for international agreements. However, economic integration meant the overcoming of nation and state limitations through the integration of various national economies. The case of West Germany truly demonstrates how Germany independently drove integration, irrespective of planning, negotiations, and agreements (Ambrosius 1984, pp. 271–272).

According to a 1957 federal government report on government activities, the close integration of various European countries was, at the time, West Germany's only chance to maintain or restore its former position within the cooperation of European countries; it was the last possible way to achieve economic prosperity and social progress (Das Presse- und Informationsamt der Bundesregierung 1957, p. 15). On the basis of this perspective, efforts were made toward ensuring a more favorable trade and economic zone created by Western European integration and a common market and customs union based on this integration. As exemplified by the automotive industry, for manufacturers, economic integration results in sales of the same model in broader markets, with opportunities to create economies of scale (Laux 1992, pp. 175–176). As observed by L. Erhard or O. Brenner, the committee chairman of IG Metal, a large-scale economic zone that transcended the nation and states was necessary to effectively use production capacity through sufficient automation and increase fixed cost rates through automation and mechanization (D.W.I.-Berichte 1960, p. 12), emphasizing the significance of European integration.

The realization of European integration was of peculiar significance to Germany, which heavily relied on exports in the region. It could attain the German objective of opening new sales markets in the German economy, achieving its goal of economic growth (Ambrosius 1984, p. 293). In the latter half of the 1950s, West Germany, with its competitive edge and productive forces against neighboring countries in Western Europe, considered the formation of regional economic zones such as the EEC as an important new mechanism for stable growth; this replaced the OEEC and EPU frameworks that created conditions for a so-called "protected market," which were discriminatory to the US (Furuuchi 2006, pp. 90, 100–102, 109–111). Trade within Europe was initiated as a strategy to achieve prosperity within the region (Carreras 2006, p. 312).

European integration and the formation of the EEC were, to West Germany, the agents that could create a reproduction (accumulation) structure for German capitalism within a framework of the postwar economic system at a European level. They were also the building blocks of a market control system for German corporations on a Western European scale, against the background of gaps in productive forces and competitiveness gaps with Germany's neighboring countries. With expanded markets in the European region, efforts toward European integration laid the foundation for corporate, industrial, and economic progress, which was based on further increases in exports within the heavy and chemical industries—a sector in which Germany had been internationally competitive since before the war. These efforts for European integration show that the state's role in regard to corporate development had extended beyond domestic Germany and into Europe at large.

In addition to the above changes in national, economic, and corporate relations, a new framework of labor relations was formed on the basis of the codetermination system, another new and important change in political economy. We will examine this development in further detail in the next chapter.

References

Abelshauser W (1983) Wirtschaftsgeschichte der Bundesrepublik Deutschland 1945–1980. Schrlkamp, Frankfurt am Main

Abelshauser W (2004) Deutsche Wirtschaftsgeschichte seit 1945. C. H. Beck, München

Aizawa K (1991) Dai Doitsu Keizaiken no Taito (Rise of Germany large economy). Toyo Keizai Shinposha, Tokyo

Ambrosius G (1984) Europäische Integration und wirtschaftliche Entwicklung der Bundesrepublik Deutschland in den fünfziger Jahren. In: Berding H (ed) Wirtschaftliche und politische Integration in Europa im 19. und 20. Jahrhundert. Vandenhoeck & Ruprecht, Göttingen, pp 271–294

Angster J (2004) Wirtschaftswunder und Wohlstandsgesellschaft in der Bundesrepublik. In: Wolfrum E (ed) Die Deutschen im 20. Jahrhundert. Primus, Darmstadt, pp 124–133

Auswärtiges Amt (1959) Deutsche Außenpolitik 1949–1959. In: Das Presse und Informationsamt der Bundesregierung (ed) Deutschland im Wiederaufbau und Tätigkeitsbericht der Bundesregierung für das Jahr 1959. Kommissionsverlag, Bonn, pp 5–15

Benz W (1999) Währungsreform. In: Benz W (ed) Deutschland unter alliierter Besatzung 1945–1949/55. Akademie Verlag, Berlin, pp 190–194

Berghahn V (1985) Unternehmer und Politik in der Bundesrepublik. Suhrkamp, Frankfurt am Main
Berghahn VR (1986) The Americanization of West German industry 1945–1973. Berg Publishers, Leanington
Blücher F (1951) Das Bundesministreium für den Marshallplan. In: Das Presse- und Informationsamt der Bundesregierung (ed) Deutschland im Wiederaufbau. Tätigkeitsbericht der Bundesregierung für das Jahr 1951, Kommissionsverlag, Bonn, pp 11–27
Bundesministrium für Wirtschaft (1959) Der Sprung in die Marktwirtschaft—Entwicklung zum Wohlstand. In: Das Presse- und Informationsamt der Bundesregierung (ed) Deutschland im Wiederaufbau 1949–1959 und Tätigkeitsbericht der Bundesregierung für das Jahr 1959, Kommissionsverlag, Bonn, pp 18–25
Burckhardt H (1981) 25 Jahre Kohlepolitik. Nomos-Verlagsgesellschaft, Baden-Baden
Carreras A (2006) The twentieth century: from break with the past to prosperity (II). The great stages. In: Vittorio AD (ed) An economic history of Europe. From expansion to development. Routledge, London, pp 289–334
Chandler AD Jr (1990) Scale and scope: the dynamics of industrial capitalism. Harvard University Press, Cambridge
Chemelnizkaja J (1962) Der westdeutsche Monopolkapitalismus. Verlag der Wirtschaft, Berlin
Das Presse- und Informationsamt der Bundesregierung (ed) (1957) Erklärungen des Bundeskanzlers und der Bundesregierung 1957. Zur auβenpolitischen Lage. In: Deutschland im Wiederaufbau. Tätigkeitsbericht der Bundesregierung für das Jahr 1957. Kommissionsverlag, Bonn, pp 5–33
Der Volkswirt (1955a) Demag nutzt ihre Chancen. Der Volkswirt 9(24):29–30
Der Volkswirt (1955b) Orenstein-Koppel geht auf 8 vH. Weiter Verflüssigung—trotz dem Kapitalerhührung. Der Volkswirt 9(21):36–37
Deutscher Bundestag (1958) Bericht des Bundeskartellamtes über seine Tätigkeit im Jahre 1958 sowie über Lage und Entwicklung auf seinem Aufgabengebiet (§50GWB). Drucksache 1000
Dienel H-L (2004) Linde. History of a technology corporation 1879–2004. Palgrave Macmillan, Basingstoke
Djelic M-L (1998) Exporting the American model. The postwar transformation of European business. Oxford University Press, Oxford
D.W.I.-Berichte (1955) Der wesdeutsche Steinkohlenbergbau. D.W.I.-Berichte 6(6):2–30
D.W.I.-Berichte (1959) Der Stand der Konzentration des Kapitals in Westdeutschland. D.W.I.-Berichte 10(3):1–36
D.W.I.-Berichte (1960) Methoden und Auswirkungen der Rationalisierung in der westdeutschen Industrie. D.W.I.-Berichte 11(13):1–23
D.W.I.-Berichte (1965) Investitionen, Selbstfinanzierung und Kreditpolitk in Westdeutschland. D.W.I.-Berichte 16(18):14–19
Dyas GP, Thanheiser HT (1976) The emerging European enterpreise. Strategy and structure in French and German industry. The Macmillan Press, London
Erhard L (1951) Das Bundesministerium für Wirtschaft. In: Das Presse- und Informationsamt der Bundesregierung (ed) Deutschland im Wiederaufbau. Tätigkeitsbericht der Bundesregierung für das Jahr 1951. Kommissionsverlag, Bonn, pp 85–105
Erhard L (1952) Das Bundesministerium für Wirtschaft. In: Das Presse- und Informationsamt der Bundesregierung (ed) Deutschland im Wiederaufbau.Tätigkeitsbericht der Bundesregierung für das Jahr 1952. Kommissionsverlag, Bonn, pp 97–116
Erhard L (1953) Das Bundesministerium für Wirtschaft. In: Das Presse- und Informationsamt der Bundesregierung (ed) Deutschland im Wiederaufbau. Tätigkeitsbericht der Bundesregierung für das Jahr 1953. Kommissionsverlag, Bonn, pp 129–153
Erhard L (1954) Das Bundesministerium für Wirtschaft. In: Das Presse- und Informationsamt der Bundesregierung (ed) Deutschland im Wiederaufbau. Tätigkeitsbericht der Bundesregierung für das Jahr 1954. Kommissionsverlag, Bonn, pp 147–176
Erhard L (1957) Das Bundesministerium für Wirtschaft. In: Das Presse- und Informationsamt der Bundesregierung (ed) Deutschland im Wiederaufbau. Tätigkeitsbericht der Bundesregierung für das Jahr 1957. Kommissionsverlag, Bonn, pp 35–94

Eymüller T (1953) Wem gehören Rationalisierungs-Gewinne? Der Volkswirt 7(12):9–10
Fack FU, Hort P (1985) Soziale Marktwirtschft: Stationen einer freiheitlichen Ordnung. Ploetz, Freiburg
Feldenkirchen W (2004) DaimlerChrysler Werk Untertürkheim. Motorbuch-Verlag, Stuttgart
Furuuchi H (2006) Gendai Doitsu Keizai no Rekishi (A history of the modern German economy). Tokyo Daigaku Shuppankai, Tokyo
Hafer E (1949) Sachwalter der gewerblichen Wirtschaft. Zum Wiedererstehen des deutschen Industrie- und Handelstags. Der Volkswirt 3(44):11–12
Haley JO (2001) Antitrust in Germany and Japan. The first fifty years, 1947–1998. University of Washington Press, Seattle
Hellborn R (1963) Der westdeutsche Imperialismus erobert Westeuropas Markt. Akademie Verlag, Berlin
Heβ P (1958) AEG. Energie—Profit—Verbrechen. Verlag Die Wirtschaft, Berlin
Hirota L, Nagamine M (1992) Yoroppa no Sengo Kaikaku (Postwar reform in Europe). In: The Socio-Economic History Society (ed) Shakai-Keizaishigaku no Kadai to Tenbo (Problems and prospects of socio-economic history). Yuhikaku, Tokyo, pp 321–334
Idemizu K (1978) Sengo Doitsu Keizaishi (German economic history after WWII). Toyo Keizai Shinposha, Tokyo
IFO-Institut für Wirtschaftsforschung (ed) (1953) Fünf Jahre Deutsche Mark. Der Wiederaufbau der westdeutschen Wirtschaft seit der Währungsreform. Duncker & Humblot, Berlin
Ifo-Schnelldienst (1953) Erneuerungs-Investitionen aus Abschreibungen insbesondere Möglichkeiten der degressiven Abschreibungsweise. Ifo-Schnelldienst 6(34):7–10
Inoue T (1992) Shakaiteki Shijyo Keizai (Social market economy). In: Onishi T (ed) Doitsu no Keizai (The German economy). Waseda Daigaku Shuppanbu, Tokyo, pp 11–29
Keichel A (1951) Investitionshilfe wird Gesetz. Der Volkswirt 5(26):7–9
Keller H (1979) Innovation und Technologietransfer. Rationalisierung 30(5):107–114
Kipping M (2004) 'Importing' American ideas to West Germany. In: Kudo A, Kipping M, Schröteret HG (eds) German and Japanese business in the boom years. Transforming American management and technology models. Routledege, London, pp 30–53
Krieger W (1988) General Lucius D. Clay und die amerikanische Deutschlandpolitik 1945–1949, vol 2. Aufl. Klett-Cotta, Stuttgart
Krohne H (1955) Investitionen und Abschreibung. Der Volkswirt, 9.Jg, Beilage zu Nr.38 vom 24. September 1955, Deutsche Wirtschaft im Querschnitt, vol 33. Folge, Maschinenbau, pp 13–17
Laux JM (1992) The European automobile industry. Twayne Publishers, New York
Maekawa K (1970) Doitsu Dokusen Kigyo no Hatten Katei (Development of monopolistic enterprise in Germany). Mineruva Shobo, Kyoto
Masamura K (1983) Sengo Nihon Shihonshugishi (History of Japanese capitalism after WWII). Nihon Hyoronsha, Tokyo
Mercedes-Benz AG (1990) Werk Sindelfingen. Karosserie- und Montagewerk der Mercedes-Benz Aktiengesellschaft. Ein historischer Überblick. Mercedes-Benz AG, Sindelfingen
Miwa R (2005) Dokusen Kinshi Ho (Monopoly prohibition law). In: Sasaki T, Tsurumi S, Tominaga K et al (eds) Sengoshi Daijiten (Encyclopedia of postwar Japan 1945–2004), new enlarged edn. Sanseido, Tokyo, pp 664–665
Molitor R (1958) Sozial Marktwirtschaft. Hamburger Jahrbuch für Wirtschaft- und Gesellschaftspolitik 3:57–75
Möller H (1976) Die westdeutsche Währungsreform von 1948. In: Deutsche Bundesbank (ed) Währung und Wirtschaft in Deutschland 1876–1975. Fritz Knapp, Frankfurt am Main, pp 433–483
Mötteli C (1961) Licht und Schatten der sozialen Marktwirtschaft. Leitbild und Wirklichkeit der Bundesrepublik Deutschland. Rentsch, Zürich
Müller-Armack A (1956) Soziale Marktwirtschaft. In: von Beckerath E, Brinkmann C, Gutenberg E et al (eds) Handwörterbuch der Sozailawissenschaften, Bd.9. Gustav Fischer, J.C.B. Mohr, Vandenhoeck & Ruprecht, Göttingen, pp 390–392

Nakamura T (1980) Nihon Keizai (The Japanese economy), 2nd edn. Tokyo Daigaku Shuppankai, Tokyo
Neebe R (1996) German big business and the return of the World market after World War II. In: Berghahn VR (ed) Quest for economic empire. Berghahn Books, Oxford, pp 95–121
Noda S (1998) Doitsu Sengo Seijikeizai Chitsujo no Keisei (Formation of political-economic order in Germany after WW II). Yuhikaku, Tokyo
Petzina D (1992) Zwischen Neuordnung und Krise. Zur Entwicklung der Eisen- und Stahlindustrie im Ruhrgebiet seit dem Zweiten Weltkrieg. In: Dascher O, Kleinschmidt C (eds) Die Eisen- und Stahalindustrie im Dortmunder Raum. Wirtschaftliche Entwicklung, soziale Strukturen und technologischer Wandel im 19. und 20. Jahrhundert. Gesellschaft für Westfälische Wirtschaftsgeschichte E.V, Dortmund, pp 525–544
Plettner B (1994) Abenteuer Elektrotechnik. Siemens und die Entwicklung der Elektrotechnik seit 1945. Pieper, München
Rationalisierung (1950) Rationalisierung und Leistungssteigerung. Rationalisierung 1(4):98–99
Reindl R (2001) Wachstum und Wettbewerb in den Wirtschaftswunderjahren. Die elektorotechnische Industrie in der Bundesrepublik Deutschland und in Groβbritannien 1945–1967. Ferdinand Schöningh, Paderborn
Roesler J (2006) Momente deutsch-deutscher Wirtschafts- und Sozialgeschichte 1945 bis 1990. Eine Analyse auf gleicher Augenhöhe. Leipziger Universitätsverlag, Leipzig
Sato S, Jungfer J (1997) Kyoso Seisaku (competition policy). In: Sakura Institute of Research, Ifo Institut für Wirtschaftsforschung (eds) Nihon to Doitsu no Keizai Sangyo Sisutemu no Hikaku Kenkyu (Comparative study of economic and industrial systems in Japan and Germany). Springer, Tokyo, pp 179–197
Schmitz E (1974) Analyse der Wettbewerbseffekte der Kontorverträge von 1967 und der Verträge zur Gründung der vier Rationalisierungsgruppen von 1971. In: Röper B (ed) Rationalisierungseffekte der Walzstahlkontore und der Rationalisierungsgruppen. Dunker & Humblot, Berlin, pp 14–29
Schröter HG (1997a) Cartelization and decartelization in Europe, 1870–1945: raise and decline of an economic institution. J Eur Econ Hist 25(1):129–153
Schröter HG (1997b) Zur Übertragbarkeit sozialhistorischer Konzepte in die Wirtschaftsgeschichte. Amerikanisierung und Sowjetisierung in deutschen Betrieben 1945–1975. In: Jarausch K, Siegrist H (eds) Amerikanisierng und Sowjetisierung in Deutschland 1945–1970. Campus, Frankfurt am Main, pp 147–165
Schröter HG (2005a) Americanization of the European economy. A compact survey of American economic influence in Europe since the 1880s. Springer, Dordrecht
Schröter HG (2005b) Deutschlands Reintegration in die europäischen Wirtschaft. In: North M (ed) Deutsche Wirtschaftsgeschichte. Ein Jahrtausend im Überblick, 2.,völlig überarbeitete und aktualisiert Auflage. C.H. Beck, München, pp 362–388
Smyser WR (1992) The economy of United Germany: colossus at the crossroads. Hurst & Co., London
Stahl und Eisen (1952) Das Investitionehilfe-Gesetz. Stahl und Eisen 72(3):156–157
Stelter H (1955) Gestiegene Maschinenproduktion—erfolgreiche Wirtschaftsexpansion. Der Volkswirt, 9.Jg, Beilage zu Nr.38 vom 24. September 1955:11–13
Stolper G, Häuser K, Borchardt K (1964) Deutsche Wirtschaft seit 1870. J. C. B. Mohr, Tübingen
Takagi K (1962) Nishi Yoroppa ni okeru Seisansei Undo (The productivity movement in Western Europe). Nihon Seisansei Honbu, Tokyo
Takahashi I (1997) Doitsu Kyoso Seigen Kinshiho no Seiritsu to Kozo (Formation and structure of the restrictive trade practices act in Germany). Sanseido, Tokyo
Thomas BG (1951) Investitionen ohne Kapitalmarkt. Der Volkswirt 5(9):9–11
Tolliday S (1995) Enterprise and State in the West German Wirtschaftswunder: Volkswagen and the Automobilindustry, 1939–1962. Bus Hist Rev 69:273–350
Triebe K (2001) The 1948 currency reform: structure and purpose. In: Hölscher J (ed) 50 years of the German mark. Essay in honour of Stephen F. Frowen. Palgrave, Basingstoke, pp 15–51

Tsusho Sangyo Sho Tsusho Sangyo Seisakushi Hensan Iinkai (ed) (1990) Tsusho Sangyo Seisakushi (History of international trade and industry policy), vol 6. Tsusho Sangyo Chosakai, Tokyo

Uegusa M (1975) Nishi Doitsu no Sangyo Sosiki (Industrial organization in West Germany). In: Eikawa H (ed) Nishi Doitsu no Keizai to Sangyo (Economy and industry in West Germany). Chikura Shobo, Tokyo, pp 165–220

Walter R (2003) Wirtschaftsgeschichte, 4th edn. Böhlau, Köln

Wettengel EB (1963) Bürgerliche Legenden vom Wesen der kapitalistischen Rationalisierungin Westdeutschland. Jahrbuch für Wirtschaftsgechichte, Teil I:61–126

Wormer H (1960) Wer finanziert die Investitionen? Der Volkswirt 14(52/53):125–132

Yanagisawa O (1991) Doitsu ni okeru Sengo Kaikaku to Shihonshugi no Tenkan (Postwar reform and conversion of capitalism in Germany). In: Tanaka T, Yanagisawa O, Ono J et al (eds) Kindai Sekai no Henyo (Transformation of the modern World). Ribro Port, Tokyo, pp 65–87

Yanagisawa (2006) Shihonshugishi no Renzoku to Danzetsu (Continuity and discontinuity in the history of capitalism). Nihon Keizai Hyoronsha, Tokyo

Zeitlin J (2000) Introduction: Americanization and its limits: reworking US technology and management in post-War Europe and Japan. In: Zeitlin J, Herrigel G (eds) Americanization and its limits. Reworking US technology and management in post-war Europe and Japan. Oxford University Press, Oxford, pp 1–50

Zickler E (1954) Die Konjunktur im chemischen Apparatebau hälten. Chem Ind 6(8):448

Chapter 4
Development of the Codetermination System

Abstract Postwar Germany built a systematic framework for labor relations based on the Codetermination Act. A new framework for labor relations in the codetermination system provided an alternative to the US model, and was an important element that regulated Germany's "Rheinland Model of capitalism" or the "coordinated market economy." Therefore, this chapter discusses post WWII changes in labor relations under the codetermination system. First, it views characteristics of postwar labor relations in Japan, then considers the new framework for labor relations in Germany called the "dual system," followed by the mechanism of corporate governance based on the codetermination system. On the basis of these discussions, this chapter examines the codetermination system's significance from the perspectives of improvement in the flow of information between labor and management, promotion of cooperative and stable labor–capital relations, and safety net functions.

Keywords Codetermination • Corporate governance • Labor relations • Safety net • Works council

In this chapter, we will discuss changes in labor relations in conjunction with the postwar codetermination system. The framework for the labor relations system had a peculiar German style even after the war and remains characteristic of the institutional framework and corporate governance till date.

A problem common to OEEC member nations, according to the US, was the need to remove restrictive practices by labor unions, thus strengthening the development of free labor unions (Takagi 1962, p. 17). Through its assistance to West Germany, the US expected to resolve union collective bargaining at the corporate level, not the national level (Takagi 1962, p. 40). In Europe, US business and political leaders pushed for the adoption of labor relations along the lines of the US model, which would be based on the "human relations" approach. To demonstrate the benefits of US-style labor relations, the US Technical Assistance and Productivity Program supported trips to the US for workers and employer representatives from

T. Yamazaki, *German Business Management: A Japanese Perspective on Regional Development Factors*, DOI 10.1007/978-4-431-54303-9_4, © Springer Japan 2013

Europe; however, these initiatives were complete failures. This was true even in West Germany, which was directly influenced by the US occupation authorities.

Germany's systematic framework for labor relations was based on the Co-determination Act and emanated from the issue of power distribution between workers and employers under the unique postwar conditions. As a result, the US-style labor relations system had little influence. This is clearer in comparison with France, where the effects of the law for establishment of enterprise committees, enacted at the end of 1940s, quickly faded, and Italy, where the establishment of work councils for decades was limited to two state-owned corporations (Schröter 2005a, pp. 197, 199).

Because of the failure of transitioning to US-style labor relations under the US-led productivity movement, a new framework for labor relations through the establishment of the codetermination system acted as an alternative to the US model. This new framework was an important element that regulated the characteristics of German capitalism known as the "Rheinland Model of capitalism." Further, with the labor market consisting of a social economic system as per the "coordinated market economy" (Albert 1991; Hall and Soskice 2001a, b), and a system of corporate governance with worker participation in management, the framework was an integral part of German-style business management. Because the framework was regulated by law, its coordinating functions were combined with the market economy through the codetermination system, thus creating important issues for the postwar development of labor relations.

In this chapter, we will consider this new framework for labor relations through the codetermination system, with focus on its coordinating functions. In doing so, we will show the historical significance and relevance to current German-style mechanisms for corporate governance and the social economic system.

4.1 Characteristics of Postwar Labor Relations in Japan

Comparing the framework for postwar labor relations in Japan and Germany, we see that labor relations in Japan had three basic pillars: lifetime employment, seniority wage systems, and enterprise trade unions, which revolved around regular employees (OECD 1977). Lifetime employment is the employment throughout one's entire life, and on the basis of this system, workers in large Japanese corporations were given opportunities to earn higher wages (i.e., increments) and designations (i.e., promotions), given their loyalty to the company. With such rigidity in the labor market, the seniority order system, one of the principles of the order of personnel and their wages, was formed through lifetime employment relations. Japanese-style enterprise trade unions were formed only from labor relations built on lifetime employment. Labor unions' basic units of activity were formed according to individual corporations; thus, labor conditions were negotiated and agreed upon according to individual corporate conditions, and would generally not go beyond those bounds. In this sense, Japanese labor unions were not horizontally organized by industry, but divided by and walled within each corporation. Therefore, a unified labor movement, as in Europe and the US, were difficult to develop. Also, the power of collective bargaining was hampered and cooperative labor relations integrated into the corporation as a whole were the norm. Agreements through collective bargaining or collective agreement were mostly at the corporate level (Okouchi 1980, pp. 10–13, 105–106; Mori 1981, pp. 367, 371–372; Takahashi 1970, p. 9). On this note, the collective agreement system was vastly different from Germany's industry-wide system.

The system of worker participation in management did not wait for new laws or other forms of governmental intervention. Rather, participation voluntarily occurred in small group activities with QC circles or joint labor-management consultation systems, which negotiated and discussed labor-management issues on the basis of premise of creating trust–worthy relationships between labor and management. However, a legal codetermination system, such as that in Germany, did not exist at the plant level and certainly not at the top-management level. Joint labor-management consultation systems proliferated with the collaboration of labor and management as per the productivity movement of 1955, and gradually took shape through discussions of productivity improvement issues (Urabe and Omura 1983, pp. 101–102; Hirano 1976, pp. 205–206, 210; Roshikankei Chosakai 1963, pp. 17–18). In Japan, joint labor-management consultation systems differed from collective bargaining and were established on the foundation of horizontal corporate labor relations through enterprise trade unions. Taken from systemic and functional perspectives, that collective bargaining and joint labor-management consultation systems, essentially heterogeneous, became tightly woven together were characteristic to Japan's systems (Urabe and Omura 1983, pp. 105, 108–110, 112–113; Roshikankei Chosakai 1963, p. 55). In other words, official collective bargaining as defined by collective agreements was done formally and tended to be extremely rare; collective bargaining became a mere façade (Hirano 1976, pp. 209–210). Further, matters of labor conditions were the focus of not only collective bargaining but also the joint labor-management consultation system, which occupied a greater position. Japanese-style labor relations were oriented toward labor-management consultation, and even in collective-bargaining matters, in which there existed conflicts of interest, issues tended to be resolved harmoniously and in the unique manner of the joint labor-management consultation system (Urabe and Omura 1983, pp. 117–118, 123–124). In Japan, as the floor managers in shops became union members and leaders, they took on the function of labor management. This type of industrial partnership between labor and management was not common to large corporations in Europe or the US (Maekawa 1997, pp. 247, 310, 313; Aoyama 1981, pp. 94–96).

Based on the above framework for labor relations, Japan's labor protection did not face hindrances as did Germany's codetermination system. This led to circumstances enabling easier dismissals and reassignments (Maekawa 1997, p. 87). Moreover, the wage gap between large corporations and small and medium enterprises, and that between medium and small enterprises became was greater in Japan than in Germany (Maekawa 1997, pp. 119–120, 126; Sugaya 1977, p. 105).

Germany's circumstances were quite different from those of Japans. In Germany, labor unions were organized by industry, and a large framework was created based on a collective agreement system and labor conditions that varied by industry and region. Furthermore, there was a system of participation in work councils at the plant level for specific labor conditions within each company that assumed collective agreements. A system of codetermination at the top management level also existed. Under the capitalist system, a response to issues and inconsistencies of market economies, such as safety nets, was called for. Examining the codetermination system and its relevance to a social market economy, the foundation of the postwar economic order—the codetermination system—played a significant role in addressing these issues and inconsistencies.

In Sect. 4.2, we will examine the characteristics of the framework for labor relations within postwar Germany. In Sect. 4.3, we will discuss the codetermination system from the perspective of corporate governance. Finally, in Sect. 4.4 we will show the significance of the codetermination system.

4.2 New Framework for Labor Relations in Germany Post World War II

First, we discuss the basic characteristics of the new framework for labor relations in postwar Germany. These can be seen as a dual system: (a) the autonomy to negotiate agreements regulating sales conditions for labor unions and the general framework for labor unions and employer associations; (b) works constitutions, which are works agreements that specifically regulate labor conditions between work councils and management based on collective agreements (Jentsch 1995, p. 218). Collective agreements were applied to corporations within a region's particular industry, and as a result, regardless of corporate size, wages tended to be applied horizontally. Collective agreements by the industrial sector were supplemented by work councils, which were labor-management negotiating organizations in corporations for labor conditions not covered by collective bargaining (Allen 2006, p. 77); these two systems shared a mutually complementary relationship. In general, the larger the corporation the more work councils it had and were covered by collective agreements at the industry level (Allen 2006, pp. 81–82). This dual system was composed of concentrated collective bargaining by multiple industrial unions on one hand and a statutory institute for labor participation at the plant level through autonomous work councils, which were formally separated from trade unions, on the other. This framework for systematic coordination to resolve labor-management conflicts contributed to stable and harmonious coordination. Additionally, with the political and market power of labor unions weakening, legal authority of plant-level work councils helped support central union power (Thelen 1991, pp. 2, 13). With such mechanisms, an employment system in which dismissals were difficult and a wage security system took shape.

A relatively strong and stable system for legal labor participation at the plant and corporate levels was embedded in the national control system of collective bargaining. The German codetermination system was also a decisive element in coordination through negotiations in the German model (Thelen 1991, pp. 14–15). Streeck noted that codetermination at the supervisory board level cannot be understood separate from a work council's right of codetermination and the structure of labor unions; these three were structurally and functionally connected (Streeck 1992, p. 137). The fall of fascism characterized the beginning of the new era of business policy by positioning workers as the most important element within corporations, implementing codetermination, and coinciding institutional acknowledgement of employees as central, independent elements of production (Pirker et al. 1955, pp. 431–432). Collective agreements, with their adoption at the industry level, and a system of labor markets such as work councils enabled the creation of a long-term employment perspective as well as industry- and corporation-specific skills (Hall and Soskice 2001a, pp. 24–25; Allen 2006, pp. 4, 7). This dual system of labor relations was closely connected with the state of the employment system and labor market.

4.3 Corporate Governance Based on the Codetermination System

Next, we consider the relevance of the codetermination system to German-style corporate governance mechanisms. Within the German system, the multi-layered structure with mutually complementary relationships linked codetermination at the top levels of management to the shop floor level by division, and codetermination exhibited the ability to get things done from both sides (Yoshida 1994, p. 24). However, from the perspective of corporate governance, labor was able to influence corporate policy decision-making and capital through the enactment of the 1976 Law on Codetermination. The law equalized labor representation on the supervisory board in industries other than coal and iron and steel. It enabled the monitoring of corporate policy decision-making by personnel rights of directors and withholding of the approved rights for board of directors (Kaido 2005, p. 12). All supervisory board members had equal authority and responsibility according to the 1978 Constitutional Court, and the 1976 Law became the foundation for a German-style labor relations structure (Streeck 1992, p. 150). This law was also important to the structure of corporate governance.

Supervisory boards, the nucleus of codetermination at top management levels, were not originally management organs; however, in Germany, because the supervisory board was necessary for capital control, workers and labor unions aimed at equal codetermination in the supervisory board (Ohashi 1982, p. 171). The supervisory board was, institutionally speaking, a supervisory organ of business execution through the board of directors, but was not solely responsible for executing business.

Its direction was fairly comprehensive, with the ability to appoint and dismiss directors and approve important matters of business. The supervisory board was an important method of controlling managers, with the CEO mostly being responsible for business execution. Thus, workers' participation in this supervisory organ was also important (Futagami 1995, p. 141). Checks on business execution through labor participation in supervisory organs or at the top level of management were particularly significant from the aspect of inadequacy in management capabilities of labor and information. An affirmed company constitution with industrialists (or investors) at its core, and "with the codetermination system, members of a company's supervisory board had the important function of providing governance over despotic control on capital" (Kaido 2005, p. 107). However, when analyzing issues of corporate governance related to this type of restraining function, one can see several aspects that were influenced by this condition. We will illustrate these issues below.

First was the degree of influence made possible by the differences in the interests of investors and workers. While many divergent interests of customers, suppliers, and banks represented the shareholder side, those of workers were more uniform. As a result, shareholders were relegated to minority status. Also, labor unions had an advantageous position on supervisory boards that had an equal composition of labor and management (Deutsche Industrieinstitut 1968, p. 49). However, even in such cases, by nature of inter-corporate relations with German characteristics the unification of investor interests through collaborations and partnerships, between not only banks and corporations but also banks themselves, strengthened this foundation.

Corporations also had the unique German opportunity of autonomous management. A possible decrease in the influence of external members on the supervisory board was relative to the decrease in investor composition of the supervisory board; this was made possible by having employees account for half of the supervisory board members. This resulted in opportunities to increase the autonomy of corporate members on the supervisory board and applied to management autonomy within the board of directors. Supervisory boards, with the an equal composition of labor and management within the coal and iron and steel industries, created conditions wherein members responsible for commerce and technology on the board of directors frequently enjoyed greater freedom and independence from bank and shareholder representatives (*Bayer Archiv*, 302-0500, Vorstellungen und Überlegungen des DGB zur Mitbestimmung, p. 21).

Thus, labor participation on supervisory boards, half of which comprised labor representatives as mandated by the Codetermination Act for the Coal, Iron and Steel Industries and the 1976 Law on Codetermination indicated a relative decrease in the composition of external members on the supervisory board, such as banks and corporate shareholders or even general investors. Accordingly, to corporations and internal supervisory board members as well as directors responsible for business execution, this was an opportunity for less external influence and involvement. In particular, a majority of supervisory board seats were seized by obtaining the approval of labor representatives through prior internal discussion with the supervisory board and between its employee members and directors (Mitbestimmungskommission 1970, p. 63); this made it possible to greatly mitigate or even circumvent external influence, resulting in a chance to increase autonomous execution of business functions for both the supervisory board and the board of directors. This is noteworthy especially when considering the characteristics and nature of German corporate governance.

Today, codetermination at the supervisory board level raises the possibility of suppressing or mitigating pressure from short-term shareholders, such as foreign investment funds, through the semi-representation of worker representatives. Among corporations to which the 1976 Law on Codetermination applied, when management and labor representatives on the supervisory board were in cooperation, external forces found it difficult to enforce their interests, particularly if they did not control all supervisory board members who were investor representatives. As seen in the share buyback movement of recent years, that is, with corporations wanting to regain ownership of their stocks, securing even one investor representative on their supervisory board makes control for external forces possible by cooperation with labor representatives on the supervisory board. To secure and stabilize employment, the interest in maintaining and improving labor conditions and developing and strengthening of labor relations based on the codetermination system built a foundation for a partnership between labor and management.

Moreover, when the composition of investor representatives on the supervisory board was limited to half, strengthening defensive functions by cooperating with banks became possible. In these cases, even if external influences planned to take control of management authority by gaining majority voting rights in general meetings, in reality, it was difficult to grasp the reins of business management.

A fundamental point in the "Rheinland Model of capitalism" can be seen here. Unique German conditions were wavered with increasing pressures in the capital market and the progress of financial globalization (Vgl. Zugehör 2003, Teil III, Teil VI; Lompe et al. 2003, pp. 61, 327); however, when compared with other countries, the possibility for corporations to maintain management autonomy relatively increased.

4.4 Significance of the Codetermination System

4.4.1 Improvement in Labor-Management Information Flow

Next, we will examine the significance of the codetermination system. The system of worker participation in management through codetermination contributed to the formation of cooperative relations between labor and management that were based on trust established through better flow of information between the two parties. Thus, the readiness to cooperate manifested by free information flow was essential for the proliferation of codetermination elements, resolution and mitigation of social conflict, and cooperation between work councils and management with complete trust (Tegtmeier 1973, p. 140). Codetermination not only forced the provision of information to management regarding corporate conditions and behavior but also contributed to the establishment of a culture of trust (Bertelsmann Stiftung and Hans-Böckler-Stiftung 1998, p. 98). In regard to quality and density of information flow, codetermination became further advantageous because labor and management were on equal footing. Similarly, it was said to be stronger in the coal, iron and steel industries than in regions where the 1972 Works Constitution Act was applied (Tegtmeier 1973, p. 148). In this way, the improvements in conditions for worker participation in management through the 1976 Law on Codetermination were greatly significant. For example, a 1970 report by the Codetermination Committee noted that responses from employee members of supervisory boards in the coal, iron and steel industries showed that information was mostly sufficient, while general industries where the Works Constitution Act was applied often complained of insufficient information (Mitbestimmungskommission 1970, p. 93).

While the complexity of decision making under codetermination increased, the transparency of processes improved compared to the past, and for workers, the trend was toward increasing availability of information. It is understood that information flow and cooperation between management and those responsible for codetermination at the plant level as well as between capital and labor representatives on the supervisory board helps create a common, integrated decision-making process (Tegtmeier 1973, pp. 150–151). These types of improvements in information flow, and the decision-making processes based on them, were complemented by preliminary discussions between labor representatives on the supervisory board and directors, which formed an important part of corporate-wide information processes (Mitbestimmungskommission 1970, pp. 62–63). For managers in these conditions, information channels among work councils, employees, and management were clearly not easily replaceable with other methods (Hans Böckler Stiftung and Bertelsmann Stiftung 2003, p. 17).

4.4.2 Promotion of Cooperative and Stable Labor–Capital Relations

The codetermination system laid the foundation for improving labor-management information flow as well as strengthening harmonious relations between labor and management by reflecting the interests of labor through participation in management and changing the conditions under which labor opposed capital.

Within the codetermination system, the regulation of capitalistic labor relations and workers' dependency on the corporation was a result of subordination, which is an important issue even today (Vgl. Mitbestimmungskommission 1970, pp. 104–105). The codetermination system contributed to maintaining economic order in the market by providing workers with the opportunity to recognize the economy as part of their responsibility, and experience and understand the decentralization of decision-making functions within the corporation as preliminary conditions for exercising their influence (Vgl. Mitbestimmungskommission 1970, pp. 121–122). In other words, codetermination became necessary for sustained cooperation between labor and management within corporations and political stabilization of the market economy by decreasing arbitrary or excessive exercising of management and leadership authority connected with this "worker dependency" (Murata 1987, p. 201). For example, according to a report by the Codetermination Committee, codetermination by equal numbers of labor and management on the supervisory board promoted reconciliation and cooperation. As long as sufficient attention was given to maintaining the social standing of workers, rationalization measures to lower costs were possible without the strong opposition by labor representatives on the supervisory board (Mitbestimmungskommission 1970, pp. 61, 73).

Codetermination significantly changed workers standings and relations between labor and management as well as those within management. Under the codetermination system, modernization of management structures and business processes through the emphasis on objective data and free flow of information within organizations, discussions, agreement, and cooperation were benefits of codetermination that brought about management independence from shareholders. Codetermination also brought about an integration of joint decision-making processes by having labor representatives take on certain management functions, in particular sharing in work councils the responsibility of decision making. While codetermination added organizational rigidity to the effective use of labor, it provided a solution to deal with the same issue (Streeck 1992, pp. 160–164). For example, in the iron and steel industry, the codetermination system promoted cooperation between labor and management within the labor market as well as at the factory level. Those in this industry, whether on the side of labor or management, understood they belonged to the same group, with mutual obligations and responsibilities. This type of mutually accepted structure, institutionalized by codetermination, granted critical flexibility in mass production such as allowing various lot sizes for production or reallocation of labor and materials within a factory. This type of flexibility was considered much greater than that found in US iron and steel firms (Herrigel 2000, pp. 380, 383; Zeitlin 2000, p. 39).

Another important influence of codetermination was that supervisory boards were forced to pay attention to personnel development policy or employment policy more than companies without codetermination (Bertelsmann Stiftung and Hans-Böckler-Stiftung 1998, p. 96). Social security for workers within management took on a new quality through codetermination. For example, new elements of codetermination within the personnel and economic spheres and the driving forces for worker protection in response to rationalization, typically appeared in the process of social prevention and sometimes resulted from this process (Tegtmeier 1973, pp. 247, 252). In terms of works constitutions based on codetermination at the plant level, these were historically accomplished by considering social viewpoints within management practices (Eberwein 1992, p. 501).

When viewed from its relation with employment stability, personnel policy based on codetermination improved the condition for workers already hired. Codetermination provided an institutionalized opportunity to integrate and satisfy the enterprise-specific interests of workers. Further, codetermination tended to strengthen the segmentation of labor along the borders of productive units and their internal labor market (Streeck 1992, pp. 166–167). In this way, the codetermination system was not only a control function for workers in response to management but also was forced to become a system for worker participation in management; in other words, it functioned to integrate workers within the capital side of policy. This type of policy integration on the part of capital progressed further as labor relations stabilized with the continuing internalization of leadership by labor unions, as is seen in the 1963 adoption of new basic principles by the German Federation of Trade Unions. With the 1972 Works Constitution Act, labor union activities at the plant level were suppressed and the integration policy function expanded. This is evident from the weakening of employee solidarity through the elimination of "managerial employees" from the work council, restrictions on labor union activities within plants, and approval of labor union cooperation with work councils, which were built on the premise of cooperation and collaboration with management (Hayashi 1993, pp. 121–132). The integrated effect of this type of codetermination at the plant level was the weakening of opposition in labor unions (Muszynski 1975, p. 331).

At the plant level, the codetermination system was an effective method to coordinate the conflicting interests of labor and management (Futagami 1971, pp. 266–267), and representatives of labor interests in work councils more often became mediators of individual employee demands and management decision-making (Hans Böckler Stiftung and Bertelsmann Stiftung 2003, pp. 11, 30). On one hand, work councils were exclusively guaranteed by law the right to negotiate at the corporate level, and on the other hand, fulfilled their role of preventing the expansion and worsening of disputes; they did so by handling issues as a claims resolution and welfare facility management organ within the corporation and scope of regulations obligating them to maintain peace (Tokunaga 1977, p. 301). The interaction between codetermination and wage autonomy created a foundation for social peace (Hans Böckler Stiftung and Bertelsmann Stiftung 2003, p. 7). The 1972 Works Constitution Act was generally lenient in its consideration of discussions conducted in a harmonious fashion. Labor peace generally seen within Germany was largely due to this law, which regulated codetermination at the plant level (Plettner 1994, p. 109).

In postwar Germany, strikes were rarely implemented because of codetermination regulations. Of course, there were severe labor disputes with strikes and lockouts due to wage policy or social issues, particularly payment of wage and work time. Nevertheless, these instances were chosen in the interest of the coordination process between labor unions and employer associations; the harmonious style expressed in the then occasionally used phrase—society partner—made labor disputes largely unnecessary and social compromise fairly easy (Abelshauser 2004, p. 358).

In this sense, the extremely strong cooperative relations between labor and management, which were the basis of the German model of labor relations, developed gradually (Schröter 2005b, p. 377). On this point, management's responsibility for labor representatives participating in management alongside corporate managers, contributed to the creation and strengthening of worker interest in "social partnership" and "cooperation" within the corporation (Streeck 1992, p. 137). In many cases, appropriate information and employee participation prevented the eruption of disputes (Triesch 1977, p. 205). However, work councils were institutions for negotiation with management and did not have the rights to strike, as did trade unions. This was the reason rationalization-related disputes did not often arise, particularly in the boom years (Tokunaga 1977, p. 300).

With worker representatives on supervisory boards, the legitimate exercise of authority came to be more broadly based due to consideration for work and societal interests, and not just those of capital holders. The creation of the codetermination system gave a great shock to the legitimate control of traditional power until then (Futagami 1971, pp. 278–280) and created an opportunity to change the nature of the control's legitimacy in response to the modernization of postwar labor relations and the employment system.

The ability to exercise participatory rights in management decision-making by employee representatives was dependent on the skill and knowledge of employees. For codetermination to be meaningful, it was necessary to educate and train workers who were given this type of authority by law. This meant that the historical opportunity to create a German alternative to management based on the codetermination system earnestly started with the education and training of employee representatives; in other words, it was during the latter half of the 1960s and the early 1970s when social democracy was dominant (Locke 1996, p. 80).

Codetermination was thus a positive movement as a system of labor relations and education (a two-tiered system of education in schools and vocational education) and wage policy (agreements at the sector level). The educational system and wage policy supported other unique German characteristics in inter-sector technology transfer, standardization, and inter-corporate systems (Abelshauser 1999, p. 234). When we examine this within the global stage of capitalism, particularly after the 1990s, we see that codetermination fulfilled the important role of securing the following: social peace; expansion of production strategies into upper-market segments defined by higher quality; flexible workers; higher wages, living standards, and productivity; and cooperative relations between employees and employers. These were characteristic advantages in German corporations within markets competing on quality in the European and global economies (Thelen and Turner 1999, p. 212).

4.4.3 Functions as a Safety Net

Based on the above discussion, the final topic we will raise is the issue of the coordinating function in response to "marketization limits," which is related to arguments on the varieties of capitalism and their typology. In the "Rheinland Model of capitalism," one can see signs of "stakeholder capitalism" (Albert 1991) that aimed to create a stable society by emphasizing the realization of long-term welfare while limiting the application of market principles. Because of this, the significance of the coordinating function of the codetermination system became an important issue.

Among discussions on the varieties of capitalism, Hall and Soskice differentiate between a "liberal market economy" seen in the US and UK, a "coordinated market economy" found in Germany and Sweden, and a market economy that defies classification under the two types, such as the economies of France or Italy (Hall and Soskice 2001a, pp. 19–21). Today, a tendency toward new liberalism policies has become stronger. Also, as market principles are pushed to the forefront, safety mechanisms (or safety nets) in response to market economy limitations (or marketization limits) due to the stable continuance of capitalism become important issues. In many instances these safety mechanisms are generally provided by various types of regulations and legal protections. Market economy principles in each capitalistic country are manifested as variations in response to marketization limits and issues determining the political economy system of each country and the nature of their capitalist economies (Kaneko 1997).

In this sense particularly, labor relations and safety nets were important issues. In Germany, a typical example of what Hall et al. called a "coordinated market economy," there existed institutional complementarities between collective agreements at the industry-sector level and various other systems of labor relations, particularly work councils. Such institutional complementarities at the corporate level can be seen in work councils, which comprised elected employee representatives and had a fair amount of authority in regard to layoffs and other labor conditions (Hall and Soskice 2001a, pp. 24–25). The codetermination system offered further possibilities of restraining effects on management and manager functions through organic ties between labor representatives in the supervisory board and worker representation, which was made possible by work councils. Through this possibility, the codetermination system attempted to prepare a set of safety measures within corporations in response to marketization limits based on a capitalistic economic system. References by Chmielewicz et al. (1981, p. X) to company constitutions being the overall structural regulation with long-term binding power that affect corporations clearly reflect these aspects.

The safety measures seen in the codetermination system were not merely in response to marketization limits; rather, they were proactive in nature. In addition to defending the interests of workers through codetermination of personnel (or labor) and social issues at the plant level and avoiding labor disputes, these type of measure were evident in the adoption of employment systems that made it difficult for employers to layoff workers (Streeck 1997, p. 37). It was supported by collective bargaining and legal regulations as well as the codetermination system. Thus, the codetermination system functioned as a proactive safety measure in response to marketization limits within the labor market and provided the basis for a common market for the factors of production. Codetermination at the supervisory board level led to the possibility of a board of directors with labor representatives on the supervisory board; this facilitated monitoring of directors and supporting healthy business management through participation in management policy decision-making at the supervisory board level. This codetermination system created proactive safety measures for workers in the labor market and a broad range of stakeholders in general. At the same time, the codetermination system created ex-post safety measures based on the authority to appoint and dismiss directors through the supervisory board as referees of management results.

In regard to redistribution functions of social policy (or social securities) seen in Germany's postwar social market economy, through the aforementioned proactive safety net functions enabled by the codetermination system, an opportunity to reduce the fiscal burden of social coordination beforehand was very important. Thus, the codetermination system's safety net functions embedded within the corporation created critical conditions that supported the postwar economic system, which was the social market economy.

That safety measures within the codetermination system, as seen in the aspect of labor relations, had a retroactive and proactive nature that was hugely significant to workers. It also and served as a means of corporate governance within a capitalistic economy deeply connected to broader society. However, the codetermination system also had aspects of "system stabilization measures," which were based on safety measures in response to marketization limits in a capitalistic system. This was seen in worker integration functions and labor coordination with management as well as their conciliatory and compromising solutions. In reality, there were constraints in smaller corporations that had low levels of internal codetermination dissemination or where codetermination laws were not applied. Nevertheless, these safety measures and the embedding of functions for system stabilization using these measures show characteristics of the postwar system, which were based on the codetermination system and structured according to German-style labor relations.

As noted above, the opportunity for business management to gain autonomy from external forces through the passage of the 1976 Law on Codetermination, which specified that supervisory boards must have an equal composition of labor and management, provided the possibility for avoiding or reducing the influence to workers and pressures from shareholder value-oriented management and post-hostile takeover employment. Of course, increased pressure from capital markets after the 1990s made it difficult for the codetermination system to demonstrate its safety net functions. However, in protecting the rights and interests of workers, these functions remain significant for regulation and protection against the limitations of "over marketization," or capital market influences and pressure. The use of these functions continues to be an important issue even today.

The new postwar framework for labor relations described above demonstrated the function of safety nets in the form of employment and wage security, and supported conditions for the correction of social inequities within a social market economy. However, within German corporations, labor relations promoted investment in education and training to develop workers' skills and expertise, which was important for the development of diversified quality production. This institutional framework for labor relations was based on a system of vocational education and qualification for specialized skills and expertise, and was closely related to the development of a production system in postwar Germany.

With various changes in postwar relations among the nation, economy, and corporations, as well as those to the framework for labor relations, new developments could be seen in the postwar era within industrial concentration, which was deeply rooted to the characteristics of German capitalism and business management. Therefore, in the next chapter we will consider new developments in the industrial system based on industry-bank relations and the restructuring of the system of large corporate groups through the reconcentration of monopoly enterprises that were dissolved through occupation policy.

References

Abelshauser W (1999) Vom wirtschaftlichen Wert der Mitbestimmung: Neue Perspektiven ihrer Geschichte in Deutschland. In: Streeck W, Kluge N (eds) Mitbestimmung in Deutschland: Tradition und Effizienz, Expertenbericht für die Kommission Mitbestimmung Bertelsmann Stiftung/Hans-Böckler-Stiftung. Campus, Frankfurt am Main, pp 224–238

Abelshauser W (2004) Deutsche Wirtschaftsgeschichte seit 1945. C. H. Beck, München

Albert A (1991) Capitalisme contre Capitalisme. Ed. du Seuil, Paris

Allen MMC (2006) The varieties of capitalism paradigm. Explaining Germany's comparative advantage? Palgrave Macmillan, Basingstoke

Aoyama S (1981) Gendai "Nihonteki Roshikankei" no Tokusitsu to Saihen (Characteristics and reorganization of contemporary "Japanese industrial relations". In: Hasegawa H (ed) Gendai Nihon Kigyo to Roshi Kankei (Contemporary Japanese enterprise and industrial relations). Rodo Jyunposha, Tokyo, pp 53–112

Bertelsmann Stiftung, Hans-Böckler-Stiftung (eds) (1998) Mitbestimmung und neue Unternehmenskulturen—Bilanze und Perspektiven. Bericht der Kommission Mitbestimmung. Verlag Bartelsmann Stiftung, Gütersloh

Chmielewicz K, Coenenberg AG, Köhler R et al (1981) Einleitung der Herausgeber. In: Chmielewicz K, Coenenberg AG, Köhler R et al (eds) Unternehmensverfassung. Poechel, Stuttagart, pp IX–XIII

Deutsche Industrieinstitut (ed) (1968) Mitbestimmung. Forderungen und Tatsachen. Deutsche Industrieinstitut, Köln

Eberwein W (1992) Zur Geschichte und Soziologie der deutschen Betriebsverfassung. WSI Mitteilungen 45(8):499–504

Futagami K (1971) Nishi Doitsu Kigyo Ron (West German enterprise). Toyo Keizai Shinposha, Tokyo

Futagami K (1995) Keieiteki Kyodo Kettei Sisutemu (Codetermination system in enterprise). In: Takahashi T (ed) Koporeto Gabanansu (Corporate governance). Chuo Keizaisha, Tokyo, pp 129–143

Hall PA, Soskice D (2001a) An introduction to varieties of capitalism. In: Hall PA, Soskice D (eds) Varieties of capitalism: the institutional foundations of comparative advantage. Oxford University Press, Oxford, pp 1–68

Hall PA, Soskice D (eds) (2001b) Varieties of capitalism: the institutional foundations of comparative advantage. Oxford University Press, Oxford

Hans Böckler Stiftung, Bertelsmann Stiftung (2003) Mitbestimmung für die Zukunft. Ergebnisse und Fazit aus der Arbeit des "Forum Mitbestimmung und Unternehmen" 1999–2003. http://www.bertelsmann-Stiftung.de/cps/rde/xchg/SID-OA000F14-A6259003/bst/hs.xsl/prj6504651O.htm. Accessed 5 Sept 2007

Hayashi A (1993) Gekido no Jidai no Gendai Kigyo (Modern enterprise in the era of economic shock). Chuo Keizaisha, Tokyo

Herrigel G (2000) American occupation, market order, and democracy: reconfiguring the steel industry in Japan and German after the Second World War. In: Zeitlin J, Herrigel G (eds) Americanization and its limits. Reworking US technology and management in post-war Europe and Japan. Oxford University Press, Okford, pp 340–399

Hirano K (1976) Sengo Nihon ni okeru Roshi Kankei no Tenkai (Development of labor relations in Japan after WWII). In: Kimoto S (ed) Roshikankeiron (Labor relations). Nihon Hyoronsha, Tokyo, pp 193–216

Jentsch WM (1995) Doitsu Kigyo ni okeru Roshikankei (Industrial relations in German enterprise). In: Ohashi S, Oda A, Schanz G (eds) Nihonteki Keiei to Doitsuteki Keiei (Japanese business management and German business management). Chikura Shobo, Tokyo, pp 217–234

Kaido N (2005) Doitsu no Kigyo Taisei (Company constitution in Germany). Moriyama Shoten, Tokyo

Kaneko M (1997) Shijyou to Seido no Seijikeizaigaku (Political economics of markets and institutions). Tokoyo Daigaku Shuppankai, Tokyo

Locke RR (1996) The collapse of the American management Mystique. Oxford University Press, New York

Lompe K, Blöcker A, Marquardt B et al (2003) Bilanz und Perspektiven der Montanmitbestimmung, Entwicklung, Erfahrungen, Herausforderungen. Edition Sigma, Berlin

Maekawa K (1997) Nichidoku Hikaku Kigyoron eno Michi (Comparative study of Japanese enterprise and German enterprise). Moriyama Shoten, Tokyo

Mitbestimmungskommission (1970) Mitbestimmung im Unternehmen. Bericht der Sachverständigen-kommission zur Auswertung der bisherigen Erfahrung bei der Mitbestimmung. W. Kohlhammer, Stuttgart

Mori G (1981) Nihonteki Roshikankei Sisutemu no Tokusitsu to Kongo no Tenbo (Characteristics and prospects of the Japanese industrial relations system). In: Mori G (ed) Nihon no Roshikankei Sisutemu (Industrial relations system in Japan). Nihon Rodo Kyokai, Tokyo, pp 359–385

Murata K (1987) Roshi Kyodo Kettei no Keieigaku (Management study of codetermination), enlarged edn. Chikura Shobo, Tokyo

Muszynski B (1975) Wirtschaftliche Mitbestimmung zwischen Konflikt und Harmoniekonzeptionen. Theorethische Voraussetzungen, geschichtlicher Grundlagen und Hauptprobleme der Mitbestimmungsdiskussion der BRD. A. Hain, Meisenheim am Glan

OECD (1977) The development of industrial relations system. Some implications of Japanese experience, I, II. OECD, Paris

Ohashi S (1982) Doitsuteki Keiei (German business management). In: Yoshida K, Ohashi S (eds) Doitsu Keieigaku Soron (General remarks on business administration in Germany). Chuo Keizaisha, Tokyo, pp 157–172

Okouchi K (1980) Roshikankei Ron (Industrial relations). Rodo Junposha, Tokyo

Pirker T, Braun S, Lutz B et al (1955) Arbeiter Management Mitbestimmung. Ein industriesoziologische Untersuchung der Struktur, der Organisation und des Verhaltens der Arbeiterbelegschaften in Werken der deutschen Eisen- und Stahlindustrie, für das Mitbestimmungsgesetz gilt. Ring-Verlag, Stuttgart

Plettner B (1994) Abenteuer Elektrotechnik. Siemens und die Entwicklung der Elektrotechnik seit 1945. Pieper, München

Roshikankei Chosakai (1963) Roshikankei to Ningen Kankei (2) (industrial relations and human relations (2)). Chuo Koron Jigyo Shuppan, Tokyo

Schröter HG (2005a) Americanization of the European economy. A compact survey of American economic influence in Europe since the 1880s. Springer, Dordrecht

Schröter HG (2005b) Deutschlands Reintegration in die europäischen Wirtschaft. In: North M (ed) Deutsche Wirtschaftsgeschichte. Ein Jahrtausend im Überblick, 2., völlig überarbeitete und aktualisierte Auflage. C. H. Beck, München, pp 362–388

Streeck W (1992) Social institutions and economic performance. Studies of industrial relations in advanced capitalist economies. Sage, London

Streeck W (1997) German capitalism. In: Crouch C, Streeck W (eds) Political economy of modern capitalism: mapping convergence and diversity. Sage, London, pp 33–54

Sugaya A (1977) Roshikankei Ron no Kihon Mondai (Fundamental problems of industrial relations). Horitsu Bunkasha, Kyoto

Takagi K (1962) Nishiyoroppa ni okeru Seisansei Undo (The productivity movement in Western Europe). Nihon Seisansei Honbu, Tokyo

Takahashi K (1970) Nihonteki Roshikankei no Kenkyu (A study of Japanese labor relations), enlarged edn. Miraisha, Tokyo

Tegtmeier W (1973) Wirkungen der Mitbestimmung der Arbeitnehmer—Eine sozial-ökonomische Analyse potentieller und faktischer Wirkungen der Mitbestimmung im Unternehmen und im Unternehmensexternen Breich. Vandenhoeck & Ruprecht, Göttingen

Thelen KA (1991) Union of parts. Labor politics in postwar Germany. Cornell University Press, Ithaca

Thelen K, Turner L (1999) Die deutsche Mitbestimmung im internationalen Vergleich. In: Streeck W, Kluge N (eds) Mitbestimmung in Deutschland: Tradition und Effizienz, Expertenbericht für die Kommission Mitbestimmung Bertelsmann Stiftung/Hans-Böckler-Stiftung. Campus, Frankfurt am Main, pp 153–213

Tokunaga S (1977) Doitsu Shinshugi to Roshi Kankei (German capitalism and industrial relations). In: Tozuka H, Tokunaga S (eds) Gendai Roudo Mondai (Modern labour problems). Yuhikaku, Tokyo, pp 217–314

Triesch G (1977) Gensoku seichyou ka no Roshi Kankei (Industrial relations during decelerating growth). In: Arisawa H, Okouchi K (eds) Seichou Keizai no Tenkan (Conversion of growing economy). Nihon Keizai Shinbunsha, Tokyo, pp 203–221

Urabe K, Omura K (1983) Nihonteki Roshikankei no Tankyu (A study of Japanese industrial relations). Chuo Keizaisha, Tokyo

Yoshida O (1994) Doitsu Kigyo Taisei Ron (German company structure). Moriyama Shoten, Tokyo

Zeitlin J (2000) Introduction: Americanization and its limits: reworking US technology and management in post-war Europe and Japan. In: Zeitlin J, Herrigel G (eds) Americanization and its limits. Reworking US technology and management in post-war Europe and Japan. Oxford University Press, Oxford, pp 1–50

Zugehör R (2003) Die Zukunft der rheinsichen Kapitalmarkt. Unternehmen zwischen Kapitalismus und Mitbestimmung. Leske+Budrich, Opladen

Chapter 5
New System of Industrial Concentration

Abstract This chapter discusses the development of a new system of industrial concentration post WWII. Industry–bank relationships are important issues related to the system of corporate governance and German capitalism's cooperative characteristics. These relationships developed through various mechanisms such as banks' credit and securities businesses, the shareholdings and deposited stock system, assignment of directors from banks to corporations, and the advisory board system. Post WWII, large corporate group systems evolved during the dissolution and reconcentration of monopolies. First, this chapter examines the characteristics of postwar industrial concentration in Japan and compares them with those in Germany. Next, it analyzes new developments in Germany's industrial systems based on industry–bank relationships from the perspectives of mechanisms of cooperative inter-firm relationships and corporate governance. Furthermore, it considers the restructuring of a system for large corporate groups in relation to the dissolution of monopolies under the occupation policy and their reconcentration in the latter half of the 1950s. Drawing on this discussion, this chapter explains the manner in which large business operations were restructured through reconcentration or concentration, and the resultant divisions of labor in business domains developed in response to oligopolistic competition.

Keywords Corporate governance • Industrial concentration • Industry–bank relationship • Inter-firm relationship • Large corporate groups • Universal banking system

In Chap. 5, we will consider inter-firm relationships as a problem that was deeply connected with that of postwar German business management. When examining industrial concentration, the cooperative mechanisms for corporations are the most characteristic manifestation of corporate group systems, particularly in relation to ties between industries and banks. They were the cornerstone of German capitalism's accumulation structure and were important processes in postwar German

T. Yamazaki, *German Business Management: A Japanese Perspective on Regional Development Factors*, DOI 10.1007/978-4-431-54303-9_5, © Springer Japan 2013

corporate development. Industry–bank relationships were found before the war and emerged in the postwar era as a new development in the industrial system; they served as a cooperative system between industries and banks as well as among corporations themselves. The reconcentration of monopolies, which were dissolved as part of the postwar occupation policy, and the corporate group systems progressed apace.

Thus, in this chapter we will discuss the restructuring of corporate group systems and the new developments in industrial systems and describe the characteristics and significance of the new industrial concentration system in postwar Germany. First, we will explore the issues of inter-firm relationships between industries and banks in an "organic" industrial system and describe the significance of new developments in Germany's industrial concentration. "Industry" here refers not only to the manufacturing industry but, in a broader sense, to non-financial industries, including distribution and service industries. The industrial system based on industry–bank relationships was fundamental to the development of financial capital interests, which was based on a market control system for large corporations. For corporate group systems, the postwar occupation policy dissolved the concentration of monopolies and catalyzed new developments in large corporate groups through the reorganization of business structures that were adaptive to oligopolistic competition; it was not simply a return of the prewar structure. Thus, we examine the internal restructuring of corporate group systems that formed the cornerstone of new developments in postwar industrial concentration.

5.1 Characteristics of Industrial Systems Based on Industry–Bank Relationships and Large Corporate Groups in Japan

We will examine the characteristics of postwar industrial concentration in Japan and compare them with those in Germany. In prewar Japan, major corporations in each business sector, including banks, were part of the *zaibatsu* families and *zaibatsu* parent (holding) companies. Although corporate stocks were publicly traded, the percentage of shares held by *Zaibatsu* families was high. As a result, dissolution was focused on *zaibatsu* parent companies and certain major corporations and *zaibatsu* stocks were released to the market; however, banks were not included in these dissolutions. The prohibition of holding companies and regulation of treasury stock acquisitions and ownership formed six industrial groups. In these industrial groups, enterprises were concentrated by interlocking stockholding and forming large corporations, which were horizontally rather than vertically joined within capital groups and had substantial holdings of other companies' stocks. The large corporate groups formed in postwar Japan spanned several industries, with industrial corporations, banks, and trading companies at its core. The industrial groups comprised a full set of industries and conducted financing, interlocking stockholding, mutual business transactions, and joint investments internally. Banks and trading companies played a significant role in this scheme. These groups coordinated among themselves through an organization, the Network of Presidents, with decisions primarily made be by those in a certain position, such as presidents of group companies. However, banks did not always an absolute advantage, even though financial institutions formed the core of the Network of Presidents (Maekawa 1997, pp. 23, 58–59, 247, 263–264; Miyamoto et al. 2007, pp. 246–249, 252–253; Okumura 1976, pp. 12, 21–23; Miyazaki 1966, pp. 221–222, 224–225, 227–228; Kikkawa 1992, pp. 62–63, 69, 73, 77). Moreover, although industrial groups comprising full sets of industries were broadening, from the standpoint of inter-firm information sharing, the Network did not always adopt mechanisms that supported banks–industry relationships, as was the case in Germany. However, among these types of industrial groups, interlocking shareholding stabilized shareholders. In addition, corporations were able to use supplementary functions to bridge the gaps in organizational capabilities and corporate planning for entering new industries such as oil and nuclear power (Kikkawa 1992, pp. 80–81; Kikkawa 1996, pp. 192–200). It is noteworthy that the formation of these industrial groups enforced every industrial sector to directly compete with other large corporations, and each industrial group had relatively large and competitive or evenly matched corporations (Maekawa 1997, p. 59).

The industrial groups comprised large banks that were designated main banks to each group. These banks flexibly and resiliently supplied payment and settlement money needed for credit creation. These banks adopted the *keiretsu* financing system and capital procurement methods because Japanese corporations tended to use indirect financing in the postwar era. These banks also advised the large corporations on external financing (Suzuki 1993, p. 140). *Keiretsu* financing was, from the viewpoint of the six industrial groups' main banks, a way to distribute risk and avoid extreme concentration of borrowers; moreover, it enabled the expansion of lending while saving banks' screening and monitoring costs (Miyajima 1992, p. 238). In addition to corporate financing, another important function of the main banking system was corporate governance and monitoring (Aoki and Patrick 1994, p. xxii). In corporate governance, Japanese banks and corporate groups functioned as a defense against external pressures by interlocking stockholdings within the groups. However, although Japanese banks executed financial functions within industrial groups, they failed to develop binding relationships with the large corporate groups and had rather weak control over the industries. Close examination of the banking system reveals that the Japanese banks were not universal banks and could not exercise voting rights using the deposited stocks system. Top management in Japanese corporations followed a one-tier system, which comprised board of directors which controlled management mechanisms and the assignment of directors from banks.

Compared with Japanese banks, banks in Germany broadly associated with large corporate groups rather than with a specific corporate group (Maekawa 1997, p. 58). These ties were significant for the mechanisms and functions of information sharing and coordination, particularly in the interest of industrial system-based relationships between industries and banks. In contrast to Japan, large corporate groups in postwar Germany were not full-set types that encompassed a broad range of industries, but were essentially corporate groups based on a single-industry structure.

The emphasis on functional aspects based on the division of labor among corporations was critical. Moreover, holding companies were not prohibited in Germany as they were in Japan, and were considered a mechanism of corporate concentration. The restructuring of large corporate groups formed industry-specific groups that were adaptive to postwar oligopolistic competition.

In Sect. 5.2, we will consider the new developments in the industrial systems that were based on industry–bank relationships in Germany. In Sect. 5.3, we will analyze the restructuring of the corporate group systems.

5.2 New Development of Industrial Systems Based on Industry–Bank Relationships in Germany

We examine industrial system mechanisms based on inter-firm relationships (Sect. 5.2.1), analyze them from the perspective of corporate governance (Sect. 5.2.2), and explain the significance of the postwar development of industry–bank relationships (Sect. 5.2.3). In addition to the primary focus of this book, which is the period from the 1950s to the 1970s, we will further consider the period that immediately follows as well as more current circumstances.

The supervisory board, which held a central role in the assignment of directors from banks to corporations, appointed and dismissed directors, provided the board of directors with guidance on business management, and functioned beyond deliberation by approving rights in various critical matters. According to Herrhausen (1973), supervisory boards at the time were transforming from supervisory to advisory bodies for boards of directors; they exerted necessary control on the decision-making process to proactively avoid erroneous actions or measures (Herrhausen 1973, p. 32). This observation was noted in the 1986 annual report of Deutsche Bank as well (Deutsche Bank 1986, p. 17). Supervisory boards could indirectly influence business management through the appointment and dismissal of directors (Bleicher et al. 1984, pp. 28–29). The supervisory board was also involved in corporate policy decision-making by means of deliberation (Gutenberg 1970, pp. 3, 5–6). Corporate law regulations allowed for the involvement of the supervisory board in business policy decision-making through the approval of rights by specific board of directors by means of by-laws or supervisory board decisions. In these cases, the supervisory board formed a second decision-making body along with the board of directors (Bleicher et al. 1989, p. 55; Gutenberg 1970, p. 6). For instance, if the supervisory board executed its advisory function and delivered an opinion on the board of directors' decision making, the chairman of the supervisory board played an important role as corporate policies were collaboratively created (Böhm 1992, p. 206). Although explicit guidance by the supervisory board to the board of directors was forbidden by corporate law, it was regularly observed; in fact, some research notes the significant gap between the law and actual practice (Bleicher et al. 1989, p. 55). Nevertheless, the relationship between the supervisory board and the board of directors assumed diverse forms depending on the company.

5.2.1 Industrial System Mechanisms Based on Industry–Bank Relationships

5.2.1.1 Banks' Influence on Corporations Through Credit and Securities Businesses

Let us now examine bank credit and securities businesses and the influence of banks on corporations based on these businesses. Jeidels (1905) noted that, in bank and industrial alliances, the formation of regular business relationships that were primarily financial in nature was the most basic type of alliance, and personal links through the assignment of directors to supervisory boards was a method complementing these relationships (Jeidels 1905). Regarding creditor–debtor relationships, a 1979 report by the Gessler Committee, an advisory council to the Ministry of Finance, noted that most large corporations were able to procure capital outside of bank credit. In addition, the 30 largest corporations receiving credit had a considerable number of creditor–debtor relationships with financial institutions and credit organizations. Thus, we surmise that, apart from crises with debtor corporations, banks could not exert much influence on corporations through the supply of credit and house bank relationships did not exist in large corporations (Vgl. Bundesministerium der Finanzen 1979, pp. 157–158, 160–162). However, Gerhardt (1982) noted that creditor–debtor relationships between banks and their debtors were not sufficiently examined by the Committee (Gerhardt 1982, p. 192). He emphasized that credit-based financial relationships were strongly influencing corporate business policy (Gerhardt 1982, p. 107). In addition, although Eglau (1989) mentioned instances of banks assigning supervisory board members to family-owned private corporations and German subsidiaries of large foreign corporate groups, the positions of supervisory board members usually depended on long-term house bank-like relationships with the corporation (Eglau 1989, pp. 181, 261–263). It was likely that banks' exercising of management functions was facilitated by its character as a creditor and its supervisory post (Hopt 1979, p. 237). For example, large banks and corporations formed close alliances through the creditor–debtor relationship and proposals presented at annual meetings were generally coordinated in advance (Aizawa 1994, p. 117).

Regarding securities business in financial institutions, the Gessler Committee reported concentration in only few large banks and ties between large corporations and banks, with securities business functioning as intermediaries. From the period of the 1950s to the 1970s, specifically 1966–1975, top ten financial institutions accounted for 44.7% of financial institutions participating in the Consortium for Issuance of Securities; domestic issuers of stocks, convertible bonds, and option bonds totaled 58.3% and foreign issuers totaled 70%. Among the 71 publicly traded companies, the three large banks—Deutsche Bank, Dresdner Bank, and Commerz Bank—accounted for more than 98.6% of issuances among all banks. These three banks accounted for a high percentage of consortium leaders and co-managers at 81.7% and 80%, respectively (Bundesministerium der Finanzen 1979, pp. 452, 457). Edwards and Fischer (1994) revealed that the leaders of securities issuance syndicates were normally corporate house banks of joint stock companies, namely the three abovementioned banks (Edwards and Fischer 1994, pp. 215–221).

Because the securities business grew in scale, house bank functions in the creditor–debtor relationship and the security issue business became an important pillar of the industry–bank relationship. For example, Deutsche Bank had considerable power in both corporate finance and the overall economy because it offered payment of copious accounts, working capital, and fixed investment capital and made possible the underwriting of corporate capital increases and bond issues as a universal bank (Aizawa 1994, p. 4).

Regarding industry–bank relationships, in addition to the functions of the house bank in the security issue business and the intelligence that banks obtained by acting as intermediaries in the credit business, banks also exerted influence by exercising voting rights through bank-owned and deposited stocks; this laid the foundation for close ties. Thus, it is critical to comprehensively examine the interplay between the credit and securities businesses.

5.2.1.2 Banks' Influence on Industry Through Shareholdings and the Deposited Stock System

Let us now examine banks' influence on industries in relation to bank shareholdings and the deposited stock system. According to the 1976/1977 report by the Monopoly Committee, the provision of essential competitive information to corporations by financial institutions, which owned stocks in those corporations, and the voting rights through proprietary ownership stocks or deposited stocks that were supplementary thereof, enabled banks to exert direct and indirect influence on the business policies of non-bank corporations (Monopolkommission 1978, p. 338, Tz.604). Such stock deposits in banks and banks' proxies exercising the voting rights were a long-standing practice in Germany (Vgl. Schaad 1972, pp. 14–16), and were legalized by the 1937 Corporations Law (Lindhardt 1958, pp. 169, 171; Gottschalk 1990, p. 11; Schaad 1972, p. 17). However, before World War II, a portion of shares deposited in banks was not exercised in annual meetings and large private shareholders often exercised their own shares (Kuhlmann 1949, p. 489). The exercising of voting rights as an industrial system based on industry–bank relationships and banks' assignment of members to supervisory boards were not significant until after World War II.

Regarding the banks' influence on corporations, the impact of banks exercising voting rights through the deposited stock system was more important than the banks' shareholding itself. However, even in this case, the influence from deposited stock voting rights was more often dependent on the shareholder ownership structure of these corporations, and this was most likely for publicly traded corporations with scattered holdings and no control over shareholders (Hein and Flöter 1975, p. 352; Küstler et al. 2006, p. 78).

Shares of individually or family owned corporations that were dispersed among small individual shareholders were sold through banks, which had cooperative relationships with the share issuing companies; often the voting rights associated with those shares were entrusted to the banks due to the friendly relationships with the issuing companies. The cooperative relationships between the banks and corporations were based on the latter's direction. Such reciprocal relationships could also be observed in corporations with widely distributed shares. In contrast, among management-controlled corporations with widely distributed shares, the board of directors had a commanding position over the supervisory board, particularly in the top-level decision making and selection of supervisory board members from banks during the annual meeting; there were instances where the banks cooperatively exercised voting rights with the management (Sakuma 2003, pp. 69–70, 75).

Regarding the exercise of voting rights including bank deposited stocks, the total value of deposited stocks for instance increased from DM 28.9 billion at the end of 1970 to DM 36.5 billion by the end of 1975. At the end of the 1970, 73.7% of those stocks were deposited in credit banks, and by the end of 1975, the number declined to 71.3%, which was nonetheless a high rate (Hansen 1977, pp. 161–162). According to a report by the Monopoly Committee, in terms of revenue, of the top 100 companies 56 corporations had 5% or more of their voting rights held by banks in the mid-1970s. Of those, 18 corporations had 75% of their voting rights held by banks, 12 between 50% and 75%, 11 between 25% and 50%, and 15 between 5% and 25% (Monopolkommission 1978, p. 296). In addition, examining the ratio of banks' voting rights in representative corporations effective 1975, we see that AEG had 89.29%, Hoechst 88.62%, BASF 87.15%, Siemens 81.02%, and Bayer 79.09%, all rather high figures. August Thyssen held a relatively low rate at 45.28%. However, the proportion of owner-held stock voting rights held by banks in these corporations was not greater than 1% (Vgl. Monopolkommission 1978, p. 560), whereas banks exercising voting rights through the deposited stocks system were significant.

According to a survey by Gottschalk on the 32 of the 100 largest corporations with widespread shareholding or bank-owned stocks at 50% or more, in terms of added value in 1984, the percentage of voting rights for all banks in 1986 (or for a portion of the corporations in 1987) was on average 82.67%. For 22 of those corporations, banks held voting rights greater than the 75%, required to make decisions on critical issues such as amending by-laws. Of the 32 corporations, the top three banks on average held 45.44% of the exercisable voting rights and over 50% in 15 corporations (Vgl. Gottschalk 1988, pp. 297–299). A 1992 survey by Baums and Fraune, which analyzed in terms of added value 24 of the largest 100 public corporations that had a majority of widespread shareholding, showed that the percentage of voting rights held by banks at these companies' annual meetings was on average 84.09% and those through the deposited stocks system was 60.95%. In addition, there were 11 corporations with greater than 75% of voting rights through deposited stocks alone, 18 corporations with banks holding 75% of their voting rights, and 17 corporations at more than 90% (Vgl. Baums and Fraune 1995, pp. 98, 103). A 1994 research by Edwards and Fischer also showed that German banks, in particular the top three banks, had a great deal of control over voting rights in corporations, and this control was primarily through proxy voting rights through the deposited stocks system (Edwards and Fischer 1994, p. 226).

5.2.1.3 Assignment of Directors from Banks to Corporations

The impact of exercising voting rights based on the deposited stocks system and bank shareholding was further realized though the assignment of directors from banks. The most secure foundation for banks to exert influence was built through personal ties with corporations, the assignment of supervisory board members that acted as information conduits, selection of directors, and the involvement in business policies. Thus, close ties between non-bank corporations and banks were the most important factor in generating the power held by banks (Volkmann and Kronenberg 1994, p. 481). The influence of two particular factors, capital holding and voting rights through the deposited stocks system that were executed by supervisory board members, began to be felt, and these positions became a mechanism for the transfer of this power (Vgl. Böhm 1992, p. 222). Therefore, we will next consider this point.

5.2.1.3.1 Information Sharing System and Banks' Assignment of Directors

We will first examine information sharing systems enabled by the assignment of directors from banks to corporations. By integrating finance-based information with that obtained from the assigned supervisory board members, it became possible for banks to fill an advisory and leadership capacity in these corporations and obtain information valuable to external borrowers. By obtaining information on borrowers, corporate sales, and financial statuses of supplies of credit, banks could gather substantial inside information on multiple corporations; it enabled them to act as storehouses of information and information conduits (Uetake 1997, p. 104). Specialized financial information and experience and guidance necessary to help the board of directors avoid mistakes were important factors in strengthening the role and significance of supervisory board member positions (Vgl. Deutsche Bank 1986, p. 17). Regarding corporations being assigned supervisory board members from banks, the preferential status of easier access to good information sources helped them form closer relationships (Eglau 1989, p. 192).

From a corporation's internal functional perspective, banks sharing information, particularly know-how, often acted as a type of corporate consultant. On the other hand, for external functioning, this system of information sharing among corporations, with bank representatives on the supervisory board acting as intermediaries, spread further contingent on the likelihood of contact between corporations and the supervisory board, that is, mainly through bank-assigned supervisory board member (Hopt 1979, pp. 235–238).

The assignment of supervisory board members was also important for coordination among various departments, and the most decisive point for the overall system (Hopt 1979, p. 238). Banks were familiar with issues within industries and provided advice and guidance for decision-making to corporate borrowers across the broad categories of management. For corporations receiving the directors, the assignment of directors from banks was very significant for obtaining opinions on the overall management as well as for procuring capital (Busse 1962, p. 51). Although relatively few banks were represented on the supervisory board, banks performed overall coordination in the best manner possible; however, this allowed the control of large banks' positions through supervisory board representation (Edwards and Fischer 1994, p. 220).

The supervisory board chairman could obtain all sorts of important and internal information through the directors' reports on critical matters (Bundesministerium der Finanzen 1979, p. 116). If a bank representative was assigned to a corporation and later appointed the chairman of the supervisory board, the representative could exert tremendous influence on decision-making in the corporation as opposed to other supervisory board members.

5.2.1.3.2 Assignment of Directors and Collaborative Relations Among Banks

We will now examine the assignment of directors that were based on collaborative relationships among banks. For example, we see that the top three banks, being the largest shareholders, could exercise voting rights through the deposited stocks system. Furthermore, these banks created collaborative relationships with combined capital complementing the voting rights of banks (Uetake 1997, p. 106). This could be seen in the banks' annual meetings with banks exercising voting rights. Gottschalk's survey analyzed the total number of shares and deposited stocks owned by investment firms and their parent banks and noted that the percentage of Deutsche Bank's voting rights in 1986 was 47.17% and that for the top three banks was 60.36%. Dresdner Bank's percentages of shares and deposited stocks were 47.08% and 64.04%, respectively, while Commerz Bank's percentages were 34.58% and 60.81%, respectively; these were considerably high rates (Gottschalk 1988, pp. 297–298). In addition, against the total rate of voting rights, the 1992 research by Baums and Fraune revealed that Deutsche Bank's rate of voting rights was 32.07% and that among the top three banks was 49.24%. At Dresdner Bank these percentages were 44.19% and 53.66% and at Commerz Bank they were 18.49% and 48.27% (Vgl. Baums and Fraune 1995, p. 106). Thus, the top three banks held a very high percentage of shares with voting rights, enabling them to collaboratively and effectively control their annual meetings (Böhm 1992, p. 75). H. Pfeiffer observed that the controller of large banks were the large banks themselves (Pfeiffer 1986, p. 475). These collaborative inter-bank relationships laid the foundation for control over large banks and such control influenced and controlled many industrial corporations.

In addition to the collaborative relationships that could be found in joint funding between banks (Vgl. Monopolkommission 2003, p. 231), in the exercising of voting rights through the deposited stocks system, banks could transfer voting rights deposited by customers to third parties such as other trusted banks (Yamaguchi 1981, p. 113). Even the transfer of voting rights through the deposited stocks system from smaller banks to large banks strengthened the influence of these collaborative inter-bank relationships on corporations (Busse 1962, p. 65; Bundesministerium der Finanzen 1979, p. 568).

Banks had similar collaborative systems for financing because, in the case of the top three banks' consortium for issuance of securities, positions, rankings, and allocations were approved in a fixed fashion (Poullain 1979, p. 80). Edwards and Fischer (1994) research noted that for a long period of time the structure of this bank syndicate was extremely stable (Edwards and Fischer 1994, p. 215). The top three banks acted collaboratively in the exercise of voting rights at annual meetings, and for the most part, were immovable as supervisory positions in the companies with which they dealt (Vgl. Gottschalk 1988, pp. 299–300). Other banks also tended to collaborate with the top three banks (Gottschalk 1988, p. 300; Bundesministerium der Finanzen 1979, p. 173). Further, voting rights and deposited stocks provided opportunities to constrain and suppress industrial relationships and competition among banks for industry work (Busse 1962, pp. 64, 66). This served an important role even in activities that included the assignment of members to the supervisory board. On this point, the creation of a "strong shareholder" system based on the universal banking system was important for the selection of supervisory board members, who acted as capital-side representatives during their annual meetings (Takahashi 1997, p. 51).

Assigning of supervisory board members occurred in financial institutions as well (Vgl. Bundesministerium der Finanzen 1979, p. 591). The collection and exchange of valuable information regarding borrower corporations or corporations to which supervisory board members had been assigned based on personal ties were extremely critical.

5.2.1.3.3 Assignment of Directors Between Banks and Industries

In examining the assignment of directors between banks and industries, we find that, for example, according to a Monopoly Committee 1976/1977 report, among 51 surveyed corporations, there were 137 instances of supervisory board members being selected from financial institutions and 57 instances of financial institution assignees being chairmen or vice-chairmen. The numbers coming from the top three banks were 76 board members and 35 chairmen or vice-chairmen, accounting for more than 55.5% and 61.4%, respectively, of the total assignees from financial institutions (Monopolkommission 1978, pp. 574–577). For these 51 corporations, if financial institutions had more than 25% of the voting rights, they had without exception secured at least one supervisory position, and if the financial institutions had more than 25% stock holding, they procured chairman or vice-chairman positions on the supervisory board. Among the largest 100 corporations, 31 had financial institution representatives serving as chairmen of the supervisory board, 35 corporations had representatives serving as vice-chairmen. The top three banks had 21 chairmen and 19 vice-chairmen in these corporations (Monopolkommission 1978, pp. 303–304, 307–308). The Gessler Committee reported that, in 74 publicly traded corporations surveyed in 1974 and 1975, 182 had supervisory board members assigned from financial institutions and 37 had chairmen of the supervisory board from financial institutions. The numbers of supervisory board members and chairmen assigned from the top three banks were 101 and 25, and respectively, accounted for 55.5% and 67.6% of those assigned from financial institutions. Of these 74 publicly traded corporations, that is, where a bank held at least 25% of the voting rights in a particular corporation, the same banks also held chairmanship of the supervisory board in many instances, and in an overwhelming number of cases, two supervisory positions (Vgl. Bundesministerium der Finanzen 1979, pp. 173–174, 436, 438–439, 443–445).

In subsequent periods as well, the Gottschalk survey noted that in 1986, bankers or former bankers had 69 (27%) of the 256 supervisory positions within 27 non-bank corporations. Of these, 50 positions, or roughly three-fourths, were populated by representatives of the top three banks (Gottschalk 1988, p. 300). According to Ziegler, two if not all three of the top three banks had representatives serving as supervisory board members among larger manufacturers. One decisive factor in the banks having so many representatives was the economic importance of the companies accepting the representatives (Vgl. Ziegler 1984, p. 597). Pfeiffer in 1993 found that the top three banks had assigned 1,053 directors to other corporations' supervisory boards in the 1990s, with 170 of them acting as supervisory board (or other management) chairmen, and 92 as vice-chairmen (Vgl. Pfeiffer 1993, pp. 151, 172, 182–183). At least one bank representative served as a supervisory board member in the 261 publicly traded corporations surveyed by Hansen in 1993, and 372 supervisory board members were assigned from financial institutions. Of these, 192 (51.6%) were from the top three banks and 59 companies had bank representatives serving as supervisory board chairmen. The corporations comprising the DAX30 had 73 supervisory positions filled by bank representatives, with 13 corporations having bank directors in the supervisory board chairman position. The top three banks had a total of 56 supervisory positions in the DAX30 corporations, or 76.7% of the total (Hansen 1994a, R.78). In roughly the same time period, one-fourth of the total market value of German stocks was owned by foreigners, with more than one-fifth being owned by private investors. However, the percentage of supervisory board positions in the DAX30 accounted for by these two groups of investors was no greater than roughly 5% each (Hansen 1994b, R.404).

The mutual assignments of directors from industries to banks was also common; Pfeiffer (1993) noted that there were up to 5,286 cases including assignment of (1) directors and supervisory board members from non-bank corporations to the supervisory boards or boards of directors of the top three banks, (2) supervisory board members from the top three banks to the supervisory boards or boards of directors of non-bank corporations (Vgl. Pfeiffer 1993, pp. 172, 182–183). Further, cases of corporate representatives participating in bank committees and other organizations existed as well. For example, the chairman of the board of chemical giant BASF belonged to a Deutsche Bank committee, and BASF's supervisory board chairman traditionally belonged to a similar organization at Commerz Bank (Pfeiffer 1989, p. 15). Thus, supervisory board assignments from the top three banks to non-bank corporations and vice versa accounted for many of the personal ties between banks and industries.

5.2.1.4 System of Corporate-Bank and Inter-Corporate Information Sharing Through the Advisory Board System

The banks' personnel exchange structure for the sharing of information had an important role in complementing industry–bank relationships through the assignment of directors from banks. The advisory board, created for banks' head offices and for each region, functioned as a focal point of information exchange between corporations and banks as well as among corporations themselves.

Major corporations assigned members to a central advisory board, where industry leaders regularly reported to each other on their markets' conditions. As they performed their board roles, they received advice and guidance on various business issues (Eglau 1989, pp. 192–193). The central advisory board acted as a coordinating body between banks and industrial corporations and could be seen in Dresdner Bank prior to 1966. These boards were established by banks to maintain the level of personal ties, previously enjoyed in response to the 1965 Corporations Law's regulation on the number of supervisory board members (Vgl. Pfeiffer 1993, p. 477; Stanzick 1968, p. 72). Region specific advisory boards had existed in Deutsche and Dresdner Banks since before the war and postwar in Commerz Bank. Regional advisory boards included management representatives from various corporate sectors that served large banking customers and their regional organizational units. One reason for the existence of regional advisory boards was that they strengthened relationships among various corporations across business sectors and in each region for matters of business policy (Vgl. Büschgen 1983, pp. 242–243; Koubek 1971, p. 261). Pfeiffer's (1993) research states that, among many medium-sized businesses, the supervisory board's functions of regulation, consultation, and guidance were undertaken by the advisory board (Pfeiffer 1993, p. 181; Commerz Bank 1970, p. 142). Persons appointed by the top three banks to the supervisory or an advisory board were considered "friendly" (Gottschalk 1988, p. 301). For example, it was important for Deutsche Bank's advisory board to create strong ties with the banks' customers through its business and propose new operations through those ties (Vgl. Schwarz 2003, p. 32).

In addition, several hundred business associations shared ties with banks through the top three banks' supervisory board, central advisory board, or regional advisory board members (Vgl. Pfeiffer 1987, pp. 29–31). With these personal organizational ties, close relationships between banks and industries created information conduits, and were not only based on direct relationships between the two groups but also complemented by intermediary relationships of economic associations such as business and industrial associations and industry–bank relationships (Vgl. Koubek 1971, pp. 262–266).

5.2.2 *Corporate Governance and Industry–Bank Relationships*

5.2.2.1 Collaborative System of Corporate Governance Based on Industry–Bank Relationships

The industrial system based on industry–bank relationships created a collaborative system of corporate governance that has German characteristics, a phenomenon we will now examine.

The German segregation of authority into a two-layered system of top management for supervisory boards and boards of directors facilitated debates between those outside the corporation offering much valuable advice and those actually running the business. This dynamic's ability to expand corporations' views and clearly delineate responsibility was significant (Winnacker 1972, p. 467). As bank representatives acting as supervisory board members offer guidance on the basis of the banks' wealth of information and know-how, this German management system demonstrates its importance and effectiveness as an industrial system based on industry–bank relationships. With such decision-making mechanisms, functions to monitor and regulate are exhibited by business functions centered on the board of directors.

The high percentage of voting rights held by banks, including voting rights through deposited stocks, the assignment of supervisory board members, and industry–bank relationships based on personal ties through representatives on advisory boards, enabled defensive mechanism against capital market pressures. Here, we see German characteristics in the corporate governance systems. With the progress of financial globalization since the 1990s, there was pressure on shareholder value-oriented management through investment funds, execution of business strategy, and selection of supervisory board members at annual meetings. Compared with other European countries, the US, and Japan, conditions in this environment reveal that the German industrial system enabled banks to secure management stability not only in corporations in which they held shares but also with borrowers.

However, with greater capital market pressures in today's financial globalization, this stable system is sometimes rocked to its foundation. Beginning in the 1990s, large banks transited from their traditional lending business toward investment banking, and the assignment of directors from banks to corporations declined. Further, banks began accepting fewer corporation representatives for the positions of a supervisory board chairman (Vgl. Zugehör 2003, pp. 68–70, 92–93, 173). These changes by banks were another step toward globalized capitalism, and banks themselves were regulated by changes in the conditions for capital accumulations. From the perspective of corporate relationships, banks were forced to intensify their relationships based on "selection and concentration" to achieve greater efficiency.

5.2.2.2 Codetermination and Collaborative Systems of Corporate Governance in Industry–Bank Relationships

It is important to consider the relationship between issues of corporate governance based on close ties between industries and banks and the codetermination system at the supervisory board level, as examined in Chap. 4.

The authority of the supervisory board chairman was expanded under the 1976 Law on Codetermination. The law granted two votes to the chairman in cases of conflicts between shareholders and labor representatives on the supervisory board. Conditions that were in the interest of the investors were important for coordinating interests with the supervisory board chairman. In addition, the number of labor representatives on the supervisory board being equal to that of shareholder representatives necessitated the formation of groups. Also, the supervisory board chairman held authority that enabled governance of certain types of opinions within the groups (Vgl. Eglau 1989, pp. 178–179). Primarily based on this, when bank representatives served as supervisory board chairmen in corporations, they found it easier to demonstrate the governing and coordinating functions of their role on the basis of abundant data.

With the deployment of the 1976 Law on Codetermination, the supervisory board would regulate its meetings that were occasionally conducted to eliminate controversial issues from discussion; however, some have pointed out that the supervisory board tended to lose its authoritative position in matters of corporate policy being discussed in a critical fashion. Rather than an expansive board, the supervisory board chairman often took on the role of a critical debater for the board of directors (Eglau 1989, pp. 166–167). In these circumstances, when bank representatives took over the position of the supervisory board chairman, it became easy to coordinate group interests based on, both internal and external, critical corporate information, obtained by the supervisory board chairman from banks, which were information sources.

The codetermination system decreases the rate of investors in the supervisory board and provided opportunities for autonomous corporate management. In particular, with the Codetermination Act for the Coal, Iron and Steel Industries and the 1976 Law on Codetermination requiring the proportion of labor representatives to be half of the supervisory board, the number of external members in the board fell. From the latter half of the 1970s, the 1976 Law on Codetermination tended to reduce the number of bank representatives on the supervisory boards representing German corporations (Cable 1985, p. 33). Corporations used this as an opportunity to reduce potential external influence and involvement.

However, the decrease in supervisory positions held by shareholders allowed for conditions of easier fulfillment of banks' interests, with banks and inter-bank alliances holding a superior position in exercising voting rights through deposited stocks. Further, through collaborations between banks and the corporations to which they assigned directors, the latter had greater decision-making ability, including those regarding the remaining supervisory board members and suppressing outside influences. For these reasons, collaboration with banks took on further significance for corporations.

As mentioned, the codetermination system created conditions for a more strong functioning industrial system based on industry–bank relationships, while suppressing the influence of external shareholders. For banks, this was a mechanism for regulating their own interests and fulfilling bank interests in corporations to which banks assigned directors.

Under the codetermination system, opportunities for corporations to collaborate with labor representatives on the supervisory board were fortified as a defense mechanism against external pressures, which were heavily oriented toward the pursuit of short-term interests and represented by investment funds in present-day terms. From the objectives of labor, it secured soundness and security in employment and corporate management. This feature further strengthened collaboration between corporations and labor. For capital supervisory board members, there is an industrial system based on industry–bank relationships in the form of collaborative network for broad personal ties. In this type of industrial system collaboration with supervisory board comprising capital members, such as bank representatives, the exercise of a defensive function becomes even stronger.

Thus, preconditions for effective, direct control through the assignment of bank representatives to corporate supervisory boards are met within joint-stock and limited liability companies under the 1976 Law of Codetermination or the Codetermination Act for the Coal, Iron and Steel Industries. The Act requires corporations to have codetermination with equal labor representation. In corporations with this type of codetermination, supervisory positions that banks held as creditors were effective for surveillance and providing approvals required by the management (Wiendieck 1992, p. 172, p. 176).

From the foregoing discussion, we see that Germany developed a system that had functions similar to that of corporate defense, developed to counter external pressures, and contrasted that of interlocking stockholdings, which characterized postwar Japan. This type of corporate system was supported by the industrial and codetermination systems based on industry–bank relationships at the supervisory board level, forming an important characteristic of German corporate governance.

5.2.3 Significance of New Developments in Industry–Bank Relationships

Our discussions to this point have examined new developments in postwar industry–bank relationships and the industrial system upon which they were based. We will discuss the types and possible significance of future developments that were different from those in the prewar era.

First, we will establish the development of an industrial and corporate governance system based on banks exercising voting rights through the deposited stock system. The issuance business was prominent in the securities business that was based on the prewar universal banking system. However, in the postwar era, with the expansion of general investments in securities, the position of the securities business in the secondary market also grew. As a result, a system of bank agents exercising voting rights through the deposited stocks system was fully established. This practice built the essential foundation for both capital and personal ties for the postwar development of industrial concentration and the establishment of a uniquely German industrial system, facilitating information sharing between industries and banks and regulating their interests.

Second, we will observe the full-scale development of a network for sharing information between banks and industries and among corporations through the bank's advisory board system and a system for regulating interests through that network. Although there were prewar cases of regional advisory boards, in the postwar period, central advisory boards were established and became the cornerstone of the advisory board system. Through the combination of central and regional advisory boards, a national and regional system of information sharing between banks and industries and among corporations themselves was established. These systems differed from those based on the assignment of directors and were used for regulating interests between banks and investors and those among corporations.

Third, the weakening influences and pressures from external shareholders, which emerged due to the codetermination system program proposing equal labor representation on the supervisory board, established and strengthened a corporate governance system based on industry–bank relationships; its roles differed from those featured during the prewar era. In addition, the strengthened industry–bank relationships and the industrial system on which they were based revealed the system's importance.

Examining the significance of new postwar developments in industry–bank relationships and the cooperative characteristics of German capitalism (Chandler 1990), reveals that the strong influence exerted by banks on industries was due to the collaborative relationships between the two groups, rather than the banks' desire to control the industries. The framework for bank shareholdings, the assignment of supervisory board members according to the exercising of voting rights based on the deposited stocks system, and the advisory board system resulted in information sharing and a support system dependent upon advice from banks and collaborative relationships with industrial corporations. Banks' involvement in the joint responsibility for industrial policy and several corporate business policies (Busse 1962, p. 61) was an important element supporting the collaborative system, through which banks regulated inter-corporate interests. Directors from banks and insurance firms often played an important role in the formation of personal ties among competing corporations (Vgl. Pfannschmidt 1993, p. 274). Further, the German-style system of corporate governance based on the codetermination system and the inter-corporate collaborations that the system supported complemented this industrial system's collaborative structure. The industrial system was further complemented by the inter-corporate assignment of directors and interlocking of directorates (Vgl. Schönwitz and Weber 1982; Decher 1990; Pfannschmidt 1993). This postwar German-style industrial system based on industry–bank relationships combined these elements and functioned in a framework that deeply connected each element.

Although major changes can be seen in the 1990s and thereafter, this collaborative structure in the postwar era enabled corporate management to not only plan for business expansion from a long-term perspective but also suppress the influence of external shareholders and the pressures of the capital market. This structure constituted significant German development within the Americanization of business management, as management pursued business expansion with a long-term perspective in line with German and European market structures, which were central to German exports.

5.3 New Developments in the System of Large Corporate Groups in Germany

As discussed, this postwar industrial system based on industry–bank relationships was extremely important for the expansion of German corporations. However, an important problem that changed industrial concentration was the restructuring of the system of large corporate groups within the reconcentration of monopolies, which were previously dissolved under the occupation policy, and the later concentration of enterprises. We will next consider this issue.

In Sect. 5.3.1, we will first examine the dissolution of monopolies by victorious nations such as the US and its influence. In Sect. 5.3.2, we will consider the reconcentration of monopolies beginning in the 1950s and new developments in the system of large corporate groups that accompanied reconcentration. We will explore the significance of these new developments in Sect. 5.3.3.

5.3.1 Influence of the US Deconcentration Policy on Monopolies

5.3.1.1 Expansion of Monopoly Deconcentration Policy

First, examining monopoly deconcentration policy, we note the US belief that excessive German economic and political power should be curtailed through monopoly dissolution and decartelization (Schlieper 1986, p. 156). The basic policy was to turn Germany into an oligopolistic market founded on the principle of competition, very similar to that in US (Berghahn 1985, p. 280, Djelic 1998, p. 167).

Separating the coal industry from the iron and steel industries through dissolution deeply impacted these groups (Berghahn 1986, pp. 95, 110). In heavy industries, the eight large corporate groups were eventually divided into 23 steel companies. Vereinigte Stahlwerke AG's steel division was split into 13 separate companies, which further spilt three into the coal sector, one in processing, and one in trading (Fiereder 1989, p. 237; Uebbing 1991, p. 55). Krupp had its main plant, the Friedrich–Alfred–Hütte iron works, demerge and dissolve into a separate company, Hüttenwerk Rheinhausen AG, and Essener Kruppzechen also split (Der Volkswirt 1954b, p. 24). Previously, Krupp had been able to globally produce superior products in both quality and price through its effective cooperation and complementary functioning with materials industries and processing plants. However, its ties with these production stages were terminated and the company changed completely (Der Volkswirt 1954a, p. 49; Der Volkswirt 1956c, pp. 28, 30). This type of dissolution also occurred at Mannesmann, Hoesch, and Gutehoffnung, among other corporations (Der Volkswirt 1952a, pp. 24–25; Der Volkswirt 1953b, p. 23; Der Volkswirt 1952b, pp. 23–24; Der Volkswirt 1954c, p. 24; Der Volkswirt 1953a, p. 21). However, West Germany strongly opposed the complete separation of the coal industry from the iron and steel industries, which was envisioned by the occupation forces, and the parallel management of both iron and steel and coal companies was approved with an upper limit of 75% of coke consumption (Tohara 1974, p. 141).

The chemical firm IG Farben was also dissolved, resulting in a restructured oligopoly of three main companies: BASF, Bayer, and Hoechst (Vgl. Kleinkamp 1977; Gross 1950). Major changes in capital relationships also occurred. The banking industry was split into 30 small-scale regional banks, with specific bank operations limited to a specific state regions (Pohl 1986, pp. 102–104; Djelic 1998; Stolper et al. 1964, pp. 227–228). However, the universal banking system was not reformed through these dissolutions and restructuring, a very important factor in the new development of the industrial system based on industry–bank relationships.

5.3.1.2 Significance of Monopoly Dissolution and Restructuring

The dissolution of large corporations was a huge setback to the corporations; nevertheless, it was also an opportunity for monopolistic corporations to undergo a rationalized process of restructuring. For example, in the case of Vereinigte Stahlwerke, dissolution provided an opportunity to restructure as a large company with a scope appropriate for management, with a functional monopoly or oligopolistic system. In addition, IG Farben was able to liquidate an immovable, excessive group to create a functional, large corporate group with a more rational structure that responded to postwar technological reforms while allowing them to pioneer new areas and expand their base (Tohara 1974, pp. 145–147). The US proposal for organizational restructuring of the coal and iron and steel industries, which accompanied the dissolution of monopolies, attempted to rationalize these industries, thus reducing costs and improving efficiency while increasing production (Berghahn 1986, pp. 90, 95, 108–109; Djelic 1998, p. 166). US postwar reforms primarily focused on market restructuring by terminating monopolies and cartels and the achievement of economies of scale (Herrigel 2000, p. 361).

For example, in the iron and steel industry, a great deal of production capacity was allocated to other steel production units through the dissolution of monopolies. Thus, components of the industry's rolling mill capacity spread throughout the entire industry rather than within a single corporation. This type of production capacity allocation created conditions for oligopolistic competition, and not only raised the cost of diversification but also generated possible incentives for corporate growth through an increase in the scale of corporate rolling mills (Herrigel 2000, p. 364). The prewar structure of domestic markets was replaced by an oligopolistic structure through a policy of deconcentration, and the previously existing monopolies and specialization were replaced by mass production (Herrigel 2000, pp. 352–353, 368). Such industrial restructuring created a foundation for the expansion of corporate activities suitable for oligopolistic competition, which differed from the assumptions of the prewar German iron and steel industry structure, industrial organization, and market structure.

IG Farben's dissolution in the chemical industry revived inter-firm relationships in same form taken before the company was created. However, the restructuring actually created the industry's three giants in response to the move from coal to petroleum chemistry, wherein a unique, multifaceted industrial complex was created to produce synthetic rubber, synthetic resins, synthetic fibers, and other petroleum-based products. This change was not merely a return to prewar conditions, but a rational restructuring that established a more competitive intercorporate structure (Kudo 1999, p. 378). The following two achievements resulted from the dissolutions: (1) the chemical market was restructured along competitive lines. (2) The new and sufficiently large-scale units were established to act as an engine useful for the rebuilding and growth of Western Europe and to survive in the multi-lateral liberal capitalistic world trade system dominated by the US (Berghahn 1986, p. 95).

The restructuring of corporate organizations to their prewar form was not the primary objective; rather, it was to create resilient trust structures (Maekawa 1970, pp. 147–148). Significantly, dissolution and restructuring created stronger control in the heavy equipment manufacturing industries. Krupp, Gutehoffnung, Klöckner, and others demonstrated and laid the foundation for the rapid development of the heavy machinery sector (Sasaki 1975, p. 65).

The latter half of the 1950s, although brought about the reconcentration of monopolies, new developments in the system of large corporate groups will be our next topic of discussion.

5.3.2 Development of the Reconcentration of Monopolies

5.3.2.1 Background of the Reconcentration of Monopolies

Since the end of World War II and during the 1957 and 1958 crises, Germany experienced a wave of corporate amalgamations with large corporate group structures, providing the foundation for mergers and acquisitions of subsidiaries. Enterprise concentration in the same capital groups were also central to this movement (Hahn and Tammer 1970, p. 24) and played an important part in the reconcentration of dissolved corporations.

Three factors influenced this reconcentration and new concentration from the latter half of the 1950s through the end of the decade: (1) the benefits of economies of scale, (2) the legal benefit of scale, and (3) psychological factors. First, these developments achieved economies of scale. Second, tax benefits were applied to vertically integrated corporations. Third, cartels and concentration, rather than competition, were always the *lingua franca* of Europe's economic system and were known to the market players [*National Archives*, RG59, 862A.33, Reconcentration in Iron, Steel and Coal Industries of the Federal Republic (5.10.1959), pp. 3–4].

For legal benefits, national growth policies played a significant role and four laws enacted by the government dealt with this issue. The 1956 Transformation Law and 1957 Tax Law enabled large corporate groups to concentrate their power on a previously unseen scale and rid themselves of small shareholders. Revisions to corporate law allowed corporations to enjoy tax benefits by elimination or reduction of taxes on a portion of their profits and transforming it into equity capital. Further, the Restrictive Trade Practices Act publicly acknowledged about 250 cartels in 1958 and 1959 (D.W.I.-Berichte 1961, p. 5).

The reconcentration of previously split or dissolved large corporate groups continued apace in conjunction with the European Coal and Steel Community (ECSC). Article 66 of the ECSC Convention, May 1954, allowed concentration of companies that did not obstruct market competition and were granted relatively broad freedom for merging corporations within the coal, iron and steel industries; these new rules accelerated reconcentration (Sieber 1958, p. 48; Wirtschke 2009). With reconcentration permitted for vertically integrated corporations affiliated with the coal and iron and steel plants, several coal and iron and steel companies that were previously dissolved, such as Mannesmann, Klöckner, and Rheinstahl-Phöenix, restructured their corporations on the basis of the prewar foundation, that is, the consolidation of coal and steel [*National Archives*, RG59, 862A.054, Status of Decartelized and Deconcentrated German Coal and Steel Companies (23.6.1955), p. 1]. Among the 34 instances of corporate concentration in West Germany approved by the 1962 ECSC, 14 were related to the reconcentration of corporations that were forced to dissolve postwar (Abelshauser 2004, p. 245).

This powerful concentration of production in a relatively small number of large corporations was a result of highly intensified competition (D.W.I.-Berichte 1961, p. 5), and it increased in the latter half of the 1950s in response to the competitive conditions in the market. For example, according to Thyssen's 1957/1958 annual report, the Thyssen group of corporations had the following four objectives: (1) strengthening cooperative ties that had already emerged, (2) strengthening resistance to market changes through horizontal integration of specialized production domains, (3) exploring new possibilities for rationalization and lower costs, and (4) greater competitiveness (August Thyssen Hütte 1958, p. 11). The emerging need for stronger ties within the group as a method to adapt to the market's business environment and increasing competitiveness necessitated reconcentration. EEC member nations were definitely not complementary partners in their industrial production structure, but rather competitors; this competitive environment greatly accelerated the concentration and consolidation process (D.W.I.-Berichte 1962, p. 20).

For banks, the abolition and cancelation of allied nation regulations was a great opportunity for reconcentration. With the approval from the US in 1952, banks were zoned into three operational districts—northern, western, and southern—and concentrated into nine large banks through mergers. Deutsche Bank, Dresdner

Bank, and Commerz Bank, each inherited three financial institutions [*National Archives*, RG59, 862A.14, Reconcentration of German Commercial Banks (10.1.1957), p. 1; Djelic 1998, p. 165; Pohl 1986, pp. 102–104; Horstmann 1991]. The December 1956 law abolished mutual capital participation by banks, personal ties among executives from inherited banks, and restricted issuance to only that of registered stock (Aizawa 1994, p. 49). The top three banks were authorized to re-establish themselves, except for subsidiary financial institutions in Berlin, and return to their respective pre-war institutions [*National Archives*, RG59, 862A.14, Reconcentration of German Commercial Banks (10.1.1957), p. 1; Pohl 1986, p. 105; Wandel 1998, pp. 40–41]. The reconcentration occurred in 1957. Deutsche Bank's primary reasons were to improve their international standing and the position of the new group in their handling of large accounts, gain greater flexibility in maintaining unified credit policies, and realize the economic potential of its business operations [*National Archives*, RG59, 862A.14, Present and Forthcoming Bank Merger in West Germany (3.5.1957)].

In their reconcentration efforts, the top three banks strongly lobbied the government while demonstrating their initiative (Vgl. Gall et al. 1995, pp. 526–544). At the time, government policy offered no opposition to mergers, and even most Social Democratic Party (SPD) leaders agreed to return to the concentration of banks [*National Archives*, RG59, 862A.14, United States Policy regarding Reconcentration of German Banks (15.12.1955), p. 1]. With the new order in Europe during the 1950s and with efforts through new cooperation models in a larger economic sphere, early postwar regulations on large German banks were no longer deemed appropriate, but rather unreasonable, an opinion that continued to gain momentum (Deutsche Bank 1970, p. 35).

Banks played a critical role in the concentration of monopolies and in bringing about new developments in the system of large corporate groups. Klöckner's reconcentration exemplifies concentration through bank intermediaries, from which they gained majority interests in coal companies that split from larger corporate group (Huffschmid 1954, p. 26; Der Volkswirt 1955a, p. 25).

5.3.2.2 Reconcentration of Monopolies and Development of Divisions of Labor in Business Domains

Based on the abovementioned developments, the next important issue are how large businesses operations were restructured amidst reconcentration or concentration, and how, as a result, the system of large corporate groups was restructured. The most striking manifestation of the restructuring of operations in conjunction with the reconcentration of monopolies occurred in the coal, iron and steel industries. Thus, we will focus on these industries in the next section.

In the iron and steel industry, the process of corporate concentration beginning in the 1950s essentially proceeded in two stages. The first stage was the return of a company temporarily deconcentrated through dissolution to its previous state; this stage ended in 1958 and 1959 as reorganizations ended. The second stage included the close cooperation of many large corporate groups in production and investment (D.W.I.-Berichte 1962, p. 1).

As discussed, the dissolution of monopolies in the postwar era was related to the "integrated economy" that underpinned productive forces in Germany's heavy industry. Thus, the movement to reconcentrate proceeded with the aim of expanding production units and product types and strengthening the vertical combination of coal and iron and steel industries (D.W.I.-Berichte 1955, p. 9; Yajima 1959 p. 53). These goals were also intended to integrate production capacity in the iron and steel industry and adopt advanced technologies (Herrigel 2000, p. 381).

Examining the successor companies of Vereinigte Stahlwerke AG, Phöenix and Rheinrohr corporations merged due to the relationship of the former as a supplier of semi-finished steels with the latter [*National Archives*, RG59, 862A.331, Merger of Rheinische Roehrenwerke AG and the Huettenwerke Phoenix AG with Approval of High Authority (11.2.1955)]. In 1959, Ilseder Hütte decided to convert two subsidiaries into parent companies to simplify their management structure and ease financial and other burdens [*National Archives*, RG59, 862A.053, Reconcentration of Ilseder Huette, Pein (1.4.1959), p. 1]. For Thyssen, the initial target of reconcentration was entirely related to the Duisburg region. They signed an Agreement of Community of Interests in September 1955 prior to merging capital. The next year August Thyssen and Niederrheinische Hütte AG consolidated their corporations by stock exchanges. The second target of Thyssen's reconcentration was Deutsche Edelstahlwerke AG, with which they merged in 1957. This was a result of August Thyssen lacking his own electric steel production plant in Duisburg, and in that regard, the possibility for cooperation in production technology, especially for crude steel, was considered (Uebbing 1991, pp. 60, 330). The merger of Thyssen with these two companies provided the impetus for the divisions of labor that followed. Thyssen valued the production of flat bars, semi-finished steels, and large profile iron. In response, Niederrheinische Hütte AG focused on rod wire and bar steel, whereas Deutsche Edelstahlwerke AG focused on the production of high-grade steel and other value-added steels (Treue and Uebbing 1969, p. 219). With the purchase of shares in Hüttenwerke Siegerland AG and Rasselstein-Andernach's steel rolling company in 1957 and 1958/1961, respectively, Thyssen secured sales channels for band iron. These purchases also achieved the benefit of division of production labor on a product-by-product basis (Treue and Uebbing 1969, pp. 215, 218; Kobayashi 1983, pp. 156–162). The new Thyssen group became the only capital group in West Germany with a steel production plant in the postwar stage. This plant was characterized by ultra-large scale blast furnaces, LD converters, continuous rolling to automatic rolling mills, and a steel production system on a large scale. The restructuring through post-dissolution reconcentration was also significant for such economies of scale (Kobayashi 1983, pp. 1, 179).

Among the 13 successor companies resulting from the postwar dissolution of Vereinigte Stahlwerke AG, reconcentration in the 1950s resulted in only four surviving companies by the early 1960s: August Thyssen, Phöenix-Rheinrohr, Rhein Steel, and the Dortmund-Hörde Hütten Union. Within most of these, corporate mergers and expansions did not result in direct competition with the other corporations; each company chose to expand and integrate production capacity in separate domains, seeking profit through division of labor. That is, most of Vereinigte Stahlwerke AG's steel production capacity was once again folded into the operations of either Thyssen or Phöenix-Rheinrohr. This specialization of product supply in the rolled-product markets for the most part did not overlap, and they enabled a product-based division of labor between the two companies. Specifically, Thyssen specialized in the production of lighter plate, semi-finished and finished rolled sheets, coils, rod wire, and specialty steel, whereas Phöenix-Rheinrohr specialized in the production of steel pipe, heavy plates, semi-finished steels, and raw iron. As a result of the dissolution of Vereinigte Stahlwerke AG, Rheinische Stahlwerke AG inherited Vereinigte's interests, except for those from steel production. The Dormund-Hörde Hütten Union became an important producer of crude steel; however, unlike the other corporations, it was not broadly diversified into the iron and steel industry. The Union planned for concentration in two domains, heavy plate and both bar and structural steel by the early 1960s. Other large corporate groups such as Hoesch, Klöckner, Mannesmann, Hüttenwerk Oberhausen AG, and Krupp predominantly followed the Dormund-Hörde Hütten Union's path of specialization. Each attempted to organize the production of steel and rolled products, such that companies could realize a strong position in the limited number of markets (Herrigel 2000, pp. 381–383; Huffschmid 1965, pp. 110–115, 149; Sieber 1958).

Next, we will examine companies other than Vereinigte Stahlwerke AG. Within a few years after the restructuring that occurred with dissolution, Flick, Gutehoffnung, Klöckner, Otto Wolff, and Hoesch re-emerged as an integrated organization that was larger in investment and production scale than the previous Vereinigte Stahlwerke AG (Petzina 1992, p 532). At Mannesmann, the disassociation with the coal company due to the postwar dissolution had been restored by the mid-1950s, and the restoration of an integrated organization proceeded (Der Volkswirt 1955b, p. 27; Der Volkswirt 1956b, p. 27). Thereafter, in the fall of 1958, their six most important subsidiaries merged with the parent company (Vgl. Der Volkswirt 1959, p. 1439). Similarly at Hoesch, of the three successor companies that split due to dissolution, two were returned to the parent company. The plan called for a vertical integration of coal and steel industries, as this was a condition for survival among Ruhr's coal and steel corporations (Der Volkswirt 1956a, pp. 36–37; Der Volkswirt 1957, p. 1163). Hoesch restructured as a large corporate group comprising of four core corporations in the late 1950s, with many subsidiaries established thereafter (Vgl. Der Volkswirt 1960a, p. 1092; Der Volkswirt 1960b). Even at Krupp, Hüttenwerk Rheinhausen AG assumed control over Bochmer Verein, a successor to Vereinigte Stahlwerke AG, with the primary objective of benefitting from the division of labor. Hüttenwerk Rheinhausen AG mainly produced mass products through Thomas steel, as opposed to Bochmer Verein, which focused on the production of high-grade steel using LD processes and electric furnaces. This consolidation facilitated the expansion of production programs and division of labor. Within materials supply in the processing sector, Krupp formed a lucrative consolidation with its supplier, Bochmer Verein (Yajima 1959, pp. 98–100). At Gutehoffnung, dissolution measures ended vertical ties, and the reconcentration movement affected reconsolidation of the steel and coal sectors in 1957. The energy-related consolidation of Hüttenwerk Oberhausen AG and Bergbau AG Neue Hoffnung expanded through ties with Ruhrchemie AG, in which Bergbau AG Neue Hoffnung had capital investments (Yajima 1959, pp. 124–125). Reconcentration in coal and steel industries thus generated more advantageous conditions than those before dissolution.

The reconcentration of monopolies temporarily ceased in the late 1950s, but with the growth of fierce competition and pressure from the 1958 crisis, the process of accumulation and concentration proceeded in the second stage. The new economic advances that emerged in 1959 and 1960 were already forgotten as the economy stagnated again in 1961. In addition, the Thyssen group began building close cooperative relationships with the Dortmund-Hörde and Hoesch groups at the beginning of the 1960s in response to the powerful expansion. Hoesch, in a collaborative effort with Mannesmann, begun construction of a large steel pipe factory, and the cooperation of these three groups was partially demonstrated in joint capital procurements and in the joint use of rolling facilities. In 1962, Thyssen, Mannesmann, and Hoesch formed agreements regarding cooperation in production and investment (D.W.I.-Berichte 1962, p. 2). Thus, one form of concentration resulting from increased competition at the end of the 1950s and the beginning of the 1960s was the various pacts between large corporate groups for joint research and development activities and the allocation of production equipment for joint use (D.W.I.-Berichte 1961, pp. 5–6).

5.3.3 Significance of New Developments in Large Corporate Group Systems

Based on the foregoing discussion, we will now turn our attention to the significance of new developments in the systems of large corporate groups that accompanied the dissolution of monopolies and later reconcentration. During this period, to simplify management, large companies formed scales that were suitable for management, which were founded through liquidation of large corporate groups; this was observed through the process of concentration and reconcentration of monopolies. This process created important preconditions for thorough rationalization (I.P.W.-Berichte 1960, pp. 11, 13). This type of concentration helped create a system that exhibited economies of scale through the benefits of specialization and division of labor. This approach intended to reform systems that enables large corporate groups to develop more effective operations in response to opportunities for technological reforms, provided by US implementation under the transition to a system of oligopolistic competition. In other words, this type of development strengthened the systems of inter-firm relationships; these relationships formed for the expansion of corporate activities that emphasized market segments adapted to oligopolistic competition in the form of "division of labor complementary to each product." For the iron and steel industry, this approach meant leveraging "integrated economy" benefits between the coal and steel industries to transform the system on the basis of collaborative inter-corporate relationships in pursuit of scale merit through "division of labor with complementary products" between large corporate groups.

This systemic transition aggregated production, sales, and management as the foundation of an industrial system; in terms of maintaining economic consistency, it strengthened German large corporate groups (Shimotani 2008, pp. 3–4, 8) functioning on the lines of organic parent-subsidiary corporate groups based on the principle of product-based division of labor. It created better conditions for business rationalization and facilitated the pursuit of economies of scale as well as strengthened the foundation for cooperation-based market control. This postwar business structure differed from industrial concentration systems that were based on market control with a high level of concentration through giant trusts, which included industrial sectors seen in the prewar era, particularly those in the 1920s; instead, it more carefully pursued functional benefits. Relationships with such "complementary product-based divisions of labor" proceeded between large corporate groups as well (Dyas and Thanheiser 1976, p. 92). These relationships differed from the prewar period's economic concentration through cartels, and were meaningful as a systemic transformation for monopolistic market control based on the economic benefits of the division of labor. This was a system of large-scale business, appropriate to large corporate groups; however, they differed from Japan's industrial groups and the full-set industrial structure found thereafter. These were reforms to the system of large-scale business that incorporated collaborative relationships in response to global and domestic competition. The system helped German corporations avoid intense price competition and was an important foundation for the development of management methods, which adopted a style of management that focused on competing with quality.

Building upon our previous discussions, the next issue we discuss is how German business management changed at the corporate level with the deployment of American management methods, and the developments that emerged in Germany thereafter. We will examine this issue in Chaps. 6–10.

References

Abelshauser W (2004) Deutsche Wirtschaftsgeschichte seit 1945. C. H. Beck, München

Aizawa K (1994) Oshu Saikyo no Kinyu Teikoku (The strongest financial empire in Europe). Nihon Keizai Shinbunsha, Tokyo

Aoki M, Patrick H (1994) Introduction. In: Aoki M, Patrick H (eds) The Japanese main bank system. Its relevance for developing and transforming economies. Oxford University Press, Oxford, pp xxi–xxxii

August Thyssen Hütte AG (1958) Bericht über das Geschäftsjahr 1957/58. August Thyssen Hütte AG, Duisburg

Baums T, Fraune C (1995) Institutionelle Anlage und Publikumgesellschaft: Eine empirische Untersuchung. Die Aktiengesellschaft 40(3):97–112

Berghahn V (1985) Unternehmer und Politik in der Bundesrepublik. Suhrkamp, Frankfurt am Main

Berghahn VR (1986) The Americanization of German industry 1945–1973. Berg, Leamington Spa

Bleicher K, Bortel K-D, Kleinmann R et al (1984) Unternehmungsverfassung und Spitzenorganisation. Zeitschrift Fürung+ Organisation 53(1):21–29

Bleicher K, Diethard LK, Paul H (1989) Unternehmungsverfassung und Spitzenorganisation. Führung und Überwachung von Aktiengesellschaften im internationalen Vergleich. Gabler, Wiesbaden
Böhm J (1992) Der Einfluβ der Banken auf Groβunternehmen. Steuer- und Wirtschaftsverlag, Hamburg
Bundesministerium der Finanzen (ed) (1979) Bericht der Studienkommission. Grundsatzfragen der Kreditwirtschaft (Schriftenreihe des Bundesministeriums der Finanzen, Heft 28). Stollfuss, Frankfurt am Main
Büschgen HE (1983) Die Groβbanken. Fritz Knapp Verlag, Frankfurt am Main
Busse A (1962) Depotstimmrecht der Banken. T. Gabler, Wiesbaden
Cable JR (1985) The bank-industry relationship in West Germany: performance an policy aspects. In: Schwalbach J (ed) Industry structure and performance. Edition Sigma, Berlin, pp 17–40
Chandler AD Jr (1990) Scale and scope: the dynamics of industrial capitalism. Harvard University Press, Cambridge
Commerz Bank AG (1970) 100 Jahre Commerzbank 1870–1970. Knapp, Düsseldorf
Decher CE (1990) Personelle Verflechtungen im Aktienkonzern. Verlag Recht und Wirtschaft, Heidelberg
Der Volkswirt (1952a) Beendeter Mannesmann-Umbau. Der Volkswirt 6(16):24–25
Der Volkswirt (1952b) Die Neuordning bei Hoesch. Der Volkswirt 6(31):23–24
Der Volkswirt (1953a) Gutehoffnungshütte neu geordnet. Der Volkswirt 7(31):21–23
Der Volkswirt (1953b) Mannesmann für neue Aufgaben gerüstet. Der Volkswirt 7(25):23–25
Der Volkswirt (1954a) Fried. Krupp. Nur noch Verarbeitungsgesellschaft ohne Kohle und Stahl. Der Volkswirt, 8.Jg, Beilage zu Nr.44 vom 30. Oktober 1954, Das veränderte Gesicht der Montan-Industrie. Zum Eisenhüttentag, p 49
Der Volkswirt (1954b) Kruppbetriebe im Existenzkampf. Der Volkswirt 8(1):24–25
Der Volkswirt (1954c) Liquidation der Hoesch AG. Die Nachfolgegesellschaften entwickeln sich günstig. Der Volkswirt 8(19):24–26
Der Volkswirt (1955a) Klöckner-Neuordnung abgeschlossen. Der Volkswirt 9(14):25–27
Der Volkswirt (1955b) Rückgliederung abgeschlossen. Die Mannesmann AG berichtet. Der Volkswirt 9(24):26–28
Der Volkswirt (1956a) Bald 2 Mill. t Stahl bei der Hoesch Werke AG. Der Volkswirt 10(20):36–39
Der Volkswirt (1956b) Der neue Mannesmann-Konzern. Der Volkswirt 10(27):27–29
Der Volkswirt (1956c) Weitere Konsolidierung bei Krupp. Der Volkswirt 10(14):28–30
Der Volkswirt (1957) Hoesch Werke AG geht auf 8 vH. Der Volkswirt 11(23):1163–1166
Der Volkswirt (1959) Mannesmann AG: Erfolgreiche Verarbeitung. Schulden konsolidiert—Zum dritt Mal 10 vH Dividende. Der Volkswirt 13(28):1439–1443
Der Volkswirt (1960a) Hoesch AG in solidem Fortschritt. Dividende von 8 auf 10 vH erhöht—Abrundendes Investitionsprogramm. Der Volkswirt 14(23):1092–1094
Der Volkswirt (1960b) Hoesch Aktiengesellschaft. Der Volkswirt 14(26):1282
Deutsche Bank AG (1970) 100 Jahre Deutsche Bank 1870–1970. Deutsche Bank AG, Frankfurt am Main
Deutsche Bank AG (1986) Geschäftsbericht für das Jahr 1986. Deutsche Bank AG, Frankfurt am Main
Djelic M-L (1998) Exporting the American model. The postwar transformation of European business. Oxford University Press, Oxford
D.W.I.-Berichte (1955) Der westdeutsche Steinkohlenbergbau. D.W.I.-Berichte 6(6):2–30
D.W.I.-Berichte (1961) Der Stand der Konzentration der Produktion von Produktionsmitteln in Westdeutschland. D.W.I.-Berichte 12(2):5–13
D.W.I.-Berichte (1962) Die mächtigsten Konzern der EWG und Groβbritanniens in wichtigen Zweigen der Produktionsmittelindustrie. D.W.I.-Berichte 13(23):1–21
Dyas GP, Thanheiser HT (1976) The emerging European enterpreise. Strategy and structure in French and German industry. The Macmillan Press, London

Edwards J, Fischer K (1994) Banks, finance and investment in Germany. Cambridge University Press, Cambridge
Eglau HO (1989) Wie Gott in Frankfurt: Die Deutsche Bank und die deutsche Industrie. Econ Verlag, Düsseldorf
Fiereder H (1989) Demontagen in Deutschland nach 1945 unter besonderer Berücksichtigung der Montanindustrie. Zeitschrift für Unternehmensgeschichte 34:209–239
Gall L, Feldmann GD, James H et al (1995) Die Deutsche Bank 1870–1995. C. H. Beck, München
Gerhardt M (1982) Industriebezihungen der westdeutschen Banken. Sendler, Frankfurt am Main
Gottschalk A (1988) Der Stimmrechtseinfluβ der Banken in den Aktionärversammlungen von Groβunternehmen. WSI Mitteilungen 41(5):294–304
Gottschalk A (1990) Depotstimmrecht und die Macht der Banken. Die Tageszeitung 3108:11
Gross H (1950) Material zur Aufteilung der I.G. Farbenindustrie Aktiengesellschaft. Institut für Weltwirtschaft, Kiel
Gutenberg E (1970) Funktionswandel des Aufsichtsrats. Zeitschrift für Betriebswirtschaft 40. Jg, Ergänzungsheft, pp 1–10
Hahn W, Tammer H (1970) Kapitalkonzentration in Westdeutschland an der Wende zum neuen Jahrzehnt. DWI-Berichte 21(8):21–29
Hansen H (1977) Die Wertpapierdepots der Bankkunden. Die Aktiengesellschaft 22(6):161–163
Hansen H (1994a) Das Gewicht der Banken in den Aufsichträten deutscher Aktiengesellschaften. Die Aktiengesellschaft 39(3):R76–R79
Hansen H (1994b) Die Zusammensetzung von Aufsichtsräten der DAX-Gesellschaften und die Auswirkungen auf ihre Effizienz. Die Aktiengesellschaft 39(11):R403–R404
Hein M, Flöter H (1975) Macht der Banken—Folgerungen aus der bisherigen Diskussion. WSI Mitteilungen 28(7):342–361
Herrhausen A (1973) Überwachen allein genügt nicht. Manager Mag 2(1973):32–35
Herrigel G (2000) American occupation, market order, and democracy: reconfiguring the steel industry in Japan and German after the Second World War. In: Zeitlin J, Herrigel G (eds) Americanization and its limits. Reworking US technology and management in post-war Europe and Japan. Oxford University Press, Oxford, pp 340–399
Hopt KJ (1979) Zur Funktion des Aufsichtsrats im Verhältnis von Industrie und Bankensystem. In: Horn N, Kocka J (eds) Recht und Entwicklung der Groβunternehmen im 19. und frühen 20. Jahrhundert. Wirtschaft-, sozial- und rechtshistorische Untersuchungen zur Industrialisierung im Deutschland, Frankreich, England und den USA. Vandenhoeck & Ruprecht, Göttingen, pp 227–242
Horstmann T (1991) Die Alliierten und die deutschen Groβbanken. Bankenpolitik nach dem Zweiten Welkrieg in Westdeutschland. Bouvier, Bonn
Huffschmid B (1954) In Zukunft wieder Klöckner-Werke AG. Rückkehr der Kohle zur Obergesellschaft. Der Volkswirt 8(45):26–28
Huffschmid B (1965) Das Stahlzeitalter beginnt erst. Verlag Modeme Industrie, München
I.P.W.-Berichte (1960) Die neue Konzentrationswelle in der westdeutschen Industrie. IPW-Berichte 11:10–15
Jeidels (1905) Das Verhältnis der deutschen Groβbanken zur Industrie mit besonderer Berücksichtigung der Eisenindustrie. Dunker & Humblot, Leipzig
Kikkawa T (1992) Kigyo Shudan no Seiritsu to sono Kino (Formation and functions of corporate groups). In: Morikawa M (ed) Bijinesuman no tameno Sengo Keieishi Nyumon (An introduction of business history after WWII for businessmen). Nihon Keizai Shinbunsha, Tokyo, pp 62–85
Kikkawa T (1996) Nihon no Kigyo Shudan (Japanese large corporate groups). Yuhikaku, Tokyo
Kleinkamp H-D (1977) Die Entflechtung der I.G. Farbenindustrie A.G. und die Gründung der Nachfolgegesellschaft. Vierteljahrhefte für Zeitgescichte 25(2):220–251
Kobayashi M (1983) Nishi Doitsu Tekkogyo (Iron and steel industry in West Germany). Yuhikaku, Tokyo

Koubek N (1971) Personelle und institutionelle Verbindung der Bereiche „Produktion“ und „Kapital“ in der Wirtschaftsgesellschaft der BRD. WWI-Mitteilungen 24(8/9):258–274
Kudo A (1999) Gendai Doitsu Kagaku Kigyoushi (Modern business history in the German chemical industry). Mineruva Shobo, Kyoto
Kuhlmann H (1949) Die Banken in der Hauptversammlung. Zeitschrift für das gesamte Kreditswesen 2(21):489–490
Küstler R, Zachert U, Müller M (2006) Aufsichtsratepraxis, vol 8. Aufl. Bund Verlag, Frankfurt am Main
Lindhardt H (1958) Wider das Depotstimmrecht der Banken. Die Aktiengesellschaft 3(8):169–176
Maekawa K (1970) Doitsu Dokusen Kigyo no Hatten Katei (Development of monopolistic enterpreise in Germany). Mineruva Shobo, Kyoto
Maekawa K (1997) Nichidoku Hikaku Kigyoron eno Michi (Comparative study of Japanese and German enterprise). Moriyama Shoten, Tokyo
Miyajima A (1992) Zaibatsu Kaitai (Dissolution of Zaibatsu). In: Hosei Daigaku Sangyo Jyoho Senta, Hashimoto J, Takeda H (eds) Nihon Keizai no Hatten to Kigyo Shudan (Development of Japanese economy and corporate groups). Tokyo Daigaku Shuppankai, Tokyo, pp 203–254
Miyamoto M, Abe T, Udagawa M et al (2007) Nihon Keieishi (Japanese business history). Yuhikaku, Tokyo
Miyazaki G (1966) Sengo Nihon no Keizai Kiko (Japanese economic system after WW II). Shin Hyoron, Tokyo
Monopolkommission (1978) Hauptgutachten 1976/77 (Haupugutachten II), Fortschreitenden Konzentration bei Groβunternehmen. Nomos-Verlagsgesellschaft, Baden-Baden
Monopolkommission (2003) Hauptgutachten 2000/2001 (Hauptgutachten XIV), Netzwettbewerb durch Regulierung. Nomos-Verlagsgesellschaft, Baden-Baden
Okumura H (1976) Nihon no Rokudai Kigyo Shudan (Six Japanese large corporate groups). Daiyamondosha, Tokyo
Petzina D (1992) Zwischen Neuordnung und Krise. In: Dascher O, Kleinschmidt C (eds) Die Eisen- und Stahalindustrie im Dortmunder Raum. Wirtschaftliche Entwicklung, soziale Strukturen und technologischer Wandel im 19. und 20. Jahrhundert. Gesellschaft für Westfälische Wirtschaftsgeschichte E.V., Dortmund, pp 525–544
Pfannschmidt A (1993) Personelle Verflechtungen über Aufsichtsrate. Mehrfachmandate in deutschen Unternehmen. Gabler, Wiesbaden
Pfeiffer H (1986) Groβbanken und Finanzgruppen. Ausgewählte Ergebnisse einer Untersuchung der personellen Verflechtungen von Deutscher, Dresdner und Commerzbank. WSI Mitteilungen 39(7):473–481
Pfeiffer H (1987) Das Imperium der Deutsche Bank. Campus, Frankfurt am Main
Pfeiffer H (1989) BASF und die Deutsche Bank. WSI Mitteilungen 42(1):9–16
Pfeiffer H (1993) Die Macht der Banken. Die personellen Verflechtungen der Commerzbank, der Deutschen Bank und der Dresdner Bank mit Unternehemen. Campus, Frankfurt am Main
Pohl M (1986) Entstehung und Entwicklung des Universalbanksystems: Konzentration und Krise als wichtige Faktoren. Fritz Knapp Verlag, Frankfurt am Main
Poullain L (1979) Tätigkeitsbericht. Seewald, Stuttgart-Degerloch
Sakuma N (2003) Doitsu no Kigyo Touchi (Corporate governance in Germany). In: Nakamura M (ed) Kigyou Rinri to Kigyo Touchi (Business ethics and corporate governance). Bunshindo, Tokyo, pp 65–83
Sasaki K (1975) Gendai Yoroppa Shihonshugi Ron (Contemporary European capitalism). Yuhikaku, Tokyo
Schaad H-P (1972) Das Depotstimmrecht der Banken nach schweizerischem und deutschem Recht. Schulthess Polygraphischer Verlag, Zürich
Schlieper A (1986) 150 Jahre Ruhrgebiet. Ein Kapitel deutscher Wirtschaftsgeschichte. Schwann, Düsseldorf
Schönwitz D, Weber HJ (1982) Unternehmenskonzentration, Personelle Verflechtungen und Wettbewerb. Eine Unterschung auf Basis der 100 gröβten Konzern der BRD. Nomos-Verlagsgesellschaft, Baden-Baden

Schwarz F (2003) Die Deutsche Bank. Reise auf tünerner Füβen. Campus, Frankfurt am Main
Shimotani M (2008) Shinko Kontsuerun to Zaibatsu (New large corporate groups and Zaibatu). Nihon Keizai Hyoronsha, Tokyo
Sieber G (1958) Die Rekonzentration der eisenschaffenden Industrie in Westdeutschland. WWI-Mitteilungen 11(3):46–55
Stanzick K-H (1968) Der ökonomische Konzentrationsprozeβ. In: Schäfer G, Nedelmann C (eds) Der CDU-Staat. Analysen zur Verfassungswirklichkeit der Bundesrepublik. Bd. I. Suhrkamp, Frankfurt am Main
Stolper G, Häuser K, Borchardt K (1964) Deutsche Wirtschaft seit 1870. J. C. B. Mohr, Tübingen
Suzuki K (1993) Nihon no Kigyo Shudan (Japanese large corporate groups). Otsuki Shoten, Tokyo
Takahashi T (1997) Kigyo Soshiki to Kigyo Touchi (Organization of enterprises and corporate governance). In: Takahashi T, Onishi T (eds) Doitsu no Kigyo (German Enterprise). Waseda Daigaku Shuppanbu, Tokyo, pp 34–53
Tohara T (1974) Nishi Doitsu ni okeru Sengo Kaikaku (Postwar reform in West Germany). In: University of Tokyo Institute of Social Science (ed) Sengo Kaikaku: Kokusai Kankyo (Postwar reform: international environment), vol 2. Tokyo Daigaku Shuppankai, Tokyo, pp 91–151
Treue W, Uebbing H (1969) Die Feuer verlöschen nie: August Thyssen-Hütte 1926–1966. Econ Verlag, Düsseldorf, Wien
Uebbing H (1991) Wege und Wegmarken. 100 Jahre Thyssen, 1891–1991. Siedler, Berlin
Uetake T (1997) Kinyu Kikan to Kigyo (Financial institutions and enterprises). In: Takahashi T, Onishi T (eds) Doitsu no Kigyo (German enterprise). Waseda Daigaku Shuppanbu Tokyo, Tokyo, pp 93–112
Volkmann G, Kronenberg B (1994) Bankenmacht und Aufsichtsrat. WSI Mitteilungen 47(8):481–487
Wandel E (1998) Banken und Versicherungen im 19. und 20. Jahrhundert. R. Oldenbourg, München
Wiendieck M (1992) Unternehmensfinanzierung und Kontrolle durch Banken, Deutschland–Japan–USA. Gabler, Wiesbaden
Winnacker K (1972) Nie den Mut verlieren. Erinnerungen an Schicksalsjahr der deutschen Chemie. Econ Verlag, Düsseldorf
Wirtschke T (2009) Gefahr für den Wettbewerb? Die Fusionkontrolle der Europäischen Gemeinschaft für Kohle und Stahl und die »Rekonzentration« der Ruhrindustrie 1950–1963. Akademie Verlag, Berlin
Yajima C (1959) Ruru Kontsuerun no Hukkatsu (Resurrection of corporate groups in the Ruhr district). Keizai Dantai Rengokai, Tokyo
Yamaguchi H (1981) Nishi Doitsu ni okeru Ginko to Kigyo no Kankei (Relationship between banks and enterprises in West Germany). Shoken Keizai (Financial Econ Rev) 135:103–131
Ziegler R (1984) Das Netz der Personen- und Kapitalverflechtungen deutscher und österreichischer Wirtschaftsunternehmen. Kölner Zeitschrift für Soziologie und Sozialpsychlogie 36(3): 585–618
Zugehör R (2003) Die Zukunft des rheinischen Kapitalismus. Unternehmen zwischen Kapitalismus und Mitbestimmung. Lesket + Budrich, Opladen

Chapter 6
Deployment of American Management Education

Abstract Post World War II, European and Japanese enterprises and industries, as well as their overall economies, were developed by deploying and adapting US technology and management methods; this practice was also observed in Germany around the same time. American management methods were introduced and implemented under the US-led productivity movement. The major American management methods implemented in Germany were those for management education. In Germany, however, many factors influenced the introduction of American management education. This chapter discusses the deployment of American management education in relation to universities' role in management education, eligibility criteria for executive management, and the manager promotion system in German enterprises. First, it considers Japanese characteristics in the deployment of American management education followed by that of relevant American methods. Next, it examines American initiatives in management education reform, German universities' role in management education, and the deployment of Training within Industry (TWI) and top management education methods. These discussions explain the various factors that restricted the deployment of American-style methods in management education.

Keywords Business school • Management education • Productivity movement • Role of university • Training within Industry (TWI)

In Chaps. 6–10, we will focus on management education, management and production systems, methods of adapting to the mass market, and management organization in the deployment of American management methods and systems after World War II through the early 1970s and subsequent transformations in business management. The deployment of American management methods and systems varies widely between a specific management system and method as well as between industries and corporations. Thus, in addition to analyzing the overall situation, it is important to examine the differences and various factors influencing each industry and corporation.

T. Yamazaki, *German Business Management: A Japanese Perspective on Regional Development Factors*, DOI 10.1007/978-4-431-54303-9_6, © Springer Japan 2013

In general, there is an extremely broad scope of transfer of American business culture in Germany, extending into all functional areas of management. In particular, elements of management philosophy and language, skills, technology, know-how, and specialized methods and processes are some of the aspects that have been adopted. However, unlike science and technology, for management, organizational know-how and techniques generally require extensive adaptations to the conditions of the importing country (Dyas and Thanheiser 1976, pp. 112–113). For example, even in a German subsidiary of a US company, despite the former's subordinate relationship with the latter, the deployment of American-style innovations encountered many difficulties and did not go smoothly (Hartmann 1963, p. 192). Thus, there are significant issues such as German corporate attitudes, responses, and the nature of the actual deployments in response to American management methods and systems; changes in business management itself with the deployment of management education; and the effect of German business management characteristics on specialized processes.

In this chapter, we will first consider the deployment of American management education. After World War II, the role of middle management in the function of management and top management functions increased. In such an environment, reforms in management education became critical issues in Germany. The United States viewed reforms in management education in Europe as particularly important for the American-led productivity movement. Thus, the deployment of management education was important during the 1950s and 1960s. The reforms were influenced by pragmatic business schools and the type of education-oriented universities found in American-style education systems and practices. However, the deployment of American-style methods conflicted with German universities' form of management education.

6.1 Japanese Characteristics in the Deployment of American Management Education

In regard to the deployment of American management education methods, Japan was more influenced by America than was Germany; in fact, Japanese government agencies strongly encouraged expanding education for managers and supervisors. Implementation of Training with Industry (TWI), a method for supervisors, was achieved with technical assistance from the Ministry of Labor through the Employment Security Act and its amendments. Management Training Program (MTP), a method for training managers, was also implemented with the considerable involvement of the Ministry of International Trade and Industry. MTP, originally a training system for American supervisors, was first adapted for Japanese supervisors working on American Air Force bases during the post-war occupation period. Thereafter, Japanese corporations began using MTP to train middle management, and after several iterations it was modified according to Japan's requirements. This form of MTP was developed primarily for office manager training given by the National Personnel Authority, a government bureau, and was broadly referred to under the acronym JST (Jinjin Supervisor Training). It was used to train managers at banks, insurance firms, government institutions, and other public associations. Further, Civil Communication Section (CCS) courses were implemented as a top management education method under the directive of the occupying military. These courses were implemented in Japan by GHQ based on the recognition of serious deficiencies in the management of Japan's telecommunications industry. However, since 1953, the number of courses taught began to diminish, and less influence was exerted on management thereafter. Thus, fixed-form type of education methods represented by TWI, MTP, and CCS were distinctly American in nature, and drew criticism and concern because they were not characteristically compatible with Japan's management culture, specifically paternalism, the seniority order system, and lifetime employment. Moreover, because they were standardized methods, they were not only inappropriate for the corporations' specific issues and needs but also lacked situational awareness and opportunities for decision making needed to solve day-to-day management issues. Therefore, Japanese corporations began to enact their own education policies and programs, and disseminate new management education that applied a variety of education methods, introduced by newly established management education associations. Thus, as a replacement for CCS, education for top management via external organizations saw tremendous growth. In addition to the executive management seminars sponsored by the Japan Productivity Center, there were education courses published by regional bank associations, Keio University, the Japan Management Development Association, business consultants, the Japan Federation of Employers' Associations, and the Nippon Omni-Management Association (Zennihon Noritsu Renmei Ningen Noryoku Kaihatu Senta 1981, pp. 59–63, 73–75, 77–78, 101–109; Sugiyama 1968, pp. 2–5; Okuda et al. 1987, pp. 14, 18; Noda 1969, p. 243). Issues such as those mentioned above, arising from the deployment of American-style management education, occurred because of the rigid character of fixed form education, which standardized the American style, regardless of the systemic differences in hiring, personnel change, promotion, and other functions. In Japan, industries generally relied excessively on fixed-form training courses (Kamei and Shiraki 1971, p. 129; Hasegawa 1960, p. 173; Okuda 1961, pp. 120, 150–153).

In addition, it was impossible to inject fundamental ideas of American rationalism and individualism into Japanese management training. Thus, American-style methods were adapted incorporating Japan's ideology of collectivism and efficiency, as well as skill-based education, which included industrial co-partnership, a sense of belonging within the company, and management education (Shimokawa 1976, p. 58).

According to Japan, several characteristics of Germany's deployment of American-style management education stand out. Indeed universities in both Germany and Japan did not play an important role in training executives and managers as they did in America. Nevertheless, the era's management studies boom had a tremendous impact in Japan, it was evident that in Germany, which has an extensive history of management studies, universities did not train executives and managers. Unlike those in Japan, corporations, executive management education, philosophies of and objectives for top management education, as well as the industry intentions they reflected, the internal promotion system and other factors had a greater impact in Germany.

Next, we consider the German deployment of American-style management education in Sect. 6.2. We discuss American initiatives in transforming management education and the role of German universities within the education, in Sects. 6.2.1 and 6.2.2, respectively. Next, in Sect. 6.2.3, we consider the deployment of American-style management education methods and in Sect. 6.2.4 the various factors that defined that state of affairs.

6.2 Deployment of American Management Education in Germany

6.2.1 Management Education Reform and American Initiatives

First, we examine American initiatives in management education reforms. The process of exporting American-style methods in this field to Western Europe followed three steps: (1) creation of the US Technical Assistance & Productivity Program (USTA&P); (2) combination of American universities and European management reforms; and (3) internationalization of American-style management education. The USTA&P was initiated to directly place American technology specialists and management consultants in corporations interested in implementing management and production reforms; they also provided factory observation opportunities and retraining seminars. Moreover, until business schools similar to those in America were established in Western Europe, programs run by productivity centers in each country, along with the USTA&P, played the important role of providing education. To combine American universities and European management innovations, the USTA&P constantly collaborated with American colleges and universities that were interested in providing management education courses for visiting teams, in response to the increasing numbers of managers in Europe. American universities played a decisive role in providing organization and support for TWI programs. The USTA&P's programs for management education dramatically increased contact between American and European students and scholars. Since 1958, these programs opened paths to continually disseminate management knowledge through universities and corporations. The remarkable growth of foreign students in America further internationalized American-style management education. Beginning in the 1960s, Europe became the center of academic exchange between America and foreign countries (McGlade 1998b, pp. 51–58, 62, 64).

The American perception of conditions at the time was that European executives were resistant to constructive changes, unaware of their roles in providing long-term planning, and tended to participate in many day-to-day activities of the corporation;

thus, changing their attitudes was considered imperative (OEEC 1954, pp. 5, 13–14). In such as environment, USTA&P's aim was to implement an American model of management research and executive and managerial training for European professors and universities (McGlade 1998c, p. 33). USTA&P was initiated to promote effective communication between leading industrialists and executives in America and Europe, in alliance with business associations, employer associations, and employer organizations, such as the National Management Council (NMC) and the National Association of Manufacturers (NAM) in America, through workshops and seminars conducted in collaboration with several prominent universities in America (McGlade 1998a, p. 27; McGlade 1998c, p. 18). For example, in the early 1950s, proper management education programs were conducted within the USTA&P framework in cooperation with the International Chamber of Commerce, OEEC, the European Productivity Agency (EPA), and each country's productivity center. Executives representing leading corporations such as Eastman Kodak, P&G, Ford, DuPont, and GE, as well as those from NMC, various universities, and research organizations participated in the program (Kleinschmidt 2002, p. 296). The transfer of the American model into Germany was considered for executive education and retraining projects, with the assistance of the Mutual Security Agency (MSA) and Foreign Operations Administration (FOA). The MSA had already planned to create a management education center by 1953 (Kleinschmidt 2002, pp. 75–77).

From Germany's viewpoint, intensive research focusing on management education began between 1949 and 1950 in groups of delegations sent to America (Feldenkirchen 2004, p. 120). Several special delegations for technical assistance planning in the 1950s considered education in this field as one reason for the American economy's superiority (Kipping 1998, p. 102). This perspective provides the background for Germany's deployment of American-style methods.

Thus, although the initiative shown by America was important, American support for the EPA diminished after 1956; thereafter, the Ford Foundation increased its involvement (Boel 1998, pp. 38, 42). This foundation had since the early 1950s been involved in the organizational and financial aspects of management education in Europe and, through the proliferation of focused education and research programs, had worked as a cultural intermediary in efforts to standardize management education and professional requirements. The primary goal of the Ford Foundation was to transfer the basics of America's "organizational synthesis" into Europe, rather than export educational curricula and programs (Gemelli 1996, pp. 42, 47, 55).

6.2.2 *Role of German Universities in Management Education and their Limitations*

We have shown that America's initiatives in transforming post-war management education were significant. In the 1950s and 1960s, the transfer of American-style management education into Europe varied greatly by country, and no country remained unaffected by it (Schröter 2005, pp. 104–105). This level of influence owes a great deal to traditional management education within German universities.

Viewed historically, there are three different models for management education systems: German, Latin, and American. Management education in the German model was conducted outside universities in one of two higher education institutions, the engineering college and the commercial college. In the Latin model used in France, Italy, and Spain, while overall education focused on law, economics, and organization management, micro aspects such as schools providing opportunities to systematically learn business management were neglected. The American model of management education, however, was set up from the beginning as an element of the overall system of higher education. The emphasis was on actual decision making in market conditions, and business schools played an important role. The response to and absorption of American thinking into management education was primarily dependent on that country's education system (Schröter 2005, pp. 97–99).

In terms of education systems, German universities focused on academic research rather than specialized education. The differences between the Germans, who emphasized theory and science, and the Americans, with their tendency toward pragmatism, impeded the deployment of American-style methods in German universities. In the German system, a person's compensation and promotion were determined by the type of school from which he/she graduated. Also, Germany had two qualification categories: "capable of work" ("Berufsfähig"), obtained from educational institutions, and "ready for work" ("Betriebsfertig"), obtained during on-the-job training (OJT). Although executives believed in the core pragmatic values provided during OJT, they could apply only limited pressure to modernize curricula (Schröter 2005, pp. 103–104). Efforts to change this style of education faced stiff opposition from within schools, who rejected replacing theory with practicality (Locke 1996, p. 76).

Further, German commercial colleges had not attained the status of providers of basic, broadly shared education for executives, as did American business schools. This more narrowly focused perception developed because the education obtained in German engineering colleges was recognized by manufacturing executives. However, although Germany's commercial colleges concentrated primarily on business economics rather than management, unlike American MBA programs, it was not considered a tool for nurturing executives. In the American model education aimed at management development, which differentiated between education for operational functions and that for management functions. In general, it was highly unusual for engineers in America to fill important executive roles (Amdam 1996, pp. 4–6). On this point, the American-style method regarding the function of management was not conducive to the German environment, where those with an engineering background were often leaders.

In addition, as observed in disputes concerning business administration methods, business economics needed to become a scholarly endeavor to be recognized as an academic field in universities. Furthermore, in choosing to either become pragmatically useful in management practice or maintain the traditional methods, standards of theoretical science or elements of a scientific nature inevitably received priority. In such an environment, the relationship between higher education and management practice was always tenuous. To complicate matters further, the difficult postdoctoral thesis, required to be promoted to a research professor in a university, along with the long research program it entailed, reduced any possibility of long-term work experience before becoming a professor. As a result, academicians with a high level of scholarly ability, but no actual experience in management were promoted to a professorship (Locke 1996, pp. 74–75).

Against this background, industry voiced its demands for reforms in the university system. However, the traditional German university system remained largely intact after 1945, and the academic persona was even reinforced. As a result, the business world sought alternative solutions, the most powerful of which was the American model (Kipping 1998, pp. 99, 101).

6.2.3 Deployment of American Management Education Methods

6.2.3.1 TWI Implementation

Here, we examine the deployment of American-style management education methods in greater detail. First, TWI education courses based on American education materials were useful intermediaries for promoting stability in industrial and labor relations with management, improving relationships between superiors and subordinates, guidance for subordinates, and work methods and technological knowledge (Vgl. Kleinschmidt 2002, p. 74).

Occupation authorities implemented TWI in Germany, organizing education courses for leaders of employee education in September 1948. Interest in the TWI program was heightened by many enthusiastic individuals, and the program spread further with the support of a few companies such as Bosch. It is important to note that these companies attempted to promote harmonious relationships in the workplace, and courses were conducted for both management and employee representatives. By mid-1953, 160 sessions of trainer education courses had been conducted, and about 80,000 individuals had participated in approximately 8,000 education courses (Kipping 2004, p. 35).

Because American corporate involvement in the USTA&P management education project had ended, American universities began cooperating to pick up the slack (McGlade 1998c, p. 19), and in 1951, American universities began organizing and conducting TWI programs. University participation played a decisive role in the USTA&P campaign to improve management education and support management retraining in postwar Europe (McGlade 1998c, pp. 24–25). Further, with the support of this program, thousands of European scholars and executives gained the unparalleled opportunities of observing and learning at American universities and corporations. Upon their return, they brought back these American management techniques with them (McGlade 1998c, p. 28).

The RKW (National Board for Economy and Efficiency) also contributed to management education and retraining by visiting America in response to an invite by American professionals [*National Archives*, RG469, Mission to Germany,

Productivity and Technical Assistance Division, Subject Files of the Chief, 1953–1956, Council for International Progress in Management (USA), Inc (11.12.1953), *National Archives*, RG469, Mission to Germany, Productivity and Technical Assistance Division, Subject Files of the Chief, 1953–1956, TA09-217, Program for the TA-B-Project 09–217 Top Management, *National Archives*, RG469, Mission to Germany, Productivity and Technical Assistance Division, Subject Files of the Chief, 1953–1956, Berlin Top Management Team (7.10.1953)] and conducting their own TWI education courses [*National Archives*, RG469, Mission to Germany, Productivity and Technical Assistance Division, Subject Files of the Chief, 1953–1956, Durchführung des TA-B-Projectes 09-216–Management Training, *National Archives*, RG469, Mission to Germany, Productivity and Technical Assistance Division, Subject Files of the Chief, 1953–1956, Management Program for Berlin—Management Training Team (22.6.1953)]. REFA also contributed to the implementation of TWI, and in 1954, incorporated TWI activities within its education programs (Pechhold 1974, p. 155; REFA-Nachrichten 1954, p. 75). Having REFA personnel engaged in the TWI program shows the extent of REFA's public involvement in education (REFA-Nachrichten 1955, p. 16). The long-term cooperation between REFA and TWI also demonstrates how highly TWI education material was valued in the development of REFA employees (Jaeckel 1961, p. 222).

In this historical context, when we explore TWI implementation in detail, we find three TWI courses held by the chemical industrial firm, Henkel, during work hours: job instruction, labor relations, and job design (or job improvement). Among those, job design was the most intensive, and these courses were used for the first time in 1964 within the framework of in-company retraining (*Henkel Archiv*, K160, Betriebliche Ausbildungs- und Bildungsarbeit (5.7.1960), p. 2, *Henkel Archiv*, K160, Niederschrift über die Meisterbesprechung Nr.11 vom 17.11.64, p. 2). Bayer had also implemented TWI courses in 1950. The purpose of the TWI system was to simply and quickly train employees and make supervisors, particularly foremen and gang bosses, proficient in appropriately and humanely managing employees [*Bayer Archiv*, 210–001, TWI (Training within Industry)-System, p. 1, *Bayer Archiv*, 221/6, TWI (Training within Industry)-Kursus]. In addition to the educational purposes of the system, Bayer also emphasized the importance of methods for creating and maintaining good relationships with those in the factory [*Bayer Archiv*, 210–001, TWI (Training within Industry)-System, p. 2]. Thereafter, TWI was developed to cover human relations problems in depth. TWI participants agreed that leadership and involvement by those in personnel management are crucial for good management, and that TWI is an effective way to develop this leadership [*Bayer Archiv*, 221/6, TWI (Training within Industry)-Kursus].

Similar programs on issues of human relationships and in-company retraining of middle management were undertaken at Glanzstoff, Volkswagen, Bahlsen, Continental, and other corporations. The American influence was clearly evident in TWI courses and foreman training courses, implemented during the 1950s. Beginning in the latter half of the 1950s, the foreman training and retraining courses used by these corporations were different in both form and content compared with their pre-war equivalents (Kleinschmidt 2002, pp. 192–194).

The severe shortage of young managers in the 1950s led to the idea of adopting American methods for the systematic training of managers. R. Meine, head of human resources at Siemens, sought to strengthen the continuous education program and work training based on the American model, and concentrate all of Siemens' education activities. In 1956, Siemens began preparatory management training for young employees and managers. In 1959, they began week-long master classes, with the objective of providing advanced instruction to lower and middle management (Feldenkirchen 2004, p. 128). The textile manufacturer Spinnerei und Weberei Offenburg AG had no formal training program until 1954, when they began exploring the use of the TWI program [*National Archives*, RG469, Productivity & Technical Assit Division Labor Advisor Subject Files 1952–54, TA-Work, Labor and Human Relations Survey Report for Spinnerei und Webrei Offenburg A.G. (3.3.1954)].

6.2.3.2 Deployment of Top Management Education Methods

As we consider education and retraining for executives, we find that German executives took a different path from that of America's, given the value Germans placed on acquiring what they considered to be executive attributes. They focused their studies on law, business economics, and, in particular, engineering, as they had done prior to entering the workforce, and their executive development education was primarily short training courses, wherein they researched specialized topics instead of general management issues [Locke 1996, pp. 98, 100. For information on business school issues in Germany see Locke (1989, pp. 164–176)]. Most of the content of American-style executive development programs was missing in German universities, and only a few had begun offering short-term seminars for executives in 1966; most of these followed American examples of education for top management. These courses, which reflected the demands of the business world in their non-traditional content and education methods as well as their pragmatic orientation, were held outside the university system. Their adherence to an outline dictated by industry was an important characteristic. Executive development programs supplemented university training as well as the in-house selection process of top management both within and outside of corporations (Kipping 1998, pp. 104–108). For example, among the brief 3- to 5-day training courses held by various associations for incumbent executives, certain German university professors individually conducted retraining and re-education lectures in specialized areas in their spare time. However, most lecturers were incumbent executives themselves, and this sort of retraining was different from the American model in that they conducted lectures outside of academia (Locke 1996, p. 78). Documentation for a 1956 technical assistance project mentioned that, though top management education in America was predominant within universities, such type of education in Germany was conducted outside of universities [*National Archives*, RG469, Mission to Germany, Productivity and Technical Assistance Division, Subject Files of the Chief, 1953–1956, Projekt 329/1–329/4: Ausbildung von deutschen Lehrkräften auf dem Gebiet der Betriebsführung in USA (24.11.1956)].

In this manner, private corporations and industrial associations took the initiative in advancing management education. Efforts by industrial associations included two management debates held in Baden-Baden in 1951 and 1952, and Baden-Baden seminars from 1955, and activities of the loosely aligned group known as the Wuppertal Circle (Kipping 1998, pp. 102–103). The Baden-Baden seminars not only included debates to discuss American-style management methods and promote their introduction at an industry level but also provided as a forum for the exchange of ideas and theories on retraining and re-educating executives. They supplemented commercial colleges' educational offerings by building at least a partial bridge between academic and practical experience (Kleinschmidt 1998, p. 184; Kleinschmidt 2002, p. 299). A working group established by the Federation of German Industries in 1953 reviewed many case studies from Harvard Business School and other international sources. However, the working group eventually chose not to imitate those case studies, deciding instead to work toward transmitting knowledge and developing methods unique to Germany through the exchange of ideas between two generations of top management (Kipping 2004, pp. 41–42). Germany tended to establish formal programs for executive development within each industry. One important reason for this approach was that the true role of this type of training was to instill entrepreneurial spirit, attitudes, and values (Granick 1962, pp. 117–118; Hartmann 1959, p. 264).

RKW was also involved in the deployment of methods for top management education. For example, in November 1953, 33 top executives from Berlin and their aides gathered in RKW's Berlin branch office to listen to and debate on American management consultants regarding "management development." Seeing this as an opportunity, a 7-week seminar was conducted. This event was in response to the need for better education for executives and managers in many organizations (*National Archives*, RG469, Mission to Germany, Labor Advisor, Subject Files, 1952–1954, Field Statistics, Management Development in Berlin, pp. 1–2). Consulting and intermediary institutions also participated; for example, Carl Duisberg-Gesellschaft, which was responsible for personnel development, developed a German-American exchange program in collaboration with Harvard Business School (*National Archives*, RG469, Mission to Germany, Productivity and Technical Assistance Division, Subject Files of the Chief, 1953–1956, Carl Duisberg-Gesellschaft für Nachwuchsförderung e.V., Halbjahresbericht der Geschäftsleitung für die Zeit vom 1. April bis 30. November 1955, *National Archives*, RG469, Mission to Germany, Productivity and Technical Assistance Division, Subject Files of the Chief, 1953–1956, A letter from Carl Duisberg-Gesellschaft für Nachwuchsförderung e.V.).

Along with these additional corporate efforts, in the 1950s, many German corporations began to institutionalize their management education (Kipping 1998, p. 103). Internal corporate education rose to a new level and was largely based on the American model. In addition to internal management seminars, wherein the American case method was used in discussions and debates, Bayer conducted staff training, in which board members shared their experiences within their area of expertise. However, it became clear in the mid-1960s that the business community's efforts and private initiatives, with their focus on the sharing of experiences and use of materials lacking in scientific methods, were insufficient. Thus, renewed interest arose in the establishment of business schools (Kleinschmidt 2002, pp. 300–301).

Germany's attempt to establish its first business school center, which followed the American model, failed due to the decentralized structure of its education system (Kleinschmidt 2002, p. 78). Nevertheless, the latter half of the 1960s finally saw a German business school established, and the Universitätsseminar der Wirtschaft's founding in 1968 also played an important role. However, other than the College for Business Management at Koblenz, the era had no other institutions of this sort (Vgl. Kleinschmidt 2002, p. 306; European School of Management and Technology 2009).

The use of American education materials in courses designed for top management education in universities and specialized courses began in the 1960s and increased rapidly (Dyas and Thanheiser 1976, p. 112), however, business schools failed to become a ubiquitous phenomenon at that time. In Germany, the topics studied by executives at universities were neither related to their being selected for promotion, nor was it important for their development. Executive selection remained traditionally grounded in actual experience and results, with most executives working at one company for long periods before being promoted to the top. These practices were an important factor in the strength of resistance to the American model and in delaying the introduction of business schools (Engwall and Zamagni 1998, pp. 11, 15; Kipping 1998, p. 96).

6.2.4 Factors and Limitations in the Deployment of American-Style Management Education

On the basis of the aforementioned considerations, we next examine the various factors that restricted the deployment of American-style methods in management education.

The TWI program was first seen in supervisor and foreman education, and emphasized methods for better communication that could improve the labor climate by implementing more effective information policies. However, TWI was often met with a lukewarm reception (Kleinschmidt 2002, p. 185). It originated in America, and never took hold as firmly as it did in Germany. Although it was tailored to the German environment, the number of TWI programs implemented under the USTA&P in Germany was clearly lower than in other European countries. West Germany held only 134 TWI courses from the fall of 1948 (in the western region) to the summer of 1952, whereas the Netherlands for instance held more than 6,000 courses and the UK more than 30,000 in the same period. The TWI courses had relatively few participants from German corporations (Kleinschmidt 2002, p. 75), and institutions such as business schools, which supported executive development effectively in America, did not gain popularity and were not Americanized. At the time, individual organizations conducting retraining and re-education for German executives and managers remained separated, and saw limited change. The elements that did change were the types of retraining and the content within corporations. For example, week-long or several-week seminars were held for specialists and operational personnel in middle and upper management to learn about and discuss the latest American-style management methods (Kleinschmidt 2002, p. 78).

As we examine the relationship with America from the European perspective, we notice that, for example, the EPA's improvements to management education were not an American product, but were an adaptation and fusion of European methods. Boel points out that "even in the 1950s, US-European relations in the field of management education were not a one-way affair" (Boel 1998, p. 46). The overall influence of the American drive for management education in Europe was determined by a complex matrix of several factors. Amidst this, progress was particularly dependent on each program's effectiveness and the amount of resistance from executives and educators (Gourvish and Tiratsoo 1998, p. 9).

The effects of attempting to transfer and implement the American model of management education into Europe during the period of the Marshall Plan and the productivity movement, apart from a few exceptions, were very modest. Converting traditional forms and replacing them with modern management education methods took another decade, and the impact of this process was smallest in German-speaking nations (Schröter 2005, p. 121). The direct transfer of programs from the American model, such as TWI and top management education, was also unsuccessful in German corporations because of their traditional views on managerial social policies. Within the field of management education, American development aid also had relatively little effect (Kleinschmidt 2002, pp. 79, 83). As Kleinschmidt noted, when compared with American and Western European expansion, education and retraining for German executives and managers adhered to a "special path." This "German stubbornness" is the primary cause of the poor acceptance of the American-style business school model, its low probability of adoption, and the total emphasis on theory rather than practical work in the commercial colleges' economics-focused education. It has been proposed that the German's chosen path could even be seen as a German model, an alternative to American-style management (Kleinschmidt 2002, pp. 398–399).

These observations elucidate that the American style was not always appropriate, given the nature of extant education systems and traditions, such as the role universities played within management education, the education and characteristics sought in executives, corporate promotion systems, and executives' internal labor markets arising from them. Based on this point, management values and a management climate emphasizing technology and with a relatively long-term perspective was already well-rooted in Germany even after the war. They functioned counter to a personnel policy, thoroughly grounded in a doctrine of efficiency that reflected management values and a management climate based on American pragmatism. Even in the face of strong American influence, the German system could not be transformed overnight. The most important factor behind changes to management education and executive management education was the country's overall education system and the strength of its management education system, along with cultural factors such as management styles and traditions for learning that could transcend national borders (Amdam 1996, p. 11).

Thus, in the 1990s, executive and manager development and education found in American-style business schools have attained unprecedented importance. The problem then arises that the global competition and market principles beginning in the 1990s, wrought dramatic changes to the conditions that supported German management values and management styles, causing a resurgence of Americanization.

References

Amdam RP (1996) Introduction. In: Amdam RP (ed) Management, education and competitiveness. Europe, Japan and the United States. Routledge, London, pp 1–16

Boel B (1998) The European productivity agency and the development of management education in Western Europe in the 1950s. In: Gourvish T, Tiratsoo N (eds) Missionaries and managers: American influences on European management education, 1945–60. Manchester University Press, Manchester, pp 34–49

Dyas GR, Thanheiser HT (1976) The emerging European enterprise. Strategy and structure in French and German industry. Macmillan, London

Engwall L, Zamagni V (1998) Introduction. In: Engwall L, Zamagni V (eds) Management education in historical perspective. Manchester University Press, Manchester, pp 1–18

European School of Management and Technology (2009) USW Netwerk: 30 Jahre Managerfortbildung in Schloss Gracht. http://www.esmt.org/deu/usw.-netwerk-30-jahre-Managerfortbildung-in-schloss-gracht/. Accessed 3 June 2009

Feldenkirchen W (2004) The Americanization of the German electrical industry after 1945. Siemens as a case study. In: Kudo A, Kipping M, Schröteret HG (eds) German and Japanese business in the boom years. Transforming American management and technology models. Routledge, London, pp 116–137

Gemelli G (1996) American influence on European management education. The role of the ford foundation. In: Amdam RP (ed) Management, education and competitiveness. Europe, Japan and the United States. Routledge, London, pp 38–68

Gourvish T, Tiratsoo N (1998) Missionaries and managers: an introduction. In: Gourvish T, Tiratsoo N (eds) Missionaries and managers: American influences on European management education, 1945–60. Manchester University Press, Manchester, pp 1–12

Granick D (1962) The European executive. Weidenfeld & Nicolson, London

Hartmann H (1959) Authority and organization in German management. Princeton University Press, Princeton

Hartmann H (1963) Amerikanische Firmen in Deutschland. Westdeutche Verlag, Köln

Hasegawa H (1960) Nihon no Hyuman Rireshonzu (Human relations in Japan). Otsuki Shoten, Tokyo

Jaeckel B (1961) 10 Jahre REFA-Bundesverband. REFA-Nachrichten 14(6):221–226

Kamei T, Shiraki T (1971) Keiei Kyoiku Ron (Management education). Maruzen, Tokyo

Kipping M (1998) The hidden business school: management training in Germany since 1945. In: Engwall L, Zamagni V (eds) Management education in historical perspective. Manchester University Press, Manchester, pp 95–110

Kipping M (2004) 'Importing' American ideas to West Germany, 1940s to 1970s. In: Kudo A, Kipping M, Schröteret HG (eds) German and Japanese business in the boom years. Transforming American management and technology models. Routledge, London, pp 30–53

Kleinschmidt C (1998) An Americanized company in Germany. The Vereinigte Glanzstoff Fabriken AG in the 1950s. In: Kipping M, Bjarnar O (eds) The Americanization of European business. The Marshall plan and the transfer of US management models. Routledge, London, pp 171–189

Kleinschmidt C (2002) Der produktive Blick. Wahrnehmung amerikanischer und japanischer Management- und Produktionsmethoden durch deutsche Unternehmer 1950–1985. Akademie Verlag, Berlin

Locke RR (1989) Management and higher education since 1940. The influences of America and Japan on West Germany, Great Britain, and France. Cambridge University Press, Cambridge

Locke RR (1996) The collapse of the American management Mystique. Oxford University Press, New York

McGlade J (1998a) From business reform program to production drive. The transformation of US technical assistance to West Europe. In: Kipping M, Bjarnar O (eds) The Americanization of European business. The Marshall plan and the transfer of US management models. Routledge, London, pp 18–34

McGlade J (1998b) The big push: The export of American business education to West Europe after the Second World War. In: Engwall L, Zamagni V (eds) Management education in historical perspective. Manchester University Press, Manchester, pp 50–65

McGlade J (1998c) The US technical assistance and productivity program and the education of Western European managers, 1948–58. In: Gourvish TR, Tiratsoo N (eds) Missionaries and managers: American influences on European management education, 1945–60. Manchester University Press, Manchester, pp 13–33

Noda K (ed) (1969) Nihon Keieishi: Gendai Keieishi (Business history in Japan: modern business history). Nihon Seisansei Honbu, Tokyo

OEEC (1954) Problems of business management. American opinion, European opinion (Technical Assistance Mission, No. 129). OEEC, Paris

Okuda K (1961) Ningen Kankei to Kigyonai Kyoiku Kunren (Human relations and education in enterprise). In: Nihon Rodo Kyokai (ed) Romu Kanri to Chingin (Personnel management and wages). Nihon Rodo Kyokai, Tokyo, pp 109–181

Okuda K, Takezawa S, Ootsubo D (1987) Amerikasiki Keieikanri no Jyuyo to Hukyu (Acceptance and diffusion of American management). Keiei to Rekishi (Bus Hist) 10:2–27

Pechhold E (1974) 50 Jahre REFA. Beuth, Berlin/Köln/Frankfurt am Main

REFA-Nachrichten (1954) 30 Jahre REFA. Vortrag von Herrn Min.-Dir. I. R. Dr. Kurt Magnus auf der Mitglieder-Versammlung in Bad Dürkheim. REFA-Nachrichten 7(4):73–6

REFA-Nachrichten (1955) Zur Übenahme der deutschen TWI-Arbeit durch den REFA. REFA-Nachrichten 8(1):16

Schröter HG (2005) Americanization of the European economy. A compact survey of American economic influence in Europe since the 1880s. Springer, Dordrecht

Shimokawa K (1976) Sengo no Keieisha to Keieikanri (Managers and business management after WW II). In: Kobayashi M, Shimokawa K, Sugiyama K et al (eds) Nihon Keieishi wo Manabu (Textbook of Japanese business history), vol 3. Yuhikaku, Tokyo, pp 46–65

Sugiyama T (1968) Keiei Kyoiku Shu (Materials of management education). In: Nihon Keieiseisaku Gakkai (ed) Keiei Shiryo Shutaisei III, Jinji Romuhen (Subjectivity of management materials III, personnel management). Nihon Sogo Shuppan Kiko, Tokyo, pp 1–30

Zennihon Noritsu Renmei Ningen Noryoku Kaihatu Senta (1981) Sengo Kigyonai Kyoiku Hensenshi (History of changes in corporate education after WW II). Zennihon Noritsu Renmei Ningen Noryoku Kaihatu Senta, Tokyo

Chapter 7
Deployment of American-Style Management and Mass Production Systems: Human Relations, IE, and the Ford System

Abstract This chapter discusses the deployment of American-style management and production systems. The major issues are human relations, industrial engineering (IE), and the Ford system. It first considers Japanese characteristics of the American management and production system, and then examines the deployment of human relations, IE, and the Ford system in Germany. This chapter analyzes these issues in relation to German environmental factors such as labor relations, the codetermination system, management values and traditions, and the market structure in Germany and Europe. It reviews the deployment of human relations, in particular the problems of transformation of labor relations and those in the management system. The primary issue was the implementation of the work factor method and Methods Time Measurement (MTM) for the deployment of IE. Finally, this chapter examines the deployment of the Ford system, the rollout of the mass production system, and German manufacturing on the basis of German and European market characteristics.

Keywords Human relations • Industrial engineering (IE) • Management system • Production system • The Ford system

In Chap. 7, we considered the implementation of American management education but in this chapter, we turn our attention to human relations, industrial engineering (IE), and the Ford system regarding the deployment of American-style management and production systems. Deployment of human relations (HR below) began early because it was regarded as a priority for the US, in Germany's efforts to adopt US management models as part of the productivity movement. IE is an advanced form of scientific management that originated in America and gained broad acceptance after World War II. The Ford system was implemented in Germany even before the war and became commonplace afterward. This not only enabled mass production within the processing and assembly industries, but also became the basis for the post-war mass production system. In the following sections, we will describe how American-style management systems were implemented in Germany and the resulting changes in corporate management.

T. Yamazaki, *German Business Management: A Japanese Perspective on Regional Development Factors*, DOI 10.1007/978-4-431-54303-9_7, © Springer Japan 2013

7.1 Japanese Characteristics of the Deployment of American-Style Management and Production System

We will first examine the environment within Japan during the 1950s and 1960s as a point of comparison for the deployment of these American-style management methods. Human relations played an important role in Japan's increasing corporate modernization efforts after the war, as the legal recognition of labor unions and the growing labor movement heightened the conflict between labor and management. This environment called for reforms in management methods based on the family system, feudal family relations, as well as the irrational familial and paternalistic human relations that labor management had previously relied upon. HR was deployed in response to this demand. Small- and medium-sized businesses, in particular, demanded further reforms to labor management methods and proceeded to deploy HR under the direction of business associations and the Japan Productivity Center. Within larger corporations, HR was used particularly to improve corporate consciousness and as a labor union countermeasure with regard to the lifetime employment system. Because of these factors, the broad deployment of various HR policies typically included company newsletters, suggestion systems, employee attitude surveys, human resource consultation, and employee welfare activities along with an emphasis on labor harmony within the deployment of HR (Hasegawa 1960; Nakamura 1958, p. 221; Ewatari 1954, p. 20). However, Japan's management culture, with its characteristic paternalism, lifetime employment, and seniority order system, was not fully prepared to deploy and commit to the original American-style HR model. Germany, in contrast, did not need to modernize its management as strongly as Japan. Although reforms in HR-driven labor relations were undertaken at the behest of the US rather than by Germany's own volition, the legal establishment of systems for employee participation in management, typified by codetermination, established a strong framework for labor relations. As these examples demonstrate, conditions for the deployment of HR varied greatly between Germany and Japan.

The following items constitute the main characteristics of IE deployment in Japan. Rather than adjusting IE content, Japanese companies placed greater emphasis on a reshuffling of distributed management based on work standardization (time-motion studies). They addressed various methodologies for work rationalization (production management, cost controls etc.). The general foreman, specified as a principal player in IE, was sometimes given responsibility for cost control, cost reductions, and overall labor management, and the systemization of IE was delayed (Noguchi 1968, pp. 196–197; Noguchi et al. 1965, pp. 224–225, 228; Hibi 1975, p. 30). The work measurement that was so popular in the US and Germany was not thought to be a fit for Japan, and many corporations focused entirely on continuous method engineering (Jyuji 1969, p. 2). IE was rolled out in connection with labor management functions. For example, different employment practices among Japanese corporations, such as the seniority wage system and lifetime employment, led to inconsistent labor targets for IE and differences among other IE elements (Ueda et al. 1967, p. 539). Furthermore, upon implementation of the work-factor method, reforms were made to wage systems, particularly to wage rates along with job analysis (Inoue 1976, p. 29). Compared to Japan, Germany placed greater emphasis on the production management function. Moreover, Germany had a history of activity among organizations, such as the REFA, engaged in process studies that were an important factor in the IE rollout and also the combining of German and American elements.

Further, as we explore the Ford system, Japan's small yet highly diverse domestic markets, such as the automobile industry, necessitated revisions to that system. Postwar production system reforms progressed as a hybrid of the Ford production method and the traditional craft production system (Fujimoto 1997, pp. 100–101, 120). Japan did not have a huge demand the US had, so a structure was developed wherein necessary parts were delivered in smaller lots as needed to perfectly match production trends. This was done in order to respond to a highly diverse product lineup combined with limited demand, as can be seen in Toyota. That is, the goal was to synchronize parts supply with the workflow of each process using the "just-in-time" method (Shimokawa 2004, pp. 174, 183). This method required a standardized "flow" across all production processes (Wada and Shiba 1995, pp. 126–127; Wada 2009, p. 544). The artisan production-type work organization was replaced by work standardization and direct control of the workplace. However, this reshuffling of standardized tasks created a multifunction work organization responsible for a sequence of processes rather than a single process. The reshuffling also led to the transfer of decision-making power and responsibility for work improvements through employee suggestions and total quality control (TQC) to the shop floor level. Further, through selective deployment and modifications of structural elements of the Ford system, such as moving assembly lines or transfer machines, corporations could reintegrate these elements to respond to Japan's domestic market, which was rich in diversity and change (Fujimoto 1997, pp. 116, 119, 121). Germany, in contrast, did not pursue a system of complete production process synchronization as Japan did. Although Germany did attempt to develop a mass production system that leveraged the workers' skills and technical abilities, the two countries had different markets, and so the workers' skills and abilities were dissimilar. Consequently, differences can be seen between the two nations' hybrid production systems based on Ford production methods and the artisan production system.

Next, we will consider Germany's deployment of American-style methods, examining HR in Sect. 7.2 and IE in Sect. 7.3. In Sect. 7.4, we will study the deployment of the Ford system and the resulting production system reforms, along with its relationship to German-style manufacturing.

7.2 Human Relations Deployment in Germany

7.2.1 Social and Economic Background of Human Relations Deployment

We will first consider human relations. Looking back on the decade between 1948 and 1958, the Management Technology Council reports on electrical manufacturer Siemens & Halske AG state the importance of the HR movement in their psychological climate (*Siemens Archiv Akten*, 64/Lt350, Betriebstechnische Tagung 1958, 10 Jahre Aufbau—Rückblick und Vorschau 1948–1958, pp. 15–19). A research group traveling in the US pointed out the important role of labor relations, or human relations, in American economic life in approximately 10 years after the 1940s (Der Arbeitgeber 1950, p. 12). Thus, we will first look at the social and economic background of HR deployment.

The US had observed a common problem among OEEC member nations wherein they eliminated restrictive practices by labor unions and strengthened development of the now free labor unions (Takagi 1962, p. 17). The US technical assistance plan, which was provided to improve productivity, was also considered closely related to the formation of labor relations. From the American perspective, HR was critical in responding to the clear insufficiency and slow development of post-war Germany, and was thus an important type of "development assistance" (Kleinschmidt 2002, p. 173). HR was therefore considered the most important pillar among the many projects the US initiated as part of the US Technical Assistance and Productivity Program (USTA&P), and of course the US strongly supported it. During this time, US employers' associations and the US government itself supported building labor relations through HR to avoid instability on the shop floor and conflicts with labor unions (Kleinschmidt 2004a, p. 170).

Likewise, from the German perspective, HR methods were accepted as a way to establish harmonious relations with various groups within a corporation. America's superiority in productivity could not be explained by better technology and a rationalized management organization alone; rather, one factor viewed as important in its productivity and high profitability was the stable labor relations resulting from its HR methods. The reports of nearly every study trip to the US are firm on this point (Kleinschmidt 2002, p. 177). For example, according to one official in the Federation of German Industries in 1954, there was a collegial environment existed between US management and labor that was not seen in German corporations [*National Archives*, RG469, Mission to Germany, Labor Advisor, Subject Files, 1952–54, A letter about Human Relations Seminar to Mr. C. Mahhder (3.2.1954)]. In West German corporations, American HR concepts attracted attention as a means of liberating Germany from its pre-war ideological burden (Hilger 2004, p. 244).

New methods of HR did not immediately take hold in this kind of climate. However, HR did have a tremendous impact, and the idea of the importance of workers as human beings can be seen in the period's newly Germanized HR concepts (Wiesen 2001, p. 191).

7.2.2 *Human Relations Deployment Efforts and Their Characteristics*

Next, we explore the efforts to deploy HR. The primary route for learning about HR and transferring that knowledge was international conferences and study trips to the US, in addition to educational programs.

First, with regard to international conferences, the first talks between German and US management personnel took place in August 1951at Baden–Baden. They discussed various HR issues, and the improvement of human relations became a theme of modern research [*Bundesarchiv Koblenz*, B102/37023, Management Development and Human Relations. OEEC-EPZ-Projekte im Rahmen der Technischen Hilfeleistung (8.3.1955), pp. 1–2]. At the 1954 10th annual International Management Congress as well, the improvement of human relations as a management methodology was a major theme (*Bundesarchiv Koblenz*, B393/17, Xth International Management Congress. In: *Management Methods of Improving Human Relations*, Sao Paulo, 1954), and efforts to deploy HR grew internationally. In the European Productivity Agency's Project 312 of the mid-1950s, the Agency proposed the organization of a twofold project: a debate of industrial-social research on HR in industry and an international seminar [*National Archives*, RG469, Off African & European Operations Regional Organizations Staff. European Productivity Agency (EPA) Project File, 1950–1957, Productivity and Applied Research Committee. Human Relations in Industry. E.P.A. Project No.312 (28.12.1954), p. 2, *National Archives*, RG469, Off African & European Operations Regional Organizations Staff. European Productivity Agency (EPA) Project File, 1950–1957, Productivity and Applied Research Committee, Human Relations in Industry, E.P.A. Project No.312 (26.10.1955), pp. 1–2].

Among the study trips to the US, the RKW, for example, discussed HR in their *Productivity in the USA* report in one of their 1953 study trips (RKW 1953, pp. 44–45). Additionally, an RKW study trip from March to April, 1954, included RKW representatives in addition to members from the German Federation of Trade Unions, REFA, Braunschweig Engineering College's Institute for Industrial Psychology and Personnel management, Max Planck Institute for Industrial Psychology, and the German Ministry of Labor, among others (Kleinschmidt 2002, pp. 72–73). A 1956 report pointed out that the US economy had seen strong results from its use of HR, which was far more advanced than Germany's, and noted the possibility of importing basic HR concepts (Bramesfeld et al. 1956, p. 96). In looking at HR education programs, in addition to Germany's RKW, the REFA, Braunschweig Engineering College's Institute for Industrial Psychology and Personnel Management, and others contributed to HR, for which special programs were instituted (Kleinschmidt 2002, p. 72).

Further, among corporate HR efforts, the managers of human resources and welfare departments were the first to work on HR issues. P.G. v. Beckerath, the head of Bayer's welfare department in 1951, embraced both the factory communities of 1920s' Germany and American HR methods (Kleinschmidt 2002, p. 178). This amalgamation of American-oriented thinking on human resource policy and welfare policy combined with pre-war ideas was also seen in Glanzstoff, where HR views merged with 1920s labor research in "psychotechnology." This combination of HR with human resource methodologies conforming to pre-war traditions permeated Glanzstoff for a long term (Kleinschmidt 2002, pp. 181–182). Siemens also took up HR issues in the early 1950s, strongly promoting healthy relations between superiors and subordinates and among workers. According to a 1952 document, many observations stated in a publication regarding human relations based on American thinking provided opportunities for considering and examining unique methods [*Siemens Archiv Akten*, 12799, „Human Relations" im Haus Siemens

(22.1. 1952), pp. 9, 11, *Siemens Archiv Akten*, 12799, „Human Relations“ (25.2. 1952), *Siemens Archiv Akten*, 12799, Human Relations (16.11.1953), *Siemens Archiv Akten*, 12799, Bericht Nr.2 über die Besprechung zwischen WL ZEL Berlin und BR ZEL am 30.9.53 (27.10.1953)]. Another document from the same company in the same year described particular interest in the results of US research in the field of psychological business management [*Siemens Archiv Akten*, 12799, Rationalisierung als betriebspsychologiche Aufgabe (January 1952), pp. 4, 6].

By the mid-1950s, HR had become a fashionable topic in European debates and conferences [*National Archives*, RG469, Off African & European Operations Regional Organizations Staff. European Productivity Agency (EPA) Project File, 1950–1957, Human Relations in Industry. E.P.A. Project No.312, Stage A—Florence Discussions (21.3.1955), p. 2]. Scientific discussions on this theme, particularly discussions and publications in economics and sociology, reached their peak during the 10-year period from the mid-1950s to the mid-1960s (Vgl. Kleinschmidt 2002, p. 191). All corporate efforts regarding human relations within management, employee information and education, and labor climate improvement were affected from the 1950s onward by the HR and TWI movements following US models. German corporations had previous experience in the creation of worker information, internal corporate education, and labor relations, and these aspects increased the likelihood of HR importation into Germany (Kleinschmidt 2002, pp. 195–196).

As publications focusing on workers began appearing in the early 1950s, new thinking on HR and cooperative relations spread by various means. Among those, the internal corporate newsletter, originally initiated by many corporations in the 1920s, was revived in the late 1940s and early 1950s as an important medium through which the new consideration of industrial workers could be shown. In 1951, there were approximately 200 such newsletters published by West German corporations, but within 2 years that number swelled to 400 (Wiesen 2001, pp. 192–193). In a 1955 publication, research by T. Pilker and others surveying steel corporations to which the Montan Codetermination Act (an act for the coal, iron, and steel industries) was applied, stated that at the time of the survey, corporate newsletters and the like had not yet become an effective means of disseminating extremely important information (Pirker et al. 1955, p. 427). By 1957, however, 441 different corporate newsletters were being published, with a total distribution of approximately five million copies. Particularly within medium- and large-sized corporations, these newsletters were a superior means of communication for management, clarifying management actions toward workers and facilitating the exchange of ideas between labor and management (Bundesvereinigung der Deutschen Arbeitgeberverbände 1957, p. 255).

These corporate newsletters were an attempt to understand all aspects of worker life in terms of HR concepts. Many newsletters were titled so as to suggest to employees that the corporation was attempting to embrace the technical concept of “human relations.” “*The Factory and Me*” (Hoesch AG); “*Our Factory*” (Bayer AG); “*My Factory*” (Chemische Werke Kalk G.m.b.H.); “*Touch*” (Brown, Boveri & Cie AG); and other similar titles implied to workers an identity with no special interests (Kauders 1960, pp. 23–24). One of Opel’s corporate newsletters published in 1949 raised the issue of encouraging employee trust in corporate management in non-decision making contexts. From portraying the ideal worker to displaying photographs of employees considered to be role models by the corporate leadership (Neugebauer 1997, pp. 195, 197–199, 212), corporate newsletters were used as a means to improve labor and human relations and promote competition among workers.

Even in this area, German corporations, particularly in connection with ideas for work communities, depended on pre-war traditions and experience wherein the German Technical Training Institute (Dinta) promoted the spread of corporate newsletters. However, in the 1950s, most wartime and post-war magazines that had previously suspended publication had begun anew, and German corporations aligned themselves with US models. At this time, the means of disseminating internal management information became more diverse, and some corporations used periodically published notices, informational pamphlets, a few even using video in addition to labor discussions, retraining seminars, and newsletters (Kleinschmidt 2002, p. 195).

This approach applied HR theory more broadly for an ideological and psychological impact. Unlike previous methods, its use was intended to affect workers, their families, and their surroundings in every aspect of life. Rationalization, new technology related to the productivity movement, increased labor intensity, threat of mass layoffs, and the resulting stronger pressure on wages were all veiled within HR (Kauders 1960, pp. 15–16).

Among these efforts, at least a few elements of the American model were adopted by German corporations. They affected communication between lower-level supervisors, such as foremen and supervisors, and employees, as well as information structures and labor climates within corporations. The knowledge and actions of those implementing the American model for labor relations simultaneously reproduced a corporate structure in the context of German legal regulations, modifying the original model. Thus, the American model of HR complemented the formation of labor relations within German corporations (Kleinschmidt 2002, p. 203).

7.2.3 *Human Relations Deployment Limitations and Their Factors*

HR deployment, as shown above, had a great impact on the labor climate in German corporations as well as in labor relations. However, in the areas of technology and production, there was a strong trend in favor of the American model, and while from the early 1950s onward US know-how was broadly introduced into Germany, the opposite was true of HR's introduction regarding the amount of emphasis placed on discussing and implementing HR themes. In actuality, because of the attitudes of employees and their representatives, discussions on codetermination beginning at the end of the 1940s, and societal and managerial traditions in German labor relations, only a miniscule fraction of the American HR model ended up being implemented in German corporations. C. Kleinschmidt attributed the utter failure of German corporations in implementing American HR and labor relations strategies to the realities of German management in the 1950s (Kleinschmidt 2002, pp. 173–175).

In a 1958 report of observations of Europe, two Japanese persons observed that the basic policy of activities included in the theme of "human beings and labor" was expressed in a foreign language as "human relations," but noted that this was not necessarily suitable to the US method (Osikawa and Takagi 1959, pp. 83, 67).

Many cases of great resistance by both corporations and labor against deployment of HR are recorded. For example, at Bayer, certain board members and personnel in the engineering department resisted having foremen education courses because they felt it unnecessary. Until the 1960s, most board members of large corporations in the German chemical industry had a different mindset from HR, and chemists were a primary example of those who distanced themselves from HR. Technical departments were particularly skeptical of combining human resources and welfare departments because of the common disputes over authority, making it necessary to separate the technical departments from HR; these attitudes were in resistance to HR. Similar opposition could be seen in other corporations, and there was resistance from employee representatives and labor unions. Codetermination was also an issue in which German and US traditions and influence played a role (Kleinschmidt 2002, pp. 185–186). However, in the 1950s, education initiatives for foremen were undertaken in which debates ensued amongst the participants; among the educational courses were lectures, film screenings, and exchange of information and experiences. One of the important topics raised in these debates was personnel management issues concerning foremen and subordinates [Vgl. *Bayer Archiv*, 221/6, Meisterarbeitsgemeinschaft (25.6.1956), *Bayer Archiv*, 221/6, Auswertung der Ergebnisse der Zweiten Meisterarbeitsgemeinschaft (20.7.1956), *Bayer Archiv*, 221/6, Meisterarbeitsgemeinschaft (5.9.1955), *Bayer Archiv*, 221/6, Meisterausbidung (9.7.1953), *Bayer Archiv*, 329/737, Die Schrift von Sozial- und Personal Abteilung an Zwiste am 1. Dezember 1954].

Original management models, such as the Harzburg model, also exerted a strong influence. In contrast to the authoritarian management style, this model proposed delegating not just labor but authority and responsibility of everything related to the work in an effort to greatly lighten the load of those in various management positions (Obst 1970, pp. 80, 82). Many corporations found this model attractive; after the 1950s and 1960s, it was widely adopted in Germany (Kleinschmidt 2002, pp. 198–199).

Further, because HR methodologies were promoted with the US intent for labor relations reform in mind, they met with strong skepticism and opposition in Germany. In the US, various efforts to increase productivity through technical assistance were closely linked with labor relations initiatives in promoting HR and TWI, and HR plans within German corporations were a significant part of comprehensive political objectives, or "missions" (Kleinschmidt 2004a, p. 168). For those reasons, the Germans' skepticism and opposition were naturally severe.

Great changes to the labor relations framework arising from the Codetermination Act inhibited the spread of HR. Although German businessmen had an interest in management models for direct communication between management and employees as a "management partnership," labor relations were actually shaped by the strong influence of legal regulations and state intervention. These cultural and political differences between the US and Germany underpinned the extraordinary differences in labor relations (Kleinschmidt 2002, p. 202).

For large German corporations, the codetermination debate was particularly heated in the early 1950s, when it was thought that US development would provide an attractive alternative to the German model for labor relations, which was based on the strength of labor unions. However, within the areas of TWI and "foreman training" or "worker conferences," the 1951 Montan Codetermination Act and the 1952 Works Constitution Act impeded a broader adaptation of American-style HR. These two laws are characteristic of the failed attempts to create labor relations in German corporations along the lines of those in the US. Instead, a German model for labor relations was created, based on legal regulations and rooted in the traditions of corporatism, with labor unions being an integral part and labor relations embedded therein. This model recognized far greater rights of codetermination than the American model in employee education, remuneration, labor safety, and various other issues of corporate social policies (Betriebliche Sozialpolitik). As a result, attempts to adopt Americanization in HR steadily decreased in German corporations from 1955 onward (Kleinschmidt 2002, p. 190; Kleinschmidt 2004a, pp. 169, 171). This new framework for labor relations in Germany, based on the restraint imposed by labor unions and codetermination rights, became a meaningful alternative to the American model.

Thus, we see that German corporations' deployment of HR did not lead to widespread adoption even as a labor relations model. In 1963, Hartmann noted that HR, after being imported into Germany as a trendy strategy in the early 1950s, lost its luster and was seen simply as an almost unimportable product of US economic culture (Hartmann 1963, p. 173). By the end of the 1950s, the postwar craze for new values and a society modeled upon the US abated. Many of the efforts to deploy these reforms disappeared, HR being a prime example (Hartmann 1959, p. 271).

Hence, the deployment of HR in corporations first concentrated on various issues that could not be automatically solved by legal regulations or formal regulations of codetermination. Such niche operations occurred in relations between foremen and subordinates, and improvement of "human relations" and the "labor climate" were the issues at hand (Kleinschmidt 2002, pp. 191–192). These attempts to apply HR at the corporate level, where management cooperation and discussions of codetermination were more critical, were limited, and even for the German personnel system, the use of partial knowledge from HR schools of thought was selective at best (Hilger 2004, pp. 244–245).

As the above-mentioned observations regarding HR deployment reveal, these HR management methodologies and the labor relations activities based on them were set against the background of the historically powerful, pragmatic management culture of the US, whether in the practical application of management principles like "efficiency improvement" or corporate activity mechanisms, or within the labor climate. Thus, management methodologies and practices that place the highest value on the principle of "efficiency improvement" were not necessarily appropriate for Germany. This is because of management philosophies on personnel composition issues, with managers generally coming from technical fields, as well as German management traditions in and the resulting emphasis on technology and quality. Further, because of the US' strong political motive of labor relations reform, the push for deployment and transfer of HR were not at all aligned with Germany's conditions for acceptance. In post-war Germany, labor relations derived not from management methodologies as in the US, but rather from systems embedded in the law. This point is deeply connected to post-war German capitalism, as can be seen in the phrases "Rhineland model of capitalism" and "coordinated market economy" (Albert 2001; Hall and Soskice 2001).

7.3 Deployment of Industrial Engineering in Germany

7.3.1 Development and Impact of Industrial Engineering

As we next look at IE, we see that work studies consider it the next level of development (Kirchner 1970, p. 440), and that the US had a decisively leading role in the IE field. A Siemens US study trip report in 1963, the end of the productivity movement, noted that the predetermined time method then being implemented in the world of capitalism was without exception developed and tested in the US prior to being made public. For example, WF (work factor) was developed in the US in the mid-1930s (*Siemens Archiv Akten*, 16020, Aus Theorie und Praxis des Industrial Engineering in den USA. Bericht über eine Studienreise September/Oktober 1963, p. 123), implemented after 1938, and then used internationally from 1952. In the International Management Conference held in September 1963, there was a discussion on issues of WF time standards and WF use [*Bundesarchiv Koblenz*, B393/27, International Conference on Work Factor Time Standards (26–27.9.1963)]. MTM (Methods Time Measurement) was developed by H. B. Maynard, G. J. Stegemerten, and J. L. Schwab in the 1940s at Westinghouse (*Siemens Archiv Akten*, 16020, Aus Theorie und Praxis des Industrial Engineering in den USA, p. 33), and spread after the war.

Even in Germany, according to a 1948 source, manufacturers began to place great significance on work study (Kothe 1948, p. 10). For example, electrical manufacturer AEG noted that from the 1950s to the 1960s, the rationalization of work and time studies played an important role in productivity improvement [*AEG Archiv*, GS2052, Programm für durchzuführende Arbeits- u. Zeitstudienim Geschäftsjahr 1959/60 (12.10.1959), *AEG Archiv*, GS2052, Programm für durchzuführende Rationalisierungsmaβnahmen im Geschäftsjahr 1960/61 (2.12.1960), *AEGArchiv*, GS2052, Programm fürdurchzuführende Rationalisierungsmaβnahmen im Geschäftsjahr 1961/62 (5.12.1961), *AEG Archiv*, GS2052, Programm für Rationalisierung im Geschäftsjahr 1964 (8.6. 1964), *AEG Archiv*, GS2052, Programm für durchzuführende Rationalisierungsmaβnahmen im Geschäftsjahr 1966 (21.1.1966), *AEGArchiv*, GS2052, Geschäftsbericht 1959/60 an Dir. Mempel

(2.12.1960), *AEG Archiv*, GS2052, Geschäftsbericht 1960/61 an Dir. Mempel (5.12.1961), *AEG Archiv*, GS2052, Geschäftsbericht 1962/63 an Dir. Mempel (2.6.1964), *AEG Archiv*, GS2052, Durchzuführte Rationalisierungsvorhaben im Geschäftsjahr 1963, *AEG Archiv*, GS2052, Durchzuführte Rationalisierungsvorhaben im Geschäftsjahr 1966 (5.4.1967)]. However, by the mid-1950s, the German organization REFA's activities and wage payment methods were becoming prominent (Free 1955, p. 67; Pavel 1957, p. 22). For example, in a March 1956 survey of 2,655 corporations conducted by Ifo, REFA systems accounted for as much as 80% of the work study methods used by manufacturers, with REFA systems having taken a dominant position (REFA-Nachrichten 1956, pp. 91–94; Pechhold 1956, p. 147).

However, the situation changed by the latter half of the 1950s. The increasing importance of work and time studies, along with the further development of REFA's methods, is particularly apparent in the US predetermined time method. Even in West Germany, use of such methods expanded greatly by the end of the 1950s (Schmiede and Schudlich 1981, p. 359), and REFA was instrumental in its deployment. In the early 1960s, REFA was at the IE expansion stage, and had translated a US handbook into German (Billhardt 1962, p. 249). Upon publication of this translated *IE Handbook*, the first education course in this field was conducted using improved teaching methods (REFA-Nachrichten 1964, p. 186). However, by around 1960, the original industrial engineering training had been around for quite some time in Anglo-Saxon countries, and in West Germany the opportunity to receive training in the IE field was largely nonexistent apart from the efforts of several organizations like REFA (Bramesfeld 1960, pp. 1259–1260).

IE training began to significantly increase in the 1960s. The structure of training events fundamentally changed in 1969, with IE courses comprising 24.7% of all education courses (REFA-Nachrichten 1970, p. 77). In addition, the number of work study personnel trained in WF and MTM had risen to 2,491 by 1966 (Schmiede and Schudlich 1981, p. 360). There were a total of 52IE seminars by the mid-1973, and about half of the candidates who completed the course were in IE positions, with the remainder being managers responsible for production control or business management, heads of labor science departments, or their assistants (Pechhold 1974, pp. 219–220). Regarding IE materials and books, 1967 saw the publication of a companion volume to the *IE Handbook*, thereby completing the REFA standard works for engineer training. Further, as REFA's third original report, a magazine was published for work studies and IE managers (Pechhold 1974, p. 195), and from 1971 onward, *Industrial Engineering* was published as a bi-monthly magazine (Pechhold 1974, p. 233).

Responding to wages and cost pressures was an issue in the spread of IE in the mid-1950s when Germany was at full employment. Because of this issue, the predetermined time method was implemented primarily for labor efficiency (in job design). However, the overall spread of the predetermined time method was generally first considered successful during the downturn of 1966/67 and its subsequent easing of the tight labor market (Schmiede and Schudlich 1981, p. 369). We will now examine the deployment of WF and MTM in detail.

7.3.2 Deployment of Work Factor Method

WF deployment was accomplished with the cooperation of US corporations and through licensing methods. REFA assisted in the deployment and spread of predetermined time methods such as WF (Schmiede and Schudlich 1981, pp. 400–401). On February 1, 1958, REFA and the Work-Factor Company signed an agreement on implementing WF training courses in West Berlin and West Germany (*Siemens Archiv Akten*, 7882, Beurteilung und Einsatzmöglichkeit des Work-Factor-Verfahrens. Das Work-Factor-Verfahren als Hilfsmittel der Arbeitsgestaltug und der arbeitstechnischen Vorplanung, p. 9; Jaeckel 1961, p. 223). The Work- Factor Company was a technical consulting organization that provided global IE services to economic and industrial institutions (*Siemens Archiv Akten*, 16020, Aus Theorie und Praxis des Industrial Engineering in den USA, p. 91). After extensive research into number systems (MTM, WF, BMT, DMT, etc.), the REFA Institute for Labor Science became a licensee of the Work-Factor Company (Vgl. *Siemens Archiv Akten*, 16020, Aus Theorie und Praxis des Industrial Engineering in den USA, p. 20, Jaeckel 1961, p. 223). REFA also acquired the rights to translate the Work Factor Handbook and the rights to use the German translation which was based on the Dutch company, Philips. The second WF training course held in September 1958 was conducted by two people from Philips under contract with the Work-Factor Company, and Philips was heavily involved (*Siemens Archiv Akten*, 7882, Beurteilung und Einsatzmöglichkeit des Work-Factor-Verfahrens, p. 10). However, the situation changed greatly in the 1960s; by 1964, REFA instructors were using the original German training materials (Pechhold 1974, p. 193). Other corporations, such as AEG, Bosch, Siemens, and Olympia, acquired their own WF licenses, and deployed the American system (Schmiede and Schudlich 1981, p. 360).

At the beginning of the 1960s, as the productivity movement was drawing to a close, job design was becoming more important than standard time settings because of the rapid onset of mechanization (Deininger 1962, p. 146). REFA regarded WF as an appropriate tool for job design (*Siemens Archiv Akten*, 7882, Beurteilung und Einsatzmöglichkeit des Work-Factor-Verfahrens, p. 10), and the focus of its activities shifted increasingly away from predetermined time methods toward job design in the latter half of the 1950s. In this manner, the significance of motion study increased, and WF deployment also became more significant (Votsch 1962, p. 62).

7.3.3 Deployment of MTM

Study trips under the auspices of the US Technical Assistance Plan played an important role in the study and deployment of MTM, to which REFA also greatly contributed [Vgl. *Bundesarchiv koblenz*, B102/37261, Technische Akademie Bergische Land e.V.: TA-Studienreise nach USA auf dem Gebiet des MTM-Verfahrens (Methods Time

Measurement) (13.10.1952)]. Many of REFA's regional branches saw the possibility of providing information on US time study systems (Pechhold 1974, p. 125).

According to a source in 1963, MTM saw its greatest usage in the US but was also spreading in Germany (Witte 1963, p. 104), primarily being taught and spread by foreign consulting engineers. In comparison with WF, MTM had a more long-term, subdued role; however, in 1963, companies that had executed it formed the German MTM Association (*Siemens Archiv Akten*, 16020, Aus Theorie und Praxis des Industrial Engineering in den USA, p. 20). The greatest impediment to European worker productivity, other than the delay in mass production and large-scale lot production, was supposedly job design and work flow, which was far weaker than in the US. The German MTM Association accepted the US predetermined time method in 1964/65, adapted it to German circumstances, and disseminated it throughout Germany (Birn 1968, pp. 234, 236).

The German MTM Association's membership grew 2.6 times, from 115 corporations in 1966 to approximately 300 in 1973. The employees of these member companies more than quadrupled, from roughly 500,000 to 2,000,000. More than half of these member companies were in the precision equipment (30% in 1974) and metal processing (23% in 1974) industries, and other industries included clothing (14%), steel (4%), chemical (4%), service and banking (5%) industries (Vgl. Deutsche MTM Vereinigung 2002, p. 31; Mergner et al. 1974, pp. 175–176). In many cases, activities sponsored by organizations such as the German MTM Association were made possible with the cooperation of corporations and similar organizations in the US. The new US motion and time study methods were often implemented in Germany through private US companies (Schmiede and Schudlich 1981, p. 359).

7.3.4 Deployment of the Work Factor Method and MTM in Major Industrial Sectors

Looking next at major industrial sectors, IE methodologies were first deployed in various areas within mass production management, but the primary focus was the electrical and automotive industries. At Bosch, a transition to WF methods began in the mid-1950s, but in 1960 the decision was made to use MTM, and work councils and company management signed a shop agreement. MTM deployment had special priority in the production department, and was afterward expanded for the first time, though on a smaller scale, to the maintenance and control departments (Rau 1968, pp. 169–170). Daimler-Benz also used MTM from the 1960s onward. Although in retrospect, there were but a few cases of MTM being used at Daimler-Benz, in the German automotive industry in general or even in various departments within the electrical industry, MTM proved to be the best tool for job design and time economics (Arlt 1978, p. 143).

A 1965 IG Metall report states that WF, MTM, and other predetermined time methods were gaining popularity in the metals industry. For example, corporations in the steel industry were systematically moving toward the streamlining of maintenance and repair departments using predetermined time methods based on the deployment of wage incentive systems. The shipbuilding industry also increased its usage of predetermined time methods (IG Metall 1965, pp. 127–128). Deployment of predetermined time methods in maintenance tasks could also be seen in the chemical and mining industries (Vgl. Erdmann 1969, pp. 310–311). A 1969 report noted that usage of IE methods were not limited to the machinery or transportation equipment industries, but was spreading to steel and metals, clothing, construction, chemicals, and even service industries (Schlaich 1969b, p. 6). For example, MTM was being used in the sewing industry by the 1950s (Hopf 1979, p. 67), and all sorts of MTM-based data systems could be used to locate time data within the clothing and machinery industries (Hopf 1979, p. 72). To German industries, IE was an important element in creating satisfactory management results and competitive advantage (Schlaich 1969b, p. 7).

In the electrical industry, WF attracted attention at the end of the 1950s at Siemens as an aid to job design planners and production equipment designers, and both WF and MTM were the most well-known work study methods (*Siemens Archiv Akten*, 7882, Beurteilung und Einsatzmöglichkeit des Work-Factor-Verfahrens, pp. 1, 3, 9). Siemens implemented approximately 15 WF information education courses by 1962, and in addition to sponsoring many seminars for supervisors and specialists had roughly 100 WF-trained workers in their factories. The largest portion of these trained personnel worked in production preparation and work planning departments for large-lot and mass production. The Siemens Work Factor Group comprising nine members from three Siemens companies was formed, and the results of their work were tested and then conveyed to the REFA Institute, after which they could be adopted by any company that had WF-trained personnel (REFA-Nachrichten 1962, p. 257). An "IE Theory and Practice in the US"-themed study group participated in a US IE Institute international conference and a WF international conference, and visited Westinghouse, Bell and Howell, Teletype, and the Work-Factor Company. Siemens' WF instructors were instrumental in providing guidance in the preparation of Germany's public WF manual. By April 1964, a total of 615 people had participated in 35 WF training courses held in West Germany. Twelve of these courses were taught internally for Siemens' organizations, and Siemens had approximately 150 trained WF personnel. In two particular teacher training courses, there were 31 REFA instructors qualified to teach, of which eight were Siemens employees. At the time, 27 major corporations, such as Siemens, AEG, Olympia, and Zeiss, were formally using WF, and it was becoming clear that it would be necessary to adapt WF to the overall situation in Germany as well as to the special environment within Siemens. To that end, Siemens formed a team of specialists experienced in WF. This study group was conscious of the need to modify WF for a number of reasons, and they applied Siemens' scientific human engineering research not only to psychological effects but also to specific operations. This same group published a companion volume to the internal Siemens manual so that WF could be uniformly used across Siemens organizations (*Siemens Archiv Akten*, 16020, Aus Theorie und Praxis des Industrial Engineering in den

USA, pp. 20, 22), and a document explaining WF was created in 1970 [*Siemens Archiv Akten*, 8679, Daten für die Gestaltung von Arbeitsplätzen (April 1970), Work-Factor-System (WF), Einführung].

Within the chemical industry, Glanzstoff decided to deploy WF in the REFA Institute training courses, and both four-week basic and one-week information training courses were held [*Rheinisch-Westfälisches Wirtschaftsarchiv zu Köln*, Abt 195, F5-5, Betriebs-gebundene Work-Factor-Lehrgänge (15.5.1961)]. WF specialists from US consulting firms conducted practical work and research studies as part of the WF deployment. As a result of a detailed examination of both WF and MTM methods, Glanzstoff pressed ahead in using the WF method [*Rheinisch-Westfälisches Wirtschaftsarchiv zu Köln*, Abt 195, F5-5, Anwendung des Work-Factor-Verfahrens bei Glanzstoff (12.12.1961), pp. 1–5]. A 1962 document by Glanzstoff's rationalization department showed that predetermined time methods such as WF and MTM were excellent ways to make systematic improvements (*Rheinisch-Westfälisches Wirtschaftsarchiv zu Köln*, Abt 195, F5-5, Die Schrift der Rationalisierungsabteilung von 27.9.1962, p. 2). Time units of less than 1/1000 (0.06s) became the elements of work analysis through film and predetermined time methods (WF and MTM). This was one reason BASF chose to compare results from various time measurement devices using test film and high-speed camera photography, and to compare predetermined lengths of time as well (Lorenz 1962, p. 283). Deployment, however, varied by company, and Henckel, for example, used methods like IE to a very limited extent, even in the latter half of the 1960s (Hilger 2004, pp. 181–182).

With new methods such as IE, predetermined time methods were not negotiated between workers and those making time measurements as done in the REFA methods; instead, the usage and modifications of performance measurements were negotiated between management and work councils that represented workers, or between management and labor unions (Schmiede and Schudlich 1981, pp. 371–372). There was a great deal of opposition to certain aspects of the predetermined time method, but the fact that labor unions did not oppose them in principle made it much easier for corporations to implement (Schmiede and Schudlich 1981, p. 362).

7.3.5 Characteristics of Industrial Engineering Deployment in Germany

Next, let us look at characteristics of the German IE deployment. Within IE, American methods like WF and MTM were promoted based on REFA's strong involvement, along with the cooperation of the Work-Factor Company, the German MTM Association, consultants, and others. Between the late 1950s and the first half of the 1960s, US superiority in IE had greatly diminished compared with similar standard methods used in other progressive industrial nations (Hartmann 1963, p. 125).

However, REFA had traditionally played an important role in Germany since the rationalization movement of the 1920s. K. Schlaich notes that, from an operational perspective, it is only natural that the spread of IE is mainly attributed to REFA (Schlaich

1969a, p. 234). A 1960 Hämmerling report noted that there were certainly efforts to reduce production times through a partial adoption of new methods such as MTM and WF based on US practice, but these methods would not have succeeded without their incorporation into REFA's methods (Hämmerling 1960, p. 127). A 1975 Schwartzman report noted that the German industry had built work studies based on REFA thinking over the last several decades (Schwartmann 1975, p. 205). Thus, we see that the dissemination of IE was related to REFA activities, and was also greatly affected by US-based IE.

REFA had researched and examined various predetermined time methods including MTM and WF for a long time, and as a result decided to support WF, obtaining a license to use and disseminate the method (REFA-Nachrichten 1961, p. 223; Pilz 1961, p. 124). However, REFA did not, for the most part, deprioritize its own systems in promoting WF. As a result, these US methods were not widely adopted in German industry, unlike countries such as Sweden, where the creator of MTM, H.B. Maynard and his consulting firm, were highly successful in selling the method to corporations (Kipping 2004, p. 36).

Procuring training and deployment routes for IE methodologies, like the agreement with Work-Factor Company or the use of consulting firms, provided characteristically greater opportunities for the deployment of American-style methods, unlike other management methods. An additional important characteristic was that German organizations played a major part, as can be seen in the efforts and roles of REFA and the German MTM Association. However, the deployment and dissemination of American-style methods continued with the help of REFA's leadership in work studies and their activities in the 1920s, along with the attempts to apply these methods to German circumstances under REFA's strong influence.

7.4 German Rollout of the Ford System and German Manufacturing

Next, let us look at the issues of production system innovation via deployment of the Ford system and German-style manufacturing. The US form of mass production was new to Europe in the 1950s (Schröter 2005, p. 71). In the automotive industry, which was the most pivotal, until the 1940s, the types of production organizations were definitively regulated by the markets it supplied. It has been noted that as long as that was the case, Americanism would only spread on a selective basis (Vgl. Braun 1995, pp. 67–68). In contrast, postwar market changes brought mass motorization, which enabled full-scale deployment of the Ford system.

7.4.1 General Conditions in the Postwar Deployment of the Ford System

First, let us examine the overall circumstances at the time of the Ford system deployment. Deployment occurred in processing and assembly industries such as the automotive and electrical industries (but particularly in final assembly of primary product lines such as radios, televisions, vacuum cleaners, washing machines, dishwashers, and electric ranges) (Wittke 1996, p. 153). In 1953, there were very few production fields that could economically use production lines based on American-style methods because of changes to product and component design and structure as well as fluctuations in production volume (Steeger 1953, p. 197). A 1956 report mentioned that flow production was still in its initial stages (Mennecke 1956, p. 45), but this situation changed in a major way in the latter half of the 1950s. For example, a 1958 report noted that the principles of flow production had become much more widespread and had completely eliminated the principle of organization by machine type (Lauke 1956, p. 41; Lauke 1958, p. 79). Springer also stated in 1963 that the need for rationalization increasingly led to production via work flow in manufacturing industries (Springer 1963, p. 769).

The automotive industry was the most typical sector in which American-style methods were deployed, and the end of the 1950s saw a continuous transition away from smaller cars toward mid-sized vehicles in Germany (Der Volkswirt 1959, p. 2133). The deployment of the Ford system was a response to this trend, and the industry-wide switch to Fordism accelerated during the last third of the 1950s (Wellhöner 1996, p. 16). One focus of the automotive industry effort to rationalize in the 1950s and 1960s was a large-scale production revolution using conveyor belt technology in the body production, unit assembly, and final assembly departments (Vgl. Kern and Schumann 1984, p. 40). For example, according to a 1963 report, in many cases manual work dominated assembly, despite the high standards already being achieved by machines and automation in cutting and machining of processed parts (Goos 1963, p. 152). Thus, the rollout of the flow production system and its synchronization of overall assembly processes were particularly meaningful.

7.4.2 Deployment of the Ford System and Rollout of Mass Production Systems in the Automotive Industry

Here, we will review case studies of corporations in the automotive industry. These corporations are prime examples in which Ford system deployment was most dominant.

Volkswagen: Volkswagen was the trendsetter in accepting Ford production methods and in the formation of corresponding labor relations (Vgl. Wellhöner 1996; Kapitel 3; Klenke 1996, p. 219; Abelshauser 2005, pp. 98–102). In 1946, immediately after the war ended, a number of assembly and final assembly conveyors were already in operation for transmissions, axles, and engines, producing approximately 1,000–1,200 automobiles per month (Automobiltechnische Zeitschrift 1946, p. 45). After 1954, Volkswagen worked on technical reshuffling, one objective being the creation of an external force for the work rhythm using Takt time (effective working time in a period/demand in a period) of machines and conveyors. The time required for each process was calculated and set as a standard time for workers. This technical reshuffling in the Wolfsburg plant forced the labor organization to adapt from the outset and fall in line with the US model (Wellhöner 1996, pp. 116–117). The conveyor assembly line that began operating in 1946 produced only one model, the Beetle, and by the beginning of the 1960s, a perfect flow had been built for coordinated mass production (Tolliday 1995, p. 328). In the summer of 1961, two new assembly conveyors were completed that allowed Volkswagen to produce 250,000 VW1500 vehicles per year (D.W.I.-Berichte 1961, p. 19).

In the new delivery van factory operating in Hanover in 1956, final assembly used a conveyor belt as well. Production was organized by deploying many new mechanized or partially automated routings to individual lines that fed the final assembly. Assembly using fully mechanized conveyor belts was typical, and the widespread use of conveyor belts was characteristic of the production technology of this plant. Body production conveyors were synchronized with body panel production, and these production methods reduced work time by 25% compared with stationary assembly (Automobiltechnische Zeitschrift 1957, pp. 116–117).

For the deployment of special-purpose machinery and automation technology, which was important in the expansion of Ford system type mass production methods, H. Nordhoff sought a "perfect new direction" by the spring of 1954. Automation of body frame production as well as painting and plating areas was already well underway. In contrast, press plants and machining departments were striving to gradually eliminate or drastically reduce manual work (Edelmann 2003, p. 184). In 1955, automation efforts expanded, and the company made large investments in special-purpose machine tools and general automation as they replaced old multipurpose tools. The company's continuous flow production was developed by connecting the stages of individual routings through the transfer machines of many work spaces. In all cases where planning of the production volume without frequent design and structure coordination was possible, multipurpose machinery was replaced by flexible special-purpose machinery. This type of automation was deployed early on in the production of the Beetle economy car (Abelshauser 1995, p. 284).

Technical aspects of Volkswagen's automation concentrated on two aspects: combining individual processing stages using production lines and more powerful use of special-purpose machinery (Wellhöner 1996, p. 113). However, by the end of the 1950s, despite Volkswagen possessing the most modern equipment among West German corporations (Vgl. Eberhorst 1959, p. 7), manufacturing processes were automated very cautiously until the company was sure that markets could absorb the production increases that the additional automation enabled. This kind of corporate behavior resulted from operating in product markets and factor supply conditions that were clearly different from those of the US (Zeitlin 2000, p. 37). However, the 1960s saw a more intense expansion in the automotive market, and a full-scale deployment of American-style automation technology was attempted. For example, the 1963 annual report of the "Purchasing and Materials Management Department" for the board of directors mentioned the approval of many orders for presses, equipment, and transfer machines in the Kasel and Hanover plants (*Volkswagen Archiv*,

Z174/Nr.2366, Jahresbericht 1963 des Vorstandsbericht "Einkauf und Materialverwaltung"). In 1964 at the Wolfsburg plant, new transfer machines for automated assembly of the 1200 and 1300 Beetles were in operation (Seherr-Thoss 1979, p. 476).

In the deployment of these kinds of production technology innovations within Volkswagen, Kleinschmidt maintains that with the exception of companies such as Ford and Opel, Volkswagen is the only German automotive manufacturer capable of putting the American model to use over the course of decades. Volkswagen became strongly aligned with the American model, particularly Ford's River Rouge plant, and in the 1950s, the US played a decisive role in Volkswagen's success (Kleinschmidt 2004b, pp. 75–76).

In reality however, one secret of Volkswagen's success was their selective approach to the American model. While Volkswagen followed the US expansion, they used specialized know-how such as highly mechanized proprietary transfer machines for body assembly, and could thus relax their very strict alignment with US development (Kleinschmidt 2004b, pp. 82, 88–89). One way Volkswagen pursued a German approach to production technology innovation was to replace the US style of automation called "Detroit automation," which impeded flexible production methods, with one adapted to German circumstances. As a follower, Volkswagen was able to learn from others' mistakes and avoid the difficulties first-moves had experienced in the automation process. In this manner, a new type of typical German Fordism was born, enabling Volkswagen to survive the decline of the 1970s through this application of American methods to German circumstances. The essence of this method could be seen in the diverse, high quality production that dominated the country in concert with German-style labor relations that were critical to codetermination. This system of harmonious labor relations based on labor resource cooperation in distributing shop floor power between labor and management is said to reflect the essential elements of a classic paradigm of highly skilled labor that values technical precision (Abelshauser 2003, pp. 130–133; Abelshauser 2004, pp. 376–377; Abelshauser 2005, pp. 100–102).

Opel: K40, Opel's new, large scale body and assembly plants were in full operation by August 1956, and the company was working on production system innovations. Two basic chassis types, for 1.5- and 2.5-l engine vehicles, were separately assembled on two conveyors within body assembly, and these merged onto one conveyor to produce white bodies. After undercoating, painting, and interior installation, completed bodies were sent via conveyor to final assembly, where engines and chassis also moved on conveyors. Two thirds of the main assembly conveyors comprised overhead chain conveyors whose height could be adjusted based on the work being performed (Automobiltechnische Zeitschrift 1956, p. 351). A 1957 report mentions that only one 6,500m long main conveyor remained in the Rüsselsheim plant for body manufacturing, where all six types of vehicles were produced. Production using large belt conveyors can be performed in two ways: continuous production using larger volumes of the same model or a mixed production environment for all models based on the assembly plan. Opel chose the latter method because of long work times that varied by model, and also because they could effectively use tools set up along the conveyor belt (Faensen 1957, p. 1425). The combined length of the plant's conveyor belts and assembly conveyors amounted to 28,000m. To manage the assembly of all models other than trucks on the same conveyor, a teletype system was created, making the plant one of the world's most modern automotive plants (Der Volkswirt 1957, p. 1274; Seherr-Thoss 1979, p. 443).

The Bochum plant began production in 1962. The Number 2 plant produced engines and chassis parts, with engine assembly being done using conveyors as well. The Number 1 plant produced bodies and performed final assembly using overheard chain conveyors, assembly conveyors, and other transportation equipment that totaled 31km in length over 227 pieces of equipment. The length of conveyor belts and assembly conveyors in the Number 2 plant was 11km. Bodies, pre-assembled chassis units, and engines converged on final assembly conveyors (Automobiltechnische Zeitschrift 1962, pp. 343–345; Stahl und Eisen 1962, p. 805).

Opel primarily manufactured small cars and economy vehicles, and they put great effort into deploying the Ford system. In 1962, Opel noted that conveyor belts were being used for mass production, with one automobile rolling off the line every 50s (Adam Opel 1962, p. 73).

In reviewing the deployment of special-purpose machinery and automation technology, we see that transfer machines and other automation equipment were implemented for crankshaft production in machining departments in the mid-1950s [*Mercedes-Benz Archiv*, Könecke 122, Transferstraβe für 4-Zyl.-Kurbelwelle für die Fa. Opel (5.7.1954)]. According to one source in 1956, a characteristic of this period's production was the addition to the work flow of numerous pieces of equipment that could also monitor and control the work, rather than simply automating it (Hilf 1956, p. 5). At the end of 1958, a new, large investment project was begun, and the pace of investment accelerated (Der Volkswirt 1960, p. 1852). Around this time, Opel began using cylinder piston lines along with many general transfer machines, a phenomenon unique to this plant (*Bundesarchiv Koblenz*, B149/5697, Untersuchung sozialer Auswirkungen des technischen Fortschrittes, p. 1).

The Rüsselsheim plant began production using new equipment for engines and transmissions in August 1961. At the time, the plant had 55 transfer machines, 70 multi-axis lathes, and 1,175 individual pieces of machine tools (Seherr-Thoss 1979, p. 464). In 1962, the Bochum plant began production of engines, transmissions, axles, cardan shafts, and other components using 1,147 individual machine tools. The standard of technology was high, with much of the equipment being the 47 transfer machines used to process cylinder blocks, crankshafts, connecting rods, gearboxes, and the like (Automobiltechnische Zeitschrift 1962, pp. 343–344; Stahl und Eisen 1962, p. 805). Opel also stated in their 1962 corporate history that they had begun using transfer machines to automatically transport all work-in-process inventory (Adam Opel 1962, pp. 77, 83–84).

When transferring production systems to a subsidiary of an American company, as was the case with Opel and Ford, it was sometimes necessary to know and understand subsidiary production system dynamics not present in the parent company. Even in cases where the subsidiary was most receptive, this transfer required innovation and flexibility (Tolliday 2000, p. 78). This issue also relates to the adaptation of methodologies to the conditions in postwar Germany. There was sometimes a huge gap between the potential power of GM and Ford's methods and the ability to effectively apply them. In Germany, Volkswagen serves as the best example of the selective and skillful application of the American experience in the European context (Tolliday 2000, p. 117).

Daimler-Benz: In 1950, Daimler-Benz had begun work on production lines for the 220 and 300 model automobiles. The 220 model was produced using conveyor belts beginning in the fall of 1951, and the 300 model moved to mass production, although slowly at first, beginning in November 1951 (Hiller 1952, p. 26). After the war, the Sindelfingen plant began final assembly work in addition to body production (Mercedes-Benz 1990, p. 100; Feldenkirchen 2004, p. 179). In the fiscal year 1957, the company invested in production methods that would lower costs (Daimler-Benz 1957, p. 25) and worked on improving production methods for mass production along with complete process modernization.

However, even in the first half of the 1960s, there was a serious gap in productivity between Daimler-Benz and US corporations. In the US, Ford produced a maximum of 2,500 cars per day, while Daimler-Benz required 17 manufacturing hours to assemble even the smallest passenger car. The high production capacity of US factories was due to the complete mechanization of transportation using conveyors and conveyor belts. One important way to create economies of scale was the response by standardization based on "unit system" principles that enabled both model variety and economically profitable volumes. Daimler-Benz implemented standardized mass production by using the unit system and cutting back on certain models in both the passenger and commercial vehicle departments (Vgl. Hilger 2004, pp. 175, 177).

The applicability of standardized production factors based on unit system principles and the integration work that increases their applicability were very important. In Daimler's case, when considering production methods from a work organization perspective, it appeared to be nothing more than an organized flow of work as would be found in the US. However, the skills within the key production elements between design and production were significant. Thus, emphasis was placed on the development of high quality production that encompassed labor process flexibility based on Daimler-Benz's reliance on skilled labor.

In examining the deployment of special-purpose machinery and automation, an August 1958 survey noted that production volumes were low at the Untertürkheim plant, and that its equipment were far from meeting the highest standards of modernization (*Bundesarchiv Koblenz*, B149/5697, Untersuchung sozialer Auswirkungen des technischen Fortschrittes, p. 1). An annual report on that plant in 1959 reported that there were limits to further automation for larger-scale production because of the diverse models being produced (*Mercedes-Benz Archiv*, Daimler-Benz AG, Jahresbericht 1959 des Werkes Stuttgart-Untertürkheim,

p. 3). This factor alone demonstrates that standardization critical in deploying the latest technology, and in the 1960s it became an even more important issue. Deployment of automation technology began in earnest in the 1960s at Daimler-Benz. For example, the increase in transfer machines in the Untertürkheim plant numbered 4 in 1961, 13 in 1962, 1 in 1963, 7 in 1965, 1 in 1966, 10 in 1967, and 5 in 1970. The deployment scope was not limited to engine production, but expanded to axles, transmissions, oil pans, bracing tubes, and other systems (*Mercedes-Benz Archiv*, Daimler-Benz AG, Jahresbericht 1961 des Werkes Stuttgart-Untertürkheim, pp. 40–41, Jahresbericht 1962 des Werkes Stuttgart-Untertürkheim, p. 35, Jahresbericht 1963 des Werkes Stuttgart-Untertürkheim, p. 34, Jahresbericht 1965 des Werkes Stuttgart-Untertürkheim, p. 35, Jahresbericht 1966 des Werkes Stuttgart-Untertürkheim, p. 33, Jahresbericht 1967 des Werkes Stuttgart-Untertürkheim, p. 34, Jahresbericht 1970 des Werkes Stuttgart-Untertürkheim, p. 38). An annual report on the Untertürkheim plant listed machines and their years of use, but reports after 1959 provided a simple average of machines by year of purchase and did not accurately reflect the aging of equipment because of the deployment of special-purpose machinery and the increase of high-performance transfer machines for many machining processes (*Mercedes-Benz Archiv*, Daimler-Benz AG, Jahresbericht 1959 des Werkes Stuttgart-Untertürkheim, p. 28, Jahresbericht 1962 des Werkes Stuttgart-Untertürkheim, p. 36, Jahresbericht 1965 des Werkes Stuttgart-Untertürkheim, p. 36).

Corporations such as Daimler-Benz that were pursuing a product strategy emphasizing upper-class market segments sought a German production model while deploying American-style mass production technologies and systems. Specifically, to ensure high quality and to differentiate themselves in the marketplace, Daimler-Benz relied on high quality, skilled labor that complemented the standards created by technical equipment, and integration of production factors within the unit system as they rolled out a system for diverse, high-quality production. In this context, it could be said that they chose to Germanize the model in a different way than did Volkswagen.

7.4.3 The Rollout of Mass Production Systems and German Manufacturing

As these examples demonstrate, postwar Germany's deployment of mass production systems such as the Ford system centered on typical volume production industries like the automotive and electrical industries. Overall, changes in production during the 1950s were not simply a "rebuilding" of the prewar state, as they also became more flexible and dynamic. It has been stated before that rationalization along the lines of Taylor Ford using an American-style mass production model was integrated with the management climate of the 1950s and modified based on collective experience (Radkau 1993, p. 139). On this point, Ambrosius identifies two important factors in the failure of the Taylor Ford model of rationalization in quickly spreading in 1950s West Germany: consumer goods production at the time was merely of supplementary significance and German managers had a traditionally skeptical attitude toward American-style Fordism. This not only has to do with the issue of the wide-scale management units necessary to roll out this type of rationalization model, but is also related to the "Made in Germany" brand, combined with flexible labor- and knowledge-intensive production methods instead of globally standardized mass production (Ambrosius 1993, pp. 117–118).

Mass production did progress in Germany during the 1950s and 1960s, but even there it was limited to two types of companies. First are companies like Volkswagen with a corporate policy of producing affordable cars for their broad customer base that pursue economies of scale through American-style mass production (Der Volkswirt 1969, p. 55). In contrast, companies that had developed management and product strategies, which prioritized high-end market segments with outstanding quality and technology and considered the relatively low-price elasticity of upper segments in the market, occupied an important position but applied a different strategy (Vgl. Schmidt 1993, p. 94). Companies like Daimler-Benz and BMW in particular implemented strategies to design products targeting market segments with high quality, value-added products based on a relatively long-term model policy. From the manufacturer's perspective, their product design concepts were based on their users' functional needs of quality and durability, which were different from the needs of US consumers.

For example, in the 1950s, Daimler-Benz had a corporate philosophy anchored in two production concepts: manufacturing vehicles with a utility value created in response to the demands for uniqueness and luxury, and a broad and comprehensive supply for commercial vehicles. This philosophy proved highly successful (Sörgel 1986, p. 16). Such product and production concepts are related to the production model. According to W. Streeck, there were two types of auto manufacturers in postwar West Germany: mass production manufacturers in the north (Volkswagen, Ford, and Opel) and luxury car manufacturers, a remnant of craft production, in the south (BMW, Daimler-Benz, and their competitors). These regional differences developed in response to differences in manufacturing principles and philosophies. Southern manufacturers had technical creativity and were engineering perfectionists (Streeck 1989, p. 119). For these manufacturers, specializing in these particular market segments with a value-add strategy of high quality and high performance meant that there was little necessity for cost superiority through economies of scale (Kazama 1997, p. 69). Strategies for product design concepts and market positioning greatly influenced the important characteristics of quality and flexible production concept, an inherently German characteristic.

This focus on "quality and a flexible production concept" could be seen in prewar Germany as one method of production responding to market limits (Vgl. Stahlmann 1993). The basic principles of this same production concept could also be seen in postwar Germany. That is, one can identify German characteristics in production methods and systems based on product design concepts, such as avoiding price competition, positioning, and specific niche strategies in postwar international market expansion. Even though work organization itself was a flow production system that may have been founded on a US model and although these corporations pursued economies of scale in mass production, the elements of high quality, knowledge-intensive production relying on skilled labor, and German-specific systems of vocational education and specialist qualifications, such as the meister system, were quite significant. Germany had a production system based on technical qualifications and vocational education, and production management work in corporations was dominated by skilled engineers. Thus, the skill level of production managers was very high. This was an important factor in the superiority of the design, development, production, and quality of German products (Lawrence 1980, pp. 131, 140–141, 150, 187, 190). In Germany's case, quality in the form of product functionality, durability, dependability, and safety was heavily emphasized, as was reliance on expert, skilled labor in certain jobs. This model differs from Japan's, where integration emphasizing operational capability was a major source of competitive advantage (Fujimoto 2004, Chap. 5). The distinct characteristics of German-style manufacturing can be seen in production, which reflected product design concepts emphasizing quality, function, and branding against the background of the European market's competitiveness and factors of competitive advantage.

In this context, despite the common perception of "Americanization," important aspects of German characteristics in German production and manufacturing can be observed in the midst of the postwar American influence. However, these characteristics are deeply rooted in market structures and differed with those of the US, which had a highly standardized market. Because this phenomenon was born of the uniquely German and European market emphasis on quality and function, it is important to understand that the German production and manufacturing model was a rational adaptation to the nature of these markets.

References

Abelshauser W (1995) Two kinds of fordism: on the differing roles of the industry in the development to the two German states. In: Shiomi H, Wada K (eds) Fordism transformed. The development of production methods in the automobile industry. Oxford University Press, New York, pp 269–296

Abelshauser W (2003) Kulturkamp. Der deutsche Weg in die neue Wirtschaft und die amerikanische Herausforderung. Kulturverlag Kadmos, Berlin

Abelshauser W (2004) Deutsche Wirtschaftsgeschichte seit 1945. C. H. Beck, München

Abelshauser W (2005) The dynamics of German industry. Berghahn Books, New York

Adam Opel AG (ed) (1962) ...auch das ist Opel. Adam Opel AG, Rüsselsheim

Albert M (2001) Capitalisme contre Capitalisme. Ed. du Seuil, Paris

Ambrosius G (1993) Wirtschaftlicher Strukturwandel und Technikentwicklung. In: Schildt A, Sywottek A (eds) Modernisierung im Wiederaufbau. Die westdeutsche Gesellschaft der 50er Jahre. Die westdeutsche Gesellschaft der 50er Jahre. Dietz, Bonn, pp 107–128

Arlt J (1978) Erfahrungen und Tendenzen bei der MTM-Anwendung. Ein Bericht aus der Automobilindustrie. REFA-Nachrichten 31(3):143–147

Automobiltechnische Zeitschrift (1946) Das Volkswagenwerk. Automobiltechnische Zeitschrift 48(3):45

Automobiltechnische Zeitschrift (1956) Das neue Opel-Werk K-40,2000000 Opelwagen. Automobiltechnische Zeitschrift 58(12):351

Automobiltechnische Zeitschrift (1957) Bildbericht vom VW-Transporter-Werk Hannover. Automobiltechnische Zeitschrift 59(4):116–117
Automobiltechnische Zeitschrift (1962) Das neue Opelwerk in Bochum. Automobiltechnische Zeitschrift 64(11):343–345
Billhardt H (1962) Der Arbeitsablauf als Ansatzpunkte zur Rationalisierung. REFA-Nachrichten 15(6):249–254
Birn SA (1968) Ein Amerikaner sieht Europas Wirtschaft. Wichtigstes Problem: Mangel an Rationalisierungsfachleuten. Der Arbeitgeber 20(9):234–236
Bramesfeld E (1960) Arbeitswissenschaft und Betrieb. Stahl und Eisen 80(19):1257–1261
Bramesfeld E, Herwig B, Honnacker A et al (1956) Human relations in industrie. Die menschlichen Beziehungen in der Industrie. Beobachtungen einer deutschen Studiengruppe in USA (RKW-Auslandsdienst, Heft 41). C. Hanser, München
Braun HJ (1995) Automobilfertigung in Deutschland von den Anfängen bis zu den vierziger Jahren. In: Niemann H, Hermann A (eds) Die Entwicklung der Motorisierung im Deutschen Reich und den Nachfolgestaaten. Stuttgarter Tage zur Automobil- und Unternehmensgeschichte. Franz Steiner, Stuttgart, pp 58–68
Bundesvereinigung der Deutschen Arbeitgeberverbände (1957) Jahresbericht. BDA, Köln
Daimler-Benz AG (1957) Geschäftsbericht über das Geschäftsjahr 1957. Daimler-Benz AG, Stuttgart
Deininger (1962) Arbeitsstudium als Rationalisierungshilfe. Rationalisierung 13(6):146–147
Der Arbeitgeber (1950) „Human Relations“ in der deutschen Wirtschaft. Der Arbeitgeber 10:12–13
Der Volkswirt (1957) Opel in stetiger Entwicklung. 12 (13) vH Dividende. Der Volkswirt 11(25):1273–1275
Der Volkswirt (1959) Riskovolle Kleinwagenproduktion. Der Volkswirt 13(38):2133
Der Volkswirt (1960) Hohe Gewinn bei Opel. Steiler Investitionsanstieg—200 (125) Mill. DM Dividende. Der Volkswirt 14(33):1851–1853
Der Volkswirt (1969) Hauptversammlungs-Ansprache des Herrn Dr. Kurt Lotz, Vorsitzender des Vorstandes der Volkswagen AG, in der Hauptversammlung 1969. Der Volkswirt 23(28):54–57
Deutsche MTM Vereinigung e.V. (ed) (2002) MTM—Von Anfang an richtig. Deutsche MTM Vereinigung, Hamburug
D.W.I.-Berichte (1961) Die westdeutsche Automobilindustrie und die Entwicklung auf dem internationalen kapitalistischen Automobilmarkt. DWI-Berichte 12(22):13–19
Eberhorst E v (1959) Fortschritt im deutschen Kraftfahrzeugbau. Der Volkswirt, 13. Jg, Technische Fachbeilage zu Nr. 38 vom 19. September 1959, Wirtschaft und Technik, Kraftfahrzeug am deutschen Markt, pp 6–7
Edelmann H (2003) Heinz Nordhoff und Volkswagen. Ein deutscher Unternehmer im amerikanischen Jahrhundert. Vandenhoeck & Ruprecht, Göttingen
Erdmann W (1969) Möglichkeiten und Grenzen der Zeitvorgabe bei Instandhaltungsarbeiten. Bericht über Ergebnisse eines RKW-Unterschungsprojektes. REFA-Nachrichten 22(5): 309–318
Ewatari S (1954) Romu Kanri no Kindaika ni Tsuite (Modernization of personnel management). In: Noda N, Mori G (eds) Romu Kanri Kindaika no Jitsurei (Cases of modernization of personnel management). Daiyamondosha, Tokyo, pp 15–26
Faensen HH (1957) Lochkarten und Fernshreiber als Arbeitsvorbereitung. Beispiel der Adam Opel AG, Rüsselsheim. Der Volkswirt 11(27):1425–1427
Feldenkirchen W (2004) DaimlerChrysler Werk Untertürkheim. Motorbuch-Verlag, Stuttgart
Free J (1955) Maschinenbau und Rationalisierung. In: Brandt L, Frenz G (eds) Industrielle Rationalisierung 1955. Verkehrs- und Wirtschaft-Verlag, Dortmund, pp 67–70
Fujimoto T (1997) Seisan Sisutemu no Sinka Ron (Evolution of production system). Yuhikaku, Tokyo
Fujimoto T (2004) Nihon no Monodukuri Tetsugaku (Japanese philosophy of manufacturing). Nihon Keizai Shinbunsha, Tokyo
Goos G (1963) Spezielle Fertigungsfragen im Kraftfahrzeugbau. Werkstatt und Betrieb 96(3):151–152

Hall PA, Soskice D (eds) (2001) Varieties of capitalism: the institutional foundations of comparative advantage. Oxford University Press, Oxford
Hämmerling F (1960) Die Mechanisierung von Montagen in der Elektroindustrie. In: Brandt L, Gardellini R, King A et al (eds) Industrielle Rationalisierung 1960. Verkehrs- und Wirtschafts-Verlag, Dortmund
Hartmann H (1959) Authority and organization in German management. Princeton University Press, Princeton
Hartmann H (1963) Amerikanische Firmen in Deutschland. Westdeutscher Verlag, Köln
Hasegawa H (1960) Nihon no Hyuman Rireishonzu (Human relations in Japan). Otsuki Shoten, Tokyo
Hibi S (1975) Seisan Kanri Ron (Production management). Dobunkan Shuppan, Tokyo
Hilf HH (1956) Arbeitswissenschaftliche Beobachtungen in USA. Rationalisierung 7(1):3–8
Hilger S (2004) „Amerikanisierung" deutscher Unternehmen. Wettbewerbsstrategien und Unternehmenspolitik bei Henkel, Siemens und Daimler-Benz (1945/49-1975). Franz Steiner Verlag, Stuttagart
Hiller H (1952) Alteste Automobilfabrik der Welt. Der einzigartige Wiederaufstieg der Daimler-Benz-Werke. Der Volkswirt 6(9):25–28
Hopf H (1979) Die Anwendung von MTM-Analysiersystemen in der Bekleidungs- und Maschinenindustrie. REFA-Nachrichten 32(2):67–73
IG Metall (1965) Geschäftsbericht 1962, 1963 und 1964 des Vorstandes der Industriegewerkschaft Metall für die Bundesrepublik Deutschland. IG Metall, Frankfurt am Main
Inoue H (1976) Nihon ni okeru IE no Tenkai to Mujyun (Development and contradictions of IE in Japan). Gijyutu to Ningen (Technol Human Beings) 6:26–34
Jaeckel B (1961) 10 Jahre REFA-Bundesverband. REFA-Nachrichten 14(6):221–226
Jyuji S (1969) Futatsu no Sinro wo Toru Korekarano IE (Further IE that will take two paths). IE 11(3):205
Kauders M (1960) Westdeutsche Werkzeitungen und ihre Rolle als Instrument zur Verarbeitung der „Human Relations" in den Monopolbetrieben nach 1945. Jahrbuch für Wirtschaftsgeschichte 1960, II:9–46
Kazama N (1997) Doitsuteki Seisan Moderu to Furekisibiriti (German production model and flexibility). Chuo Keizaisha, Tokyo
Kern H, Schumann M (1984) Das Ende der Arbeitsteilung? Rationalisierung in der industriellen Produkution: Bestandnahme, Trendbestimmung. C. H. Beck, München
Kipping K (2004) 'Importing' American ideas to West Germany, 1940s to 1970s. From associations to private consultancies. In: Kudo A, Kipping M, Schröteret HG (eds) German and Japanese business in the boom years. Transforming American management and technology models. Routledge, London, pp 30–53
Kirchner J-H (1970) Förderung der Produktivität in Mittel- und Kleinbetrieben durch das Arbeitsstudium. REFA-Nachrichten 23(6):440
Kleinschmidt C (2002) Der produktive Blick. Wahrnehmung amerikanischer und japanischer Management- und Produktionsmethoden durch deutsche Unternehmer 1950–1985. Akademie Verlag, Berlin
Kleinschmidt C (2004a) America and the resurgence of the German chemical and rubber industry after the Second World War. Hüls, Glanzstoff and Continental. In: Kudo A, Kipping M, Schröter HG (eds) German and Japanese business in the boom years. Transforming American management and technology models. Routledge, London, pp 161–174
Kleinschmidt C (2004b) Driving the West German consumer society: the introduction of US style production and marketing at Volkswagen, 1945–70. In: Kudo A, Kipping M, Schröter HG (eds) German and Japanese business in the boom year. Transforming American management and technology models. Routledge, London, pp 75–92
Klenke D (1996) „Wirtschaftswunder"—Weltmarkt—Westdeutscher Fordismus von V. Wellhöner. Zeitschrift für Unternehmensgeschichte 41:219–220
Kothe E (1948) Sind Arbeitsstudien noch zeitgemäβ? Werkstatt und Betrieb 81:10–11

Lauke (1956) Für und wider die Fließarbeit. Rückblick und Ausblick. REFA-Nachrichten 9(2):41–46
Lauke (1958) Tendenzen in der Weiterentwicklung des Flußprinzips. REFA-Nachrichten 11(3):79
Lawrence P (1980) Managers and management in West Germany. Croom Helm, London
Lorenz FR (1962) Zur Frage der Erfassung kurzer Zeiten bei Arbeits- und Zeitstudien. Werkstatt und Betrieb 95(5):283–287
Mennecke K (1956) Fließende Fertigung durch Stetigförderer. Der Volkswirt 10(3):45–46
Mercedes-Benz AG (1990) Werk Sindelfingen. Karosserie- und Montagewerk der Mercedes-Benz Aktiengesellschaft. Ein historischer Überblick. Mercedes-Benz AG, Sindelfingen
Mergner U, Osterland M, Pelte K (1974) Die Entwicklung ausgewählter Arbeitsbedingungen in der BRD. Soziologisches Forschungsinstitut Göttingen, Göttingen
Nakamura S (1958) Nihon Seisansei Kojyo Undoshi (History of the productivity movement in Japan). Keiso Shobo, Tokyo
Neugebauer A (1997) Etablierung der Sachzwänge. Werkzeitschrift und soziale Wirklichkeit nach dem Zweiten Weltkrieg. In: Heyl B, Neugebauer A (eds) » ... ohne Rücksicht auf die Verhältniss «. Opel zwischen Weltwirtschaftkrise und Wiederaufbau. Brandes & Aspel, Frankfurt am Main, pp 195–216
Noguchi T (1968) Seisan Kanri no Keieigaku (Business administration of production management). Zeimu Keiri Kyokai, Tokyo
Noguchi T, Ishizaka I, Sekiguchi M et al (1965) Keiei Kanri Souron (An introduction to business management). Chuo Keizaisha, Tokyo
Obst P (1970) Das „Harzburger Modell" in organisatorischer Sicht. Zeitschrift für Organisation 39(2):80–82
Osikawa I, Takagi K (1959) Yoroppa Seisansei Tsushin (European productivity report). Nhion Seisansei Honbu, Tokyo
Pavel K-H (1957) Formen und Methoden der Rationalisierung. Verlag die Wirtschaft, Berlin
Pechhold E (1956) Weitere Ergebnisse der IfO-Erhebung über die Verbreitung des Arbeitsstudiums. REFA-Nachrichten 9(4):147
Pechhold E (1974) 50 Jahre REFA. Beuth, Berlin
Pilz HE (1961) Die Einführung des Work-Factor-System in Deutschland. REFA-Nachrichten 14(4):124–125
Pirker T, Braun S, Lutz B et al (1955) Arbeiter Management Mitbestimmung. Ein industriesoziologische Untersuchung der Struktur, der Organisation und des Verhaltens der Arbeiterbelegschaften in Werken der deutschen Eisen- und Stahlindustrie, für das Mitbestimmungsgesetz gilt. Ring-Verlag, Stuttgart
Radkau R (1993) „Wirtschaftswunder" ohne technologische Innovation? Technische Modernität in den 50er Jahren. In: Schildt A, Sywottek A (eds) Modernisierung im Wiederaufbau. Die westdeutsche Gesellschaft der 50er Jahre. Dietz, Bonn, pp 129–154
Rau R (1968) Die Anwendung von MTM in einem Unternehmen der deutschen Kraftfahrzeug-Zubehör-Industrie. In: Pornschlegel H (ed) Verfahren vorbestimmter Zeiten. Bund-Verlag, Köln, pp 168–176
REFA-Nachrichten (1956) Die Verbreitung des Arbeitsstudiums und die Bedeutung der REFA-Arbeit in Zahlen. REFA-Nachrichten 9(3):91–94
REFA-Nachrichten (1961) 10 Jahre REFA-Bundesverband. Die Entwicklung von 1951 bis 1961. REFA-Nachrichten 14(6):221–226
REFA-Nachrichten (1962) Rationalisierung durch vorbestimmte Zeit. Bericht über die REFA-Tagung am 20 Juni 1962 in Darmstadt. REFA-Nachrichten 15(6):254–258
REFA-Nachrichten (1964) 40 Jahre REFA. Festvortrag von Dipl.-Ing. Antoni, Vorsitzer des REFA-Bundesverbandes, auf der Abschlußveranstaltung am 23. Mai 1964 in Hannover. REFA-Nachrichten 17(4):184–186
REFA-Nachrichten (1970) Geschäftsbericht des Verbandes für Arbeitsstudien—REFA—e.v. für die Zeit vom 1. Januar bis 31.Dezember 1969. REFA-Nachrichten 23(3):177
RKW (1953) Produktivität in USA. Eine Eindrücke einer deutschen Studiengruppe von einer Reise durch USA (RKW-Auslandsdienst, Heft 20). C. Hanser, München

Schlaich K (1969a) Die Anpassung der Aufgaben und Methoden des Arbeitsstudiums an die wirtschaftliche und technische Entwicklung. REFA-Nachrichten 22(4):229–234
Schlaich K (1969b) Inhalt und Chancen des Industrial Engineering in der deutschen Wirtschaft. REFA-Nachrichten 22(1):1–7
Schmidt V (1993) Die Mercedes-Benz AG als Dominant Firm auf dem Nutzfahrzeugmarkt—Zur wettbewerbspolitischen Problematik der Dominant Firmen. Vandenhoeck & Ruprecht, Göttingen
Schmiede R, Schudlich E (1981) Die Entwicklung der Leistungsentlohnung in Deutschland. Ein historisch-theoretische Untersuchung zum Verhältnis von Lohn und Leistung unter kapitalistischen Produktionsbedingungen, 4. Aufl. Campus, Frankfurt am Main
Schröter HG (2005) Americanization of the European economy. A compact survey of American economic influence in Europe since the 1880s. Springer, Dordrecht
Schwartmann J (1975) Praktische Arbeitsgestaltung in der Automobilindustrie. REFA-Nachrichten 28(4):205–207
Shimokawa K (2004) Gurobaru Jidosha Sangyo Keieishi (Business history of the global automobile industry). Yuhikaku, Tokyo
Sörgel A (1986) Daimler-Benz—der Multi im Musterländle. Progress-Institut für Wirtschaftsforschung, Bremen
Springer K (1963) Weibliche Arbeitskräfte am Flieβband. Werkstatt und Betrieb 96(10):769–771
Stahl und Eisen (1962) Adam Opel AG, Bochum. Stahl und Eisen 82(26):805
Stahlmann M (1993) Die erste Revolution in der Autoindustrie. Management und Arbeitspolitik von 1900–1940. Campus, Frankfurt am Main
Steeger A (1953) Flieβfertigung für Kurbelwellen während der Rationalisierungsausstellung. Rationalisierung 4(1):196–199
Streeck W (1989) Successful adjustment to turbulent markets: the automobile industry. In: Katzenstein PJ (ed) Industry and politics in West Germany. Toward the third republic. Cornell University Press, Ithaca, pp 113–156
Takagi K (1962) Nishi Yoroppa ni okeru Seisansei Undo (The productivity movement in Western Europe). Nihon Seisansei Honbu, Tokyo
Tolliday S (1995) Enterprise and State in the West German Wirtschaftswunder. Bus Hist Rev 69:273–350
Tolliday S (2000) Transplanting the American model? US automobile companies and the transfer of technology and management to Britain, France, and Germany, 1928–1962. In: Zeitlin J, Herrigel G (eds) Americanization and its limits. Reworking US technology and management in post-war Europe and Japan. Oxford University Press, Oxford, pp 76–119
Ueda S, Tumura T, Omura M et al (1967) IE Tennkai no tameno Kisoron (Fundamental theory for development of IE). Indasutoriaru Enjiniaringu (Ind Eng) 9(6):538–545
von Seherr-Thoss HCG (1979) Die deutsche Automobilindustrie. Eine Dokumentation von 1886 bis 1979, 2. Aufl. Deutsches Verlagsanstalt, Stuttgart
Votsch H (1962) Rationelle Auswertung von Zeitstudien. REFA-Nachrichten 15(2):61–65
Wada K (2009) Monozukuri no Guwa (A fable of manufacturing). Nagoya Daigaku Shuppankai, Nagoya
Wada K, Shiba T (1995) Nihonteki Seisan Sisutemu no Keisei (Formation of the Japanese production system). In: Yamazaki H, Kikkawa T (eds) "Nihonteki" Keiei no Renzoku to Danzetsu (Continuity and discontinuity in "Japanese business management"). Iwanami Shoten, Tokyo, pp 125–157
Wellhöner V (1996) "Wirtschaftswunder"—Weltmarkt—Westdeutscher Fordismus. Der Fall Volkswagen. Westfälisches Dampfboot, Münster
Wiesen SJ (2001) West German industry and the challenge of Nazi past, 1945–1955. The University of North Carolina Press, Chapel Hill
Witte IM (1963) Von den Grundlagen der Rationalisierung. Zum 85. Geburtstag von Lillian Gilbreth am 24. Mai 1963. Rationalisierung 14(5):103–104

Wittke V (1996) Wie entstand industrielle Massenproduktion? Diskontinuierliche Entwicklung der deutschen Elektroindustrie von den Anfängen der „großen Industrie" bis zur Entfaltung des Fordismus [1880–1975]. Edition Sigma, Berlin
Zeitlin J (2000) Introduction: Americanization and its limits: reworking US technology and management in post-War Europe and Japan. In: Zeitlin J, Herrigel G (eds) Americanization and its limits. Reworking US technology and management in post-war Europe and Japan. Oxford University Press, Oxford, pp 1–50

Chapter 8
Deployment of the American Method for Adapting to a Mass Market: Marketing, Public Relations, and Operations Research

Abstract This chapter discusses the deployment of American methods for adapting to a mass market. As the development of mass production progressed post WWII, Germany, along with other European countries and Japan, found it important to adapt to the mass market with methods such as marketing, public relations (PR), and operations research (OR). However, in Germany many factors affected the implementation of these American methods. First, this chapter considers the deployment of American marketing methods in Japan as a representative measure for mass market adaptation. Next, it examines Germany's deployment of American marketing methods, PR, and OR in relation to various factors such as the characteristics of domestic and European markets, production- and technology-oriented management values, the composition of executive management, and changes in the structure of competition.

Keywords Advertising • Marketing • Operations research (OR) • Pricing policy • Product policy • Public relations (PR)

Introduction of the American management system post WWII constituted a fundamental condition for the development of full-scale mass production. Eventually in the 1950s and 1960s, the mass production system was established in Germany. This was accompanied by an increase in the importance of adapting to the market. Under these circumstances, marketing and public relations became very significant as a means for supporting sales and adapting to the market. In addition, from the perspective of the entire enterprise, operations research techniques became extremely significant as a method for optimizing day-to-day operational decision making. Application of these techniques to areas such as production, sales, inventory, and transport facilitates a method for optimizing operational activities tailored to market changes. These techniques have also become an important method for supporting mass production systems.

T. Yamazaki, *German Business Management: A Japanese Perspective on Regional Development Factors*, DOI 10.1007/978-4-431-54303-9_8, © Springer Japan 2013

Under these conditions, the introduction of the American approach to marketing, PR, and OR was also promoted in Germany. Therefore, in this chapter, while considering the connection with the changes in the post-war German market and social structure, we will discuss the deployment of American methods for adapting to a mass market.

8.1 Various Japanese Characteristics in the Deployment of American Methods for Adapting to a Mass Market

First, in relation to the market adaptation measures that accompanied the evolution of post-war mass production, we address marketing as the most typical measure, and for comparative purposes, we investigate the situation in Japan. We classify marketing in post-war Japan by periods: (1) the introductory period in which leading manufactures introduced American marketing (the latter half of the 1950s through the first half of the 1960s), (2) the period of modification of American marketing and the advent of the distribution industry when Japanese marketing was established as a part of Japanese management (the second half of the 1960s through the first half the 1970s), and (3) the period of evolution of Japanese-style marketing toward the era of internationalization and technological innovation/digitalization (since the late 1970s).

In Japan, the technological innovation and capital investment boom were rather sudden. On the other hand, managerial marketing as an overall marketing technique was found to exist while introducing American marketing techniques. Therefore, Japan did not go through the American-type historical steps, starting from high-pressure marketing to consumer-oriented marketing, and subsequently to managerial marketing. Rather, Japan introduced and implemented managerial marketing and high-pressure marketing simultaneously. In other words, even while emphasizing precise market research and product policies, under the intensification of competition among enterprises brought about by the rapid expansion of mass production capacity, Japanese companies resorted to using high-pressure marketing. To bridge the gap between the market and the rapidly increasing production capacity, there were great efforts in sales promotion, high-pressure advertising, provision of consumer credit, and in particular, an extraordinary emphasis on controlling sales channels. However, under the Japanese market characteristic of intense competition, there was an emphasis on product policies that combined the importance of applied research and improved new products in new product development and R&D. This resulted in a trend of emphasizing market segmentation and product differentiation in product policies. For example, in the automotive industry, product differentiation and planned obsolescence were promoted by a full-line policy and rapid model changes. Increasing the penetration rate of automobiles on the basis of mass production focusing on one model was not pursued. Rather, there was an extremely early combination of mass production and market segmentation policies. This trend was also seen in other consumer goods such as household electrical devices and cameras.

In the "modification period" described earlier, marketing focused on product policy was established. However, due to the special inclination of Japanese business management, particularly the characteristics of organizational conduct, there were also various modifications to marketing. One of these was the abovementioned trend toward the emphasis on applied research and improved new products in new product development and R&D. In addition, because of collectivist behavior patterns, the characteristics of business organizations linked by multilayered informal human relationships within the organization, and horizontal communication among organizational departments accompanied by successful mutual adjustment, total marketing was developed for achieving overall integration according to the marketing strategy. However, even in such cases, the marketing techniques of Japan and those of America did not differ greatly; the only difference was in the way they were operationalized (Shimokawa 1991, pp. 124–127, 139–141; Noda 1969, pp. 211–214).

In Japan, another characteristic was that the revision of the traditional wholesaler-led distribution system took place under the leadership of large-scale consumer goods manufacturers. The distribution system led by large-scale consumer goods manufacturers took the form of restricted group-controlled distribution channels (Sato 1983, p. 168; Wakabayashi 1999, p. 21; Ogawa 2011, p. 208). During the period when large manufactures led the introduction of American marketing, under the Japanese-style expansion of the mass market for consumer durables characterized by a constant and continuous cycle of development progressed, particularly sales promotion driven high-pressure marketing was developed. In this progression, group-sales channels were particularly effective (Shimokawa 1991, p. 140). This trend toward group domination of distribution later brought about a special pattern in Japanese distribution and marketing.

While this is Japan's view, in Germany's case, the main influences were the characteristics of the domestic and European market, which was the main recipient of exports, as well as the production- and technology-oriented management values, which were reflected in the composition of top management. Therefore, even in the introduction of the various measures that form the important components of marketing, Germany pursued distinctive methods. Overall, because of the differences in corporate management values, the structure of the market and competition, and the introduction of American-style marketing, the introduction in Germany was not as extensive as in Japan; on the other hand, there was a special evolution in terms of the scope of the introduction and extent of its prevalence.

Hence, the introduction of American methods for adapting to a mass market in Germany is discussed below. First, in Sect. 8.2, the deployment of American marketing methods is reviewed. In Sect. 8.3, we will discuss the deployment of American methods of Public Relations. In Sect. 8.4, the deployment of Operations Research are considered.

8.2 Deployment of Marketing Methods in Germany

8.2.1 Influence of American Marketing in Germany

First, regarding the impact of American marketing, Schröter argued that in relation to the Americanization of the European economy, changes such as marketing research and publicity were a logical consequence of the U.S. direct investment, mass production, and mass distribution (Schröter 2005, p. 97). Marketing, along with business management education and divisional structure, was one of the core American management concepts that Europe began to adopt in the 1960s. In the 1950s, many Europeans perceived mass-produced products as standardized, and mass production as something that is contrary to individualism. However, the American viewpoint is that mass production promotes individualism because it enables an individual to purchase a wider variety of goods. With further integration among the European national markets and increase in consumer purchasing power, this perception started to take hold in Europe as well (Schröter 2005, pp. 121–122).

We investigate the response to sales issues in Germany and the influence of American marketing. In Europe, there was a greater lag in distribution than in production, and thus, the latent potential for learning and transfer in the former was much greater (Schröter 2005, p. 78). Germany traditionally had strong production and technology orientations. Therefore, it was assumed that a demand for a marketing "revolution" in German companies would require a change in behavior that must be accompanied by a radical reform of mental attitude and traditional management (Kleinschmidt 2002, p. 226). Under the post-war boom conditions, rationalization efforts were completely focused upon the area of production, and there was no indication of any problem in the sale of products (Remele 1963, p. 113). From the American viewpoint at that time, Germany was greatly lagging in market research even in the mid-1950s (*Rheinisch-Westfälisches Wirtschaftsarchiv zu Köln*, Abt 1,517.6, Stand der Rationalisierung in Deutschland, p. 14). Not much attention had been paid to the skills of sales personnel in European companies at that time, and the same could be said about Germany (OEEC 1954, p. 16).

In these circumstances, in the many programs supported by the US Technical Assistance and Productivity Program (USTA&P) on the topic of marketing and sales, it became clear that in Germany, knowledge of modern sales economics and various methods was insufficient. Thus, interest in American marketing methods became stronger and the negative evaluation toward American sales and market research methods began to decrease (Kleinschmidt 1998, p. 181). Until the 1960s especially, the situation of emphasizing rationalization efforts in only the production area faced a decisive change. Moreover, diverse consumer needs once again enhanced sales function to the true theme (Remele 1963, p. 114).

8.2.2 Channels Through Which Marketing Methods Were Learned and Introduced in Germany

Next, let us analyze the channels through which American marketing techniques were learned and introduced. The main channels consisted of study trips to America sponsored by the USTA&P, inviting experts from the U.S. to Germany and involving them in various events, learning through books and other published materials, involvement of advertising agencies, and direct investment by American companies.

First, the efforts of USTA&P were the most successful of the efforts made by the U.S. in the area of marketing [*National Archives,* RG469, Productivity and Technical Assistance Division, Office of the Director, Technical Assistance Country Subject Files, 1949–1952, German-General, A letter to the Economic Cooperation Administration from Dr. C. Kapfner (20.9.1950)]. Numerous businessmen who travelled to the U.S. on trips sponsored by Mutual Security Agency, Foreign Administration Organization, and Rationalisierungs-Kuratorium der Deutschen Wirtshaft (RKW) began to request to learn about the latest marketing and advertising methods (Kleinschmidt 2004, p. 83). In the 1950s, on a trip to the U.S. as part of a delegation of the productivity missions, German entrepreneurs and engineers studied sales and marketing issues to the same extent that they observed the latest technology and production methods (Kleinschmidt 1998, p. 181). Even in the programs at the European Productivity Agency, marketing and distribution issues were discussed (*National Archives*, RG469, Productivity & Technical Assist Division Labor Advisor Subject Files 1952–1954, TA-Work, Program Suggestions of PTAD/FOA for the EPA second annual Program).

Furthermore, inviting experts from the U.S. was one of the channels. In *B-Projct* of the Technical Assistance Plan, exchange programs for studying American PR and marketing techniques were planned and conducted [*National Archives*, RG469, Productivity & Technical Assist Division Labor Advisor Subject Files 1952–1954, TA-Work, TA-B-Project Berlin 09-215 Marketing and Public Relations Team Berlin (24.11.1953)]. For example, a management seminar was held in Berlin in 1953 in which the person in charge of marketing at Westinghouse's Electric Appliance Division was invited. In the seminar, there were group discussions about marketing research, product planning, sales planning, advertising/distribution, PR, publicity, distribution methods for consumer goods, product service, factory organization, and personnel development of marketing personnel [*National Archives*, RG469, Mission to Germany, Productivity and Technical Assistance Division, Subject Files of the Chief, 1953–1956, Report on Experiences German-American Management Seminars in Berlin (2.11.1953)].

In the 1950s, events such as conferences and lectures also played a central role. In the mid-1950s, the Federation of German Industries, RKW, and the Foreign Operations Administration used the Baden–Baden seminar to stage an event called

"New Methods of Sales Economy" in which there were 140 participants. The challenge was to transfer new methods of marketing, sales, and publicity under the transition from a seller's market to a buyer's market. These events indicate that the relationship between the American and German experts was the same as that between a teacher and a student (Kleinschmidt 2002, p. 225).

Further, in the case of commercial magazines and books, almost all of the German commercial publications dealing with distribution referred to the American model of selling styles, salesmanship, or organization. In addition, in many cases, related books were translated and published under the editorship of well-known Germans in the business world (Schröter 2005, p. 82).

German companies also gained knowledge about the practice of American marketing by working with advertising agencies and consulting companies (Hilger 2004a, p. 203), and this method played a very important role. In the 1950s, it was revealed that American-type advertising agencies offering full service represented an economically more successful model. Under these circumstances, German companies increasingly began to utilize the wide-ranging services offered by such advertising agencies (Schröter 1997, pp. 98–99). For example, in the case of Henkel brand products, the Stanford Research Institute (SRI) and McCann-Erickson advertising agency were the most important facilitators of American know-how. In contrast to American competitive companies such as GM, at first Daimler-Benz was critical of questionnaire surveys. However, after being in contact with Ogilvy, a specialist in American advertising, in early 1960s, they changed their evaluation method and with the cooperation of the country's experts, unlocked new marketing know-how (Hilger 2004a, pp. 187–188).

In Europe, the appearance of advertising agencies that provide full service, ranging from marketing research to the organization and realization of advertising campaigns, including the evaluation of the research results, signified Americanization of this industry. The experience of European employees at American advertising agencies also contributed to the transfer of American methods and attitudes (Schröter 2005, pp. 118–119).

The method of direct investment by American companies was also an important channel for transferring knowledge. The marketing activities in the area of consumer goods of American subsidiaries in Germany often had a very strong direct impact on the adoption of similar methods by German companies (Dyas and Thanheiser 1976, p. 112). In some American subsidiaries and branches surveyed by Hartmann et al., the independent position of marketing director, which had jurisdiction over sales and publicity, was created. In other subsidiaries and branch offices, it can be said that although both sales and advertising functions were relatively independent, they were integrated in the form of work teams such as marketing groups and committees (Hartmann 1963, p. 109). Particularly in the late 1960s, many advertising agencies were established with their headquarters in the United States capital. To better adapt to the market, many of the agencies accepted German partners or formed liaison with existing local agencies (Schröter 1997, p. 107). This also contributed to the promotion of the introduction and transfer of American know-how.

8.2.3 General Conditions of the Deployment of Marketing Techniques in Germany

Next, analysis of the overall situation of the introduction of marketing techniques reveals that in the 1950s, their introduction was an extensive movement that impacted many businesses simultaneously. For example, the motto "From Sales to Marketing" at the first Sales and Marketing Conference held in Germany in 1958 summarized the events happening all around Europe at that time. However, the management of the European manufacturing industry was skeptical of the new methods and their significance. According to the directors who focused on issues of production, marketing not only required a thorough transformation of their way of thinking but also represented loss of authority within their enterprises. In light of these circumstances, a wide acceptance of American marketing and related management methods did not occur until a generational change of managers in the early 1960s (Schröter 2005, p. 106).

In German companies, until the late 1950s, with the exception of some of the departments that were in charge of sales, advertising, and publicity, the sales policy activities were generally carried out individually without a master plan and run independently (Hilger 2004a, p. 186). In the 1950s, many European managers established a small section in the sales department as the marketing unit. In the U.S., in contrast to the sales department being in charge of short-term tactics, the marketing department developed the company's long-term strategy. In Germany, such a division did not occur until the late 1960s. By 1968, 79% of German businesses created a clear division between the two departments within the organization (Schröter 2005, p. 107).

Thus, from the beginning of the 1960s, the introduction of American marketing techniques had proceeded earnestly. We will now analyze the main techniques below.

Advertising and Publicity: In 1945, there was a significant difference between the U.S. and Europe in terms of advertising and publicity, the most important one being the attitude toward advertising. For example, American advertisers used far more sophisticated techniques that adopted modern scientific methods, and advertising was seen everywhere. For many years, American advertising had been organized on a scale considerably larger than in Europe. Full-service advertising agencies were common in the U.S., but rare in Europe (Schröter 2005, p. 118). Advertising agencies of this type were established in Germany in 1947 based on the American model (Schindelbeck 1995, p. 247). In the 1950s, advertising under the influence of the American model was increasingly regarded as a part of the marketing sphere (Kleinschmidt 2002, p. 224).

Two waves of Americanization were seen in the area of advertising and publicity. The role of American-type advertising agencies that provide full service was a characteristic of the first wave in the 1950s. However, at this stage, there was considerable social antipathy toward the American advertising being seen in Germany. Measures such as publicity campaigns based on planned obsolescence had not been introduced in Germany then. As for the 1950s, it has been pointed out that the degree of the catalytic effect of the American model and Americanization should not be overestimated. The American influence was modest in the organization form of German advertising companies as well. This type of faltering in the Americanization process was due to economic factors such as the existence of the seller's market as well as the much more powerful development of the traditional producer goods industry compared with that of the consumer goods industry. On the other hand, the second wave of Americanization can be seen from the 1960s, and at this stage, the introduction of American marketing concepts and techniques progressed (Schröter 1997, pp. 98–103).

Even in the middle of the 1960s, the administrators of publicity were in middle or lower management (Vgl. Hölzer 1964; Korte 1964, pp. 26, 30). It was very different from the situation in the U.S., where the person in charge of the advertising department in many cases reported directly to the vice president of marketing (Hallig 1965, p. 64). The American system was followed by the subsidiaries and branch offices of American businesses in Germany. In such subsidiaries and branch offices, the administrators in charge of advertising played a role different from that often would be the case in a German company, commonly directors. This point is the most noticeable difference between these businesses and business of German capital (Hartmann 1963, p. 111). Many German businesses underwent reorganization based on the American model, particularly in the early 1970s. Previously, there had been a lack of trust and conflict between advertising agencies and the departments in charge of publicity. However, this situation fundamentally improved in the new generation of management. Marketing department along with management determined the corporate goals, decisions about publicity goals, concepts, publicity planning, and to a certain extent, the budget, carrying them out primarily in cooperation with the agencies (Schröter 1997, pp. 105, 107).

In this way, publicity of sales was one area in the German economy from the 1960s that was most strongly "Americanized" (Hilger 2004a, p. 202). This is seen in the fact that in the mid-1960s, the American-type advertising agency took control (Schindelbeck 1995, p. 235). In 1960, the per capita expenditure on advertising in Germany was about one-third that in the U.S., but by 1970, it had increased to about 72% of the U.S. This was about 3.1 times greater than the amount in England, 3.8 times greater than that in France, and the largest in Europe (Schröter 1998, pp. 28–29; Schröter 2005, p. 120).

However, in the 1960s, the domination of the U.S. in the selection of advertising media was still observed, which was most conspicuous in television advertising (Schröter 1997, p. 108). For example, in 1960, P&G was already spending 90% of its publicity budget in the U.S. on television advertising. Henkel's delegation to the U.S. also showed a strong interest in such advertising efforts (Hilger 2004b, p. 202). Thereafter, in Germany, with the spread of the television, this new advertising medium came to play a greater role in publicity, though slightly later than in the U.S.

Marketing Research: Next, regarding marketing research, we see that even in 1960, the increase in the diversity and increasing demands of consumers often hampered the various efforts toward large-lot rationalized production. Under these circumstances, product testing and long-term sales forecasting methods used in modern market research facilitated the use of basic data necessary for determining the type of products that promised optimum sales (Strotmann 1960, p. 12).

Even in Europe, activities related to marketing research had already been seen before 1945. However, the U.S.'s leading position in this area was not only a result of combining scientific techniques such as OR and office equipment technology, but also the result of innovative application of new statistical techniques with polling methods. The most important technique among them was consumer panels, which was introduced in Germany after the mid-1950s.

Furthermore, from the early 1950s, American marketing research companies also established subsidiaries and offices in Germany, which played a certain role in the spread of these techniques. However, the demand for these companies majorly originated from American subsidiaries or businesses planning to expand into the European market. Thus, the major part of the expansion of marketing research was from American direct investment. During the establishment of marketing research in Europe, the American model had been so outstanding that it was common to see precise imitations of the model (Schröter 2005, pp. 111–114, 117).

Product Policy and Pricing Policy: Examining further product and pricing policies, we first see that there was often a tendency for German suppliers, in contrast to American businesses, to give priority to product policies with an emphasis on traditional brand awareness. This was particularly applicable to companies that focused on brand strength gained through high quality, such as the case with Daimler-Benz. Hilger characterized this trend as a "model policy that is not constrained by the stream of the times." Since the late 1950s, Daimler-Benz followed a product strategy that sought variation in the appearance of its vehicles at the lowest cost possible by making only slight changes to the bodies of the cars. The company, by facilitating such concession to the market, suppressed American customs, and thus prevented further shortening of model change cycles in the European market. However, even in this case, there was a tendency in Europe to regard high development costs associated with the sales technique of frequent model changes as a wasteful policy and to criticize it as "planned obsolescence." Accordingly, this trend was not limited to Germany and should instead be considered a European characteristic (Hilger 2004a, pp. 190, 192–193). With Germany's high dependence on the European market, this market characteristic provided the conditions for Germany's product policy to be effective in this region.

Regarding the pricing policy, it is seen that American pricing policies closely followed the influences of free market forces. In contrast, in Germany, there were influences such as price-fixing for brand products, and the regulation of national policies such as the gift regulations and the rebates act. In addition, German companies that gave priority before the war to the traditional mild competition policy that was part of the market agreement were not so able to follow American business practices. After the war, American suppliers coped with the disturbance of the European market with low prices and discounts. In contrast, German suppliers, in the face of slow growth in the late 1960s, sought to maintain normal, high prices. However, under the conditions of increased price competition, there was an even greater change in the stubborn attitude of Henkel because of the exceptional price cuts and ceaseless discounting in the detergent and cleaner business from the late 1960s. Subsequently, as a result of competition with P&G, Henkel's strongest competitor, it came to a compromise solution, which was a middle path between American competition policies and the traditional pricing policies. Big brands such as Persil only implemented discounts and sales to the extent that was absolutely necessary, and for other products, they protected their overall market share by adjusting their supply to meet the state of competition (Vgl. Hilger 2004a, pp. 195–197, 201).

In this way, American marketing strategy, from an overall view, had a lasting effect on the concept of German companies' sales policies. American companies' techniques and know-how were introduced in, for example, product policies and publicity, but the degree of acceptance depended on the intensity of competition. Not considering the content of advertising, from the late 1950s, there was considerably more powerful systemization of sales policies depending on the new techniques of market research and opinion surveys. However, in relation to German producers' price and terms policies that were also impacted by competition policies, it was clearly difficult for the companies to distance themselves from their existing tradition (Vgl. Hilger 2004a, pp. 211–212).

Even given the above circumstances, there were intercompany differences in the shift to market-oriented management in the 1950s and 1960s. Moreover, in terms of the change in conditions represented by the transition from a seller's market to buyer's market after the war, there was a difference between the raw materials and consumer goods industries. In addition, the perceptions about issues related to sales, marketing, publicity, and consumers differed among industries and even within individual businesses. Here, individual experiences, perceptions, and attitudes played important roles. In the heavy industry, because of historical reasons such as the existence of cartels, until the mid-1960s, sales, publicity, and marketing were considered of only secondary significance. In contrast, in the chemical and artificial fiber industries, top management paid considerably greater attention to marketing, and the introduction of marketing techniques had already started at quite an early stage (Kleinschmidt 2002, pp. 226–227; Kleinschmidt 2004, pp. 83–84). In addition, according to the Booz Allen & Hamilton report that was released in the early 1970s, the American marketing concept had been understood and introduced particularly in progressive companies in the consumer goods industry, and the function consisting of marketing such as market research, sales and sales promotion, and advertising had somewhat developed. In contrast, in many companies in the producer goods industry, the focus was not on market needs, but production as it had been before (Booz-Allen and Hamilton 1973, p. 35). Hence, next we will analyze the introduction of marketing techniques in the main industries and their representative companies.

8.2.4 Deployment of Marketing Techniques in the Main Industrial Sectors

8.2.4.1 Chemical Industry

The chemical industry is one of the sectors in which marketing became an important issue during the expansion of consumer goods and products after WWII. Here, we will examine this industry through the examples of certain individual companies.

First, consider the case of **Glanzstoff**. The company pursued a rigorous market-oriented sales strategy, which indicated a departure from the traditional sales concept. The American marketing and publicity techniques offered a completely new concept, and DuPont was the model for both. Increase in the significance of marketing also impacted the organization. In 1954, the advertising department was separated from the sales department and placed under the direct control of the board of directors. A publicity committee responsible for decisions related to publicity methods was simultaneously established. The committee conducted local research on American advertising and publicity techniques, visited American companies and organizations, and examined publications and magazines. From the late 1950s to the early 1960s, the large-scale publicity of the polyester fiber Diolen was implemented; in 1959, a new sales promotion section and team were established for this product. American orientation was also introduced and was seen in television advertisements (Kleinschmidt 2002, pp. 229–231; Kleinschmidt 1998, p. 182). Glanzstoff is a representative example of a company that more directly introduced American marketing techniques. Diffusion of such techniques is reflected in the adoption of American terminology by German management teams, and also reflects the transfer of corporate culture (Kleinschmidt 1998, p. 183).

Next consider the case of **Hüls**. We see that the concept of marketing did not play a role immediately after the war (Kleinschmidt 2002, p. 233). However, in the early 1950s, with the increase in the proportion of exports, separation of the advertising budget for domestic and foreign purposes became an issue, and the type of advertising media to be used became a concern (*Hüls Archiv*, VII-7-1/1, CWH-Werbung im Jahr 1952). Nonetheless, at this stage, they still lagged behind the U.S. [*Hüls Archiv*, VII-7, Neugestaltung der Industriewerbung (7.6.1951)]. Unlike Glanzstoff, there was lack of personnel pursuing an appropriate marketing concept, and even in the late 1950s, from an overall perspective, there was barely any attention directed toward the American model. However, with the introduction of Vestan polyester fiber in the early 1960s, the situation changed. Under the conditions of competition with other manufacturers and their brand products, along with a greater necessity to adapt accordingly to various market needs, a large-scale marketing campaign for Vestan, similar to Glanzstoff's Diolen campaign, was initiated. This campaign, however, was carried out without accepting American marketing sales policies based on direct human contact or the terminology of American management methods (Kleinschmidt 2002, pp. 234–235).

With regard to **Henkel**, the post-war publicity activities for Persil began in 1950 (*Siemens Archiv Akten*, 49/Lb457, Gömmel R, Werbeverhalten im Konsum und Investitionsgüterbereich von 1945 bis 1980, gezeigt an frei gewählten Beispielen, p. 16). However, according to internal documents from September 1953, advertising was not seen as a modern method, and the competition's publicity was always better [*Henkel Archiv*, 153/9, Niederschrift über die Postbesprechung vom 18.9.1953 (19.9.1953), p. 7]. In the fall of 1956, Henkel introduced its television publicity of Persil, thus becoming the first West German company to start television advertising. The advertising was a defensive measure against P&G's extraordinary publicity efforts in the growing all-temperature detergent and cleaner market. However, as a traditional German brand product company, Henkel's management team, even after this, remained distant from such content (Hilger 2004a, pp. 208–209).

In such circumstances, from the second half to the end of the 1950s, given the increasing demand for advertising, external experts such as market research organizations and advertising agencies became involved. In 1959, for the first time, the advertising agency Troost-Campbell-Ewald GmbH was entrusted with the Persil campaign. In the same year, a marketing department in charge of product planning and advertising was established, and the advertising and publicity center became responsible for the conception and implementation of all advertising and publicity activities (*Siemens Archiv Akten*, 49/Lb457, Gömmel R, Werbeverhalten im Konsum und Investitionsgüterbereich von 1945 bis 1980, gezeigt an frei gewählten Beispielen, p. 39). However, until the early 1960s, due to lack of capital, the management team was almost completely unable to consider implementing a strategy for pricing and advertising policies similar to that of the competition (Hilger 2004b, p. 211).

Under the increasing strength of competitive pressures from their American competitors, an analysis of market research data and their competitors provided impetus to sales policies. In the early 1960s, a central department responsible for the collection of materials related to the introduction of new American brand products and the transfer of such materials to the section in charge was established inside the marketing department (Hilger 2004a, pp. 188–189). To train personnel with expertise in market research, in 1961 and 1962, Henkel participated in the productivity subsidiary program offered by the Ministry of Economic Affairs [*Henkel Archiv*, 153/20, Niederschrift über die Postbesprechung Henkel vom 31. Juli 1962 (2.8.1962), p. 3]. In addition, with the cooperation of representative producers of American brand products, merchandisers, and sales companies, they aimed at acquiring information about new trends in sales methods and marketing (Hilger 2004b, p. 200). Henkel had already, since the late 1950s, introduced a wide variety of products in cooperation with German advertising agencies, but in 1963, they entrusted the advertising campaign for the new detergent "Amba" to an American advertising agency (Hilger 2004a, p. 203).

Thereafter, the competition in the European market became a competition between two companies, Henkel and P&G. As a result, a detailed analysis of P&G's management policies was undertaken since the mid-1960s (Hilger 2004a, p. 189). It was thereby proposed that Henkel should seek a smooth and consistent treatment of all marketing factors comparable to that of their rival P&G [*Henkel Archiv*, 451/55, Auszug aus dem Protkoll Nr. 3/1968 über die Sitzung des Verwaltungsrates der Persil GmbH am 4. April 1968, *Henkel Archiv*, 153/42, Niederschrift über die gemeisame Post PERSIL/HENKEL/Böhme/HI vom 9.1.1968 (10.1.1968), p. 7]. To prepare for future competition, it was necessary for Henkel to have a detailed analysis of P&G's methods, goals, and organization; in the late 1960s, a committee was organized to study P&G's sales [*Henkel Archiv*, 451/55, Auszug aus dem Protokoll Nr. 1/68 über die gemeinsame Post vom 9. Januar 1968, p. 2, *Henkel Archiv*, 153/42, Niederschrift über die gemeisame Post PERSIL/HENKEL/Böhme/HI vom 9.1.1968 (10.1.1968), p. 7]. Around that time, there was a decline in brand value because of intensification of competition, and from the prediction that the differentiation between brands will be even weaker, countermeasures to thoroughly reduce the number of product items were implemented (*Henkel Archiv*, 451/55, Auszug aus dem Protokoll Nr. 1/68 über die gemeinsame Post vom 9. Januar 1968, p. 1). Under these conditions, in 1968 the American consulting company SRI suggested that there should be separate cost centers for each unit and group within the marketing organization, and also that existing sales-oriented activities should be transformed into a comprehensive customer-oriented marketing program (*Henkel Archiv*, 251/2, Stanford Research Institute, Langfristigen Planung für Persil/Henkel, Phase II:Strategische Plaung, 2. Bd, Juli 1968, pp. 339, 344–346).

Thus, in the chemical industry, the intensified competition that resulted from progress in mass production in the consumer goods products industries and America's export stance made responding to the marketing techniques an even more important theme. However, in this situation, along with companies that addressed these issues by having close contact with America, including the use of advertising agencies, there were also companies that addressed these issues from a certain distance.

8.2.4.2 Electrical Industry

In the electrical industry, we see that **Siemens**, with the currency reform of 1948, shifted the focus of activities of its advertising center, established in 1938 to support publicity of sales. In the 1950s, publicity research made it possible to empirically analyze the various factors impacting the effectiveness of publicity [*Siemens Archiv Akten*, 9871, Schwabenthan O, Unternehmenskommunikation für Siemens 1847 bis 1989, München, 1995 (Selbstverlag), pp. 62–63, *Siemens Archiv Akten*, 49/Lb457, Gömmel R, Werbeverhalten im Konsum und Investitionsgüterbereich von 1945 bis 1980, gezeigt an frei gewählten Beispielen, pp. 6, 8]. For Siemens to demonstrate their technological nature and to create trust in their products, there was a unified style created in the formation of the advertising media. In response to the fierce competition in the consumer goods market, illustrative advertising to the masses was initiated in 1954. In the investment goods sector, because of numerous new developments in technology, it was necessary for sales staff to have excellent information measures to support the development of human relations. In this, there was an emphasis on publicity brochures, printed materials, and advertising in media such as newspapers (*Siemens Archiv Akten*, 49/Lb457, Gömmel R, Werbeverhalten im Konsum und Investitionsgüterbereich von 1945 bis 1980, gezeigt an frei gewählten Beispielen, pp. 7–9). The company's 1961 internal documents indicate that the challenges of sales promotion, marketing research, sales planning, and production planning surfaced under the intensification of competition (*Siemens Archiv Akten*, 37/Lk975, Illmer H, Warum materialorientierter Vertrieb? p. 30).

In particular, the general economic breakthrough, an increase in the dynamism of the market combined with the introduction of more powerful advertising, and progress made in international competition lead to a movement towards modern American marketing in terms of product and sales policies oriented towards market conditions and customer needs. In relation to the organization of advertising activities beginning in 1962, specialized units other than advertising and publicity groups were formed to ensure effective generation of necessary publicity techniques and to maintain Siemens advertising style [*Siemens Archiv Akten*, 9871, Schwabenthan O, Unternehmenskommunikation für Siemens 1847 bis 1989, München, 1995 (Selbstverlag), pp. 85, 87, 92].

In the 1960s, the results of image analysis began to provide the basis for the formation of a modern advertising style of a corporate identity strategy. In Germany, scientific analysis was first used for advertising goals in the 1950s (Feldenkirchen 2004b, p. 130), but in the 1960s, scientific research in relation to Siemens corporate image was implemented by a neutral institution. In addition, activities such as research related to the corporate brand and its symbolic characteristics, analysis of the popularity of the company and its products compared with its competitors, and comparison of advertising expenditures of Siemens and AEG were carried out. Moreover, market research, market observations, and publicity research served as supplementary measures for the improved planning (*Siemens Archiv Akten*, 49/Lb457, Gömmel R, Werbeverhalten im Konsum und Investitionsgüterbereich von 1945 bis 1980, gezeigt an frei gewählten Beispielen, p. 25). In the late 1960s, GfK Nürnberg, a research company for consumption, marketing, and sales, was entrusted with a survey related to the concept of "Siemens' product series." Siemens obtained survey results on three aspects: visibility, information, and image [Vgl. *Siemens Archiv Akten*, 37/Lk975, Siemens-Serienfabrikate. Eine Untersuchung bei ausgewählten Abnehmerkreisen von Siemens-Erzeugnissen (März 1967)]. In addition, Siemens' electrothermal equipment company, which manufactured and sold household electric products, conducted a research trip to the U.S. in 1968 with the objective of applying the knowledge gained from analysis of the American small electric products market to the conditions of the European market and demonstrating the possibility of expanding their business. There, it conducted a questionnaire survey dealing with six points: (1) market conditions, (2) product characteristics, (3) product planning and product development, (4) production, (5) sales, and (6) advertising and sales promotion. Besides meeting with top management at the SMEs, it visited larger enterprises and held discussions with the people responsible for small electrical products, and investigated topics such as sales and organization methods by visiting companies such as Westinghouse (*Siemens Archiv Akten*, 68/Li137, Analyse des

USA-Kleingerätenmarktes. Reise der Herren Fromm, Prahl und Dr. Rumswinkel vom 15.5. bis 29.6.1968).

In this way, in the 1960s, Siemens' advertising activities had developed into an important part of marketing and were able to adapt to the market conditions according to the times. However, at the beginning of the 1970s, advertising went beyond its function as part of marketing mix in sales issues, as it had been in the 1960s, and began to function as part of communication mix which is an enterprise-wide issue (*Siemens Archiv Akten*, 49/Lb457, Gömmel R, Werbeverhalten im Konsum und Investitionsgüterbereich von 1945 bis 1980, gezeigt an frei gewählten Beispielen, pp. 49, 57).

8.2.4.3 Automotive Industry

Next, we look at the automotive industry. **Volkswagen** was one of the most advanced companies in its various marketing polices, in that it had a strong customer and sales orientation. American know-how gave H. Nordhoff impetus, and the company thoroughly undertook the planning of a wide-range and large-scale sales organization in as early as 1948–1950 (Vogelsang 1961, p. 6; Hiller 1952, pp. 26–27). Thereafter, the building of a national and international sales network was actively promoted. In 1947, the company's sales network merely consisted of 10 core distributors and 14 dealers, and factory-authorized repair shops did not exist. However, two years later, the sales organization consisted of 16 core representative agents, 31 wholesale distributors, 103 dealers, and 84 authorized repair shops (Kleinschmidt 2004, p. 84). In contrast to other German automotive companies, Volkswagen could not rely on their existing dealership network after the war, and the development of a sales network became an important issue. After the currency reform of 1948, the number of sales locations greatly increased, and in addition to developing a system of independent retailers that also was in charge of the wholesale stage, they expanded their customer service network. As for the method of maintaining their sales points, in the 1960s, they also used the method of acquiring other companies (Borgward and Auto Union) (Vgl. Linne 2008, pp. 8, 25–26, 31).

In each issue of the public relations magazine "VW Information Service" ("*Volkswagen Informationsdienst*") launched in August 1949, Volkswagen was early in pointing out the importance of market analysis, advertising, and the customer service function, and the company worked on the development of survey questionnaires, statistics, and the customer service function [*Volkswagen Archiv*, 61/2036, Volkswagen G.m.b.H., *Volkswagen Informationsdienst*, Nr. 1 (1.8.1948), Nr. 2 (5.10.1948), Nr. 3 (16.12.1948), Nr. 4 (10.2.1949), Nr. 5 (20.5.1949), Nr. 6 (1.9.1949), Nr. 7 (16.12.1949), *Volkswagen Archiv*, 174/1588, Nordhoff H, Ein offenes Wort zu unserer Situation, *Volkswagen Information*, Nr. 19, September 1954]. In the fourth quarter of 1945, the customer service department had already been re-established, and in the following year, the organization was expanded to include the three departments of replacement parts, technique and customer service training (*Volkswagen Archiv*, 174/1033, Bericht der Verkaufs- und

Kundendienstorganisation für das Geschäftsjahr 1946). The organization of the center for sales and customer service included sections for domestic sales, oversees trade service, technology, and advertising in 1948. Publicity departments were established in July of the same year (*Volkswagen Archiv*, 174/1033, Tätigkeitsbericht der Hauptabteilung VERKAUF und KUNDENDIENST für das Jahr 1948). In the fiscal year of 1950, as part of the restructuring of the department in charge of domestic sales, the sales promotion department was established. In addition to incorporating the publicity department with the organization, there was the integration of sales statistics techniques and various sales promotion policies into it. That fiscal year was the first time that the development of aggressive publicity existed on a considerable scale (*Volkswagen Archiv*, 174/1033, Geschäftsbericht 1950 der Hauptabteilung VERKAUF und KUNDENDIENST, p 13). The 1951 fiscal year was the first time that the sales promotion/publicity section performed systematic and planned activities (*Volkswagen Archiv*, 174/1033, Geschäftsbericht 1951 der Hauptabteilung VERKAUF und KUNDENDIENST, p 17). Among these movements, direct publicity methods began to be focused in 1953 (*Volkswagen Archiv*, 174/1588, Direktwerbung—methodisch betrieben, *VW Informationen*, Nr. 14, 1953.8, Sonderheft: Die hohe Kunst des Verkaufens und des Umgangs mit Menschen), and great emphasis was also placed on advertising. In addition, in the 1958 "*Volkswagen Information*," the emphasis on sales promotion and publicity as basic advertising principles was pointed out (*Volkswagen Archiv*, 174/1588, Grundsätzliches zur VW-Werbung, *Volkswagen Informationen*, Nr. 14, August 1958, Sonderheft: Die hohe Kunst des Verkaufens und des Umgangs mit Menschen), and policies such as training of sales staff were carried out on a larger scale (Vgl. *Volkswagen Archiv*, 174/1035, Geschäftsbericht 1958 der Hauptabteilung VERKAUF und KUNDENDIENST, pp. 7–8; Linne 2008, pp. 20–21). In the 1959 fiscal year, the dealer network and repair shop network were strengthened, and regional customer service, especially in the big cities, was expanded (Der Volkswirt 1960, p. 2047). Furthermore, support policies for contractual dealers were actively pursued. Examples of these efforts include the holding of the 1962 dealer advisory council and the dealer financial advisory system (Vgl. *Volkswagen Archiv*, 174/742, Remarks by Professor Nordhoff at Dealer Advisory Council Breakfast, *Volkswagen Archiv*, 174/1043, Jahresbericht 1960 der Hauptabteilung VERKAUF und KUNDENDIENST, *Volkswagen Archiv*, 174/1035, Geschäftsbericht für das Jahr 1962 der Hauptabteilung VERKAUF und KUNDENDIENST, *Volkswagen Archiv*, 174/1035, Geschäftsbericht für das Jahr 1964 der Hauptabteilung VERKAUF und KUNDENDIENST, *Volkswagen Archiv*, 174/1035, Geschäftsbericht für das Jahr 1965 der Hauptabteilung VERKAUF und KUNDENDIENST).

The development of such sales networks and service systems were also pursued overseas as a measure to expand exports. In 1950, Nordhoff already pointed out the importance of exports to the U.S., and on the basis of a market analysis of the U.S., the company chose a favorable time to start this activity (*Volkswagen Archiv*, 174/1588, Ansprache von Generaldirektor Dr.-Ing.e.h. HEINZ NORDHOFF anläßlich der Presskonferenz am 14. Oktober 1950, *Volkswagen Information*—Ausschnitt zu Heinrich Nordhoff). In 1955, there were 2,800 retailers and repair shops abroad, and the "*Volkswagen Information*" of that year reported that they had the best sales and customer service organization in Europe, and were also ahead of their American counterparts (*Volkswagen Archiv*, 174/1588, Ansprache von herrn Generaldirektor Prof. Dr. Nordhoff zur Presskonferenz am 6. August 1955 anläβlich der Fertigstellung des millionsten Volkswagen, *Volkswagen Information*—Ausschnitt zu Heinrich Nordhoff, p. 4; Der Volkswirt 1955, p. 11). The source of the company's competitiveness in the U.S. market was largely because of the quality of the service network as well as high productivity they developed after the war (Abelshauser 1995, p. 289).

Nonetheless, Nordhoff concentrated on the expansion of customer service, and hence, advertising continued to be limited and played only a minor role until the end of 1950 (Kleinschmidt 2004, pp. 84–85). There was still a strong emphasis on production. He had taken a cautious attitude toward modern marketing and until 1963, a publicity budget, as we understand it today, did not exist. However, with the beginning of the 1960s, the automotive market in the West Germany slowly transformed from a seller's market to a buyer's market, and Volkswagen planned entry into advertising and its expansion as measures to deal with this change in the economic environment (Wellhöner 1996, p. 130).

From the early 1960s, the German automotive industry growth rate showed a decline. The reason for this was not only the changes in the domestic market but also the greater inroads made by foreign suppliers into the German market with various aggressive marketing policies (Feldenkirchen 2004a, p. 158). Under such circumstances, the introduction of American marketing techniques was undertaken earnestly. In the 1960s, the scale of advertising activities using publicity agencies increased further. For example, in the 1964 fiscal year, the new style of advertising and publicity created in 1963 was rigorously continued, and advertising of new cars and spot commercials were developed in cooperation with various advertising agencies (*Volkswagen Archiv*, 174/1043, Jahresbericht für den Vorstandsbereich VERKAUF 1964, *Volkswagen Archiv*, 174/1043, Jahresbericht für den Vorstandsbereich VERKAUF 1965; Köhler 2008, pp. 232–233).

In general, the manager at Volkswagen headquarters only slowly came to have confidence in the quality of American publicity and gradually began to accept American publicity methods. However, American influence was extremely significant. New ways of thinking, different terminology, elements of new styles, and knowledge was introduced into German publicity. In 1960, in addition to television publicity for the first time, Volkswagen started advertising in illustrations, woman's magazines, and television magazines. For the first time in the 1966 annual report of the sales/customer service department, publicity, sales promotion, and customer service were referred to as "marketing" and expressed as a unified strategy combining these elements. Two years later, the corporate group's sales department and subsidiary companies developed a unified marketing plan, which determined the necessary measures to achieve the set sales targets on the basis of a detailed analysis of domestic and foreign market factors. In this way, the introduction of the company's new sales strategy and publicity methods was closely tied to the American model because they used American publicity and marketing methods as a standard or "role model" (Vgl. Kleinschmidt 2002, pp. 250, 255–256).

At Volkswagen, an important driving force of the strengthening and implementation of publicity was exports to the U.S. market. Here, C. H. Hahn, the president of Volkswagen of America, played an important role. A publicity committee was established to facilitate a stronger deployment of publicity in the U.S. under the pressure of wholesalers and American companies' first introduction of a small-sized car in 1959. The publicity of the "Beetle," which was handled by a local advertising agency, was the first time that sophisticated American advertising methods were introduced. In the late 1950s, in contrast to the wide use of professional advertising agencies for publicity in the U.S., this was an exception in case of German companies. In light of this situation, it can be said that Volkswagen was ahead of its time by introducing American marketing techniques (Kleinschmidt 2002, p. 254; Kleinschmidt 2004, p. 80). Particularly in the company's expansion of exports in the 1960s, it became an even more important theme to develop marketing for promoting exports. For example, due to the development of planned supply of advertising materials to importers, financial support for several markets, and the introduction of international merchandizing catalogs, there was an effort for sales promotion activities to be adjusted as much as possible to international levels (*Volkswagen Archiv*, Z174/N.2366, Jahresbericht 1966 des Vorstandsbereich Verkaufs, p. 18, *Volkswagen Archiv*, 174/1039, Jahresbericht 1969 der Hauptabteilung Verkauf und Kundendienst).

In this way, Volkswagen adopted an independent approach to marketing, while in their efforts to enter the American market and expand exports, the company heavily depended on individuals such as Hahn (Kleinschmidt 2004, p. 85). In addition, the introduction of American marketing techniques progressed in their use of advertising agencies. There was further expansion of the use of such techniques in the company's development in the German domestic market. In the 1960s and 1970s, there was an integration of the scattered individual marketing functions within the company, and in this process, there was an evolution from marketing as an auxiliary function of operational planning toward being a strategic planning method for business policies. However, consumer-oriented marketing management that integrated the various functions of product, sales, advertising, and price policies evolved even more earnestly in the 1970s and 1980s, when the business environment became even harsher (Vgl. Köhler 2008, pp. 216–239).

8.2.4.4 Steel Industry

For comparison with the industries discussed till now, we next analyze a producer goods industry; the steel industry. In the framework of Technical Assistance Project an example of a coordinated effort to learn about American marketing techniques was the Federation of German Iron and Steel Industry's implementation of a study trip to the U.S. in October 1954; the trip was related to marketing research, management organization, and industrial relations. On the trip, in relation to the organization of sales of commercial transactions, the participants learned that sales management comprises various staff departments such as the department of general production planning for preparation of orders, pricing department, market research, advertising department, and claims department. In this case, U.S. Steel served as a model [*Thyssen Krupp Archiv*, WVS/148, USA-Reise Oktober 1954: Marketing Research, Management Organisation, Industrial Relations (TA Projekt 09-288) (8.12.1954)]. In addition, there were efforts of individual companies. For example, in 1955, Thyssen conducted a study trip to their affiliate Armco in relation to the former's sales organization and market development department (*ThyssenKrupp Archiv*, A/1207, Untersuchung über die Organisation des Verkaufs und der Abteilung Market Development). Following this, in 1956, Thyssen signed an agreement with Armco to establish a market research and sales company [*ThyssenKrupp Archiv*, A/34272, Vertrag mit der Armco über die Marktforschungs- und Vertriebs GmbH (14.1.1956)].

However, since the products of the steel industry are producer goods, the market characteristic issues are different from those of the consumer goods industry, in which there are a variety of purchaser tastes and needs. Moreover, the nature of the development of marketing has aspects different from those of the previously described industrial sectors. As described above, until the mid-1960s, in heavy industries, there was a trend among companies to show only secondary interest in sales, advertising, and marketing (Kleinschmidt 2002, p. 226; Kleinschmidt 2004, p. 84). The steel industry is a representative of one of these industries.

8.2.5 German Characteristics of the Deployment of Marketing Techniques

Based on the above discussion, we will now discuss the German characteristics of the introduction of American marketing techniques.

In terms of the introduction of advertising and publicity, the scale of the second wave of Americanization from the mid-1960s to the early 1970s, particularly the acceptance of marketing based on mass consumption, was so large that it is incomparable to the first wave of Americanization in the 1950s. It affected almost all the large and medium-sized companies. Although American influence from the 1970s was not as large as before, there was a steady flow of American concepts and ideas. However, even thereafter, considerable differences continued to exist in many areas between German and American advertising and publicity. Americanization never meant the disappearance of traditional German behavior replaced by American behavior. It has been pointed out that the respect for individuality in advertising was never been Americanized (Schröter 1997, p. 114).

The adoption of American marketing and advertising methods was not a natural process of movement toward convergence; rather, it needed active and innovative entrepreneurs and managers. Even in the 1950s such entrepreneurs and managers were opposed to the practices in their own companies, such as the cartels and syndicates' model-oriented, traditional sales policies. Based on their experiences and discoveries in the U.S., they were instrumental in transitioning the country toward the market-oriented American model. However, it was not uncommon that they had to overcome resistance from within their companies (Kleinschmidt 2002, pp. 258–259).

There was hardly any economic field that strongly felt the innovative pressure from the U.S. to the extent of the advertising and publicity sector. From the perspectives of economic and cultural history, no model was more typically American than the advertising agency model. However, there barely existed an occupation with as much widespread antipathy toward the U.S. as the German advertising experts. In the history of the spread of American advertising in Germany, it is said that there was a convergence process between German tradition and modern American methods over a 40-year period that began in the mid-1920s and continued until the mid-1960s, with a temporary interruption during the Nazi period (Vgl. Schindelbeck 1995, p. 236).

Indeed, with the increase of competitive pressures, the need to introduce marketing increased. However, in German companies, there were expectations related to the sales function in terms of quality, delivery, and after-service, as well as the mindset that good quality products and services will be purchased. Because of the emphasis on providing high-quality products and services, concerns about pricing policies and distribution channels tended to be small (Lawrence 1980, p. 94). These points were also reflected in Germany's approach of introducing American marketing techniques.

In this way, compared with America's strong trend toward pragmatic thinking, in the German product market, consumer purchasing characteristics and behavior that emphasizes on technology, quality, and function can be seen. Also in case of companies, there were trends, management practices, and management cultures that emphasize on quality, technology, and production. Under these conditions, intense price competition was suppressed, and quality competition in Germany was more significant compared with other countries. This German characteristic, which was seen in areas such as product strategy, was a major background factor in the introduction and growth of marketing techniques in the development of post-war mass production.

8.3 Deployment of Public Relations in Germany

8.3.1 Overview of the Deployment of Public Relations

After World War II, corporate relations with society have gained importance beyond consumer relations or market perspectives. Therefore, we focus on the deployment of American-style public relations (PR below) in such areas.

First, we review the background and overall situation in regard to the deployment of PR. The first thesis on PR to appear in Germany was in an advertising magazine in 1937. Although there were no prominent reactions to it, a 1947 thesis, written by a different author and using the same terminology (Hundhausen 1957, p. 9), gained recognition. Efforts, or PR activities in the broad sense, could be seen in Germany before World War II (Vgl. Kunczik 1997, pp. 353–355). However, in comparison with the US, such activities were neither promoted in public interest, nor in economic or political environments prior to 1945. Nevertheless, after the 1950s, PR activities by German corporations gained new impetus through US PR concepts (Hilger 2004a, pp. 259, 261).

PR concepts were thus first accepted during German corporations' postwar recovery period (Barthenheier 1982, p. 4). However, with the acceptance of these concepts during the 1950s and 1960s, significant inconsistencies in the definition and expectations as well as inadequate distinctions were realized (Kleinschmidt 2002, p. 204). Although deployment of PR was said to have gathered steam only after the 1960s, Hartmann demonstrates that PR was still not widely used in 1963 (Hartmann 1963, p. 145). In 1971, Hoechst's K. Winnaker observed that no press conferences were held in the German industry prior to the war, but this situation completely changed after the war. During this time, PR departments began to maintain constant public contact through the radio and television, and thus, became indispensable within large corporations (Winnacker 1972, p. 391).

During the 1960s, with the advent of the mass consumer society, establishing a corporate image became more important than ever before. To create a corporate image, image advertising, similar to that widely used in the US, was even more assertively rolled out as a PR strategy. For example, through PR activities, Henkel aimed at gaining corporate name recognition in the product category of cleaning products and detergents. It went as far as sponsoring presentations and panel discussions as well as advertising in popular magazines in Germany (Hilger 2004a, pp. 270–271). Siemens, an electronics and electrical engineering company, also placed increasing emphasis on establishing and clarifying their corporate image in their communications planning and implementation, and pioneered the use of image analysis among large electrical industry corporations [*Siemens Archiv Akten*, 9871, Schwabenthan O, Unternehmenskommunikation für Siemens 1847 bis 1989, München, 1995 (Selbstverlag), p. 85]. To modernize their corporate image, Siemens conducted experiential surveys of its image in consumer society to tackle increasing competition, emerging in the latter half of the 1960s, they released increasingly aggressive image advertising that used new methodologies and content (Hilger 2004a, pp. 273, 275). However, within German corporations, unlike their American counterparts, providing financial support for cultural, humanitarian, and social activities had no strategic role until the 1980s (Hilger 2004a, pp. 260–261).

Expanding international operations increased the importance of international PR efforts. During the 1960s, departments and positions were created that were primarily responsible for international PR and creating PR concepts that could be applied both domestically and internationally; Henkel established such a department in 1969 (Hilger 2004a, p. 264).

US corporations that provided PR services were involved in such efforts and played an important role. For example, in the early 1950s, Julius Klein Public Relations, Inc. was already in the process of planning and making proposals for Bayer, a chemical corporation, and continued into the 1960s [Vgl. *Bayer Archiv*, 81/2.7.1, Public Relations an absolute Essential for Business Success in Ameria, *Bayer Archiv*, 81/2.7.1, A Public Relations Proposal for American Linen Supply Company—Steiner Sales Company, *Bayer Archiv*, 81/2.7.1, Die Schrift von Julius Klein an Farbenfabriken Bayer Aktiengesellschaft am 12. Juli 1954, *Bayer Archiv*, 81/2.7, Die Schrift von Julius Klein an Farbenfabriken Bayer Aktiengesellschaft am 12. Dezember 1955, *Bayer Archiv*, 81/2.7, Die Schrift von Julius Klein an Farbenfabriken Bayer Aktiengesellschaft am 16. Juli 1962, *Bayer Archiv*, 302–0261, Die Schift an Kurt Hansen von F. W. Haas & Company (11.5. 1966)]. By the mid-1950s, Bayer took initiative and activities of PR firms very seriously (*Bayer Archiv*, 81/2.7, USA/allgemeine Public Relations, *Bayer Archiv*, 81/2.7, Julius Klein Public Relations), and discussed appropriate PR measures to portray themselves in a stronger light in American society. These PR firms also supported companies other than Bayer, and worked toward building the image of German corporations in the US (Kleinschmidt 2002, p. 212). Julius Klein assisted Daimler-Benz with their PR activities during the 1960s [Vgl. *Mercedes-Benz Archiv,* Könecke 2, Die Schrift von Daimler-Benz AG an Julius Klein (9.1.1964), *Mercedes-Benz Archiv*, Könecke 2, Julius Klein, Public-Relations-Inc. (10.1.1964), *Mercedes-Benz Archiv*, Könecke 2, Die Schrift von Julius Klein an die Daimler-Benz AG (28.2.1964), *Mercedes-Benz Archiv*, Könecke 2, General Julius Klein, Public-Relations, Inc. (3.4.1964)], as Daimler-Benz reported during a visit to the US in 1963, and stated that advertising via PR was indispensable [*Mercedes-Benz Archiv*, 272, Persönliche Gedanken und Betrachtungen der Aufgaben der Werksleitung Sindelfingen nach der USA-Reise (9.5.1963), p. 3].

8.3.2 Prime Examples of the Deployment of Public Relations

Deployment of American-style PR methodologies progressed within Germany after World War II. However, the use of PR depended not only on West Germany's political and cultural traditions, which differed from those in the US, but also on the specific circumstances within the corporations (Kleinschmidt 2002, p. 206). We examine examples of these variations exhibited by major corporations.

Bayer began PR activities in the beginning of the 1950s to advertise and restore social trust both domestically and internationally. Although they had a long track record with PR, they often aligned themselves with the PR model applied in the US. Such efforts to improve recognition and corporate image could also be seen at Hüls, Phoenix-Rheinrohr, Henkel, amongst others (Kleinschmidt 2002, pp. 210–212, 215–217).

In 1960, Henkel created a PR department (Kleinschmidt 2002, p. 217) that reported directly to the board of directors at its headquarters. The department's purview included five areas: corporate inquiries, publishing, press relations, facility tours, and corporate archives [*Henkel Archiv*, 451/55, Bericht über die Aufwendungen der Kostenstelle "Public Relations" und des "Public Relations"-Etats im Geschäftsjahr 1968 (7.8.1969), pp. 1, 3–4]. They were tasked with clarifying PR concepts for three reasons: (1) a change in management after January 1, 1969, to the legal structure of a holding company for all corporations within the Henkel group, (2) a restructuring of group business according to divisions, functional departments, and regional departments on March 1, 1969, and (3) the establishment of a PR department responsible for all PR activities [*Henkel Archiv*, 451/55, Das PR-Konzept des Unternehmens Henkel (13.6.1969), p. 1]. From the perspective of rolling out PR activities across an entire corporation, including subsidiaries and affiliates, it was necessary to create a PR department directly under the management of the holding company. This department became responsible for resolving issues, both internal and external, by using organizational information policy methods [*Henkel Archiv*, 451/55, Der Unternehmenszweck Persil/Henkel (1968) und seine Auswirkung auf das PR-Konzept (12.9.1968), pp. 1–2]. Further, in 1969, the head of the department responsible for international PR, assumed responsibility for all PR activities, including planning PR initiatives, creating their structure, and implementing them. The department head was also engaged in merging the PR work of foreign subsidiaries with corporate-wide PR concepts, in addition to advising foreign subsidiaries on diverse PR issues [*Henkel Archiv*, 451/55, Organisation und Stellung der "Public Relations International" (23.1.1969), p 1, *Henkel Archiv*, 451/55, Überlegungen zur Einordnung der Stabsstelle Public Relations in die hierarchischen Ebenen (1.8.1969), p. 3]. Henkel's PR work was also remarkable because they also responded to marketing as well as personnel issues, such as hiring high-quality workers and managers [*Henkel Archiv*, 451/55, Überlegungen zur Einordnung der Stabsstelle Public Relations in die hierarchischen Ebenen (1.8.1969), pp. 2–3].

As for corporate image creation, the public was not entirely aware of Henkel's diversification, which was very broad in scope even in the beginning of the 1960s. Thus, Henkel used the expertise of management consulting firms to establish their corporate identity. SRI from the US advised Henkel to concentrate on a flexible pricing policy, while remaining true to their branded item philosophy and image of high-quality, long-lasting products (Hilger 2004a, pp. 271–272). On the basis of several surveys conducted in the early 1960s regarding their corporate image, Henkel moved forward with their efforts to further establish their corporate image. These efforts complemented their product advertising (Hilger 2004b, pp. 204–205), and methodologies included sample surveys and facility tours for consumers, such as housewives. The sample surveys were considered the inception for a large-scale PR campaign in the first half of the 1960s. Henkel's initial press and PR activities referenced the pre-war model, and not the US model. However, during the 1950s and 1960s, Henkel pursued PR efforts aligned with the US model, using scientific US methods and elevating the importance of a PR department within the company. The same pattern characterized the chemical firm Hüls (Kleinschmidt 2002, pp. 217–218).

BASF was also working on their PR during the 1960s to tackle problems with their communication vehicles [*BASF Archiv*, C19/14, Werbebeilage in BASF-Organen (23.5.1962), *BASF Archiv*, C19/14, Public Relations—Diskussion im Fernsehen (5.11.1962)] and organizational changes in the PR department. In 1962, the PR department continued to be responsible for PR activities and corporate advertising, whereas their sales department was responsible for product advertising; the advertising and product information groups in the PR department were transferred to the sales department [*BASF Archiv*, C19/13b u C19/14, Zuständigkeiten und Abgrenzung Öffentlichkeitsarbeit—Werbung (8.8.1962)]. In 1966, BASF's PR department underwent organizational restructuring and was given archival and editing groups, expanding to eight units from the original seven sections which were press, corporate newsletters, factory newspaper, PR publications and advertising, film and visitor relations, government relations, and overall PR (*BASF Archiv*, C19/13b, Organisationsschema der Abteilung Öffentlichkeitsarbeit (Stand: 2.1.1963), *BASF Archiv*, C0, Abteilung Öffentlichkeitsarbeit (AOA) [Stand: August 1966), *BASF Archiv*, C19/13b, Organisatorische Änderungen bei AOA (16.2.1966)].

Krupp, the steel manufacturer, was also working toward its PR under the direction of PR pioneer C. Hundhausen. It made efforts to gain "social trust" in Germany and internationally via several PR activities, not only in West Germany but also in England and France, in magazines and other print media as well as in schools and through radio broadcasts. The full color covers and pictures of their factory facilities in their US annual reports were regarded as exemplary models (Kleinschmidt 2002, pp. 209–210).

8.3.3 German Characteristics in the Deployment of Public Relations

Based on the above-mentioned examples, we describe German characteristics specific to their deployment of PR methods. Kleinschmidt emphasizes three aspects of the deployment of PR methods. First, the importance of PR grew with the growing interest of many German companies to establish a foothold in the US market. Second, the US model had an important directional function for German corporations from since the early 1950s, and served as a motivational factor for imitation until the 1980s. Third, beginning at least in the nineteenth century and into the twentieth century, Germany followed PR traditions that were clearly different from the US style of PR in the post-war period. PR in the US was not only based on new social science methods but also went beyond newspaper advertising, and was based on the broader understanding of the masses that considered closer connections with advertising, marketing, and other management methods (Vgl. Kleinschmidt 2002, pp. 219–220). In fact, American-style PR propagated throughout the operations of German corporations for the first time in the 1960s. However, German corporations' PR was subordinate to their marketing, and this divergence increasingly took the form of sales marketing methods (Barthenheier 1982, pp. 11–12).

Hilger noted that German corporations frequently held tight to their time-honored traditions, and until the 1970s, "continuity," "durability," and "quality" were typical German corporate values that received priority (Hilger 2004a, p. 277). For example, Daimler-Benz's management opposed a policy of "openness," and their communications model never coincided with the US model. Similarly, at Siemens, some parts of the organization were uninformed of the importance of PR. However, as systematic information management gained importance, unified PR activities finally began with the setting up of a central information headquarters in 1968. In fact, it was realized that Henkel was more serious than other US corporations when it came to communications policies specific to PR efforts. Germany had a tradition of political PR that was passed down from the pre-war era, and that viewpoint continued to be seen as important even after the war as a reflection of business culture after the late nineteenth century (Hilger 2004a, pp. 262–268).

In regard to these German characteristics, core PR policies aimed at the creation of good societal relationships, and were firmly integrated in a sales policy that responded to customers and the market. Even then, from the viewpoint of management and management culture based on German values emphasizing quality and technology, the pragmatic values of the US style that prioritized market principles were not necessarily appropriate.

8.4 Deployment of Operations Research in Germany

We next examine the deployment of operations research (OR). Several large German corporations had been debating OR issues from very early on. Even among US corporations, and prior to the 1940s, OR methodologies were for the most part not in use. Bayer, for example, had begun to use them only 2 or 3 years after US corporations. Bayer gathered information on US corporations from a report in the specialty magazine *Chemical & Engineering News*. In 1956, they also attended conferences and functions in New York, sponsored by organizations such as the American Management Association, and subsequently relayed information on OR methodologies to West Germany. Further, the creation of professional journals and the first series of lectures on OR in Munich in 1957 created further dissemination channels (Kleinschmidt 2002, pp. 286–287). In Germany, OR was added to business management curricula in 1945, although at the time it was not considered as significant (Schröter 2005, p. 104).

However, exponential technological advancement and intense competition in the 1960s, introduced studies on the use of OR methodologies and value analysis in calculating optimal order amounts in an RKW series of publications and other periodicals (Rationalisierung 1966, p. 189). According to Pentzlin (1964), the changes dictated a decade of progress that are most clearly defined by the American phrase "moving from scientific management to management science," and one of the important manifestations of this progress is in OR, or operational research (Pentzlin 1964, p. 4).

We now focus on examples of deployment of OR in German corporations. The Henkel group began using electronic data processing and technology such as OR in the latter half of the 1960s, although Henkel's scale of OR efforts were smaller than that of a few other corporations (*Henkel Archiv*, 251/2, Stanford Research Institute, Langfristige Planung für Persil/Henkel, Phase II, 2.Bd, Juli 1968, p. 318). However, rationalization of inventory and sales required the use of modern methodologies for business management, and it provides one good example of how OR, IE, and other scientific methodologies for business management enabled them to achieve this goal (*Henkel Archiv*, 251/2, Stanford Research Institute, Langfristige Planung für Persil/Henkel, Phase II, 2.Bd, Juli 1968, p. 343). Siemens also used OR methodologies after World War II (Eidenmüller 2002, p. 107), and deployed a management game system called "DELPHI" at the end of the 1960s. DELPHI modeled complex business conditions over time to reveal the results of corporate decision-making and the response of competitors, increasing users' awareness of economic laws. Data processing was finally considered as an investment for systems and methods enabling future activities, and OR methodologies were recognized as an aid to this end (*Siemens Archiv Akten*, 2-2600-829, DELPHI—ein handelsorientiertes Unternehmensspiel, *Siemens Archiv Akten*, 2-2600-829, DELPHI—A commercially-orientated Management Game).

It is important to view the deployment of OR methodologies in relation to that of electronic data processing technology. With the progress of corporate reorganizations after the mid-1960s and the increasing importance of business planning, electronic data processing gained more importance within the framework of OR methodologies and linear graph technology, and management information systems (MIS) deployed by the US. For example, executives at Glanzstoff and Freudenberg conducted surveys of PERT systems and linear graph technology developed in the US at the end of the 1950s. A strong orientation to the US among German corporations could be seen in management accounting and control systems after the war, but the deployment of electronic data processing was a critical prerequisite for the deployment of methodologies such as OR, linear graphs, and MIS (Kleinschmidt 2002, p. 291).

However, use of OR methodologies in Germany began only at the start of the 1960s, which was relatively late, and remained largely unused in corporations by the end of the decade. Even at the start of the 1970s, OR methodologies were primarily used to resolve operational issues. OR was rarely used to solve planning issues and basic executive management problems. Moreover, the acute lack of OR specialists made it difficult for these methodologies to gain further traction (Booz-Allen and Hamilton 1973, pp. 27–28, 30, 65).

After the war, marketing, PR, and OR maintained its management foundation of supporting the large company constitution based on competition in the oligopolistic market and the market control of large companies. However, with the German tradition of quality- and technology-oriented management values/management culture and market characteristics, the American management methods, which were created and developed under the advanced stage of standardization of both production and consumption based on the pragmatic tradition stressing the efficiency principle in the U.S., were not necessarily appropriate for Germany. For example, "planned obsolescence," one of the typical oligopolistic behaviors that are most widely promoted in the U.S. as a sales policy technique that contributes to the creation of competitive advantage (Busch 1966, p. 159), was not necessarily appropriate in Germany. Companies such as Daimler-Benz had a product development-oriented product strategy that reflected the social responsibility of providing the highest quality in terms of safety and comfort regardless of whether the vehicle was a luxury car, utility vehicle, passenger car, or commercial vehicle (Vgl. Daimler-Benz 1972, pp. 196, 202, 210; Daimler-Benz 1983, p. 127; Walz and Niemann 1997, p. 178). In the same way, in companies such as Volkswagen that had an orientation toward mass production, from the early stages of the post-war period, the factor ensuring competitiveness in the world market was the emphasis on quality (Volkswagen 1955, p. 26). The characteristics of German management behavior were also seen in these types of situations, and market characteristics, consumer purchasing characteristics, and corporate behavior principles based on these characteristics can be said to have influenced the German way of adapting to the market under the development of mass production. However, this type of German development and way of being was not only something that reflected the structure and characteristics of the market. The fact that the problem did not surface under favorable historical conditions, as seen in the competitive structure and relationship between the market and productive forces of the boom years of the 1950s and 1960s, is also important.

References

Abelshauser W (1995) Two kinds of Fordism: on the differing roles of the industry in the development to the two German states. In: Shiomi H, Wada K (eds) Fordism transformed. The development of production methods in the automobile industry. Oxford University Press, New York, pp 269–296

Barthenheier G (1982) Auf der Suche nach Identität—Zur historishen Entwicklung der Öffentlichkeitsarbeit/public relations. In: Haedrich G, Barthenheier G, Kleinert H (eds) Öffentlichkeitsarbeit: Dialog zwischen Investitionen und Gesellschafte. Ein Handbuch. W. de Gruyter, Berlin, pp 3–13

Booz-Allen & Hamilton (1973) Herausforderungen des deutschen Managements und ihre Bewältigung. Ott Schwartz, Göttingen

Busch KW (1966) Strukturwandlungen der westdeutschen Automobilindustrie. Ein Beitrag zur Erfassung und Deutung einer industriellen Entwicklungsphasen im Übergang vom produktionsorientierten zum marktorientierten Wachstum. Dunker & Humblot, Berlin

Daimler-Benz AG (ed) (1972) Chronik. Mercedes-Benz Fahrzeuge und Motoren, 5. Aufl. Daimler-Benz, Stuttgart

Daimler-Benz AG (1983) Werk Untertürkheim. Stammwerke der Daimler-Benz Aktiengesellschaft. Ein historischen Überbild. Daimler-Benz, Stuttgart

Der Volkswirt (1955) Eine million Volkswagen. Der Volkswirt 9(32):10–1

Der Volkswirt (1960) Volkswagenwerk mit hohen Zuwachsraten. Rund 256 Mill.DM Gewinne—Auflösung stiller Reserven. Der Volkswirt 14(36):2046–2050

Dyas GP, Thanheiser HT (1976) The emerging European enterprise. Strategy and structure in French and German industry. Macmillan, London

Eidenmüller B (2002) Das Jahrhundert der Massenproduktion. Siemes AG, München
Feldenkirchen W (2004a) DaimlerChrysler Werk Untertürkheim. Motorbuch-Verlag, Stuttgart
Feldenkirchen W (2004b) The Americanization of the German electrical industry after 1945. Siemens as a case study. In: Kudo A, Kipping M, Schröteret HG (eds) German and Japanese business in the boom years. Transforming American management and technology models. Routledge, London, pp 116–137
Hallig K (1965) Amerikanische Erfahrungen auf dem Gebiet der Wirtschaftswerbung im Hinblick auf ihre Anwendung im westeuropäischen Raum. Duncker & Humblot, Berlin
Hartmann H (1963) Amerikanische Firmen in Deutschland. Westdeutscher Verlag, Köln
Hilger S (2004a) „Amerikanisierung" deutscher Unternehmen. Wettbewerbsstrategien und Unternehmenspolitik bei Henkel, Siemens und Daimler-Benz (1945/49-1975). Franz Steiner Verlag, Stuttgart
Hilger S (2004b) Reluctant Americanization? The reaction of Henkel to the influences and competition from the United States. In: Kudo A, Kipping M, Schröteret HG (eds) German and Japanese business in the boom years. Transforming American management and technology models. Routledge, London, pp 193–220
Hiller H (1952) Das Volkswagenwerk legt Rechnung. Der Volkswirt 6(22):26–29
Hölzer H (1964) Werbung ist Führungsaufgabe. Der Volkswirt, 18. Jg, Beiheft zu Nr. 39 vom 25 September 1964. Werbung ist Führungsaufgabe, p 5
Hundhausen C (1957) Industrielle Pablizität als public relations. W. Girardet, Essen
Kleinschmidt C (1998) An Americanized company in Germany. The Vereinigte Glanzstoff Fabriken AG in the 1950s. In: Kipping M, Bjarnar O (eds) The Americanization of European business. The Marshall plan and the transfer of US management models. Routledge, London, pp 171–189
Kleinschmidt C (2002) Der produktive Blick. Wahrnehmung amerikanischer und japanischer Management- und Produktionsmethoden durch deutsche Unternehmer 1950–1985. Akademie Verlag, Berlin
Kleinschmidt C (2004) Driving the West German consumer society: the introduction of US style production and marketing at Volkswagen, 1945–70. In: Kudo A, Kipping M, Schröteret HG (eds) German and Japanese business in the boom year. Transforming American management and technology models. Routledge, London, pp 75–92
Köhler I (2008) Marketingmanagement als Strukturmodell. Der organisatorische Wandel in der deutschen Automobilindustrie der 1960er bis 1980er Jahre. Zeitschrift für Unternehmensgeschichte 53(2):216–239
Korte FK (1964) Der Werbeleiter in der Unternehmens-Hierarchie. Der Volkswirt, 18.Jg, Beiheft zu Nr. 39 vom 25 September 1964, pp 26–31
Kunczik M (1997) Geschichte der Öffentlichkeitsarbeit in Deutschland. Böhlau Verlag, Köln
Lawrence P (1980) Managers and management in West Germany. Croom Helm, London
Linne K (2008) «[…] bisher nur Sonnentage […]». Der Aufbau der Volkswagen-Händlerorganisation 1948 bis 1967. Zeitschrift für Unternehmensgeschichte 53(1):5–32
Noda K (ed) (1969) Nihon Keieishi: Gendai Keieishi (Business history in Japan: modern business history). Nihon Seisansei Honbu, Tokyo
OEEC (1954) Problems of business management. OEEC, Paris
Ogawa K (2011) Nihonteki Maketing no Genryu to sono Sengoshi (The origin of Japanese marketing and its history after WW II). In: Kikkawa T, Kubo F (eds) Grobaruka to Nihonteki Keieisisutem no Henyo (Globalization and transformation of the Japanese management system). Mineruva Shobo, Kyoto, pp 199–220
Pentzlin K (1964) In der modernen Industrie. Der Volkswirt 18.Jg, Beilage zu Nr. 16 vom 17. April 1964. Rationalisierung, Chancen und Grenzen in der Praxis, pp 2–4
Rationalisierung (1966) Betriebswirtschaftliche Rationalisierung. Rationalisierung 17(8):186–191
Remele H (1963) Rationalisierungsreserven in Klein- und Mittelbetrieben. Ergebnisse einer Analyse des RKW-Betriebsbegehungsdienstes. Rationalisierung 14(5):113–5
Sato H (1983) Nihon no Ryutsu Kiko (The Japanese distribution system). Yuhikaku, Tokyo

Schindelbeck D (1995) „Asbach Uralt" und „Soziale Marktwirtschaft". Zur Kulturgeschichte der Werbeagentur in Deutschland am Beispiel von Hannes W. Brose (1899–1971). Zeitschrift für Unternehmensgeschichte 40(4):235–252

Schröter HG (1997) Die Amerikanisierung der Werbung in der Bundesrepublik Deutschland. Jahrbuch für Wirtschaftsgeschichte, 1997/1:93–115

Schröter HG (1998) Advertising in West Germany after World War II. A case of an Americanization. In: Schröter HG, Moen E (eds) Une Americanisation des Enterprises? Eska, Paris, pp 15–33

Schröter HG (2005) Americanization of the European economy. A compact survey of American economic influence in Europe since the 1880s. Springer, Dordrecht

Shimokawa K (1991) Maketingu (Marketing). Bunshindo, Tokyo

Strotmann K-H (1960) Marktforschung als Voraussetzung für Typenbeschränkung. Rationalisierung 11(1):12–14

Vogelsang G (1961) Über die technische Entwicklung des Volkswagens. Automobiltechnische Zeitschrift 63(1):1–13

Volkswagen GmbH (ed) (1955) Ein Rechenschaftsbericht für die Belegschaft und für die Auβenenorganisation des Volkswagenwerks. Geschäftsverlauf und Rechnungsabschluβ 1951 bis 1954, Werks-Chronik bis 1955. Volkswagen, Wolfsburg

Wakabayashi Y (1999) Nihon no Maketingshi Kenkyu no Igi to Kenkyu Wakugumi (Significance and framework of studies on the history of marketing in Japan). In: Kondo F, Wakabayashi Y (eds) Nihonkigyo no Masu-Maketingushi (History of mass marketing in Japanese enterprise). Dobunkan, Tokyo, pp 3–24

Walz W, Niemann H (1997) Daimler-Benz. Wo das Auto anfing, 6. Aufl. Friedr. Stadler, Konstanz

Wellhöner V (1996) „Wirtschaftswunder"—Weltmarkt—Westdeutscher Fordismus. Der Fall Volkswagen. Westfälisches Dampfboot, Münster

Winnacker K (1972) Nie den Mut verlieren. Erinnerungen an Schicksalsjahr der deutschen Chemie. Econ Verlag, Düsseldorf

Chapter 9
Deployment of a Divisional Structure

Abstract This chapter discusses the deployment of a divisional structure in relation to changes in business strategies, management systems and practices, and managers' traditional attitudes. It examines Japan's and Germany's methods of deploying a divisional structure, the progress of diversification in German corporations and its connection to organizational structure reforms, and the overall situations post the deployment of the divisional structure. It also considers case studies of representative corporations in major industries such as the chemical, electric, and iron and steel industries. This chapter reviews the deployment of a control system as an internal control organization and the role of US corporations and management consulting firms in management organization reforms. These discussions explain various characteristics of the deployment of German-style divisional structure such as (1) the impact level of delegation of authorities and responsibilities, (2) the traditions and roles of the board of directors and collegiate management, (3) the characteristics of the board majority system, (4) the significance of divisional executive management, and (5) the use of a compensation system linked to divisional results.

Keywords Control systems • Decentralization • Diversification strategy • Divisional structure • Functional structure

After World War II, the expansion of domestic markets and market opportunities resulting from advances in mass production served as a basis for business diversification that in turn stimulated changes in management organization. Once again, the American-style management system was established as an effective model. A prime example was the decentralized divisional structure implemented first in several pioneering corporations in the 1920s (Chandler 1962, 1977, 1990) and spreading after the war. German corporations as well sought to restructure organizations along the lines of the US model.

T. Yamazaki, *German Business Management: A Japanese Perspective on Regional Development Factors*, DOI 10.1007/978-4-431-54303-9_9,

In this chapter, we consider the deployment of divisional structures using case studies of typical corporations from major industries, and examine the impact and role of US corporations and consulting firms in order to understand German characteristics of management organization structure. We will explore these deployments based on their relationship to the traditional attributes of German business management.

9.1 Various Japanese Characteristics of the Deployment of Divisional Structure

Observing the situation in Japan for comparison of these organizational changes, it can be seen that the deployment of organizational divisional structure was facilitated by diversification of business. However, with Japan's high economic growth, one could notice not only diversification in large corporations but also an increase in corporations taking the opposite approach of vertical integration. Therefore, the level of diversification was low compared to that of US corporations and the pace of diversification was slow (Yoshihara et al. 1981, pp. 58, 64–65). Further, there were relatively few examples of qualitative, aggressive diversification in Japanese corporations focusing on changing patterns of resource accumulation and utilization (Yoshihara et al. 1981, pp. 49, 65–66, 209, 235).

Still, diversification caused significant changes in the organizational structure. With increased diversification, adoption rate of functional structure became lower and that of divisional structures had an almost equally inverse growth (Yoshihara et al. 1981, pp. 205–207, 225). However, Japanese corporations' adoption rate of divisional structures was relatively lower and slower than that in Europe and especially lagged behind that of the US. A major reason for the lower adoption rate of divisional structure was the low level and slow pace of diversification (Yoshihara et al. 1981, pp. 58, 64–65, 201, 203, 225). The relationship between diversification strategies and the shape of an organization was not so strong that a particular strategy would require to use a particular organization form. In fact, there was a great deal of freedom of choice on the selection of organization form. This is particularly true for a moderate scope of diversification (Yoshihara et al. 1981, pp. 205–207). In addition, among corporations that adopted a divisional structure, many deployed trendy divisional structures rather than one based on a rational comparison of the relative merits and demerits of divisional and functional structures. However, from 1965 onward, corporations began to examine the strengths and weaknesses of divisional structure and reflect more carefully on the shape of the organization. During this period, some companies discontinued divisional structures and returned to a centralized functional structure. A characteristic of this period was a trend toward re-centralization (Yoshihara et al. 1981, pp. 200, 203, 224–225; Ono 1979, pp. 125–128; Imanishi 1988, p. 61).

Moreover, this same period was characterized by a certain percentage of organizational structures that were a mixture of divisional and functional structure wherein functional structures were retained for core business lines, while non-core businesses were organizations of independent divisions. Within this form of organization, business decision-making power for non-core businesses was left to the division, whereas for core business lines, no differentiation was made between headquarters and the organization conducting the business (Yoshihara et al. 1981, pp. 191–192; Kagono 1980, pp. 205, 271).

Further, Japanese corporations had many "pseudo" divisions that were unlike the typical US divisional structure. In US divisional structures, the division typically bore profit responsibility as an autonomous unit. However, in Japanese corporations, many divisions lacked the requisite functions for autonomy (Ishii et al. 1996, pp. 132–133). Traditionally, for an organization to be autonomous, it had to have production, sales and marketing, technology, R&D, and other functions necessary for business—a rare situation for a Japanese corporate division (Yoshihara et al. 1981, p. 193).

In Japan, divisions were never granted complete authority, and even with the adoption of a divisional structure, headquarters provided a great deal of direction and exerted control over divisions, a characteristic of headquarters-driven centralization (Choki 1993, p. 44; Kagono et al. 1983, p. 37; Urabe 1960, p. 198). Given the above-mentioned conditions, the connection between results and compensation was also weak compared to the US (Ishii et al. 1996, p. 133). Divisions in Japanese corporations lacked a high degree of self-sufficiency, division performance evaluations were simpler, and divisional organizations tended to be adopted after a revision of their traditional form (Kagono et al. 1983, p. 38). After 1965, importance began to be placed on divisional independence and their traditional status as profit centers because customer- or market-oriented management systems responded to changes in corporate environments, which necessitated restructuring (Ono 1979, p. 128).

Such Japanese corporations deployed divisional structure with certain similarities to and differences from German corporations. One similarity is that a certain percentage of the largest industrial enterprises had a mixed organization that differed from a divisional structure. Another is the low level of self-sufficiency resulting from the weak connection between the delegation of authority, results, and compensation. However, as we will reveal below, regarding various factors in which Germany and Japan differed from the US, such as delegating authority to divisions, correlating general manager compensation to division results, there were differences between Germany and Japan reflecting circumstances behind decentralization, and Germany's traditions of collegiate management and the board-majority system.

Below, we will consider the deployment of divisional structures in Germany. First, we review the expansion of diversification in German corporations in Sect. 9.2. In Sect. 9.3, we consider organizational structure reforms along with case studies of divisional structure deployment in representative corporations in major industries. In Sect. 9.4, we examine the role of US corporations and management consulting firms in management organization reforms. In Sect. 9.5, we explain various characteristics of German-style divisional structure deployment based on these discussions.

9.2 Transformation of Business Strategy in Germany: Expansion of Diversification

9.2.1 Social and Economic Background of Postwar Diversification

We will first look at the expansion of diversification, one of the most important factors in postwar management organization reforms. At the time, diversification in German corporations was regulated by changes in the environment of industry competition. Specifically, changes in demand patterns and the pace of technological advancement caused changes in competition, with innovations in products and marketing method supplanting traditional factors such as pricing and quality. In addition, increased consumer affluence related to technological potential gave birth to many new product and market opportunities that enabled corporations in many industries to experience fast growth and high profits. Major corporations operating in more traditional boundaries with no potential of absolute or relative growth encountered a difficult choice. For example, at the chemical company Hüls, it became apparent that the reductions in revenue and profit at the beginning of the 1960s far exceeded those of IG Farben's three major successor companies, and heightened the necessity for diversification [Vgl. *Hüls Archiv*, I-5-8, Aktennotiz (8.8.1962), p. 1]. In addition, many corporations that had quickly accumulated resources rather than reinvesting in mature products or markets, particularly the most successful companies, needed to find growth opportunities outside their own industry. Diversification was an important element in the strategic response to these circumstances (Dyas and Thanheiser 1976, p. 132). Particularly at the end of the 1960s, competition due to the opening up of new markets and the lowering of tariffs in EEC countries was an important factor in this re-orientation toward diversification (Wengenroth 1997, p. 162).

However, the characteristics of German corporate ownership, particularly financial and management constraints in family-owned corporations, restricted diversification (Dyas and Thanheiser 1976, p. 133). Other factors limiting diversification included the necessity for rebuilding in the post-war years; extremely rapid growth in the automotive, electrical, and capital goods industries; tax laws; and tradition of cartels and trusts linked to relatively weak anti-trust laws (Dyas and Thanheiser 1976, p. 100). Technological relevance was a dominant factor of the diversification movement in Germany. However, analysis of the top 100 industrial enterprises reveals that diversification was not the only direction taken after the war, but in fact diversification also occurred simultaneously, or nearly so, with horizontal and vertical integration (Dyas and Thanheiser 1976, pp. 90, 101).

9.2.2 *Advancement of Diversification and Its Characteristics*

Next, as we look at strategic changes in the advancement of diversification, 34 out of the top 100 industrial enterprises' business structures in 1950s Germany were single types and 26 were dominant types. In contrast, 32 companies were related types and 7 were unrelated types. Although single-type firms decreased to 22 by 1960, the most important change in the 1950s was the diversification that occurred in 12 such corporations. In this diversification, nine of these corporations became dominant types, two related types, and one an unrelated type. As a result, dominant-type firms increased slightly to 28 by 1960. From 1950 to 1960, nine corporations diversified away from being dominant types, with eight of these becoming related types and one an unrelated type. While 40 corporations had become related types by 1960, unrelated types slightly increased to 9, a minor change.

In contrast, in 1960 and 1970, the greatest changes were in diversification to related types (5) and unrelated types (10). In 1970, 56% of corporations had significantly diversified in this manner. Although related types had decreased slightly to 38, unrelated types had greatly increased to 18.

Further, as we examine changes in the 20-year period between 1950 and 1970, the channel diversification often adopted was from single type to dominant type to related type to unrelated type. It was rare for a company to stray from this channel and move from a single type to a highly diversified related type or unrelated type. That is, 35% (9 out of 26) of the corporations that were dominant types in 1950 had changed over 10 years, and 25% (7 out of 28) of the corporations that were dominant types changed by 1970 (Dyas and Thanheiser 1976, pp. 26, 63–72). For an index on types and classifications of diversification, refer to Rumelt (1974, Chap. 1).

Thus, we see that in Germany, the striking expansion of diversification to unrelated types, such as that among US conglomerates, had not occurred in the 1960s, as Germany emphasized diversification in related types.

9.3 Deployment of Divisional Structure in Major German Industries

9.3.1 *Overall Circumstances of the Deployment of Divisional Structure*

9.3.1.1 Expansion of Diversification and Changes in Organization Structure

We will next look at the changes in organizational structure and their relationship to the expansion of strategy. In comparing the number of top 100 industrial enterprises using a functional structure in the years 1950, 1960, and 1970, 36 companies used a functional structure, which then decreased to 21 and finally to 20. In 1950, 15 companies had a holding company structure, which fell to 14 and then to 12. Companies with a mixture of functional and holding company structures increased from 43 to 48, and then fell dramatically to 18. In contrast, companies with a divisional structure numbered a mere five in 1950, tripled to 15 in 1960, and greatly increased to 50 by 1970. Observing the 78 German capital firms, companies with a divisional structure were unheard of in 1950 and by 1960 there were still only three; however, by 1970, they accounted for 40% of the total. Nevertheless, when compared to the 78% and 72% adoption rates of the US and UK, respectively, Germany's rate was still low.

In 1950 and 1960, 25 of the top 100 companies implemented organizational structure reforms, out of which the most common change was a shift from a functional structure to a combination of functional and holding company structures (12 companies), while a change to a divisional structure was largely unseen. Deployment of divisional structures progressed strongly in the 1960s, and between 1960 and 1970, 36 out of 47 companies chose to adopt this type of organization. In the 20 years between 1950 and 1970, the most common pattern was a change from a functional structure to a combination of functional structure and holding company, and then to a divisional structure. Of the 45 companies that adopted a divisional structure, only four moved from a functional structure and six from a holding company structure. In contrast, 35 companies changed from a functional structure/holding company combination to a divisional structure (Dyas and Thanheiser 1976, pp. 65–73).

Regarding such changes, Gabele has noted that among the overall changes to management structure, change processes resulting in divisional structures were overwhelmingly common. However, there was a great difference in adoption between large firms and small- and medium-sized firms. For example, at the end of 1974, although 46.7% of large corporations had implemented a divisional structure, among medium-sized firms, the implementation rate was only 38% (Gabele 1981, pp. 1–2). In 1982, Harrmann pointed out that during the prior decade, many corporations had restructured, with one of the characteristics of this change being apparent in operational field-, division-, and product-oriented organizations. However, when viewed overall with small- and medium-sized firms, many corporations did not replace their functional structures with divisional structures. Among the large companies that primarily moved to a divisional department or divisional structure during the late 1960s and early 1970s, some had product divisions and regional divisions, among which overseas and European business regions were problematic (Harrmann 1982, pp. 202–203).

Next, as we look at the relationship between strategy and organizational structure, in 1950, only 7% of the top 100 industrial enterprises that had implemented diversification (both related and unrelated) were also using a divisional structure. This proportion had reached 20% by 1960 and 67% by 1970. Of the 78 West German capital firms, a mere 8% had this structure in 1960 which increased up to 63% by 1970 (Dyas and Thanheiser 1976, p. 66). However, when compared with the 500 largest US companies, not only was there a difference in the adoption rate of divisional structures, but there also was a time lag in implementing diversification and divisional structures. Among the 45 corporations that had shifted to this organization form between 1950 and 1970, 14 had made the change within 10 years, seven between 10 and 20 years, and nine took more than 20 years to change. In addition, 60% of corporations that had expanded to include greater varieties in products and markets during the 1950s had adopted a divisional structure during that 10-year period. Although this figure rose to 75% by the 1960s, the most remarkable wave of divisional structure deployment was witnessed in the late 1960s (Dyas and Thanheiser 1976, pp. 73–74). In 1967, the domain of corporate organization was regarded as a new frontier (REFA-Nachrichten 1967, p. 263), and deployment of divisional structures in more than half of the 100 largest corporations occurred after that year (Dyas and Thanheiser 1976, p. 129). On this point, Siegrist noted that divisional structures first began to truly penetrate German corporations in the late 1960s, approximately 10 years after overall penetration in the US (Siegrist 1980, p. 88).

9.3.1.2 Generational Change in Management and Deployment of Divisional Structures

Divisional structure deployment in German corporations was significantly affected by management systems and practices as well as managers' traditional attitudes. Compared with a country such as the US, where management had evolved, business management specialization in German corporations was stagnant, and there was a strong differentiation between daily operational and top executives, who were highly autonomous (Vgl. Hartmann 1968, pp. 47, 75, 78, 91, 281, 291). The ideological foundation of top management authority that had become entrenched as a traditionally strict gap kept between executives at the board of directors level and the lower, laborer level was diametrically opposed to broader delegation of responsibility and strategic information sharing between vertical strata required by a divisional structure. In such cases, adoption of a new form of organization typically depended on one person or alternatively a group of a few people. The departure of certain individuals from the ranks of top management and handoffs to successors became decisive points in the timing of organizational change (Dyas and Thanheiser 1976, p. 136).

The fact that organizational restructuring occurred after the beginning of the 1960s generally resulted from opposition by one or two key individuals in the power structure of a given corporation rather than a lack of either top management knowledge regarding divisional structures or confidence in its appropriateness for solving problems in their organization. Therefore, a change in corporate control resulting from a generational change in management was an important method of eliminating obstacles to organizational restructuring (Dyas and Thanheiser 1976, p. 114). As V. Berghahn noted, the generational change in management began slowly at the beginning of the 1960s (Berghahn 1985, p. 293), and shifts from a functional structure to a divisional structure occurred relatively slowly as a result of dependence upon these generational changes in corporations (Hilger 2004, p. 278).

9.3.2 Case Studies of the Deployment of Divisional Structures

Based on the previous overview of the deployment of divisional structures, we will next consider case studies of typical corporations in major industries.

9.3.2.1 Deployment of Divisional Structures in the Chemical Industry and Its Characteristics

9.3.2.1.1 Henkel Case Study

Let us first look at the chemical industry, an archetype of the expansion of diversification and deployment of divisional structures.

Henkel was a typical corporation that implemented organizational reforms based on a proposal from the Stanford Research Institute (SRI), a US consulting firm. SRI made three proposals regarding long-term business planning, strategic business planning, and organizational structure [Vgl. *Henkel Archiv*, 251/1, Stanford Research Institute (SRI), Einführung einer verbindlichen langfristigen Planung in die Persil/Henkel Gruppe—Phase I, April 1967, *Henkel Archiv*, 251/2, SRI, Langfristigen Planung für Persil/Henkel, Phase II: Strategische Planung, 1.Bd, 2.Bd Juli 1968, *Henkel Archiv*, 314/133, SRI, Langfristigen Planung für Persil/Henkel, Phase III: Organisationsstruktur der Unternehmensspitze und des leitenden Management, Dezember 1968]. The proposal for organizational restructuring made in December 1968 was approved in 1969 (Henkel GmbH 1969, p. 33), and on this basis, a new organizational structure was deployed. At Persil/Henkel, where diversification was in progress to a certain extent, top management had extraordinary difficulty in operating the company at peak efficiency with middle and lower levels of management organized according to function (*Henkel Archiv*, 251/2, Stanford Research Institute, Langfristigen Planung für Persil/Henkel, Phase II, p. 315). In SRI's proposal, Persil/Henkel had arrived at the point where they needed to make fundamental changes to their oranizational structure due to corporate scale and diversity (*Henkel Archiv*, 314/133, Stanford Research Institute, Langfristigen Planung für Persil/Henkel, Phase III, pp. 3, 24). In Henkel's existing functional structure, specific obstacles had become apparent, including the delegation of profit responsibility, manufacturing methods to reduce overall corporate costs, optimization of costs for marketing and other functions, and inadequate information exchange among various functional silos during operational planning. A lack of clarity on responsibilities and authority in addition to a lack of delegation of authority at all levels of the company caused major problems. Therefore, top management was forced to deal with issues in excessive detail, which resulted in problems because insufficient time remained for basic corporate policy decision-making and planning [*Henkel Archiv*, 314/133, Stanford Research Institute, Langfristigen Planung für Persil/Henkel, Phase III, pp. 24–26, 28–30, *Henkel Archiv*, 314/96, SRI-Besprechung am 16. Oktober 1968 (17.10.1968), p. 3, *Henkel Archiv*, 251/10, SRI. Mündliche Präsentation. Struktur der Unternehmensorganisation von Persil/Henkel].

It was decided that increasing profits and decreasing costs required cost centers and profit centers in lower groups with authority and responsibility delegated to them (*Henkel Archiv*, 251/2, Stanford Research Institute, Langfristigen Planung für Persil/Henkel, Phase II, 2.Bd, p. 440). Thus, responsibilities for specific markets were delegated to each division, and organizational restructuring was conducted with the concept that various activities such as product development, production, and marketing in any given market orientation should be consolidated into divisions (Zeitschrift für Organisation 1970d, p. 199). The restructuring resulted in (1) six product divisions, (2) regional departments, (3) eight functional departments, and (4) an executive committee that acted as the representative executive organ of the board of directors.

The organization comprised six divisions: (1) detergent and cleaners, (2) packaging materials, (3) organic chemical products, (4) home care pharmacology, (5) toiletries, and (6) inorganic chemical products and adhesive substances. Operational management in each division was responsible for the authority the executive committee delegated to them, and for operations as defined by a framework of policies. Each division was in charge of the various operational functions necessary for the efficient execution of divisional business activities and operational function such as production, marketing, development of new products through product release, and exportation. Responsibility for all necessary operations in the division rested with a general manager, and each division was organized as an independent profit center.

As we look at regional departments, the SRI proposals included the establishment of two departments: one for Europe and the other for non-European regions. However, in actuality, only the department responsible for non-European regions was set up. In addition, functional departments were created with the primary responsibilities of (1) advising and supporting divisions, other operational departments, and regional departments; (2) providing aid and information to executive committees for various functional areas and issues; and (3) establishing policies, standards, and processing methods for the company overall, providing major service functions, and estimation of each functional activity. Functional departments were set up for (1) business planning, (2) finance and accounting, (3) legal affairs, (4) logistics, (5) organizations and scientific management, (6) production and engineering, (7) R&D, and (8) human resources and social affairs. These were all cost centers.

Among top management organization reforms, Henkel GmbH became the executive body acting as general office managing all domestic and foreign operations. This office supervised Henkel & Cie GmbH and Henkel International GmbH, which were responsible for European operations and non-European regions, respectively. By creating a headquarters' organization as well as divisions, the executive team, comprising the headquarters' board of directors, was freed from individual operational problems of each division, and dedicated its time and energy to activities such as general issues in operational management of each division as well as planning, management, and control. Furthermore, these executives established five corporate-wide staff departments to support their activities: (1) management support, (2) European industry, (3) international public relations, (4) audits, and (5) secretarial

[Vgl. *Henkel Archiv*, 314/133, Stanford Research Institute, Langfristigen Planung für Persil/Henkel, Phase III, pp. 1–114, *Henkel Archiv*, 314/96, Niederschrift über eine auβerordentliche gemeinsame Postbesprechung am 20. Februar1969 (20.2.1969), *Henkel Archiv*, 251/10, Einrichtung von Sparten und Funktionen (31.10.1968), *Henkel Archiv*, 25/10, Faktoren, die für eine produktionorientierte Organisationsstruktur sprechen (11.7. 1968), *Henkel Archiv*, 153/42, Niederschrift über die gemeinsame Post PERSIL/HNKEL/BÖHME/HI vom 12.11.1968 (14.11.1968), *Henkel Archiv*, 251/10, Neuorganisation. Unterlage für Gemeinsame Post am 12.11.1968 (9.11.1968), *Henkel Archiv*, 251/10, Oranisation der Unternehmensspitze (30.5.1968), *Henkel Archiv*, 153/42, Präsentation einer Organisationsstruktur für das Management Persil/Henkel durch das Stanford Research Institut (SRI), *Henkel Archiv*, 314/96, Zentral-Geschäftsführung Henkel GmbH, *Henkel Archiv*, 314/96, Die Unternehmensorganisation nach Sparten (18.7.1968), *Henkel Archiv*, 314/96, Neuordnung (10.3.1969), *Henkel Archiv*, 314/96, Neuordnung. Organisationsvorschlag für Funktionen—Produktion/ Ingenieurwesen. Besprechung am 12. Februar 1969 (13.2.1969), *Henkel Archiv*, 251/9, Kurz-Referat. Gewinn- und Kosten-Verantwortung der Sparten/Funktionen (6.5. 1969), *Henkel Archiv*, 251/9, Kostenverantwortung der Funktionen, insbesondere der Funktion Finanzen/Rechnungswesen. Notiz Mr. Cavender vom 17.4.1969 (23.4.1969), Henkel GmbH 1968; Feldenkirchen and Hilger 2001, pp. 200–202; Zeitschrift für Organisation 1970b, pp. 196–198].

By 1967, SRI had conveyed the principle of return on investment (ROI), an important concept for management in a divisional structure requiring a self-support account system (Hilger 2004, p. 233). This acted as an efficient system foundation for profit planning and budgetary control.

9.3.2.1.2 Bayer Case Study

Our next subject, Bayer, had no need to move away from a functional structure until the beginning of the 1960s. However, as with Henkel, corporate growth and competition set corporate management on a new path (Kleinschmidt 2002, pp. 266–268). It was proposed that everyday operational management be relegated to lower level managers to lighten the operational burden of directors, and it was decided that these operations would be conducted by divisions. The separation of production and sales organizations ended, and the consolidation of production and sales created "partial companies" that were defined in the same terms as US-style divisions [*Bayer Archiv*, 001-004-003, Vorschlag für einen Organisationsplan der FFB (ohne Agfa), pp. 1–2, 4].

The deployment of a divisional structure in Bayer began with the restructuring in February 1970 [*Bayer Archiv*, 001-004-002, Die Schrift von Kurt Hansen an die Leitenden Angestellten der Werke Leverkusen, Dormagen, Elberfeld und Uerdingen sowie der deutschen Aueβnstellen (25.2.1970), p. 1, *Bayer Archiv*, 001-004-002, Neuorganisation der Farbenfabriken Bayer AG—(3.2.1970), *Bayer Archiv*, 010-004-005, Neuorganisation der Bayer AG, S.1, *Bayer Archiv*, 010-004-005, Die

Schrift von Kurt Hansen an die Leitenden Angestellten der Werke Leverkusen, Dormagen, Elberfeld und Uerdingen (2.9.1965), *Bayer Archiv*, 001-004-003, Neuorganisation], and the new organization was implemented on January 1, 1971 [*Bayer Archiv*, 001-004-002, Vorstandsrundschreiben Nr.63 (14.10.1970), p. 1]. The new organization featured three primary elements (*Bayer Archiv*, 010-004-005, Neuorganisation der Bayer AG, p. 2): divisions, a central staff department, and staff for the board of directors. Bayer created a thorough division of labor and delegation of authority, thereby allowing managers to concentrate better on managerial activities (Vgl. *Bayer Archiv*, 210-001, Führungsgrundsätze der Bayer AG, p. 4). The general objective of the new organization conceived by Bayer's W. Knauff was to take measures in tackling the changes caused by rapid growth, technological development, and market expansion, which would place Bayer in a position where the growing number of operations in the future could be effectively managed. In this aim, maximizing flexibility and efficiency became an objective. In addition to the formation of sales-oriented divisions, Bayer clearly delineated administrative boundaries; delegated authority and responsibilities; architected an efficient information system appropriately for the new organizational structure; developed a corporate group-wide integrated planning system; and clearly divided functions within lines, staff, and committees.

Bayer was divided into nine product divisions: (1) inorganic chemical products, (2) organic chemical products, (3) rubber, (4) plastics and lacquer, (5) polyurethane, (6) dyes, (7) textiles, (8) pharmaceuticals, and (9) plant protection chemicals. These divisions were managed on the basis of policies established by the board of directors from which general managers would seek approval for their division plans at the appointed time each year. They then bore the responsibility delegated by the board of directors to achieve divisional goals on the basis of those plans. The division into nine product divisions was deemed important to give appropriate operational scale to the divisions. Each division had an integrated set of functions: production, sales, applications engineering, and research. Division management was in general delegated by the board of directors to two people: an individual responsible for commercial affairs and the other responsible for technological affairs. Each was a director with equal authority.

Manufacturing plants and their related auxiliary plants (such as drying plants) were integrated on a division production basis appropriately for their locations. As long as the various departments within each division were not consolidated into service departments that worked across divisions (such as central staff departments), a particular division's sales oversight included all other departments or groups necessary for the success of the respective division's marketing such as market development, customer support, market research, and order processing. In addition, research operations were integrated into divisional research departments, with research groups working in divisional research departments and researchers outside the central scientific research laboratories consolidated into the division's research department. Placing technology departments into divisions, Bayer intended to stimulate close contact between sales, development, research, and production. Regarding divisional staff departments, division offices were composed of staff units, and had technical and commercial staff managed by one person. These staff organizations acted as planning, direction, and control organizations and would provide services within the division's purview.

Among the top management organizational changes, the board of directors had corporate-wide operational management responsibility and was in charge of divisional and central staff department operation management; corporate policy; making corporate-wide or semi-corporate-wide objectives; decision-making for investments or other basic organizational issues; decision-making and approval for opening up negotiations on stock acquisition and sale; and important personnel issues such as manager selection and support for appointment, advancement, and transfer. Even among directors, a division of labor was implemented for production, sales, corporate group adjustment, research, engineering, finance and accounting, legal and tax affairs, and human resources and social issues. In addition, a staff for the board of directors was created to aid directors in their work. This staff organization served several purposes: prioritizing activities and avoiding information loss; jointly conducting staff functions between those responsible for commercial and technical areas as a means of planning, direction, and control for the board of directors to provide corporate-wide management; and establishing and allocating staff functions appropriate for new organizations. Furthermore, central staff departments were established. Their functions were services provided to divisions as well as the company as a whole, and oversight for each of them was given to one individual reporting to the board of directors. These staff departments were (1) human resources and social issues, (2) engineering, (3) finance and accounting, (4) purchasing, (5) advertising, (6) legal and tax affairs, (7) central research, (8) patents and licensing, and (9) applications engineering. These central staff departments, along with the board of directors' staff, served as connecting points for all nine divisions, both domestic and international, of the corporation. Specialized management for each central staff department was undertaken by directors representing specialized fields. Moreover, extra-divisional committees and council organizations were established for effective information exchange. In 1972, 10 committees and council organizations were formed: (1) general manager council, (2) investment council, (3) plant manager council, (4) central personnel committee, (5) central production committee, (6) central sales committee, (7) central research committee, (8) central engineering committee, (9) central technical committee, and (10) central corporate group coordination committee [*Bayer Archiv*, 001-004-002, Neuorganisation der Farbenfabriken Bayer AG (3.2.1970), *Bayer Archiv*, 001-004-002, Organizational Rearrangement of Farbenfabriken Bayer AG—Objectives, Functions and Tasks, *Bayer Archiv*,001-004-002, Organisationplan der Farbenfabriken Bayer AG, Leverkusen, Stand: 1.4.1971, *Bayer Archiv*,001-004-001, Farbenfabriken Bayer A.G., Leverkusen-Bayerwerk. Organisationspläne der Verkaufsabteilungen, *Bayer Archiv*, 001-004-002, Vorstandsrundschreben Nr. 64 (22.10.1970), *Bayer Archiv*, 001-004-003, Die Schrift von Kurt Hansen an W. Knauff über den Vorschlag des Organizsationsplanes von Knauff (24.2.1964), pp. 3–4, 8, *Bayer Archiv*, 010-004-005, Organisatiorische Gliederung der Bayer AG, Stand: 1.7.1972, *Bayer Archiv*,010-004-005, Neuorganisation der Bayer AG, *Bayer Archiv*, 001-004-002,

Die Schrift von Kurt Hansen an die Leitenden Angestellten der Werke Leverkusen, Dormagen, Elberfeld und Uerdingen sowie der deutschen Aueβnstellen (25.2.1970), pp. 2–3].

Overall, the new organization helped increase the company's competitiveness in global markets. Moreover, the organization had the objectives of improving the workforce's awareness of revenues and costs, delegating authority and personnel management, and strengthening market consciousness across the corporation (Kleinschmidt 2002, p. 269).

9.3.2.1.3 BASF Case Study

Furthermore, BASF was busy restructuring their organization from the late 1960s to the early 1970s and instituted a new organization in June of 1970 [*BASF Archiv*, C0, Organisatiorische und personelleänderungen bei AOA (5.6.1970), p. 1; Koch 1970]. After the war, BASF adopted a functional structure covering production, sales, research, engineering, finance, human resource and social issues, and legal affairs [*BASF Archiv*, C0, Die Neuorganisation der BASF unter Marketingssichtspunkten, p. 2, *BASF Archiv*, C19/14, C0, Organisatorische Maβnahmen (19.12.1961), *BASF Archiv*, C19/14, Organisatorische Maβnahmen (21.12.1961), *BASF Archiv*, C19/13, Organisation im Verkauf (24.6.1960)]. In addition, by the early 1960s, manufacturing department was divided into four sections by product line [*BASF Archiv*, C0, Organisation der BASF (1.1.1964), *BASF Archiv*, C19/14, Werksinterner Verteiler (25.1.1962), *BASF Archiv*, C19/15, Rundschreiben an alle Abteilungen des Werkes (20.12.1963), *BASF Archiv*, C19/15, Die Schrift an alle Vertrauensleute (22.7.1963). For information on organization changes at this level, refer to Abelshauser 2002, pp. 571–573]. However, the scope and growth rate of the chemical industry rendered review of a functional structure's functional domain impossible. At BASF, just as at Bayer, Hoechst, and Siemens, splitting up the company into relatively independent divisions for greater overall visibility and delegating responsibilities to divisions for the production and sales of specific product lines was the only method to restore visibility (*BASF Archiv*, C0, Die Neuorganisation der BASF unter Marketingssichtspunkten, p. 2). Not only did BASF's revenues more than double between 1960 and 1970, but with additional progress achieved through business expansion and external acquisitions, other group companies' revenues also increased by more than 20 times during the same period. In addition, with forward and backward integration into the oil and gas areas, the dramatic growth of the company and expansion of industry scope and business lines, it became impossible to maintain the company's existing organization management. The first crisis in terms of profit and finance emerged in mid-1967, forcing the company to acknowledge the necessity of organizational restructuring (Selinger 1977, p. 17; Abelshauser 2002, pp. 570, 574).

The organizational restructuring aimed to resolve these issues by transferring management functions from the board of directors to operational divisions. The role of a division's general manager was to implement and realize optimal production and sales strategies that could achieve planned revenue goals. The general manager was entrusted with domains worth between 100 and 600 million Deutsche Marks, and great value was placed on having them act as actual managers. Therefore, broad commerce and technical responsibilities were transferred into each division (Koch 1970). There were four product divisions at the operational activity level: (1) basic chemicals, oil, gas, and agricultural chemical products; (2) plastics and textiles; (3) dyes, chemicals, and pharmaceuticals; and (4) consumer products and sales coordination. The duties of these product divisions, in addition to the domains of production and sales, included planning, development, and applications engineering functions, and acted as profit centers with responsibility for revenues and profits [*BASF Archiv*, C0, Neuorganisation der BASF-Gruppe (in: *BASF Information,* Sonderausgabe, Oktober 1969)]. BASF's own internal documents regarding this organizational restructuring focused on particularly one large issue the organization experienced until that time with operational departments in that, although the operational departments were responsible for costs, they were not responsible for profits (*BASF Archiv*, C0, Die Neuorganisation der BASF unter Marketingssichtspunkten, pp. 3–4). Thus, a divisional general manager was given a division that was formed as a profit center under the direction of the board of directors with that issue in mind, and each division was consolidated according to their group under the purview of an executive director [*BASF Archiv*, C0, Bemerkungen von Professor Dr. Timm über die Neuorganisation der BASF (29.8.1973), p. 6]. The board of directors comprised nine members, seven of whom acted as divisional general managers [*BASF Archiv*, C0, The Badische Anilin- und Soda-Fabrik AG (BASF), some information worth knowing, p. 5. For more information on personnel changes in primary BASF departments and positions, refer to *BASF Archiv*, C0, Organisation der BASF (Stand: Juli 1975)]. In addition, the divisions took responsibility for executing long-term strategies for not only operational planning but also other areas of activity. Inter-divisional connections in production and sales were secured with planning systems, transfer pricing, and a common sales network (Selinger 1977, p. 17).

The internal structures of divisions such as basic chemicals, oil and gas, and agricultural products were organized into narrower categories according to products such as basic chemical products, oil and gas, chemical fertilizers, and plant protection chemicals. Each unit had a staff organization and a support system for operational activities. The consumer products and sales coordination division had three departments: (1) dyes and paints, (2) magnetic technology and printing plates, and (3) sales coordination. In contrast to the former two, which were product departments, the sales coordination department was responsible for marketing methods, organization, sales staff coordination, publicity, and European branches (including customer coordination) [*BASF Archiv*, C0, Neuorganisation der BASF-Gruppe (Juni 1970)].

In addition, regional departments responsible for non-European regions were established in response to the increasing importance of overseas operations. Regional departments comprised four regional sections: (1) North America, (2) Central and South America, (3) Africa and West Asia, and (4) South Asia, Southeast Asia, and Australia. Each had its own staff organization [*BASF Archiv*, C0,

Neuorganisation der BASF-Gruppe (Juni 1970), pp. 12–13, Neuorganisation der BASF-Gruppe, *BASF Information*, Sonderausgabe, Oktober 1969 (*BASF Archiv*, C0)]. Product divisions were responsible for products primarily limited to Europe, whereas the four regional departments were responsible for all products in their region. BASF's international activities were always overseen by legally independent companies; hence, the main function of regional departments was the coordination of these companies' revenue goals. Regional departments, such as product divisions, were evaluated on their results (Selinger 1977, p. 19). In that respect, regional departments acted as regional divisions in areas outside of Europe, and product divisions focused on Europe as well as regional departments responsible for non-European areas had integral management organizations.

At the top management level, directors had responsibility for management of corporate group strategy along with direct responsibility for parts of new organizational subsets. A new staff group called the "headquarters planning department" supported the board of directors' activities. Modern technologies such as management information systems (MIS) were used for selecting and processing of information. In Addition, their use made possible management activities informed by data-based planning and the clear delegation of authority within large work domains at appropriate management levels (*BASF Archiv*, C0, Direktionssitzung am 17.10.1969 zum Thema "Neugestaltung der Organisation der BASF-Gruppe", pp. 1–3). This headquarters planning department had five sections: (1) investment appraisal, (2) national economy, (3) planning systems, (4) strategic planning and investment, and (5) annual planning and budgeting. Planning function work was divided, with a unit responsible for market analysis being placed in the national economy [*BASF Archiv*, C0, Dem Vorstandsvorsitzenden direkt unterstellte Einheiten, pp. A, 2A, *BASF Archiv*, C0, Organisation der BASF-Grupe (Dezember 1972), p. 3, *BASF Archiv*, C0, Neuorganisation der BASF-Gruppe (Juni 1970), p. 3]. In these planning departments, the production, sales, and investment plans created by the various departments of each division were scrutinized and elaborated upon, with alternative plans also created. Through this process, many more corporate strategy and investment plans were submitted to directors, who would then be better able to select a plan more likely to be optimal (Koch 1970). The development of such headquarters mechanisms enabled by these planning departments was a response to the need for delegation of operational authority as well as to the growing need to connecting functions in the centralized elements that followed decentralization [*BASF Archiv*, C0, Neuorganisation der BASF-Gruppe, *BASF Information*, Sonderausgabe, Oktober 1969 (*BASF Archiv*, C0)]. At the headquarters level, functional staff departments were created to provide corporate group services. These four departments were (1) research, (2) legal and tax affairs, (3) finance, and (4) human resources and social issues [*BASF Archiv*, C0, Die Schrift an die Mitarbeiter (2.2.1970), Neuorganisation der BASF-Gruppe, *BASF Information*, Sonderausgabe, Oktober 1969 (*BASF Archiv*, C0)].

These new forms of organization were developed with the cooperation of the influential US management consulting firm, McKinsey (*BASF Archiv*, C0,

Direktionssitzung am 17.10.1969 zum Thema "Neugestaltung der Organisation der BASF-Gruppe", pp. 2–3). As we will describe later, this US consulting firm had a large impact on subsequent organizational restructuring in BASF.

9.3.2.1.4 Glanzstoff Case Study

Furthermore, the developments noted in the aforementioned three companies were observed at Glanzstoff from the late 1960s through the early 1970s, when Glanzstoff also deployed a product divisional structure. When we examine the feinchemical division, for example, two integral principles were applied. One was a concept of divisions organized vertically by product domain, integrating all activities in Glanzstoff as well as AKU and other affiliated companies. The other principle sought international business structures for chemical products that include sulfur and feinchemicals. This division managed organic and inorganic sulfide products except intermediate products resulting from Viscose production, agricultural chemical products, feinchemical and products related to these three areas. R&D and production of these products in various EEC countries as well as all sales and marketing activities globally were consolidated in this division. Engineering and other various activities in the other operational domains of AKU and Glanzstoff's central department were coordinated by divisions.

Each division was placed under a general manager, who was responsible for its operational results in addition to coordination of all divisional functions such as production, sales, and revenue as well as further expansion of the division. General managers held authority over all departments and specialized bureaus in AKU and Glanzstoff in order to perform their role and obtained various reports, statistics, and other materials critical to their divisions. Moreover, each division had a deputy general manager who acted as a proxy in the general manager's absence or when problems arose. Divisional activities were monitored by a governing body comprising three members from AKU and Granzstoff's executive team.

For division investments, the general manager annually submitted the following year's investment plan to the governing body. Authority for a discretionary amount of money was granted in an investment plan framework approved by the governing body that reviewed each investment application. The amount varied by position. A divisional general manager's discretionary range was between 20,000 and 100,000 Deutsche Marks, and anything above that amount required the governing body's approval. Investment limits within the discretionary amount were set at a maximum of 20,000 Deutsche Marks for production or sales divisional operations managers, and a maximum of 10,000 Deutsche Marks for anyone lower in the division [*Rheinisch-Westfälisches Archiv zu Köln*, Abt 195, F7-4, Vorschlag über die Bildung einer gemeinsamen AKU-Glanzstoff Schwefelchemie-Division unter der Bezeichnung Feinchemikalien-Division (FCD) (1.10.1968)].

Similarly, all AKU and Glanzstoff wool domain activities were integrated in a vertically organized wool division that was a business unit organized as an independent division. The function of the division, responsibility and authority of its general manager, and discretionary investment amount were nearly identical to those of the feinchemical division [*Rheinisch-Westfälisches Archiv zu Köln*, Abt 195, F7-5, Vorschlag über den Aufbau einer gemeinsamen AKU/Glanzstoff Vliesstoff Division unter der Bezeichnung Colbond Division (1.12.1968)].

9.3.2.1.5 Hoechst Case Study

Hoechst's organizational restructuring of 1952 divided all the company's domestic and foreign plants and subsidiary companies into five divisions: (1) inorganic chemical products, nitrogen fertilizer, and plant protection chemicals, (2) dyes and other materials and textile auxiliaries, (3) plastics and solvents, (4) pharmaceuticals, and (5) textiles and film. That structure would later be further reorganized into seven divisions. Each division was placed under a director responsible for technology. Coordinating departments were established for finance and accounting; legal affairs, patents, and tax affairs; sales; research; engineering; plant management; and technology (which was later eliminated). In addition, a technical management department and commercial management department were established. In this manner, Hoechst undertook broad management decentralization, though one domain was always simultaneously connected to a division and a coordinating department. Because of this structure, all important decisions needed the approval of at least two directors, which was a joint responsibility (Farbwerke Hoechst 1969, p. 14; Winnacker 1972, pp. 178–179, 504). Under the directors, work group committees were formed with rather broad decision-making authority, which for example could comprise administrative directors and important engineers in plant. In this structure, Hoechst followed IG Farben AG's model (Winnacker 1972, p. 184).

However, with the increase in global revenues, greater number of manufacturing facilities, continually expanding operations, and additional domains that came with Hoecsht's rapid growth during the 1960s, management could no longer be contained by the existing organizational framework. As a result, Hoechst decided an organizational restructuring was in order and decided to more broadly and clearly delegate authority so that the board of directors could take more time to consider basic issues and make decisions. To that end, all operations were split into 14 separate divisions. Each division had consolidated functions for production, sales, research, applications engineering, planning, and profit and loss accounting. The divisions operated within a pre-determined operational scope for which they were responsible globally. The management groups of each division comprised scientists and technicians as well as sales and production management staff members, and domains were restructured with clearly delineated operations.

Half of the directors were in charge of divisions while the other half oversaw the ten coordination departments: (1) plant and technical management (domestic), (2) international production, (3) sales, (4) research, (5) applications engineering, (6) engineering, (7) finance and accounting, (8) legal affairs, patents, and taxes, (9) procurement, and (10) human resources and social issues. Performance evaluations for each division were, as a principle, conducted by two directors who were entrusted by the board of directors to audit each division as a part of their overall set of responsibilities. Additional staff departments were deployed and they had two critical roles: producing preparatory communications for all work committees and securing broad cooperation within the company (Farbwerke Hoechst 1969, pp. 14–17; Winnacker 1972, pp. 451, 463–464, 505).

A system of collegiate management for the divisions was thus put in place. Advantages of this organization, launched on January 1, 1970, included securing effective cooperation in each division, logically allocating functions, global coordination, and prompt attention to any coordination needed in intra-divisional areas of small groups (Farbwerke Hoechst 1969, pp. 14–15). At this stage, the board of directors decided to return to the specialization of production and sales held by board of directors' members for all divisions reporting to them (Dyas and Thanheiser 1976, pp. 122–123).

9.3.2.1.6 Hüls Case Study

Hüls had begun to deploy a divisional structure by the mid-1950s in the areas of rubber, catalysts, and textiles (Kleinschmidt 2002, p. 270). Until a divisional structure was fully deployed in the 1970s, they used what was a fundamentally functional structure, comprising four functional departments: production, research, commerce, and human resources and legal affairs (Der Lichtbogen 1970, p. 26; Lorentz and Erker 2003, p. 270). However, due to increasingly intense competition in global markets, the growing scale of production and rapid advances in science and technology, greater changes in production and marketing became necessary (Der Lichtbogen 1970, p. 26). Along with these changes, the serious problems that occurred in the postwar era under the existing organizational structure, particularly with diversification during the 1960s, were a major factor in restructuring. The restructuring addressed the crucial need for directors to be freed from daily activities and detailed matters so that they could attend to more fundamental duties that are larger in scope, the need for stronger efforts to mobilize workers with specialized knowledge in managing plant groups, and the need to entrust these workers with details so that they could participate in decision-making systems and processes [*Hüls Archiv*, I-5-8, Einige überlegungen zu den Möglichkeiten einer Organisationsänderung bei CWH, p. 1, *Hüls Archiv*, ohne Signatur, Niederschrift über die Sitzung des Vorstands am 3. April 1970 in Münster, Sitzungssaal der Landesbank (11.5.1970)].

In this manner, the process of divisional structure deployment moved forward with new vigor in the early 1970s (Kleinschmidt 2002, p. 270), and was finally deployed in 1972 (*Hüls Archiv*, ohne Signatur, Niederschrift über die Besprechung in Hüls am 14. Juni 1971, p. 2; *Hüls Archiv*, ohne Signatur, Vorstandssitzung vom 6.7.70, p. 4; Der Lichtbogen 1970, p. 26). The organizational structure deployed to realize these goals was a product divisional structure with six divisions: (1) raw materials and inorganic chemicals, (2) organic chemicals, detergents and cleaners, (3) thermoplastics, (4) polycondensates and paint materials, (5) rubber, and (6) energy (later nitrogen and agricultural chemicals). These divisions were designed to function as independent units both technically and financially, each with its own production and sales operations. Each division acted as a quasi-independent company with business policies set by the board of directors. Responsibility for management of their spheres of operation was given to two people, a production and sales specialist, creating a collegiate management structure based on a board-majority system. In addition, the organization had ten central corporate departments which contained for example R&D, finance and accounting, legal and tax affairs and patents that operated on a corporate-wide basis. Seven staff departments provided advice and assistance to the board of directors, divisions, and the central corporate departments. In this manner, broad areas of authority and responsibility were delegated to the divisions for short-term, daily operations, and in doing so, top management created an organization in which they could focus on the creation of long-term plans, their primary job, rather than daily operational work [*Hüls Archiv*, ohne Signatur, Niederschrift über die Sitzung des Vorstands CWH am 17. Juli 1970 in Schloβ Raesfeld (5.8.1970); Der Lichtbogen 1970, pp. 26–27; Lorentz and Erker 2003, pp. 270–271]. Moreover, a new concept for business planning and control was implemented, with a standing corporate planning committee. This committee was involved with deploying new control mechanisms and in improving short-, mid-, and long-term planning [Vgl. *Hüls Archiv*, VI-8-3/1, Die Schrift über die ständige Kommission "Unternehmungsplanung" und Sachbearbeiter für die Planung (15.12.1969), *Hüls Archiv*, VI-8-3/1, Besprechungsbericht von 1. Sitzung der Kommission "Unternehmungsplanung" (5.2.1970), *Hüls Archiv*, VI-8-3/1, Besprechungsbericht von 2. Sitzung der Kommission "Unternehmungsplanung" (27.2.1970), *Hüls Archiv*, VI-8-3/1, Besprechungsbericht von 3. Sitzung der Kommission "Unternehmungsplanung" (1.10.1970), *Hüls Archiv*, VI-8-3/1, Langfristige Unternehmungsplanung (11.12.1969); Lorentz and Erker 2003, p. 271].

As we have seen, in deploying a divisional structure, US consulting firms played a significant role at BASF and Henkel. In contrast, Hüls used Bayer, BASF, and Hoechst as examples to follow [*Hüls Archiv*, ohne Signatur, Niederschrift über die Sitzung des Vorstands am 3. April 1970 in Münster, Sitzungssaal der Landesbank (11.5.1970), pp. 1, 5; Lorentz and Erker 2003, pp. 270–271], and this was a major difference.

Furthermore, although other chemical companies, such as Continental and Freudenberg, deployed divisional structures, these deployments had unique characteristics defined by their corporations. As noted above, generational changes acted as important mechanisms in effecting organizational restructuring. For example, Glanzstoff's change to a divisional structure was mediated by older entrepreneurs like R. Vits and L. Vaubel. Other corporations accepted the advice of US consulting firms; however, they adopted an organizational structure that was different from a US-style divisional structure. For example, Continental was being advised by McKinsey and restructured on the basis of their consultation, establishing divisions that were an amalgamated organization that maintained functional departments. Thus, one can find examples of different structures as well as combined divisional and functional structures even in corporations that have deployed divisional structures and have undergone decentralization (Kleinschmidt 2002, pp. 269–270). That said, the following management issues inevitably arise under functional structures as diversification advances. One issue was the difficulty encountered by each department's head manager in keeping pace with basic functions such as the production, sales, and procurement of a division in which multiple, vastly different product lines are managed together. Another was the top management's frustration with making administrative decisions rather than entrepreneurial, executive decisions, such as allocating corporate or long-term business resources (Kroos and Gilbert 1972, p. 253). As observed in these case studies of representative corporations, most companies that underwent diversification were forced to pursue organizational restructuring to resolve these managerial issues. Therefore, reforms based on restructuring principles found in divisional structure were the norm.

9.3.2.2 Deployment of Divisional Structures in the Electrical Industry and Its Characteristics

9.3.2.2.1 AEG Case Study

We will next consider the deployment of divisional structure in the electrical industry, where diversification proceeded as in the chemical industry, and the divisional structure was important because of the nature of the business.

At the time that AEG restructured its corporate group after the war, the decision-making structure was based on principles of centralization. All important decisions were managed by the board of directors or by the chairman himself. Production management was simply organized into work domains, and its authority remained small (Hautsch 1979, p. 151). However, the breadth of these functions subsequently grew considerably both in scale and from the addition of new activities, and the first post-war organizational restructuring began in 1957. The organization had previously accommodated small, simple corporations, and AEG was in danger of losing its ability to obtain a clear overall picture of the corporation. In their organizational reforms, each product group was restructured vertically, operational departments were integrated into divisions and authority for business execution was delegated to the division's general manager. However, they lacked, for example, horizontal departments for management of such functions as managerial economics of overall corporate group finance, human resources, or marketing (Strunk 2000, p. 70). Divisions took responsibility for overall operations in their domains of specialization, in particular development, factory worker placement, production, production planning, sales planning, pricing policies, and sales strategies. The goal of this organization was to deal with the various needs that were derived from the increasing amounts of business by (1) enabling divisions to make their own business policies based on a clear overview of the entire business from a technical and commercial perspective, (2) accurately grasping the overall costs and performance for each division, (3) creating unified pricing policies, (4) simplified operations, (5) a strict integration of activities related to shared technology, and (6) more clearly defined responsibilities [*AEG Archiv*, GS839, Rundschreiben Nr.14/57, Neue Organisation der AEG (9.7.1957), pp. 1, 3].

However, changes beginning in the late 1950s made organizational reform an important issue, such as rapid technological advances, expansion of activities, greater competition due to internationalization efforts in a better integrated EEC, more products, expanded sales channels, and the development of business policies more focused on the creation of demand for new products (AEG 1963, p. 53; Hautsch 1979, p. 151). Confronted with worsening revenue situation at the close of the 1950s, implementing corporate group reorganization became a crucial topic, and the use of US consulting firms' experience was deemed necessary. However, the new organization established on October 1, 1963 employed a new management structure based on that used by GE in the US, with small- and medium-sized business units empowered with authority and an executive team that simply acted as a coordinating unit. The organization was vertical in terms of business domains, rather similar to those seen in the US or UK. The new organization had five departments: (1) energy production and distribution, (2) energy use, (3) transportation, (4) industrial supply, and (5) home appliances. These departments each managed their own procurement, research, production, and sales. Therefore, strengthening of the department head's responsibility, greater flexibility and stricter management in each division were pursued [Vgl. *AEG Archiv*, GS839, Rundschreiben RO2, Bildung von Horizontalen und Vertikalen Bereichen (30.5.1963), AEG 1963, pp. 53, 55; Strunk 2000, pp. 70–74; Hautsch 1979, p. 151; Der Volkswirt 1963, p. 492; Reindl 2001, p. 138; Der Volkswirt 1964, p. 1241]. In addition to these five vertical departments, the new organization featured eight horizontal departments: (1) marketing, (2) R&D, (3) production, (4) commercial business, (5) finance, (6) a general secretariat, (7) public relations, and (8) exporting. Apart from the exporting department, these departments were responsible for assisting and coordinating with the entire corporation, though they had no command authority over the divisions [*AEG Archiv*, GS839, Rundschreiben RO2, Bildung von Horizontalen und Vertikalen Bereichen (30.5.1963); AEG 1963, pp. 53, 55].

Though the board of directors thus remained the body responsible for final decision-making for various problems, operational functions were further decentralized. Sixteen departments were created in the five divisions, and each division acted as a quasi-independent company solely responsible for all actions related to development, production, sales, and commerce within the scope of each division's policies (AEG 1963, p. 54). The reorganization maintained the independence of subsidiary companies, and decentralized at a high level. However, coordination among the various departments and subsidiaries alone was insufficient, and it was obvious that the extremely decentralized organization had exceeded the objectives. As a result, the latter half of the 1960s brought a retrenchment of the relative independence at the division level, with departments and subsidiaries being consolidated into divisions. Divisions were integrated into five business fields (energy and industrial technology, communications and transportation technology, mass-produced goods, consumer goods, and office technology), and the newly-integrated subsidiaries were folded into these business fields as departments. Control over the horizontal departments of (1) finance, (2) planning and control, (3) human resources, (4) technology, and (5) regional affairs and materials was divided among five directors. Thus, it became possible for the corporate board of directors to maintain direct control of everything down to the field level, and mechanisms were put in place for decision-making (Hautsch 1979, pp. 151–152). Later, in 1967, three additional business fields were added for a total of eight: communications equipment; components; and radio, television, and recording equipment (Vgl. AEG-Telefunken AG 1967, pp. 33–44). In 1969, these were once again reorganized into seven product divisions: (1) energy engineering, (2) communications and data systems technology, (3) transportation, (4) industrial supply, (5) components, (6) home appliances, and (7) radio, television, and recording equipment. In addition, horizontal departments were reorganized into seven groups: (1) marketing, (2) R&D, (3) production, (4) office management, (5) human resources and social issues, (6) finance, and (7) international affairs [Vgl. *AEG Archiv*, GS3501, Struktur-Organisation, Gesamt-Stellen-Übersicht, Ausgabe 1970 Organisationsplan (Stand 1.11.1969), AEG-Telefunken AG 1969, pp. 39–50].

9.3.2.2.2 Siemens Case Study

Furthermore, US principles of organization played an important role in Siemens' organization during the 1960s. The rapid growth of all Siemens' business units after the war not only encouraged the integration of power engineering and low-voltage technology, but also caused redundancies in development and production. This trend eventually forced an organizational restructuring. The first step in 1966 was the consolidation of the three parent companies of Siemens & Halske, Siemens–Schuckert, and Siemens–Reininger–Werke into one business unit called Siemens AG. This bold move created a very positive corporate image for global markets. However, Siemens needed to create manageable business units without redundancies to respond to rapid advances in technology (Feldenkirchen 2004, pp. 126–127).

Moreover, market conditions provided impetus for organizational restructuring in Siemens (Zeitschrift für Organisation 1970a, p. 338). The latter half of the 1960s had increased Siemens' scale to the point where centralized management became impossible, and the diversity and breadth of product programs required the creation of divisions. It was already becoming impossible to maintain a traditional split along the low-voltage current sector and heavy current sector lines, and a significant amount of redundancy would result between the two sectors. Moreover, there were redundancies in authority causing conflict between the sectors. As a result, it was believed that strengthening competitiveness might have a synergistic effect. Further growth for the group required greater transparency in operations, making organizational reforms an urgent issue (Hilger 2004, pp. 214–215).

The new company was reorganized into six groups on October 1, 1969, with regional offices and regional companies as well as five corporate departments.

Siemens' divisional structure into six business domains comprised (1) components, (2) data systems technology, (3) energy engineering, (4) installation technology, (5) medical technology, and (6) communications technology, with each of these divisions being given the most independence in business affairs. In addition, the organization had five functional corporate departments that dealt with corporate-wide affairs: (1) managerial economics, (2) finance, (3) human resources, (4) technology, and (5) sales. These departments acted in an advisory and coordinating capacity, and the organization as a whole took on a matrix-like character (Siemens 1969, pp. 14–15; Zeitschrift für Organisation 1970a, p. 338; Feldenkirchen 2004, p. 127; Hilger 2004, p. 216).

Each business domain or component unit within a domain was organized primarily on the basis of technological and market relationships, and with the decentralization of decision-making according to products and product groups, much effort was put into making themselves self-sufficient, taking on responsibility for everything from development to sales (Zeitschrift für Organisation 1970a, pp. 338–340). Business domains held profit responsibility along with authority over investment and human resources within the scope of corporate policy (Yamamoto 1993, pp. 152–153). The slowdown in Siemens' growth in the latter half of the 1960s motivated the deployment of profit centers as they were critical to decentralized management (Hilger 2004, p. 229). In contrast, the five corporate departments were there to ensure cooperation and control conflict between the six business domains (Yamamoto 1993, p. 152). The five corporate departments performed an advisory role to both the board of directors and the business domains, though they had no command authority (Tacke 1977, p. 277).

Siemens' organizational restructuring was intended to foster "independence" as a concept and as a means for organizational reforms; thus, Siemens differed from other corporations in that they chose not to use outside consultants. This resulted in differences between Siemens' organizational restructuring during the 1960s and US corporations' deployment of divisional structures (Hilger 2004, p. 215). New organizational concepts were based on principles of responsibility for products, functions, and regions, and the Siemens organization matrix differed significantly from the typical divisional structure used in US corporations on several points (Feldenkirchen 2004, pp. 127–128). Although Siemens aligned themselves with basic principles of divisional structures as developed in the US, they based their organizational changes on differing German conditions and focused on maintaining their integrated Siemens culture, prioritizing the company as a whole ahead of individual components (Feldenkirchen 2004, p. 131).

9.3.2.3 Organizational Restructurings in Other Industries and Their Characteristics

As is clear from the foregoing discussion, diversification occurred at high-levels in the chemical and electrical industries, and the deployment of divisional structure was significant if only for that reason. For comparison, we will also examine the iron and steel industry, where diversification seen in the chemical and electrical industries did not occur.

Mannesmann implemented organizational reforms in the late 1960s, dividing their corporate group into autonomous groups along the US model. In Rheinische Stahlwerke AG, a management shift in August 1968 (making T. Schmücker head of the company) prompted an organizational restructuring. The organization had previously been that of a holding company, managing only financial control and performing no other functions of a corporation. The countless redundancies encountered by the management of this multi-layered corporate group in production and sales stemmed from among its more than 30 subsidiaries. Mannesmann felt that a top-down, rather than bottom-up, "attack" style of management was not feasible. The plan for the new organization divided a variety of activities into the lowest level production domains, and then integrated them into 15 divisions. The deciding factors in the appropriation of divisions were the domains' alignment with markets and technological commonalities in addition to seeking to eliminate the redundancies and disruptions that had existed. At the top level, divisions consisted of five integrated groups, each under a corporate group director. The purpose for establishing a new group was to make responsibility and management clear at the production domain, divisional and corporate group board of directors' levels, in terms of management results and to enable greater flexibility and more rapid decision-making.

Similarly, Krupp, which operated in the iron and steel industry, had both an organizational restructuring and management change in 1968. Akin to Rheinische Stahlwerke AG, Krupp suffered from structural weaknesses as observed in their manufacturing companies, which were made up of many parts, and sales companies, in which many redundancies existed. This resulted in their decision to adopt organizational principles employed by major US corporate groups and to organizationally integrate similar or identical activities. They aimed to realize a more effective product classification than other corporate groups and the formation of a small number of large-scale business units, with each member of the Krupp group being given a high level of managerial responsibility (Der Volkswirt 1969, p. 70).

9.3.3 Deployment of Divisional Structures and Establishment of Internal Control Organizations: Deployment of Controlling Systems and Its Significance

An important point in the deployment of divisional structures was the issue related to setting up internal control organizations. Controlling, which is a method of evaluation used to get a financial overview of overall business progress and performance, is in general known as the "controller" in the US. Although this office had already become an indispensable business organization in US business management by the early 1950s, it was still in its infancy in Germany at that time (RKW 1957;

Zusammenfassung; Hilger 2004, p. 226). A post-US study trip report by RKW in 1957 noted that the controller's work in the US is future oriented, and that it builds an important foundation for planning and control functions. In contrast, German corporations sorely lacked future forecasting and calculation ability for profit planning and budgetary control (Auffermann 1957, pp. 43–44, 54–56).

However, circumstances changed greatly after that period. Factors increasing the complexity of work, such as corporations' expanding scale, deployment of new technologies, increases in the pace of change, and changes in environmental conditions, increased the need for corporate information, coordination, and control as the planning function expanded (Kleinschmidt 2002, p. S276). Moreover, with corporate expansion and changes in competition, accounting systems needed to be revamped to allow more powerful control and planning of a company's flows and processes. It was in these circumstances that US controlling methods as their answer (Hilger 2004, p. 278).

In addition to these factors, the deployment of divisional structures made the need for deployment of an accompanying controlling system absolutely critical. As deployment was conducted, controlling became a way for top management to monitor the results of each division, rather than a tool for middle management to perform after-the-fact evaluations. The position of controller or chief financial officer (CFO) as a director was born of this objective. For German corporations, these changes were extremely important, and as a result, they retained the original English words of "controlling" or "controller" for use as loan words (Schröter 2005, pp. 109–110).

The delay in deploying divisional structures was an important reason for the delay in deployment of controlling systems in German corporations. Unlike US corporate law, German corporations had a sufficient control mechanism in the supervisory board. Thus, the use of controllers was not organizationally necessary until the 1960s (Kleinschmidt 2002, p. 278). Literature introducing the US controller system could be found as early as the 1950s (Vgl. Abromeit 1953; Fünftes Kapitel; RKW 1957; Horváth 1992, p. 54), and Germany became familiar with it over time. However, the accounting system as a management system or alternatively a controlling system that integrated control, planning, and coordination functions began to be deployed along with organizational restructuring in corporations more commonly during the latter half of the 1960s, after which US controlling methodologies spread more vigorously (Kleinschmidt 2002, pp. 276, 282).

Controlling was aligned with the US model, and the integrated coordination system comprising planning, execution, and control functions was actually superior in functionality to that of the three functions operating separately. On this point, there was an essential characteristic of the deployment of these methodologies that provides evidence of how US management methods could cover such a broad spectrum of corporate management domains in German organizations, one section after another (Kleinschmidt 2002, p. 277). However, the responsibility of German managers engaged in the controller function was narrower than that of their US counterparts, and their participation in strategy setting and active problem solving of actual product and market issues was not common (Dyas and Thanheiser 1976, p. 137).

In addition, management of cost-effectiveness, analysis of economic efficiency and profitability, calculations for planning, budget revisions, and other controller responsibilities being undertaken by a central managerial economics department or other decentralized department was characteristic (Kleinschmidt 2002, p. 282). Through the 1970s, a gap existed in the two countries' breadth of a controller's functions (Siegwart 1982, p. 99). However, controlling as both a combination of roles and a management concept did occur in West German manufacturing corporations (Hahn 1979, p. 80) and saw a trend toward emulation of its US counterpart. From the latter half of the 1960s, changes in the economy and market policies guided German corporations to gradually deploy systematic corporate management aligned toward profit as was the American model. However, the modern US management perspective that corporate performance could be controlled clashed with that of traditional bookkeeping traditions of German accounting (Hilger 2004, p. 239).

In reviewing individual case studies such as Henkel, we find that the use of controlling methodologies advanced in response to the organizational restructuring that occurred in the latter half of the 1960s, and a unified system of accounting on a corporate group scale began. In Siemens AG, unification of accounting systems or modern controlling was first implemented in the latter half of the 1960s as they underwent organizational restructuring (Hilger 2004, pp. 227–228). In addition, the head of the managerial economics department, one of their five corporate departments, would become Siemens AG's "controller" (Tacke 1977, p. 277). However, other corporations had a longer history of the deployment and persistence of this position. For example, the concept of "controlling" finally became more commonly used as an everyday term in Freudenberg as they entered the 1980s. Moreover, at Volkswagen, the controller was the head of the managerial economics department, which was divided into the fields of "general managerial economics," "technical managerial economics," and "strategy and investment" until the mid-1980s. Planning and controlling were important functions of the controller (Kleinschmidt 2002, p. 283).

Based on the foregoing discussion, one can see German characteristics in the following points: First, the scope of managers engaged in the controlling function as a support mechanism for profit planning and budgetary control after the deployment of divisional structures was much narrower than that of their US counterparts. Second, it was not common for controlling to be actively involved in strategy setting or other critical functions. Third, the controlling function existed not only at the corporate level, but also in the decentralized operational departments.

9.4 The Role of US Corporations and Consulting Firms in Management Organization Reforms

9.4.1 Management Organization Reforms and the Role of US Corporations

We will now discuss the role played by US corporations and consulting firms in management organization reforms and the deployment of the divisional structure.

First, let us look at the role of US corporations. Among the largest German corporations, several, including Siemens, AEG, Bayer, Bosch, and Hoecsht, made the transition from a functional structure or holding company organization to a divisional structure on their own, without the help of consulting firms.

At AEG, for example, close ties with GE's top management played an important role. Specialists from GE participated in a study of organization-related solutions undertaken for organizational restructuring in 1966 and 1967, and they supported AEG in restructuring their organization (Dyas and Thanheiser 1976, pp. 121–122). According to G. Tacke, then the Siemens chairman of the board, Siemens performed organizational restructuring without relying on consultants for the following six reasons. (1) It was impossible for outside consultants to obtain a comprehensive overview of the company in a timely manner, given Siemens' size. (2) Because of their size, Siemens also needed their own internal consultants, and expected them to have continual communication with the outside world in their areas of specialty. (3) A new organization had been in the works by a handful of people for several years, and their work had progressed to at least include the principles of the restructuring and a large framework had reached a certain level of maturity by the time they were ready to begin work on organizational reforms. (4) Siemens neither pandered to the latest fads, nor completely changed their mature ideas. (5) Not much credence was given to external ideas because they thought that implementing homegrown ideas was simpler than implementing outside ideas. (6) Siemens was concerned about being manipulated by outside consultants. Because of these factors, when time came for organizational restructuring, Siemens carefully researched what was performed at other corporations in Europe and the US, and sought their own organizational theory (Zeitschrift für Organisation 1970c, pp. 343–344).

The principles behind the US developed vertical or divisional structure were widely debated in European management and financial publications, and this greatly influenced Siemens' new organization. Siemens had developed the basic concept of the organization by 1966. However, the US organization model aided Siemens' restructuring as Siemens entrenched themselves in their own concepts and by providing insight to the internal organizational limits and weaknesses of such organizations by observing the US system, which was already in use among their competitors (Feldenkirchen 2004, pp. 127–128). In addition, Hoechst sought their own solution rather than relying on outside consultants (Dyas and Thanheiser 1976, pp. 121–122), though they referenced case studies of US corporations. Hoechst's board of directors and supervisory board chairman, K. Winnacker, noted that US corporations were happy to supply information on the state of their own organizations (Winnacker 1972, p. 231).

Even among corporations that did not rely on consulting firms and instead worked on organizational reforms on their own, contact with US corporations and the know-how obtained from this contact had a great impact. Moreover, with Henkel, where SRI made important contributions to organizational reforms, the experiences of DuPont, P&G, Westinghouse, and other typical US corporations that had adopted a divisional structure were found to be useful, as we noted above (Kleinschmidt 2002, p. 264).

9.4.2 Management Organization Reforms and the Role of US Consulting Firms

Next, let us look at the impact and role of consulting firms. Unlike the knowledgeable partner's role in technology transfers, US management consulting firms took on the role of intermediaries for the US model and contributed significantly to the deployment of corporate organization forms found in US corporations primarily in the period after the mid-1960s (Kleinschmidt 2002, p. 274). The most important management reform promoted by US consulting firms was the divisional structure (Kipping 1999, p. 209). If one observes the top 100 German firms, more than half deployed divisional structure only after 1967, and as such these corporations lacked experience in undertaking such new measures or processing the paperwork required to make use of organizational structures (Dyas and Thanheiser 1976, p. 129). For that reason alone, US management consulting firms had the opportunity to make a great impact. Outside consultants were particularly important not only in their contributions made on the basis of their know-how, but also their recommendation regarding redistribution of responsibilities at the board of directors level, where the directors themselves most probably would not have worked on these issues internally (Dyas and Thanheiser 1976, pp. 114–115).

After the 1950s, as corporations increasingly concentrated on strategies and issues of corporate organization, McKinsey and other new-generation US consulting firms emerged with their expansion into Europe as the 1950s came to a close (Kipping 1999, pp. 205–207). A striking characteristic of the Americanization of industry in the period shortly after the war ended was the relatively limited impact of US management consultants. However, upon entering the 1960s, and with the deployment of divisional structures, US management consultants took a leading role in the international businesses of their clients (Zeitlin 2000, p. 26; Schröter 2005, p. 110).

Thus, we see that US consulting firms were powerful intermediaries in the implementation of management organization reforms. Among them, McKinsey had the most influence (Wengenroth 1997, p. 162). Booz Allen & Hamilton had a special reputation for production management systems in the sphere of production and manufacturing. Arthur D. Little was famous for its marketing advice and specialized knowledge of operations research. In contrast, McKinsey concentrated on the issues of top management, and had a decisive role in reforms leading to divisional structures in European corporations (Schröter 2005, p. 66, 110; Kipping 1999, pp. 209–210). It was involved in the deployment of divisional structures in 12 largest corporations of Germany, and other consulting firms worked with at least 6 corporations in the top 100 (Dyas and Thanheiser 1976, pp. 112, 120).

For example, BASF researched group organization and structure, both domestically and internationally in 1968, and requested a recommendation and proposal on organizational structure from McKinsey. Organizational reforms based on the advice and proposal from this most powerful consulting firm was given great significance because of the effective utilization of their diverse experiences [*BASF*

Archiv, C0, Die Schrift an die Mitglieder der Direktionssitzung (26.8.1968), pp. 1–2, *BASF Archiv*, C0, Die Schrift an die Mitglieder der Direktionssitzung (21.10. 1969)]. Although BASF had worked on additional organizational reforms from the late 1970s through the early 1980s, they terminated their cooperation with McKinsey as a management consulting firm in mid-February of 1981 because that project was completed [Vgl. *BASF Archiv*, C0, Die Weiterentwicklung der Organisation (20.3.1981), *BASF Archiv*, C0, M. Seefelder, Weiterentwicklung der Organisation. Direktionssitzung am 5. März 1981, *BASF Archiv*, C0, Die Weiterentwicklung der Organisation (20.3.1981), *BASF Archiv*, C0, Weiterentwicklung der Organisation kommt voran (in: *BASF Information*, 23.7.1980), *BASF Archiv*, C0, Neuorganisation der Aufgabengebiete in der BASF (in: *BASF Information*, 17.7.1980)].

As US management consulting firms planned to expand into Europe in the early 1960s, they sold US know-how to managers in the region who were working on organizational structure reforms (McKenna 1995, p. 57). In comparison with foreign countries, however, the role of McKinsey and other consulting firms in Germany was much smaller, particularly, in comparison with their impact in the US and UK (Guillen 1994, p. 149; Kipping 1996, pp. 117–121). Apart from certain corporations, their influence in Germany was relatively limited.

9.5 German Characteristics of Deployment of Divisional Structure

Based on the foregoing discussion, let us now examine German characteristics of the deployment of divisional structure. Thus, we can observe the impact level of delegation of authority and responsibility, the traditions of the board of directors along with collegiate management and the board-majority system, the role of top management in divisions, the use of a compensation system linked to divisional results, and the high number of holding companies among the largest manufacturing firms.

9.5.1 Divisional Structure Mechanisms and Their German Characteristics

We now examine various German characteristics from the perspective of divisional structure mechanisms. In the role of top management, one can observe many different applications of collegiate management in new organizations, and it is believed that there were three main alternatives. The first was having directors act as divisional general managers. Of the largest 100 enterprises, this alternative was most often seen in relatively small scale corporations. The responsibility for divisional profits in these cases rested upon top management, who were also collectively responsible for corporate-wide results. In these corporations, a controller or a position with an equivalent function existed, with a member of the top management taking such a position. The second alternative was placing divisions underneath directors who specialized in particular functions, with joint management of divisions further performed by managers who had specialized in particular functions. This was primarily conducted in corporations in the chemical industry, and in these cases profit responsibility resided in specialized management teams that were collectively responsible for directors. The directors themselves were typically responsible for a division's technical or commerce aspects and coordinating with staff or were responsible for both aspects. The third alternative was to have directors manage a group of divisions as observed in extremely large corporations such as Siemens, AEG, and Bayer. In these instances, two or sometimes more directors managed jointly, though sometimes a single director would be managing the group. Directors were usually the heads of either the division group or staff, and sometimes both (Dyas and Thanheiser 1976, pp. 123–125).

Regarding compensation systems, unlike the US where the compensation of a general manager, who was responsible for the profit of a division, is often tied to that division profits, use of performance linked financial incentives for general managers based on profit and profit responsibility are extremely rare. The introduction of incentives of this sort were often even deemed undesirable (Dyas and Thanheiser 1976, p. 138). Of the 19 capital corporations with divisional structures for which information is available, all had some type of payment system for special allowances. However, in an overwhelmingly high number of cases, these incentives neither built a large portion of the general managers' net income, nor was there a clear connection to divisional profits. Apart from 1 company that paid special allowances based on actual performance versus target performance and 2 companies that considered division results via a special allowance system that included corporate profits and divisional profits, the remaining 16 corporations made special payments based on corporate-wide profitability. In many cases, the US concept of divisions as profit centers had not been implemented. Thus, German corporations in general partially followed their own path in using the opportunities inherent in divisional structures. The possibility to strengthen profit orientation through the use of compensation systems or methods to generate internal competition, both based on divisional profits was not consciously considered in nearly all the 100 largest enterprises. Some of the reasons for the dismissal of such concepts are that German managers feel that creating direct links between divisional profits and a general manager's compensation was incompatible with corporate tradition or that the profit base was too unstable (Dyas and Thanheiser 1976, pp. 126–127). Even in cases where management responsibility was delegated to a general manager who reported to the board of directors, there was a great deal of opposition to providing the general manager with sufficient freedom and authority along with profit responsibility (Dyas and Thanheiser 1976, pp. 118–119). Of course, few of the largest corporations had delegated division management to lower levels and abolished the strict collegiate management tied to divisional management responsibility at the director level. In these methods, characteristics of the divisional structure in Germany and the US appear increasingly similar. However, there were also many other companies that left division management and the profit responsibility at the board of directors level (Dyas and Thanheiser 1976, p. 129).

Related to the nature of management decentralization, the ratio of holding companies in the largest German manufacturing corporations (see Sect.9.3.1) was relatively higher than that in the US [The percentage of companies using a holding company as a management structure in the largest US industrial firms (189 in 1949; 207 in 1959; 183 in 1969) was no more than 3.7% in 1949; 1.4% in 1959; 2.4% in 1969; Rumelt 1974, p. 65]. In transitioning from a holding company to a divisional structure, the holding company expanded and strengthened its control over subsidiaries. Changes of this type were characteristic of the aggressive contribution of holding companies to subsidiaries' internal issues. As we saw with transitions from functional structures to divisional structures, departments responsible for operations tended to have relatively low independence. A change from a holding company structure to a divisional structure could be seen in the 1960s; however, in several cases, such as Gutehoffnung, these were incomplete as of 1971 (Dyas and Thanheiser 1976, pp. 115–117). The high ratio of holding companies was based on the characteristics of large German corporations (see Chap. 5) wherein "corporate group structures developed around a single industrial system as its foundation," a characteristic of large German corporations. It could be said that a holding company style management structure is simply the most compatible in such cases.

9.5.2 Management Traditions in German Corporations and Their Influence on the Deployment of Divisional Structures

When we examine traditional management in German corporations, as we see in all instances of "Americanization" up to that time, one characteristic can be seen in the new wave of organizational reforms formed along German traditions of cooperative corporate culture that emphasize technical skills (Wengenroth 1997, p. 162). Similarities in the organizational structure compared with that in the US certainly reflected the relatively competitive, open business environment that created high technical standards in abundant markets along with industrial corporations' strategies that leaned toward increasing diversity of product and market. However, differences in culture between Germany and the US were one factor in the differences in organization. Some of these differences are as follows. Management authority that was foundational to functions in US corporations, and that had broadly spread with decentralization, sharply contrasted with the hierarchical relationships and highly centralized hierarchies that were a cornerstone in German corporations during the first few years after the war (Dyas and Thanheiser 1976, p. 128). Originally, management authority in Germany tended to be exclusive, closely held by the managers themselves because authority based on trust in top management was considered to be superior to authority based on function. These ideas changed in response to the

US influence, and the exclusiveness of management status decreased (Hartmann 1968, pp. 271–272, 282–283, 286–289; Hartmann 1959, pp. 261, 271–272, 274–277). However, traditions like these, rooted deep within the ideological foundations of management authority, greatly influenced the adoption and operation of divisional structures.

Another factor in the influence of traditional culture on German corporate management was the tradition of collegiate management and the board-majority system, which were unheard of in US corporations. In German corporations, the position of CEO, with one person having the independent authority to make decisions for the company as a whole, did not exist. The tradition of collegiate management (Dyas and Thanheiser 1976, pp. 106–107), with the board of directors generally making decisions according to a majority vote, differed greatly from the US in its pattern of delegation of responsibility as well as the relationship with reporting and management mechanisms (Dyas and Thanheiser 1976, p. 137). The practice of collegiate management was applied to the division management level for its allocation of assignments and responsibilities as well as to top management. This form of management was an important element in the cultural differences that emerged in organizational development (Dyas and Thanheiser 1976, p. 129).

Financial incentives for general managers via compensation systems linked to division results were extremely rare, reflecting the difference between German and US culture and values. US compensation systems ran the risk of potentially causing a general manager to lose objectivity in business judgment, with the plans negotiated between the division and corporate intensely conflicting with the interests of the division. Nevertheless, it has been pointed out that in general such notions are not based on actual experience with such compensation systems, they are reflections of cultural values and attitudes that clearly differ between the two countries (Dyas and Thanheiser 1976, pp. 137–138). In such cultural factors, German corporate management traditions such as collegiate management were particularly influential.

In regard to the impact of these cultural and systemic factors, analysis and research of Hilger's case studies on Henkel, Siemens, and Daimler-Benz based on differing economic, political, cultural, and systemic conditions demonstrates that the adoption of the divisional structure in German corporations frequently led to results that varied from those in the US (Hilger 2004, p. 213). Although Germany heavily relied on US know-how, in adopting the divisional structure, German corporations did not view the adoption as the simple imitation of a process, but, to a certain extent, as an adaptation to local conditions. The unquestioned acceptance of American knowledge had become a thing of the past, and was replaced by greater selectivity and confidence stemming from German managers' own ways of thinking and methods (Dyas and Thanheiser 1976, p. 138). Thus, organizational changes were not merely adaptations to strategy but were a cultural phenomenon (Dyas and Thanheiser 1976, p. 102). The further development of new organizations in the late 1960s indicates a generally decreased reliance on US innovations by German management, demonstrating that unquestioned acceptance of US solutions were a thing of the past. The priority had changed from seeking US models and knowledge to the selection of only those US ideas deemed worthwhile to Germany from the many offered by research literature and consultants (Dyas and Thanheiser 1976, p. 129).

Our discussions till now have examined the deployment of divisional structures in German corporations. In considering the compatibility of a new corporate structure based on the expansion of business domains in conjunction with diversification and the benefits of product division restructuring for an organization, we see that a German method of performing tasks was used in conducting such considerations. Specifically, a corporation's actual structure, management mechanisms and systems, and the use thereof reflect a corporate culture. It emphasizes technology rather than a sales and marketing point of view, a culture of collegiate management by a board of directors, the board-majority system tradition, the historical arc of delegation of authority, a large corporate group structure founded on a single industry structure. In the deployment of management organizations such as the divisional structure, there was in fact a method compatible with the German method, and German corporations pursued those elements that could be adapted to German corporate culture.

References

Abelshauser W (2002) Die BASF seit der Neugründung von 1952. In: Abelshauser W (ed) Die BASF: Eine Unternehemensgeschichte. C. H. Beck, München, pp 359–637, 688–713

Abromeit H-G (1953) Amerikanische Betriebswirtschaft. Die Praxis der Unternehmungen in den USA. Betriebswirtschaftlicher Verlag Th. Gabler, Wiesbaden

AEG (1963) Bericht über das Geschäftsjahr vom 1. Oktober 1962 bis 30. September 1963. AEG, Berlin

AEG-Telefunken AG (1967) Bericht über das Geschäftsjahr 1967. AEG-Telefunken, Berlin

AEG-Telefunken AG (1969) Bericht über das Geschäftsjahr 1969. AEG-Telefunken, Berlin

Auffermann JD (1957) Der Controller—eine unternehmerische Persönlichkeit. In: RKW Betriebsführung durch Planung und Kontrolle: Eindrücke von einer Studienreise deutscher Betriebswirtschaftler aus Wissenschaft und Industrie. Team-Bericht (RKW-Auslandsdienst, Heft 51). C. Hauser Verlag, München, pp 42–57

Berghahn V (1985) Unternehmer und Politik in der Bundesrepublik. Suhrkamp, Frankfurt am Main

Chandler AD Jr (1962) Strategy and structure: chapters in the history of the industrial enterprise. MIT, Cambridge

Chandler AD Jr (1977) The visible hand: managerial revolution in American business. Harvard University Press, Cambridge

Chandler AD Jr (1990) Scale and scope: the dynamics of industrial capitalism. Harvard University Press, Berkeley

Choki T (1993) Sengo Hattenki no Nihon Kigyo no Keieigenri (Business principles of Japanese enterprise in the boom years after WWII). In: Gendai Keieigaku Kenkyukai (ed) Gendai Keieigaku no Kihon Kadai (Fundamental problems of modern business management). Bunshindo, Tokyo, pp 37–56

Der Lichtbogen (1970) Neue Organisation bei Hüls. Der Lichtbogen 22(160):26–27

Der Volkswirt (1963) Reorganisation bei wachsender Rentabilität. Relativ geringe Exportquote—Bau eines Atomkraftwerkes. Der Volkswirt 17(1):492–495

Der Volkswirt (1964) AEG. Ein Konzern wird neu organisiert. Geschäftsjahr umgestellt—Verlustaufträge bei Schwermaschinen. Der Volkswirt 18(25):1240–1243
Der Volkswirt (1969) Wachablösung an der Ruhr. Bewährte Sechziger und nüchterne Vierziger. Der Volkswirt 24(45):70–72
Dyas GP, Thanheiser HT (1976) The emerging European enterprise. Strategy and structure in French and German industry. Macmillan, London
Farbwerke Hoechst AG (1969) Geschäftsbericht 1969. Farbwerke Hoechst AG, Frankfurt am Main
Feldenkirchen W (2004) The Americanization of the German electrical industry after 1945. Siemens as a case study. In: Kudo A, Kipping M, Schröteret HG (eds) German and Japanese business in the boom years. Transforming American management and technology models. Routledge, London, pp 116–137
Feldenkirchen W, Hilger S (2001) Menschen und Marken. 125 Jahre Henkel 1876–2001. Stürtz, Düsseldorf
Gabele E (1981) Die Einführung von Geschäftsbereichsorganisation. Mohr, Tübingen
Guillen MF (1994) Models of management. Work, authority, and organization in a comparative perspective. University of Chicago Press, Chicago
Hahn D (1979) Organisation des Controllings in der deutschen Industrie. In: Goetzke W, Sieben G (eds) Controlling, integration von Planung und Kontrolle: Bericht von der 4. Kölner BFuP-Tagung am 22. und 23. Mai 1978 in Köln. GEBERA, Köln
Harrmann A (1982) Steigert ein Wechsel der Strukturorganisation die Unternehmenseffektivität? REFA-Nachrichten 35(4):202–204
Hartmann H (1959) Authority and organization in German management. Princeton University Press, Princeton
Hartmann H (1968) Der deutsche Unternehmer: Autorität und Organisation. Europäische Verlagsasnstalt, Frankfurt am Main
Hautsch G (1979) Das Imperium AEG-Telefunken: Ein multinationaler Konzern. Verlag Marxistische Blätter, Frankfurt am Main
Henkel GmbH (1968) Geschäftsbericht 1968. Henkel GmbH, Düsseldorf
Henkel GmbH (1969) Geschäftsbericht 1969. Henkel GmbH, Düsseldorf
Hilger S (2004) „Amerikanisierung" deutscher Unternehmen. Wettbewerbsstrategien und Unternehmenspolitik bei Henkel, Siemens und Daimler-Benz (1945/49-1975). Franz Steiner Verlag, Stuttgart
Horváth P (1992) Controlling, 4th edn. Vahlen, München
Imanishi S (1988) Jigyobu-sei no Kaimei (A study of divisional structure). Manejimentosha, Tokyo
Ishii J, Okumura A, Kagon T et al (1996) Keiei Senryaku Ron (Business strategy), new edn. Yuhikaku, Tokyo
Kagono T (1980) Keiei Soshiki no Kankyo Tekio (Adaptation of management organizations to the environment). Hakuto Shobo, Tokyo
Kagono T, Nonaka I, Sakakibara K et al (1983) Nichibei Kigyo no Keiei Hikaku (Comparison of business in Japanese and American enterprise). Nihon Keizai Shinbunsha, Tokyo
Kipping M (1996) The U.S. influence on the evolution of management consultancies in Britain, France, and Germany since 1945. Bus Econ Hist 25(1):111–123
Kipping M (1999) American management consulting companies in West Europe 1920 to 1990. Bus Hist Rev 73(2):190–220
Kleinschmidt C (2002) Der produktive Blick. Wahrnehmung amerikanischer und japanischer Management- und Produktionsmethoden durch deutsche Unternehmer 1950–1985. Akademie Verlag, Berlin
Koch E (1970) Offene Tore für das schöpferische Potential. Neuorganisaton der BASF—Die WELT sprach mit Vorstandsvorsitzen dem Bernhard Timm. Die Welt 193
Kroos HE, Gilbert C (1972) American business history. Prentice-Hall, Englewood Cliffs
Lorentz B, Erker P (2003) Chemie und Politik. Die Geschichte der Chemischen Werke Hüls 1938–1979: Eine Studie zum Problem der Corporate Governance. C. H. Beck, München

McKenna CD (1995) The origins of modern management consulting. Bus Econ Hist 24(1): 51–58
Ono T (1979) Nihon Kigyo no Sosiki Senryaku (Organizational strategy in Japanese enterprise). Manejimentosha, Tokyo
REFA-Nachrichten (1967) Wo liegen noch Rationalisierungsmöglichkeiten im Betrieb? REFA-Nachrichten 20(6):259–263
Reindl R (2001) Wachstum und Wettbewerb in den Wirtschafyswunderjahren. Die elektorotechnische Industrie in der Bundesrepublik Deutschland und in Groβbritannien 1945–1967. Ferdinand Schöningh, Paderborn
RKW (1957) Betriebsführung durch Planung und Kontrolle: Eindrücke von einer Studienreise deutscher Betriebswirtschaftler aus Wissenschaft und Industrie. Team-Bericht (RKW-Auslandsdienst, Heft 51). C. Hauser Verlag, München
Rumelt RP (1974) Strategy, structure and economic performance. Harvard University Press, Boston
Schröter HG (2005) Americanization of the European economy. A compact survey of American economic influence in Europe since the 1880s. Springer, Dordrecht
Selinger K (1977) Die Organisation der BASF-Gruppe. Zeitschrift für Organisation 46(1): 17–22
Siegrist H (1980) Deutscher Groβunternehmen vom späten 19. Jahrhundert bis zur Weimarer Republik. Geschichte und Gesellschaft 6(1):60–102
Siegwart H (1982) Worin unterscheiden sich amerikanisches und deutsches Controlling? Management-Zeitschrift 51(2):97–104
Siemens AG (1969) Bericht über das Geschäftsjahr vom 1. Oktober 1968 bis 30. September 1969. Siemens AG, München
Strunk P (2000) Die AEG. Aufstieg und Niedergang einer Industrielegende, 2nd edn. Nicolai, Berlin
Tacke G (1977) Ein Beitrag zur Geschichte der Siemens AG. Gerd Tacke, München
Urabe K (1960) Jigyobusei to Kindai Keiei (Divisional structure and modern management). Daiyamondosha, Tokyo
Wengenroth U (1997) Germany: competition abroad—cooperation at home, 1870–1990. In: Chandler AD Jr, Amatori F, Hikino T (eds) Big business and the wealth of nations. Cambridge University Press, Cambridge, pp 139–175
Winnacker K (1972) Nie den Mut verlieren. Erinnerungen an Schicksalsjahr der deutschen Chemie. Econ Verlag, Düsseldorf
Yamamoto K (1993) Gendai Doitsu no Chiiki Keizai (Contemporary German regional economy). Hosei Daigaku Shuppankai, Tokyo
Yoshihara H, Sakuma A, Itamai H et al (1981) Nihon Kigyo no Takakuka Senryaku (Diversification strategy in Japanese enterprise). Nihon Keizai Shinbunsha, Tokyo
Zeitlin J (2000) Introduction: Americanization and its limits: reworking US technology and management in post-War Europe and Japan. In: Zeitlin J, Herrigel G (eds) Americanization and its limits. Reworking US technology and management in post-war Europe and Japan. Oxford University Press, Oxford, pp 1–50
Zeitschrift für Organisation (1970a) Die Neuorganisation des Hauses Siemens. Zeitschrift für Organisation 39(8):337–342
Zeitschrift für Organisation (1970b) Die organisatorische Neuordnung der Henkel-Gruppe „Sparten, Funktionen und Regionen". Zeitschrift für Organisation 39(5):196–198
Zeitschrift für Organisation (1970c) Interview der Z Für O mit Herren Dr. Gerd Tacke, dem Vorsitzenden des Vorstandes der Siemens AG, über die Neuorganisation des Hauses Siemens. Zeitschrift für Organisation 39(8):343–347
Zeitschrift für Organisation (1970d) Interview der Z für O zur Reorganisation der Henkel-Gruppe. Zeitschrift für Organisation 39(5):199–200

Chapter 10
Features and Significance of German-Style Management

Abstract Following the previous chapters' topics, this chapter re-evaluates the changes in business management in postwar Germany through the early 1970s by applying the two frameworks described in Chapter 1—the total system of business management and the re-framing of Americanization. First, it summarizes the environmental factors of business management on the basis of mutual relations. Next, it considers problems stemming from the German approach to conform to American methods, affected by traditional and cultural factors in business management and institutional factors. In addition, it discusses influences of the structural characteristics of German capitalism such as the structures of productive forces, industries, and markets. It also examines the development of German-style business management in relation to the reproduction (accumulation) structure of German capitalism, which was appropriate for the European region. This chapter also explains the significance of the German business management model that developed in the European environment by comparing Germany's situation in Europe with that of Japan's in Asia.

Keywords Americanization • Hybridization • Market structure • Re-framing • Total system of business management

Based on the preceding chapters, we will re-examine changes in Germany's business management in the postwar period up to the early 1970s. This chapter will also elucidate how German-style business management and its particular characteristics, conforming to European conditions while still bearing on the German management style, surfaced during the deployment of the American management method. We will do so by analyzing the original framework, that is, the "total system of business management" and "re-framing of Americanization", as noted in Chapter 1.

T. Yamazaki, *German Business Management: A Japanese Perspective on Regional Development Factors*, DOI 10.1007/978-4-431-54303-9_10, © Springer Japan 2013

In Sect. 10.1, we will discuss the overall relevance of the total system of business management in postwar Germany. In Sect. 10.2, we recapture "Americanization" from the angle of "re-framing."

10.1 Overview of the Total System of Business Management in Germany After World War II

With regard to the analysis framework for the total system of business management, we will provide an overview of the environmental factors of business management on the basis of mutual relations. The total system of business management comprises eight elements: (1) state–enterprise relations, (2) labor relations, (3) an industrial system based on inter-firm relationships, (4) the financial system, (5) the structure of productive forces, (6) the industrial structure, (7) the market structure, and (8) the enterprise–market relationship.

In the state–enterprise relations, regulatory mechanisms under the Restrictive Trade Practices Act, which dealt with regulative and anti-monopoly policies, were linked to an industrial system based on inter-firm relations. They influenced business development based on trust, which replaced cartels, and a complementary division of labor in the product fields within large-scale corporate groups. Within industrial policy, investment aid policy along with currency reform and re-evaluation of company assets greatly affected the financial market by promoting corporate self-financing and lowering the rate of direct financing by issuing securities. Industrial policy also influenced the overall industrial structure, and in particular, the heavy and chemical industries. It supported international competitiveness in the capital goods market structure, which was the foundation of the industrial structure and heavily weighted toward goods-producing industries. In addition, trade policy efforts were underway to form a common market structure, such as that in Western Europe; however, the government's response to the policy significantly influenced the structure of commodities markets. The formation of a common market served to further strengthen and complement the global linkage of markets within the European region. It also promoted the formation of a foreign trade pattern based on German international competitiveness, which was biased toward exportation in markets of that region and a "complementary division of labor in industrial and product fields."

For labor relations, a system of industry-specific collective agreements in each region was an important source of regulatory power for trade unions. The systems also played a role in the reduction of intra-corporate wage gaps in the industries which along with codetermination at the plant level reinforced the basis for employment and wage security and social redistribution in a social market economy. These safety nets coordinated labor markets and expanded commodities markets by creating and strengthening domestic markets. Further, the codetermination at the top levels of management secured autonomy in response to capital market pressures on business management caused by worker participation in supervisory boards. This autonomy was further strengthened by ties between an industrial system based on industry–bank relations. The systems even promoted investment in vocational education for the corporate workforce. The investments in education and training laid the foundation for diversified quality production that relied on skilled workers and developed production and marketing strategies in Germany. Thus, the system fostered German corporate competitiveness and contributed to the building and maintenance of a foreign trade pattern that complemented industrial and product fields in European markets.

Industrial systems based on inter-firm and industry–bank relationships secured autonomy through coordination among banks and between industries and banks, and the inclusion of bank representatives on corporate supervisory boards. This type of industrial system brought about a German-style system of corporate governance. The codetermination system under the Codetermination Act in 1976 was based on a structure comprising an equal number of labor and capital market members at the supervisory board level. This type of system weakened the influence of shareholders in capital markets. Moreover, because the system of corporate governance was based on industry–bank coordination, it further strengthened in collaboration with the codetermination system. Further, the postwar system of large corporate groups founded on trust-like unions, influenced the effects of anti-monopoly and ensuing regulations prescribed by the Restrictive Trade Practices Act. This system of industrial concentration promoted the formation of complementary relationships in product fields on the basis of product quality in the market, which further restricted price competition among corporations.

Next, we will examine the financial system that had strong connections with the industrial system based on industry–bank relationships. Mutual ties between credit businesses and securities businesses based on the universal banking system, along with the role of the house bank among large-scale banks, served as an organizational foundation that developed the industrial system based on industry–bank relations. The mutual ties also regulated the financial market structure, in which credit and securities businesses were combined; this type of market structure is a factor that determines the system of corporate governance in Germany.

In addition, one of the most important characteristics of the "structure of productive forces," an element of German capitalism, was a production system based on vocational education and specialist qualifications, such as those provided under the Meister system. This fostered the creation of experience and skill and encouraged investment in vocational education for corporate workers. Germany had a history of production system development that used prewar concepts of flexible production emphasizing quality and development of production systems that aimed at achieving improved scale merit through lower production volume and flexibility in response to changes in product demand (von Freyberg 1989; Siegel and Freyberg 1991; Stahlmann 1993). These laid the foundation for the development of diversified quality production that relied on skilled workers.

Industrial structures rapidly developed in the postwar era in the durable consumer goods industries as well as in considerably represented producer goods industries and the heavy and chemical industries, which were internationally competitive even before the war. The characteristics of the industrial structures included (1) formation of German-style production systems, (2) international competitiveness in and skewed exporting toward European markets, and (3) a foreign trade pattern that complemented these industrial and product fields.

Further, characteristics of German and European markets, which emphasized product quality and functionality, were significant in the development of postwar business management and the Americanization of technology and management. Under such market conditions, German competitiveness in European markets, along with the bias toward exporting to these regions, formed a pattern of foreign trade with a division of labor in a form complementary to their industrial and production fields. These market structures developed diversified quality production focused on niche market segments and a foundation that supported a labor division system that complemented production fields in large corporate groups. German heavy and chemical industries had competitive strength in the European market since before the war, and the complementary relationship of industrial and production fields was evident from the rapid development of processing and assembly industries postwar; this type of complementary relationship was stronger in Europe than in other regions. Given European markets that were regulated by such a structure of productive forces, the characteristics of the German industrial structure and the mutually complementary relationship were strong in comparison with other regions. This further heightened the significance of Germany's diversified quality production. In addition, credit and securities businesses were combined in financial markets, which became the basis of a system that jointly formed the cornerstone of the universal banking system.

Based on the foregoing analysis, in enterprise–market relations, which are related to the state of marketization, one can see the characteristics of a coordinated market economy in the labor market and its connection with labor relations. In the industrial system, based on the financial system and industry–bank relations, there are characteristics of a coordinated market economy in the financial market. Further, in its connection with market structure, a relationship with a coordinated market economy in the commodities market exists, as it avoided price competition by emphasizing competition in quality through product specialization. It is noteworthy that the market economy, coordinated at the top levels of management through the codetermination system, and the industrial system based on industry–bank relations were problems deeply tied to enterprise–market relations. These issues were facilitated by the development of a German-style system of corporate governance that differed from the market-oriented corporate governance system and emphasized financial markets. Measures to deal with the "limitations of marketization" included social redistribution functions based on the principles of a social market economy, a framework of labor relations based on the codetermination system, and a system of interest coordination in an industrial system based on the universal banking system and industry–bank relations.

Figure 10.1 is a graphical overview of the total system of business management in postwar Germany based on our discussions

10.2 "Re-framing" in the Americanization Process and German-Style Management

The following section discusses the development of business management by the introduction of the American management method from the angle of "re-framing". This issue was raised in Chapter 1. "Re-framing" is defined by the following five factors: (1) cultural factors such as management values and business management traditions, (2) institutional factors, (3) structure of productive forces, (4) industrial structure, and (5) market structure. Factors (3), (4), and (5) are structural characteristics of German capitalism. We will consider the problems stemming from the German method of conforming to the American method, impacted by traditional and cultural factors in business management as well as institutional factors, and its relationship to the structural characteristics of German capitalism.

10.2.1 The "Americanization" of Business Management and German-Style Adaptation

First, examining the German-style adaptation of Americanization in regard to the post-WWII introduction of American technology and management methods, the management value in German capitalism, business management traditions, and institutional and cultural factors had relatively little impact on the introduction of technology. From a comprehensive perspective, the introduction of American technology, for which strong efforts were made, was considered an effective method for developing productive forces. In contrast, various factors related to "re-framing" impacted the introduction of the methods of American management, which was unavoidable and thus strongly expressed. Moreover, there were differences observed among industrial sectors and companies as well as in each area and method.

From the perspective of this book, to improve productivity at the time of introducing the American management method, the measures and elements that were directly related to improving "efficiency" (economic efficiency) were concerned with the development of productive forces; therefore, these principles were relatively, proactively, and widely introduced. These included (a) Ford's assembly-line system of mass production; (b) the basic principles of industrial engineering, such as production management and labor management; (c) the basics of marketing philosophy and measures; and (d) organizational principles compatible with companies' diversified businesses and divisional structures.

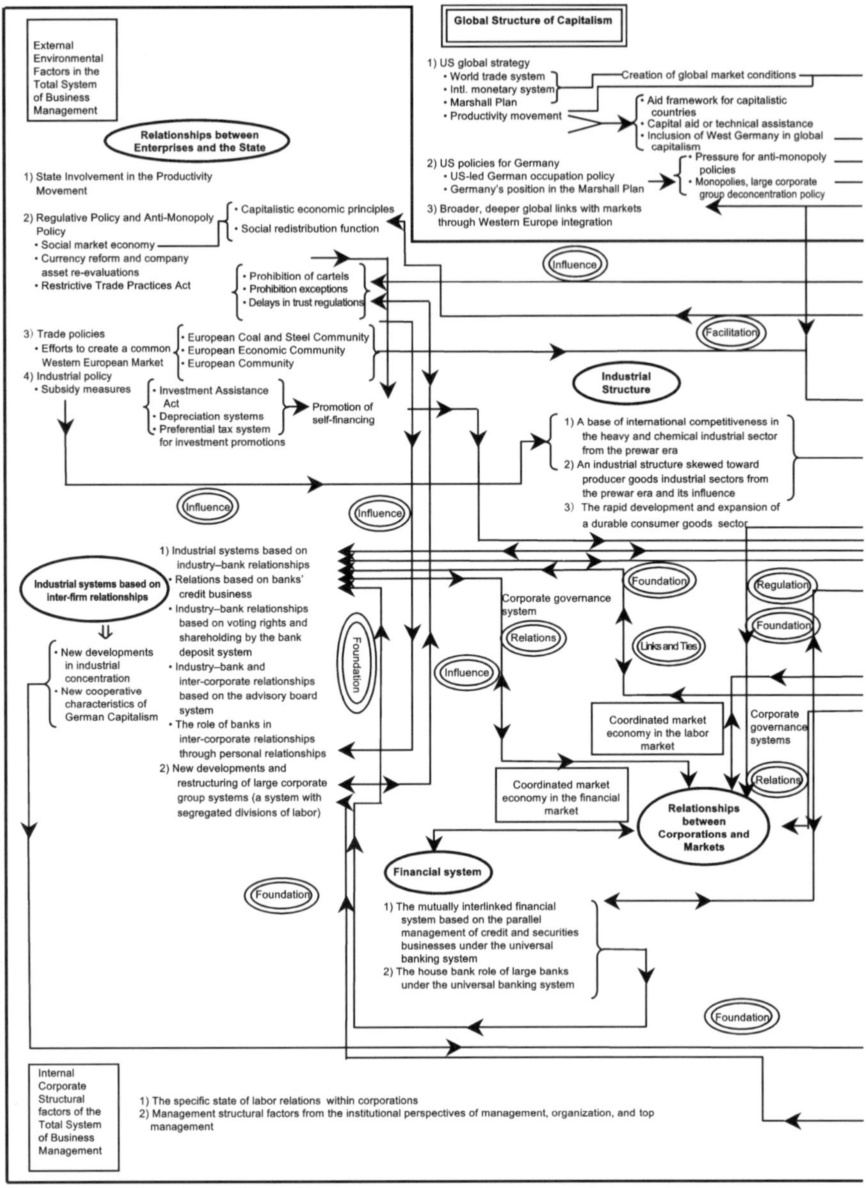

Fig. 10.1 Overview of postwar Germany's total system of business management.
Source: This figure was compiled by the author based on discussions in this chapter and previous chapters. Also available at http://extras.springer.com/

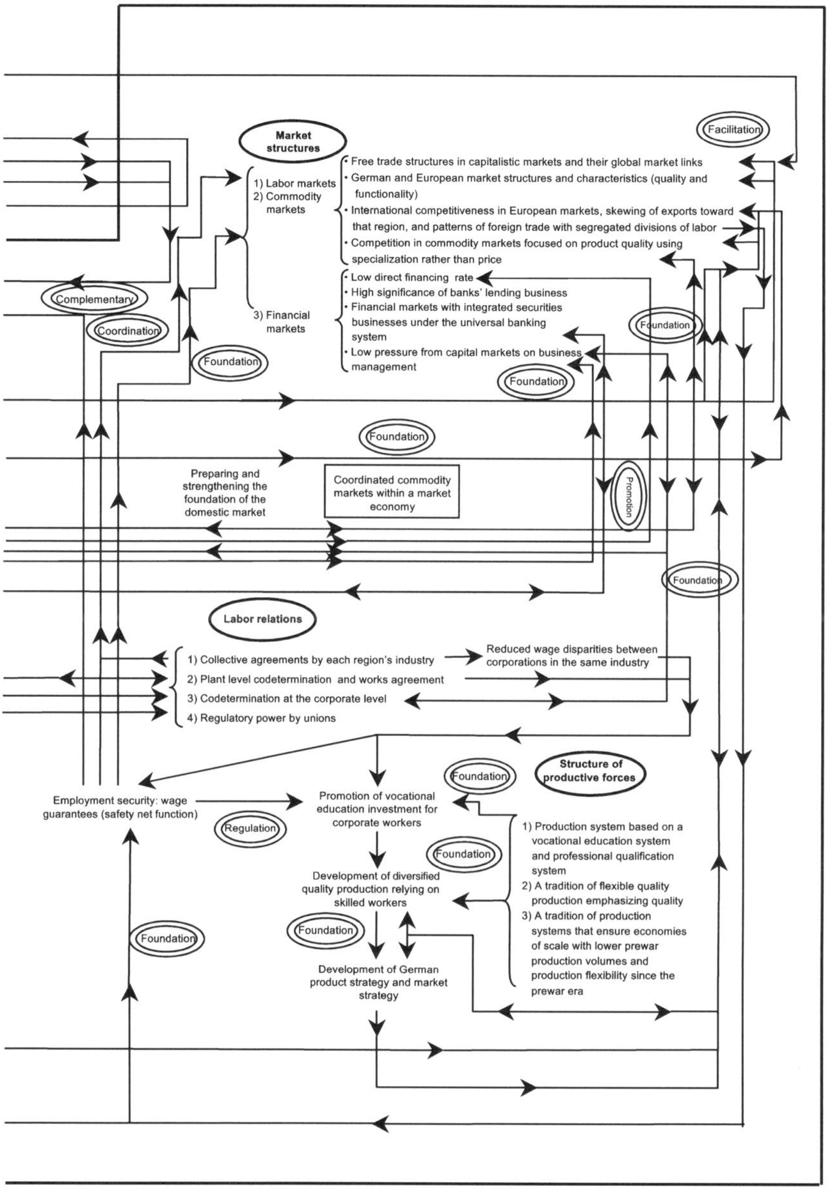

Fig. 10.1 (continued)

In contrast, there were many aspects of American-style management that did not necessarily conform at the time to the conditions in Germany. These included productive forces as well as conditional and environmental factors that supported market adaptation measures, in particular, aspects with American characteristics, such as the culture and relationships shared among labor and management, value for management, management style, and management tradition/culture. Therefore, in many cases, there was strong resistance and opposition that prevented the introduction of these aspects, and it was only possible to introduce them by modifying them in the process. These problems were most prominent in the areas of human relations and management education, which together were the most emphasized in America to transfer to the European countries under the productivity movement.

Furthermore, in reality, there were many cases wherein they pursued the German method of management, in regard to productive factors and market adaptation measures, even though mechanisms and principles for improving efficiency were introduced. In particular, due to the influence of German corporate traditions and management values and various systemic factors within companies, market characteristics, and industrial relations, many German companies sought the German-style adaptation. Such cases were observed in marketing and public relations (PR), as well as in the introduction of the Ford System and divisional structure.

The spread of the consumer society to technical and cultural adaptation, or more accurately the American influence in terms of adopting American management and production methods within German corporations, were generally included in the concept of "Americanization"; Kleinschmidt believes that the expressions "America-Concentrated" or "American Model" are better reflected in the concept. America represents technological progress, rationalization, and modernization, demonstrated as one of the successful economic models (Kleinschmidt 2004b, p. 75). In addition, Feldenkirchen comments that to keep up with international development in the field of technology, German companies relied on relationships with their international partners, particularly technologically leading American corporations. In contrast, in areas such as organization, human resources, and marketing and sales, there was no direct incorporation of the American methods; rather, the American model served as useful guide for the development of corporate strategies within these areas (Feldenkirchen 2004, p. 131).

This trend is also seen in the other European countries. For example in their research, Bjarnar and Kipping stress that the fundamental results of Americanization was not the complete adoption of the American management model, but rather a selective and partial adaptation. He emphasizes both the effectiveness and limitations of the process (Bjarnar and Kipping 1998, p. 14), and points out that it is rare for Europeans to mimic the American model; they do not perceive the model as good or excellent; rather, they select those aspects they feel are appropriate for the environment in their countries (Schröter 2005, p. 59). Zeitlin's research emphasizes the active altering of the American Model. Here, Zeitlin points out that there was selective adaptation of American technology and management that was tailored to the local environment, and that creative modifications and innovative hybridizations were observed. However, these modifications and hybridizations should not be understood as a negative phenomenon or indications of domestic resistance to the transfer process, or even as the mark of inevitable compromise. Rather, they should be realized in the positive light, i.e., the modifications originate from experimental work and innovative learning (Zeitlin 2000, pp. 11, 15–20). Thus, the people involved in the industry took advantage of their experience, accumulated while decomposing, modifying, and re-concentrating the elements of the American model to best fit the local environment. By doing so, they reinterpreted, modified, and at times changed their country's practices and systems.

However, not all practical modifications were equally successful. It is important that European and Japanese industrialists had significant existing knowledge of American-style practices. Zeitlin points out that "European and Japanese industrialists' prior familiarity with American-style practices…enabled them to treat US technology and management not as a unitary model to be imitated wholesale, but rather as a suggestive point of departure for selective adaptation, creative modification, and innovative hybridization" (Zeitlin 2000, pp. 38, 40–41).

Thus, there were certain limitations in adaptation, and hence Germany did not completely adapt the American management model. While modifying the American management model to accord with the circumstances in their country, Germans developed their own style of management that had specific developmental characteristics. A mixed form was created due to the hybridization of the American and German management practices and factors, and by the late 1960s to the early 1970s, it was no longer possible to draw fine distinctions between aspects that were originally German and those that were foreign. This was because American management practices had been widely absorbed into German companies' thinking and behavior. Thus in the 1970s, German managers were no longer oriented toward the American model to the same extent as they were 20 years ago. In particular, the adaptation of American management and production methods succeeded because it was possible to combine American management methods and technology with German methods of business management as well as Germany's own technological development (Kleinschmidt 2002, pp. 120, 398–399).

In relation to the aspect of hybridization and considering the discussion results in this book, we observe the following mix of American and German factors in management and production systems. First, industrial engineering methods such as the Work-Factor Method and Methods-Time Measurement were incorporated into the traditional German REFA system. Second, there was a mix between American orientation of corporate personnel policies and social policies introduced by human relations with the German orientation of the prewar works community philosophy. Third, there was a fusion of human relations aimed at improvement of the "working atmosphere" with the perspective of the prewar labor science research. Fourth, there was a coalition of various American elements in the introduction of the Ford system with those of Germany's own prewar production system as well as the standardized "unit system." Finally, management education fostered manifestations of fusions, such as that in the transfer of knowledge and exchange of opinions between different generations and the network of managers centered in business and industrial associations, using of American educational materials and methods.

In addition, there are examples of fusions between American and German methods in the area of marketing. For example, we see the development of the American-style marketing while German factors were incorporated. An example of this is the approach to marketing and sales that combine market characteristics with an emphasis on values (respect for individual characteristics and quality). This was prevalent since before the war, and was a product policy that emphasized quality and function as well as the price policy. Fusions in PR were also observed to occur, for example between the American methods based on new social science methodology and the tradition of prewar German corporate image advertising and publicity activities. Moreover, in the introduction of divisional structures and the formation of a matrix organizational structure, there was a fusion between the principles of the American-style product-based divisional structure and the German-style regional and functional departments. This was in addition to the German-style structure based on collegial management and the principle of board-majority system in the board of directors.

10.2.2 German-Style Adaptation and the Influence of Business Management Tradition and Culture in the Americanization Process

Having examined the German-style adaptation in the process of Americanization, let us now examine the influence of cultural factors such as the German business management tradition and values.

German entrepreneurs' and managers' willingness and speedy acceptance of American business management and production methods were not simply the outcome of objective political and economic conditions. Instead, they largely resulted from the existence of dynamic and agile entrepreneurs and managers having qualities of openness, adaptability, and orientation toward global markets (Kleinschmidt 2002, pp. 312, 396). Germany's strong culture combined with its tradition of non-compliance and skepticism of the "American vogue" was the reason there was no fundamental Americanization of business management. Further, faced with the situation of having to regain lost markets and keeping pace with technological innovation, German companies demonstrated a relatively high level of readiness to accept American know-how.

When analyzing the changes in the European market from the 1950s, i.e., the midst of the evolution of mass consumption, mass production, and mass-marketing, we see a change in the disposition of entrepreneurs. However, in the Americanization process, under the conditions of intense competition, there was tension due to the conflict between the high interest toward and readiness to accept American ideas and cautious skepticism. American management thinking and systems were and still are firmly rooted in American economic culture (Hilger 2004, pp. 279–282). However, in Germany as in Japan, despite initial enthusiasm, their manifestation of management continued to be uncertain (Locke 1996, p. 54). Kleinschmidt points out that "a broad adoption of values, behavior, norms and behavior and their implementation on the corporate level did not occur" (Kleinschmidt 2004a, p. 172). According to McCreary's (1964) research, as to the question of whether Americanization has occurred in Europe, the answer is "Yes," if you consider American goods, methods, and organizational forms, and "No," if you consider American philosophy and attitudes (McCreary 1964, p. 23).

In regard to these points, Berghahn (1985) indicates that in the Americanization of industrial capitalism in West Germany, a fusion between the elements of American industrial culture and those of Germany was born (Berghahn 1985, p. 330). The successful synthesis of modern American industrial culture and traditional West German economic spirit and structure built one of the important foundations for sustained growth of the post-WWII economy (Neebe 1989, p. 75). According to Hilger (2004), the Americanization of German companies can be understood on the basis of appropriate and selective adaptation to market changes based on the use of America's modern managerial techniques, new technology, and product innovation. However, such adaptation, at the same time, strengthened the unique German-style corporate culture, which in a way was a limited movement (Hilger 2004, p. 287).

The important aspect concerning these types of traditions, values and cultural factors of German business management is the influence of management values that emphasize technology, quality, and production. In post WWII Germany, there was a trend toward contemptuous perception of the spread of American consumer-oriented management practices (Wengenroth 1997, p. 161). Rather than an orientation toward marketing and more direct pursuits of profit, there was a strong trend toward production orientation that emphasized technology and quality. This not only had a great impact on the introduction of American-style management methods but also led to the birth of German-style business management characteristics.

This type of management orientation is observed in a high proportion of engineers, who are also directors and managers, and in individuals at relatively high positions within their respective companies. In addition, their designations and size of roles regulate the methods of German-style management. In Germany, knowledge, skills, and expertise related to production are emphasized; there are many engineers who have higher levels of expertise and more vocational qualifications than other professional managers. Management values and this type of thinking, which emphasize technology, support the important role of engineers in industrial management. The philosophy of emphasizing technology also affects the disposition of typical German companies in general, and is related to top management ideas concerning goals and the methods for achieving them (Lawrence 1980, pp. 80, 83, 96–100, 186, 190).

The impact of this situation can be seen in the introduction of many management methods and values. For example, American pragmatic management forms the background for the introduction of management methods such those in human relations and industrial relations. This method emphasizes the management principle of "increased efficiency" in corporate behavior mechanisms for management practices and the labor environment. Hence, there were certain aspects of the various types of American measures that were strongly incompatible with German traditions and management values, emphasizing technology, quality, and production, as well as with managerial philosophy related to personnel structure, populated by managers with technological backgrounds. With management values that only emphasized technology in the background, modern technologies of planning and control, for example the use of mathematical methods for decision making such as OR, did not interest German companies (Lawrence 1980, p. 98). It was the same in the case of marketing. Under German-style management values, rather than following producer-oriented measures such as planned obsolescence, a typical oligopolistic behavior, German companies tended to emphasize sales policies that prioritized consumer interests. Traditional influences from the pre-WWII period were also seen, such as priority given to moderate pricing policies based on market agreements. In addition, a look at the introduction of management education methods also reveals that methods such as TWI were unsuccessful due to the tradition of the German companies' managerial social policy and actual management behavior; this was because the education methods were not necessarily compatible with German management values and personnel philosophy. In Germany, management values and culture with long-term orientation and emphasis on technology existed, and differed from the management values based on the American vogue of pragmatism, reflected in radical "efficiency-first principle" personnel policies. Even under strong American influence, these German management values and culture could not be reversed immediately. In addition, even after the introduction of the divisional structure, there were still many cases wherein strong influences were exerted by the operational traditions of collegial management and the principle of board-majority system in the board of directors. While inheriting organizational structural principles, German companies sought to develop their own structure that differed from the American one. Concerning organizational innovations, there was a traditional influence of authority, whereby a strict separation was seen between top management against middle management and those at the lower level. In Germany, traditional family-controlled companies were widely maintained. This demonstrated stronger continuity of management and manager values than those in Japan. Thus, the hesitation and resistance toward the introduction of the American way of thinking, technology, and management was evidently strong (Kudo et al. 2004, pp. 20–21).

However, these types of German management traditions, management values, and cultural factors do not simply reflect culture in general; rather, they reflect market characteristics and are compatible with the German and European markets. This indicates the significance of German-style business management. We consider this point in more detail in Sect. 10.2.4.3.

10.2.3 German-Style Adaptation and the Influence of Institutional Factors in the Americanization Process

Examining the institutional factors impacting the German-style of adaption in the process of Americanization, we first see that aspects of industrial relations were an important issue. The deep-rooted differences between the United States and Europe in terms of understanding and implementing working participation in the management process were one of the hindrances in the Americanization of European economic life (Schröter 2005, p. 193). In Germany, the legally prescribed co-determination system was one of the most important factors. The labor agreement that was complementary with co-determination at the plant and top management levels formed the framework of industrial relations during the post-WWII period. Thus, the politically motivated attempt by America to promote the introduction of HR to transform industrial relations was unsuccessful. The traditional German-style industrial relations, emphasizing technology and skills, was an important background factor in the quest to design a method compatible with the German adaptation of American management style and system. This can be said to have had a strong influence on the view of management of companies as well as the issues of management, in general, based on the "efficiency principle."

In relation to the impact of institutional factors such as industrial relations, two aspects are important in the analysis: (a) the necessary changes in the process of "re-framing" the American-style system as a result of the power exerted by industrial relations regulations and (b) the harmonious nature of industrial relations facilitating the introduction of management measures proposed by the companies. Thus, it is important for a system with a management nature to be compatible with Germany's conditions such that strategic responses could be produced among the influences of regulatory functions and promotional efforts.

For example, the introduction of human relations was greatly limited by the industrial-relations traditions and the resistance of labor dating back to before WWII. In addition, there were factors such as the new framework of industrial relations stemming from the co-determination system. However, employment and wage security based on the dual system and the characteristics of German-style industrial relations were factors in promoting investment in vocational education, particularly for the labor force within corporations. Such investment in education and training was the foundation for the development of diversified and high-quality production dependent on skilled workers. Ensuring labor flexibility was important in terms of the development of diversified and high-quality production. Further it was essential for the formation of the type of expertise and skills required to complement the level of technical facilities and realize high quality promoted by the development of the German-style production system.

There were more than a few cases in which the nature of industrial relations was harmonious with facilitating the introduction of management measures proposed by the companies. For example, in companies that used the method of job evaluation in payment of wages, the introduction of the method was conducted only with the approval of the work council, and not the trade unions (Vgl. Industriegewerkschaft Metall 1956, pp. 97, 101, 104). There were also cases in which IE methods were introduced by work councils in the form of work agreement (refer to Chap. 7).

One of the institutional factors that impacted the Americanization process after WWII was the education system. The traditions and nature of the German university educational system tended to focus on the reasoning and understanding of the topics and exerted great influence on management education. The institutional characteristics of these German universities played a major role in the introduction of a more practical American-style management education method. Specialized skills and qualifications systems, such as the Meister system and the vocational education system, which were vital for training skilled workers, were deeply related to the introduction of the American production system and the nature of German-style production.

In comparing the situation in Japan, in terms of the impact of institutional factors on the process of Americanization, several important issues may be mentioned. In general, the extent of Americanization, on both corporate and national economy levels, was much wider and deeper in Japan than in Germany. Therefore, the shock of the superiority of America was much greater. Most technology experts and managers in Japan desperately attempted to introduce all the aspects of American technology and management practices; moreover, learning and re-learning became an enterprise-wide movement. In contrast, in Germany the appetite for such practices was very limited, and the country tried to incorporate American technology and management techniques into their existing methods. During the productivity movement, there was much greater influence exerted by country-specific systems in Germany than in Japan, both on the scale of Americanization and the impact of adapting selective American management thinking and practices, given the country's specific systems. The factors that defined the difference between the two countries, in terms of the scale of Americanization, were the differences in willingness to learn and study, and the difference in levels of introduction of American methods as defined by the level of development in each country. Furthermore, differences in the scale of post-War reforms during the occupation and reconstruction period were important. In West Germany, despite post-WWII reforms, legislation involving corporations were maintained. As a result, the supervisory board authority is as strong as it was before and the older generation of managers continues to be active, such that a comparison cannot even be made with the situation in Japan (Kudo et al. 2004, pp. 19–24; Schröter 2005, p. 219). In contrast, in Japanese business world experienced a shift between generations due to the removal of the top business leaders from older generations. Many new managers of post-War "zaibatsu"-type companies were promoted from the ranks of middle management. There were many cases in which they had not received sufficient training as top management at the time of their promotion (Miyajima 1991, pp. 139–140; Miyajima 1992, pp. 212–213; Miyazaki 1966, p. 224), which was one of the factors that called for the active introduction of American management methods. With respect to the differences between Germany and Japan, Kudo (1999) offers two factors in terms of the acceptance of American-style management: "the difference in the development stage between Germany, which was a leader in the secondary industry revolution, and Japan which was a late developing country" and "the wave of extensive institutionalization in Germany during the 1950s." In regard to the latter, he points out that "the institutionalization brought about in the 1950s along the length and breadth of corporate society, including inter-firm relationships, internal organizational structure, and industrial relations, gave power to the traditional management philosophy and subsequently constrained the new generation of managers" (Kudo 1999, pp. 507–508).

Thus, the post-WWII institutional reforms had a significant impact on the configuration of management, and were deeply related to traditional management philosophy and values. In 1950s and 1960s Germany under the American influence, a pragmatic model of behavior was gradually formed. However, representatives of the old elite tended to stick to the uniqueness of the "German spirit" (Lüdtke et al. 1997, p. 25). The exclusivity and monopoly of management indicated that authority was bestowed upon the managers themselves, but after WWII this changed under the influence of America, resulting in a reduction in the exclusivity of manager positions. However, at the end of the 1950s "authority based on credentials" dominated over "authority based on function" (Hartmann 1959, pp. 261, 271–272, 274–277; Hartmann 1968, pp. 271–272, 282–283, 286–289). The German method in relation to authority was also a factor that greatly impacted the decentralization and delegation of authority. In the development of post-war Americanization, the significance of a generational shift in management was great. According to Berghahn, this process started in the early 1960s (Vgl. Berghahn 1985, pp. 249–252, 255–257, 293). However, it must also be noted that the promotion of Americanization occurred in some cases, regardless of a generational shift in management, as seen in the role of the Vaubel initiative in Glanzstoff (Kleinschmidt 1998, p. 186).

10.2.4 The Structural Characteristics of German Capitalism and the Development of Post-war German Business Management

Based on previous discussions, next we consider how the structural characteristics of German capitalism defined the development of post-WWII German business management. In particular, we will examine the relationship between German characteristics and their structure of productive forces, industrial structure, and market structure.

10.2.4.1 Impact of the Characteristics of the Structure of Productive Forces

First, in relation to the context of the characteristics of the structure of productive forces prior to WWII, there was the tradition of "the flexible production concept with an emphasis on quality" as seen in the automotive industry (Vgl. Stahlmann 1993). Germany had tried various methods of mass production, mainly in the automotive, electrical, and the machinery industries, that aimed at securing a certain level of flexibility for dealing with demand fluctuations between products and obtaining some of the benefits of mass production even with a decreased production output under the conditions of market constraints (Vgl. von Freyberg 1989; Siegel and Freyberg 1991). After WWII, both the domestic and export market conditions were equipped to introduce American-style mass production. However, Germany sought market positioning by pursuing competitiveness in Europe's relatively high share of exports that was compatible with the characteristics of high-quality European goods. Given these circumstances, German companies pursued a suitable production system. Here, they pursued constructing a quality- and functionality-focused production system with the support of the German-specific method of specialized skill qualification system and vocational education system.

As we will see later, the German-specific method since before WWII was more compatible with the market structure and conditions given that a large portion of sales went to the European and German markets. The German method served as an alternative of sorts, even while the country's companies continued to accept American-style methods. The foundation of product differentiation based on the post-WWII, diversified, high-quality production system, in particular product policies and pricing policies, impacted the introduction and development of marketing methods. In this way, the characteristics of the structure of productive forces were strongly involved in the broad re-framing of American management methods not only in various ways relating to increasing production capacity, but also including measures adjusting to the market.

10.2.4.2 Impact of the Industrial Structure Characteristics

These types of characteristics of the structure of productive forces define the characteristics of the industrial structure. Therefore, here we will examine the context of the industrial structure. In pre-WWII Germany, the core of the industrial structure comprised the coal, iron, and steel industry, chemical industry, electrical industry, and the machinery industry that was the cornerstone of the producer goods industry. There was, in addition, the slow but expanding automotive industry forming the industrial structure characteristics. Consequently, this slow start of the consumer goods industry became a distinguishing character. After WWII, the development of the automotive industry and the home appliances of the electrical industry progressed rapidly. However, as pointed out by Wengenroth in 1997, despite the universal Americanization of both the consumer goods market and the management style, the traditional dominance of the producer goods industry in West Germany strengthened rather than weakened due to the new competitive advantage pattern among post-War European manufacturers. Of course, there was the establishment of a mass consumer society after WWII; however, there were certain industrial structure characteristics that allowed Germany to keep its own consumer society without developing a consumer goods industry that was strong enough to rival America (Wengenroth 1997, p. 161).

Under such circumstances, and for these reasons, strengthening the producer goods industries' international competitiveness became an important issue. As in the case of the machine tool industry, the quality and functionality of the producer goods were largely responsible for the quality improvement of final products and had great significance in the pursuit of competitiveness by differentiating quality and functionality. As for production systems compatible with this, it was important to expand by keeping their reliance on experienced workers. These points are also valid in the automotive industry, a durable consumer goods sector. These industrial sectors are ones in which Germany has high export competitiveness in terms of quality. Here, a different production system was developed from the American-style mass production systems.

In this way, the development of heavy industries, processing, and assembly industries, prior to WWII, and the further development of these industries, post-war, progressed and promoted the German-style development of management systems and production systems, within the American management system. The industries that form the basis of the secondary industry's revolutionary development became the most likely foundation for international competitiveness after WWII. In these industries the production methods that emphasized quality and functionality to make product differentiation possible were meaningful for establishing of competitive advantage. These factors became an important background for the "re-framing" of American-style methods. The characteristic of having the producer goods industry as the core of the industrial structure from pre-WWII and the characteristic of the producer goods industry still being so prominent even after the development of the post-War consumer goods sector, were defining factors in the delay of marketing in the producer goods industry. They also led to the German-style development with its emphasis on production rather than marketing.

10.2.4.3 Impact of the Market Structure Characteristics—European Market Structure and German Business Management

Looking at the context of market structure characteristics, the labor market structure characteristic is influenced by labor market factors, such as talents needed by the managers and directors and the companies' internal promotion systems. Hence American-style business schools for management development training were incompatible within German. These labor market characteristics became the factors defining German-style management training. However, the strongest market structure factor determining the development of German-style business management was in the commodities markets.

Here, let us look at the context of the structural characteristics of the commodities markets. Historically, America has had a tradition of emphasizing the efficiency principle based on standardization. This stemmed from a strong necessity for unification of procedures due to the large immigrant population, the potential demand expansion due to the vast domestic market, and pragmatic values/culture and customs defined under these conditions. For many years the American market has been more homogeneous compared to other countries (Chandler 1977, p. 498), and, thus, the standardization of consumption advanced. Given these market and consumption characteristics, mass production and market competition aimed at fully standardizing production and consumption became a perquisite. American management styles and methods based on the principle of "efficiency improvement" were hence created to reflect free competition and were compatible with those conditions in such markets.

In contrast, Germany did not have the same advancement in standardization of consumption as in America. The market characteristics and consumer behavior trended towards emphasizing technology, quality, and functionality, and focus was put on competition in terms of quality. These market characteristics are not just seen in Germany, but also at the European level, the core market for German exports. Thus, under the different market characteristics from the aggressive American-type price competition (Streeck 1997, pp. 39–40), where the primary management issue is the efficiency principle, Germany, on the other hand, placed a higher significance on product differentiation based on technology, quality, and functionality. This German method of management is also compatible with the European market. On this point, similarities were seen in German and European markets, for example, in the negative perceptions and resistance towards planned obsolescence, which is one of the important American marketing measures, as well as in the strong reluctance of consumers toward standardized products. Of course, the terms for a technological and qualitative competitive advantage are vastly different depending on the product and in product groups where differentiation is difficult the American method has more meaning. However, generally the differences in the American and European market conditions are important factors in defining the nature of business management in Germany. The impact from these market structure factors are also observed in the areas of market adaptation, such as marketing and PR, as well as in the area of production.

After WWII, because of the type of market structure, divisions with international competitiveness mainly developed compatible product strategies and production systems supporting them. It became significant for German companies during the development of this type of management to have a high degree of dependency exporting to the European market (Vgl. Statistisches Bundesamt 1956, pp. 282–283; Statistisches Bundesamt 1961, pp. 316–317; Statistisches Bundesamt 1971, pp. 296–297, 299–300; Statistisches Bundesamt 1981, pp. 258–259) with a relative importance placed on having basic similarities in market conditions and characteristics. The post-War Americanism-led free-trade market system and the international monetary system supported the establishment of an international economic system of the capitalist bloc. Moreover, the formation of the common market in Western Europe supports the conditions for favorable trade, and, as a result, Germany's export structure is even more dependent upon Europe. Under conditions that greatly differ from those of pre-WWII, a complementary relationship has been formed in industrial sectors and goods areas. Overall, in addition to chemical products, automobiles, and machineries, Germany has a competitive advantage in areas and products that have industrial and product characteristics based on technology, quality, and functionality, in particular capital goods, investment goods, and consumer durable goods, Germany has established a competitive advantage. Germany's trend has been to establish export competitiveness by specializing in sectors based on so-called med-ranking technology (Lindler and Holtfreich 1997, pp. 418, 420–421). With a main focus on the competitiveness of the key industry sectors in the European market, a division of labor was established to supplement existing industries and products. For example, even observations during the period leading up to the formation of the EEC show that West Germany's competitiveness leveraged the disparity in productive forces among the neighboring high-income level countries, particularly in the heavy chemical industrial sectors. This helped in penetrating the Western European export market, and later, with the progressive expansion of imports from the countries comprising the ECC, a horizontal multilayered trade structure was built (Furuuchi 2006, pp. 89–100). After the Second World War, against the background of Germany's highly nonprice competitive industrial products, a trade structure was formed among the surrounding advanced economies on the basis of mutually complementary division of labor of trade goods (Sato and Hermann 1997, p. 218). In that sense, West Germany succeeded in extracting maximum profits not by forming an industrial structure within the country's boundaries but by relying on the principle of optimal division of labor within the EEC (NHK Shuzaihan 1988, p. 91). Accordingly, within the product and industrial competitive structure, the dominance of German companies have strengthened. By doing this, the development of German-style management, job security through the codetermination system, and the foundation of capital accumulation under the high-cost structure of wages were supported.

European-style development is defined by reflecting characteristics of the European market: from the fact that German companies have a high dependency on the regional market, together with a German-style development of business management, within the Americanism movement, along with German capitalist reproduction structure (accumulation structure). The post-WWII accumulation system or so-called "German model" is supported by quality competitive sector as a core, industrial structure differences among European nations and a trade structure that is closely related (Furuuchi 2006). Such European-style reproduction structures (accumulation structures) greatly differ from the Japanese case. At the very beginning of the post-WWII period Japan did not seek out Asia as an export base, such was the case with Germany and Europe, but in turn depended on exports to America, where the dependency continued to deepen. Therefore, it is important to analyze and understand Germany's business management by taking into account phrases such as "Germany in Europe" and "Europe for Germany."

In this way, the German domestic market and structure of the European market, which accounts for a majority of Germany's exports, act as important factors with a deep relationship to the problem of "re-framing" when introducing the American management style. These facts have strongly defined the German-style development of business management. Under Germany's capitalistic reproduction structure, a business management style compatible with European conditions was pursued. This type of business management style was also an important linchpin of Germany's capitalistic reproduction structure. Table 10.1 visualizes the conditions surrounding the introduction of the American management system as well as "re-framing" and the factors defining it, based on the discussion so far in this book.

Table 10.1 Americanization and re-framing: German characteristics of business management. Also available at http://extras.springer.com/

Management Methods / Deployment and Factors Affecting Them	Management Education		Management & Production Systems		
	Top Management Education	Manager Education	Human Relations (HR)	Industrial Engineering (IE)	The Ford System
Overall Conditions in the Deployment of American Management Methods	• Top Management education efforts using US education materials • Delay in adoption of business school programs	• TWI deployment in foreman education • Slow pace of TWI adoption compared to the US and other countries	• Sparse deployments in German corporations • Failed US attempt to transfer US labor relations on the basis of HR deployment • Use of HR focusing on issues that are not automatically solved by codetermination or legal regulations (e.g., relations between the foreman and subordinates, etc.)	• Deployments focused on the Work-Factor Method and MTM • Deployments focused on processing and assembly, steel and metal, chemical, shipbuilding, and clothing industries • The delay in the spread of IE relative to other countries • Inter-industry and inter-corporate differences in the selection of the Work-Factor Method and MTM	• Deployment of flow production system mechanisms and production organization principles
Deployment Characteristics of American Management Methods	• Strong US initiative and support in technical assistance and productivity programs • Development of organizational planning through the EPA • RKW efforts and involvement • The pursuit of US methods of business management education as an alternative to the lack of practical training in German universities • Education through executive networks in business associations • US university cooperation and its roles • The deployment of TWI relating to human relations issues		• Strong US support and promotion of technical assistance and productivity programs as a priority • Involvement of institutions such as RKW and universities • HR deployment as a means of stabilizing labor relations to advance rationalization	• Strong involvement and leadership of the REFA (e.g., IE introduction, launch of education courses, etc.) • REFA's prioritization of their own system • Deployments based on REFA's license agreement with the Work-Factor Company • The establishment of the German MTM Association and its efforts	• Differences in production systems among companies • The development of diversified quality production based on skilled or specialized labor • Case of deployments of mixed-model assembly line
Modifications in American Management Methods	• The development and distribution of German top management and manager education according to individual organizations (e.g., short-term seminars on the latest US management methods, etc.)		• Alternatives to improving psychological aspects of HR by improving labor environment under the codetermination system	• Creation and development of work study based on REFA thinking despite the influence of IE • Case of the application of human engineering research (Siemens)	• The pursuit of economies of scale by using unit systems

Source: This table was compiled by the author based on discussions in this chapter and previous chapters.

Market Measures		Organizational Reforms in the Divisional Structure
Marketing	Public Relations (PR)	
• Deployment of divisions of labor between sales (short-term tactic) and marketing (long-term strategy) departments	• Deployment of methods based on US PR concepts and new sociological methods	• Expansion of deployment of principles for modifying divisional structures
• Basic marketing philosophies and principles, and the deployment and spread of advertising and publicity methods	• Adoption throughout German corporations in the 1960s	• Low rate of divisional structure adoption compared to the US and UK
• Progress of deployments in the consumer goods sector and sluggishness in the producer goods sector	• Establishment of international PR departments and positions	• Vast differences in divisional structure deployment among large corporations and small- or medium-sized businesses
		• High proportion of holding company structures in the largest companies compared with that in the US
• Marketing was the most successful field among the various efforts undertaken by the US Technical Assistance and Productivity Program	• Development of PR activities within sales policies and marketing	• Existence of matrix organizations in divisions and regional and functional departments
• Role of US advertising agencies and consulting firms	• PR's significance as a response to personnel issues	• Amalgamations of divisional and functional structures
• Low status of the head of publicity in the corporate hierarchy	• US PR and consulting firms' involvement and role	• Deployments dependent on US consulting firms and corporations
• Differentiated product strategy emphasizing quality and functionality	• The development of PR activities aiming to establish a foothold in the US market	• Relatively less impact of consulting firms in Germany than in the US and UK
		• Specific motives for changing the structure from a holding company to a divisional structure (more efficient strategies and better coordination in formerly independent subsidiaries)
• Prioritization of long-term product policies and focus on quality and functionality rather than planned obsolescence	• Trends toward information policies and communication policies used with more prudence than in US corporations	• Operations based on principles of collegiate management under a board of directors and a board-majority system
• Premium pricing policy through product differentiation	• Emphasis on governmental and political public relations activities	• Systems of collegiate management within divisions
		• Cases of divisional structure deployments that were not self-support account systems
		• The deployment of compensation systems for general managers not linked to the division's performance
		• Points where the controlling function was responsible at the operational level as well as in headquarters

(continued)

Table 10.1 (continued)

Deployment and Factors Affecting Them \ Management Methods		Management Education		Management & Production Systems		
		Top Management Education	Manager Education	Human Relations (HR)	Industrial Engineering (IE)	The Ford System
Amalgamation of American and German Elements		• Knowledge dissemination based on executive networks in business associations and the amalgamation of methods for intergenerational opinion exchange and materials and methods from the US		• US orientation in corporate personnel policy and social policy and its amalgamation with prewar works community concepts • Amalgamation of HR viewpoints and prewar labor science research viewpoints • The return of prewar company publications based on HR perspectives	• Integration of IE methods into the REFA system	• Linking unique prewar production system elements in Germany • Use of knowledge-intensive skills relying on skilled workers • Linking standardization systems through the unit system
Factors of "Re-framing" in Americanization	Influence of Traditions and Cultural Factors and Management Values on Business Management	• Management values and traditions emphasizing the value of technology and skills • Traditions of managerial social policy in German corporations		• Constraints in management values emphasizing technology, quality, and production • Management values reflecting the high proportion of executives and managers from technical fields • Influence of uniquely German management models such as the Harzburg model	• Traditional German adaptations through modifications of the Taylor system to REFA in the 1920s	• Technology-, quality-, and functionality-oriented management values • Management values and manufacturing views based on understanding customer needs, rather than production perspectives • The tradition of prioritizing skilled engineers in the production management function
		• High proportion of executives with a technical background	• Executives' and educators' resistance to the deployment of TWI			
	Influence of Institutional Factors	• The state of the German education system and its traditions • Characteristics of business management education (negligence of practical viewpoints) • Limits of universities' role in business management education • The older generations of executives continuing on due to corporate legislation despite postwar reform • Education systems based on executive networks		• Conflict between the US' intention to reform labor relations through HR deployment and Germany's traditional labor relations • Traditional labor relations and constraints from labor resistance and opposition • Codetermination system's inhibitory influence	• Systematic foundation of REFA efforts in time and work studies • Promotion of implementation and execution based on acceptable views by unions • Case of implementation and execution through work agreements with work councils	• Production systems with the foundation of the vocational education system and professional qualification system (the Meister system)
	Influencing factors of the Structure of Productive Forces	—		—	• The development of management through the REFA system since the prewar era	• Pursuit of economies of scale based on lower production volumes since the prewar era and the development of production systems that ensured production flexibility • Prewar tradition of flexible quality production

Market Measures		Organizational Reforms in the Divisional Structure
Marketing	Public Relations (PR)	
• Combining US-style thinking and methods of mass marketing, with product and price policies that emphasize Germany's respect for individuality, quality, functionality, and brand	• Combining US PR methods based on the latest sociological methods and Germany's prewar tradition of image advertising and PR	• Combining of mechanisms based on the principles of German collegiate management under a board of directors and the board-majority system with mechanisms in US-style divisions • Combining of principles of US-style product division systems and principles of German-style functional and regional departments • Cases on combinations of prewar German corporate organizations with a sub-committee in the board of directors and US committee organizations
• Management values emphasizing technology, quality, and production • High proportion of executives from technical fields	• Business management traditions and management values with corporate values of technology, quality, and functionality • The high proportion of executives from technical fields	• Ideological foundation of top management authority that strictly divides the board of directors from the overall labor hierarchy that is below middle management • The tradition and practice of collegiate management principles under the board of directors and the board-majority system
• Prewar tradition of prioritizing moderate competition policies based on cartels • Historical tendency to take sales and marketing viewpoints lightly • German corporations' persistent influence of traditional pricing and terms policies	• Executives' resistance to corporate open house and information policies	• Executive resistance to providing sufficient authority and responsibility toward general managers • The tradition of cooperative corporate culture emphasizing technology
• Historical influence of traditional cartels on heavy industry's low recognition of marketing value • Influence of state regulations such as gift regulations and the Rebates Act • Influence of competition order in the prewar acceptance of cartels	—	• German corporations' slow pace of delegation of authority and decentralization of management • Slow pace of business management specialization (strong differentiation between top and daily management) • Diversification's suppressive effects through characteristics of ownership (particularly family ownership) in German corporations and their influence on divisional structure implementations • Large German corporations' institutional characteristics in large corporate group structures as a basis for industrial structures and the influence of the proportion of holding company structures among the largest corporations
• Progress of mass production and reforms to the structure of productive forces in the durable consumer goods sector • Foundation of product differentiation based on a structure with diversified quality production and the structure of productive forces	—	—

(continued)

Table 10.1 (continued)

Deployment and Factors Affecting Them \ Management Methods		Management Education		Management & Production Systems		
		Top Management Education	Manager Education	Human Relations (HR)	Industrial Engineering (IE)	The Ford System
Factors of "Re-framing" in Americanization	Influence of Industrial Structure Factors	—		—	• Development of the metals industry and the processing and assembly industries since the prewar era • Postwar development and expansion in the processing and assembly industries	• Expansion of processing and assembly industries since the prewar period • Further development and expansion of the processing and assembly industries after World War II • Foundation of international industrial competitiveness based on a second industrial revolution
	Influence of Market Structure Factors	• Desired traits in executives and managers and the influence of corporate promotions and appraisal systems on the labor market for executives and managers		—	—	• Market characteristics of the German and European emphasis on quality and functionality • Postwar expansion of the mass consumer market • Patterns of foreign trade based on complementary relationships among European industrial and product fields

Market Measures		Organizational Reforms in the Divisional Structure
Marketing	Public Relations (PR)	
• Characteristics of industrial structures centered on producer goods industries since the prewar period • Relatively high proportions of producer goods industries in the postwar era	—	• Influence of a high proportion of producer goods industries on the largest corporations' industrial sector composition (and its influence on adoption of each type of organizational structure)
• Market characteristics emphasizing quality and functionality • Consumer resistance to product standardization • Resistance to planned obsolescence as a product policy • Differences in recognition of marketing and deployment among industrial sectors due to competitive conditions and a competitive structure	• Market characteristics emphasizing quality and functionality	• Market characteristics of quality and functionality and their reflection of the collaborative corporate culture that emphasized technology • Great reliance on exports to Europe (cases of European operations in product divisions and the separation of other regions' operations in regional departments)

References

Berghahn V (1985) Unternehmer und Politik in der Bundesrepublik. Suhrkamp, Frankfurt am Main

Bjarnar O, Kipping M (1998) The Marshall plan and the transfer of US management models to Europe. In: Kipping M, Bjarnar O (eds) The Americanization of European Business. The Marshall plan and the transfer of US management models. Routledge, London, pp 1–17

Chandler AD Jr (1977) The visible hand: managerial revolution in American business. Harvard University Press, Cambridge

Feldenkirchen W (2004) The Americanization of the German electrical industry after 1945. Siemens as a case study. In: Kudo A, Kipping M, Schröteret HG (eds) German and Japanese business in the boom years. Transforming American management and technology models. Routledge, London, pp 116–137

Furuuchi H (2006) Gendai Doitsukeizai no Rekishi (A history of the modern German economy). Tokyo Daigaku Shuppankai, Tokyo

Hartmann H (1959) Authority and organization in German management. Princeton University Press, Princeton

Hartmann H (1968) Der deutsche Unternehmer. Europäische Verlagsanstalt, Frankfurt am Main

Hilger S (2004) „Amerikanisierung" deutscher Unternehmen. Wettbewerbsstrategien und Unternehmenspolitik bei Henkel, Siemens und Daimler-Benz (1945/49–1975). Franz Steiner Verlag, Stuttgart

Industriegewerkschaft Metall (1956) Geschäftsbericht 1954/1955 des Vorstandes der Industriegewerkschaft Metall für die Bundesrepublik Deutschland. IG Metall, Frankfurt am Main

Kleinschmidt C (1998) An Americanized company in Germany. The Vereinigte Glanzstoff Fabriken AG in the 1950s. In: Kipping M, Bjarnar O (eds) The Americanization of European business. The Marshall plan and the transfer of US management models. Routledge, London, pp 171–189

Kleinschmidt C (2002) Der produktive Blick. Wahrnehmung amerikanischer und japanischer Management- und Produktionsmethoden durch deutsche Unternehmer 1950–1985. Akademie Verlag, Berlin

Kleinschmidt C (2004a) America and the Resurgence of the German chemical and rubber industry after the Second World War. Hüls, Glanzstoff and continental. In: Kudo A, Kipping M, Schröteret HG (eds) German and Japanese business in the boom years. Transforming American management and technology models. Routledge, London, pp 161–174

Kleinschmidt C (2004b) Driving the West German consumer society: the introduction of US style production and marketing at Volkswagen, 1945–70. In: Kudo A, Kipping M, Schröteret HG (eds) German and Japanese business in the boom year. Transforming American management and technology models. Routledge, London, pp 75–92

Kudo A (1999) 20 Seiki Doitsu Shihonshugi (20th-century German capitalism). Tokyo Daigaku Shuppankai, Tokyo

Kudo A, Kipping M, Schröteret HG (2004) Americanization. Historical and conceptual issues. In: Kudo A, Kipping M, Schröteret HG (eds) German and Japanese business in the boom years. Transforming American management and technology models. Routledge, London, pp 1–29

Lawrence P (1980) Managers and management in West Germany. Croom Helm, London

Lindler L, Holtfreich C-L (1997) Four decades of German export expansion—an enduring success story? In: Fischer W (ed) The economic development of Germany since 1870, vol II. Edward Elgar, Cheltenham, pp 402–435

Locke RR (1996) The collapse of the American management Mystique. Oxford University Press, New York

Lüdtke A, Marβolek I, Saldern AV (1997) Amerikanisierung: Traum und Alptraum im Deutschland des 20.Jahrhunderts. In: Jaraush K, Siegrist H (eds) Amerikanisierng und Sowjetisierung in Deutschland 1945–1970. Campus, Frankfurt am Main, pp 7–33

McCreary EA (1964) Die Dollar-Invasion. Amerikanische Firmen und Manager in Europa. Moderne, München

Miyajima A (1991) Zaikai Tsuiho to Shin Keieisha no Tojyo (Expulsion of managers from the business world and appearance of new managers). Will (Will) 10(7):36–44

Miyajima A (1992) Zaibatsu Kaitai (Dissolution of Zaibatsu). In: Hosei Daigaku Sangyo Jyoho Senta, Hashimoto J, Takeda H (eds) Nihon Keizai no Hatten to Kigyou Shudan (Development of Japanese economy and corporate groups). Tokyo Daigaku Shuppankai, Tokyo, pp 203–254

Miyazaki G (1966) Sengo Nihon no Keizaikiko (Japanese economic system after WW II). Shin Hyoron, Tokyo

Neebe R (1989) Technologietransfer und Auβenhandel in den Anfangsjahren der Bundesrepublik Deutschland. Vierteljahrschrift für Sozial- und Wirtschaftsgeschichte 76:49–75

NHK Shuzaihan (1988) Nihon Nishi Doitsu (Japan West Germany). Nihon Hososhuppan Kyokai, Tokyo

Sato S, Hermann A (1997) Boeki Shihontorihikiseisaku (Trade policy and capital transactions policy). In: Sakura Research Institute, Ifo Institut für Wirtschaftsforschung (eds) Nihon to Doitsu no Keizai Sangyo Sisutemu no Hikaku Kenkyu (Comparative study of economic and industrial systems in Japan and Germany). Springer, Tokyo, pp 199–218

Schröter HG (2005) Americanization of the European economy. A compact survey of American economic influence in Europe since the 1880s. Springer, Dordrecht

Siegel T, Freyberg TV (1991) Industrielle Rationalisierung unter dem Nationalsozialisumus. Campus, Frankfurt am Main

Stahlmann M (1993) Die Erste Revolution in der Autoindustrie. Management und Arbeitspolitik von 1900–1940. Campus, Frankfurt am Main

Statistisches Bundesamt (ed) (1956) Statistisches Jahrbuch für die Bundesrepublik Deutschland 1956. W. Kohlhammer, Stuttgart

Statistisches Bundesamt (ed) (1961) Statistisches Jahrbuch für die Bundesrepublik Deutschland 1961. W. Kohlhammer, Stuttgart

Statistisches Bundesamt (ed) (1971) Statistisches Jahrbuch für die Bundesrepublik Deutschland 1971. W. Kohlhammer, Stuttgart

Statistisches Bundesamt (ed) (1981) Statistisches Jahrbuch für die Bundesrepublik Deutschland 1981. W. Kohlhammer, Stuttgart

Streeck W (1997) German capitalism: do it exist? Can it survive? In: Crouch C, Streeck W (eds) Political economy of modern capitalism. Mapping convergence and diversity. Sage, London, pp 33–54

von Freyberg T (1989) Industrielle Rationalisierung in der Weimarer Republik: Untersucht an Beispielen aus dem Maschinenbau und der Elektroindustrie. Campus, Frankfurt am Main

Wengenroth U (1997) Germany: competition abroad—cooperation at home, 1870–1990. In: Chandler AD Jr, Amatori F, Hikino T (eds) Big business and the wealth of nations. Cambridge University Press, Cambridge, pp 139–175

Zeitlin J (2000) Introduction: Americanization and its limits: reworking US technology and management in post-war Europe and Japan. In: Zeitlin J, Herrigel G (eds) Americanization and its limits. Reworking US technology and management in post-war Europe and Japan. Oxford University Press, Oxford, pp 1–50

Chapter 11
Conclusion: German Corporate Expansion and the Path to European Integration—Germany's Development Based on Complementary Relationships in European Markets

Abstract How are capitalism and business management in Germany, a European nation, to be understood from the perspective of Japan, an Asian nation? Drawing on the previous chapters, the present chapter uniquely addresses this question from the perspective of a Japanese researcher. Post WWII, both Germany and Japan developed their enterprises and economies by deploying and adapting US technology and management methods, becoming major trading countries. However, current economic and business conditions greatly differ between Germany and Japan. In the trade sector, America continues to strongly influence Japanese business operations. However, Japan could not and cannot establish a complementary relationship with American industrial sectors and products in the American market. Exacerbating matters, unlike the European Union, Asia has no common market structure. In contrast, Germany has developed independent of American influence and become part of a well-integrated regional economy. This chapter explains the origins of these differences, and how the transformation of German business management in the 1950s and 1960s underpinned the formation of today's European Union. This section also suggests viewpoints for analyses on current problems affecting Germany's role and possible initiatives in the European debt crisis.

Keywords European debt crisis • European integration • Europeanization • German business management • German capitalism

We have examined the relationship between Germany's corporate growth and development and the movement toward European integration during the postwar boom years through the early 1970s, including the issue of the Americanization of business management. From our discussions thus far, we may draw various implications, such as on how the development of German corporations during this period affected subsequent periods. Given the development process of business management during the postwar boom years, this issue explains the root of present-day

T. Yamazaki, *German Business Management: A Japanese Perspective on Regional Development Factors*, DOI 10.1007/978-4-431-54303-9_1, © Springer Japan 2013

circumstances in Germany and its corporations as they Europeanize, even in the midst of Americanization and globalization. As we come to the end of this book, the author would like to conclude with an individual perspective on this point.

Germany and Japan were defeated in World War II and developed through US assistance and the deployment of US technology and management methods. However, shortly after the war, Japan did not have markets nearby as did Germany in Europe; this is primarily because many Asian countries had been colonies. Therefore, Japan's development of productive forces could sufficiently absorb only the expansion of its domestic markets and exports to the US, forcing a stronger reliance on America. Under these conditions, even though Japan attempted to expand by restructuring the system of large corporate groups and implementing American management methods, Japanese corporations could create only accumulation structures in the form of stronger reliance on the US for exports. Later, in the 1970s and 1980s, Japanese corporations strengthened their competitiveness in the processing and assembly industries, particularly the automotive industry by using low costs and quality, measured by few defects, as a weapon to intensify the Japanese production system. This strategy resulted in even greater exports to the US. However, because Japanese industrial sectors that had international competitiveness and expanded export were US key industries, it could not build complementary relationships with US producers and industries in the US market and had to maintain a competitive relationship with the US. Under these conditions, Japan's independent development became rather complicated. Even today, Asia has formed no regional economic integration comparable to that of the EU, leaving Japan vulnerable to fluctuations in yen versus dollar exchange rates because it relies on exports to the US. This has resulted in a hollowing out of industries, putting corporations in difficult straits.

From Japan's perspective, Germany evidently has the capacity develop independently. Although German corporations experienced an Americanization of business management, they could developed by re-framing the structure of productive forces and industrial structures in line with European market structures and competition. In addition, they have been able to develop diversified quality production, relying on skilled workers, market structures, and characteristics focusing on quality and functionality. Further, German corporate management values reflect these market characteristics within Germany and core export regions in Europe. The promotion of investments in vocational education for corporate workers, employment security, and wage guarantee systems through the codetermination system were also significant. German corporations have expanded consistent with European conditions and markets. They have developed a production system that enables product differentiation in quality and functionality that rely on the specialized experience and skill of their workers, rather than US-style mass production that is based on the principles of thorough standardization or Japanese workers' multi-process skills. German product quality focuses on functionality and durability and the German production system attempts to differentiate on quality, not price. German corporations have developed on the foundation of a German strategy that builds competitiveness through quality differentiation. As a result, Germany has become internationally competitive in durable consumer goods, investment goods, and capital goods, and has built foreign trade patterns that complement products in the European region on the basis of differences in the industrial structures of other European nations. In doing so, Germany has developed corporate and economic independence without having to follow the US global strategy.

However, this type of development that focuses on quality and functionality was particularly effective because of European market conditions. Thus, Germany sought to form and reinforce a European reproduction structure and progressed with European integration, leading to today's EU, to build a foundation conforming to that strategy. This movement toward European integration that enabled development rooted in the integrated region of Europe, although isolated inside Europe, was created at the business management level. The development of German corporations during the 1950s and 1960s set the direction toward European integration and laid the foundation for today's EU. The fact that Germany is forced to preserve the EU during the European debt crisis is deeply related to the European-style accumulation of German capitalism as well as the problems of stabilization in the financial system.

Although Germany and Japan both are among the world's leading manufacturing and trading nations, Germany has regionalized, building complementary relationships with other European nations in industrial and production areas. In contrast, Japan continues to lack a common market and have no complementary relationships with the US. The conditions that caused these differences arose from the process of corporate development during the postwar boom years' economic growth and were shaped by regional characteristics. The implication of this book are that these regional differences, in not only markets but also cultures, explain Germany's capitalism and business management, including the Americanization of business management, during this period.

Index

Printed by Printforce, the Netherlands